SENTENCES

CHARLES KLOPP

Sentences:
The Memoirs and Letters of Italian Political Prisoners from Benvenuto Cellini to Aldo Moro

UNIVERSITY OF TORONTO PRESS
Toronto Buffalo London

© University of Toronto Press Incorporated 1999
Toronto Buffalo London
Printed in Canada

ISBN 0-8020-4456-5

Printed on acid-free paper

Toronto Italian Studies

Canadian Cataloguing in Publication Data

Klopp, Charles
  Sentences : the memoirs and letters of Italian political prisoners from Benvenuto Cellini to Aldo Moro

  (Toronto Italian studies)
  Includes bibliographical references and index.
  ISBN 0-8020-4456-5

  1. Prisoners' writings, Italian – History and criticism.   2. Italian prose literature – History and criticism.   3. Political prisoners' writings – History and criticism.   4. Politics and literature – Italy.   5. Liberty in literature.   I. Title.   II. Series.

  PQ4055.P74K56 1999   850.9'9206927   C99-931161-1

University of Toronto Press acknowledges the financial assistance to its publishing program of the Canada Council for the Arts and the Ontario Arts Council.

This book has been published with the help of a grant from The Ohio State University.

University of Toronto Press acknowledges the financial support for its publishing activities of the Government of Canada through the Book Publishing Industry Development Program (BPIDP).

It is truly strange how many times the history of art, literature, and thought has taken a turn through a prison door. To amuse myself the other day, I tried to make a list of all the names of famous prisoners I could dredge from memory. The list is a truly astonishing one ...

Mario Alicata from Regina Coeli, *Lettere e taccuini*, 67–8 (16 March 1943)

Comparing an explorer to a prisoner is not all that forced. Anyone acquainted with games and crafts requiring patience knows that such activities were the prerogatives of monks and prisoners, women and sailors, people for whom time is lengthy and moves slowly: woven or knotted handiwork, ships in a bottle, letters from prison ...

Adriano Sofri, *Le prigioni degli altri*

Stone walls do not a prison make,
Nor iron bars a cage;
Minds innocent and quiet take
That for a hermitage;
If I have freedom in my love
And in my soul am free,
Angels alone that soar above
Enjoy such liberty.

Richard Lovelace, 'To Althea from Prison,' ll. 25–32 (1649)

From your letter and also from those before this, it appears that you have formed or others have formed in you, through inexact information, a too idyllic and mannered concept of my life, which is empty, terribly and squalidly empty of any interesting content, of any cerebral or mental stimulation, of any satisfaction that makes life worth living. I live barely and badly, an animal and vegetative existence.

Antonio Gramsci, *Letters from Prison* (1932), 2: 200

L'uccello che canta nella gabbia
Non canta d'amore ma per rabbia.

[A bird that is singing in a cage
Sings not from love but from rage.]

Italian proverb

Contents

PREFACE xi

Introduction: Writing As Survival 3

1 Predecessors: Prison Writing before 1800 12

2 The Spielberg: Concealment and Refutation 38

3 Bodies Politic 67

4 Authority, Desire, and Dissent: Serving the Revolution 106

5 Answering Gramsci: The Anti-Fascists 131

6 The Death of a President / The Effacement of an Author 177

Conclusion: Sentences and Convictions 186

NOTES 197
WORKS CONSULTED 237
INDEX 263

Preface

The research that has now resulted in this book began many years ago. Its most distant inspiration may have been a remark by a student at Robert College in Istanbul where I was teaching in the 1960s. During a discussion of politics and literature, this young man – he was about fifteen at the time, I think – told me calmly how he knew that in the next few years he would have to spend time in prison because of his political beliefs. While I never found out whether my student was in fact jailed during the period of terrorism and repression that came soon afterwards in Turkey, his readiness for this eventuality left a lasting impression on me. Years later, when I came across the place in Antonio Gramsci's *Lettere dal carcere* where the Italian Communist leader, physically shattered by a long and painful incarceration and now near death, recalls to his wife how, from the beginning of their relationship, imprisonment 'was not altogether unforeseeable' for a person like him for whom political activity was a 'going off to war,' I was reminded of the conversation I had had with my student in Istanbul.[1]

Some time after leaving Turkey, I read another classic of Italian literature, this time one whose place in the canon is much less secure today than it used to be: Silvio Pellico's *Le mie prigioni*. Perhaps because I encountered Gramsci's and Pellico's texts in reverse chronological order, I was struck not so much by the obvious differences between the two works as by their similarities. For even though Pellico's is a deliberately apolitical account of a spiritual crisis in an Austrian prison in the 1820s whose resolution leads to the strengthening of the prisoner's faith in both mankind and the Christian religion, while Gramsci's is the chronicle of the stubborn keeping of a different kind of faith in a Fascist prison in the 1930s, both works describe incarceration as a supreme moment of moral testing. Although their experiences after prison were very different, Pellico going on to live another twenty-five years after his release from the Spielberg while Gramsci died shortly after leaving Turi, both men were victorious in their prison struggles. Thanks in part, it has been said, to the unforeseen effect of Pellico's book on world opinion, northern Italy was eventually liberated from the Austrians and united with the south into a single nation. As for Gramsci, even though he was severely tested and finally broken by imprisonment, he managed, while in jail, not only to write what became the *Lettere dal carcere* but also to produce the immensely influential notebooks later published as the *Quaderni del carcere*, a comprehensive account of his thought on a variety of issues that constitutes his legacy to twentieth-century political philosophy.[2]

Bearing in mind these similarities, and tentatively placing Pellico and Gramsci at opposite poles, in both a chronological and an ideological sense, of a history of prison writing in Italy, I began to discover that many other works on this topic had been composed between 1832, when *Le mie prigioni* was first published, and 1947, when Gramsci's *Lettere dal carcere* appeared posthumously. Not only had an unusually large number of prison texts by Italian writers and political activists been written between these dates, the stories told in them were often set in the same prison buildings, in some cases even in the same cells where those of their predecessors had been played out years, decades, or centuries earlier. The works these men and women produced, moreover – whether letters like Gramsci's or memoirs like *Le mie prigioni* – were so similar to one another in style and content that I began to wonder if these texts could not be said to constitute a kind of tradition – an ongoing many-voiced discussion if not exactly a literary genre – in the history of Italian literature. I knew that, even before Pellico, a number of Italian writers had composed famous works in prison, among them Boethius' *Consolation of Philosophy*, Marco Polo's *Il Milione*, and Torquato Tasso's letters from Sant'Anna. I also knew that at least two widely read Italian autobiographies, those by Benvenuto Cellini and Giacomo Casanova, contained famous episodes about prison escapes, and I began to wonder how much these works had served as precedents for later writing on this theme.

So, leaving aside somewhat arbitrarily the pre-moderns Polo and Boethius – but not omitting Cellini, Tasso, or Casanova, all of whom seemed crucially present to the literary memories of later prisoners – and focusing mainly on texts from or about prison written after 1815 (the year of the Congress of Vienna that marked the beginning of the Restoration in Italy that in some ways is the start of the modern period in that country),

I selected some three dozen additional texts that, when considered in chronological order, would trace a history of prison writing in Italy from Napoleon's time to the present. This history, which runs parallel to the country's civil and political development, highlights the issue of coercion that is so important in much of the fiction and poetry of the period. In the nineteenth century especially – probably because during and after the Risorgimento problems of political freedom and government limitations on that freedom dominated the imaginations of all Italians – constraint of the individual by a superior force was an important theme in literature and other creative work.[3] The topic is central, for example, in Alessandro Manzoni's *I promessi sposi* of 1827–42, where a pivotal episode in this historical novel of fundamental importance for the future of Italian narrative is the forced abduction of a working-class bride-to-be, who is held in prison-like confinement until her captor is converted to Christianity by her guileless innocence assisted by divine grace. So, too, the poetry of Manzoni's contemporary Giacomo Leopardi (1798–1837) – a materialist thinker otherwise quite unlike *I promessi sposi*'s very Catholic author – takes as one of its central topics the conflict between the infinite desires of the imagination and the limits enforced on this faculty by the frailty of the human condition. Although the constraints evoked in Leopardi's poetry are existential and metaphysical rather than ethical and social as they are in Manzoni, both writers focus on conflicts between the individual and forces of constraint that reflect the political struggles of the day. In Italian opera as well – to turn to the best known and most widely celebrated artistic form of this period in Italy – prisons and prison scenes are everywhere, from those in Verdi's *I due Foscari* (1844) and *Aida* (1871) to the Castel Sant'Angelo of Puccini's *Tosca* of 1900, with Verdi's *Il trovatore* (1853), Boito's *Mefistofele* (1868), and Giordano's *Andrea Chenier* (1896) among many others in between.[4] Throughout the century, from Leopardi to Puccini, constraint and the lack of liberty as exemplified by prison and other places of detention occupied an important place in the Italian creative imagination.

In twentieth-century Italy, too, prison has continued to be an important motif in Italian writing. This was especially true during the twenty-year incubus of Fascism, when confinement of this sort was not just a metaphor for Italian intellectuals, many of whom were physically jailed under Mussolini. During the so-called 'years of lead' of more recent times, the theme was once again thrust into public consciousness when former prime minister Aldo Moro was kidnapped and then killed by the Red Brigades, to the horror of almost everyone in the country. Throughout the modern and contemporary periods too, then, the Italian literary imagination seemed possessed by the idea of prison and constraint.[5]

The analyses I provide in the pages that follow are of texts that in some cases were written by well-known authors whose names can be found in any history of Italian literature. Others are by writers unfamiliar even to specialists or were written by individuals usually celebrated more for their contributions to their country's civic welfare as public servants, teachers, professors, and the like, than as writers. About half the texts considered are memoirs, the other half letters – two very different kinds of writing, composed, in the case of prison letters, from the midst of a painful and often dangerous experience of uncertain outcome; in the case of memoirs, recalled in relative tranquillity but through the sometimes distorting filter of memory. Since what interests me here is the tradition that these texts trace and the social history that they mirror, I have treated these different types of writing together. While I am mindful that concentration on letters alone, for example, would have been more respectful of the limits of genre that separate these two non-fictional kinds of writing, and would have led to a tidier book, I cannot imagine a study of Italian prison writing that does not include the memoirists Pellico or Cellini or Casanova on the one hand, and the letter-writers Gramsci, Settembrini, or Moro on the other. I have therefore treated examples of these two different genres as equivalent components in the history of this particular literary mode. The reader will find, however, that the texts discussed in the first two chapters are in every case memoirs or other sorts of public writings, while in the next two chapters letters and memoirs are both used and in the final two chapters the emphasis is on letters alone. The works selected, while not literally an exhaustive survey of this kind of writing, do include almost all of the significant work on this topic during the period indicated.[6]

In addition to the major debt acknowledged in this book's dedication, I should like to acknowledge the help afforded me by the late Professor Luigi Bulferetti of the University of Genoa, the staff of the municipal library in Mantua and at the Casa di Mazzini in Genoa. The College of Humanities of The Ohio State University has nudged this project forward with grants. Dawn Michael helped with some of the proofreading. My colleagues Albert Mancini and Bob Cottrell read the manuscript in its entirety and were generous with helpful suggestions, while Steve Summerhill forced me to confront some of the more fundamental issues that the work raises. Richard Drake was helpful and supportive in regard to the Moro section of chapter 6 and Cynthia Craig kindly turned her expert eyes to the material on Casanova. Maria Ponce De León generously e-mailed me a copy from Rome of her just-completed dissertation on prison writing of the past twenty-five years, a work that arrived just as I was putting the finishing touches on this manuscript and that I have been able to make use of only in part. This is also the place to thank the anonymous readers for the University of Toronto Press for their intelligent and helpful comments. I should also like to thank the editors of the journals *Italica, Italiana, Il veltro,* and *Esperienze letterarie* for permission to use material on Pellico, Pignata, Frignani, and the Martyrs of Mantua that originally appeared in a somewhat different form or a different language in the pages of the journals they edit. I owe a debt as well to all the editors and publishers of the many collections of prison letters and memoirs that I have examined in my research for this project. That many of these texts were printed during the 1970s provides reassuring proof that at least some of the lead expended during this difficult decade in Italian life was utilized by typesetters rather than expended by terrorists and police.

In what follows, translations from Italian and French are my own unless otherwise indicated. References to the originals will be found in the notes, though in order not to make this book and its supporting apparatus even longer, I have there provided references only and not the passages translated.

SENTENCES

Introduction:
Writing As Survival

One writes to populate the desert; to no longer be alone in the ecstasy of being alone; to distract one's attention from the temptation of nothingness or at least put off considering it. Like the young princess of the *Thousand and One Nights*, everyone always talks to postpone the execution, to bribe the executioner.[1]

I have often been asked if I wrote to keep from going crazy. Absolutely. Writing can be an experience at the edge and in prison it is even more so.[2]

The letters and memoirs of political prisoners to be considered in what follows were written from the Renaissance to the 1970s and beyond. The places of detention described in them range from the Emperor Hadrian's second-century Roman mausoleum later known as Castel Sant'Angelo, where Cellini was incarcerated in the 1530s, to the block of modern apartments where the Red Brigades kept Aldo Moro prisoner in a 'people's jail' in 1978. But wherever held in whatever place for whatever reason by whatever forces of order or disorder, all the writers considered here were sent to jail for their personal and thus in the broadest sense their political views – not for serious contraventions of the criminal code. Although some of them may today seem little more than harbingers of social views not yet absorbed into the mainstream, in their own times most were considered dangerous subversives if not traitors deserving harsher punishments than those meted out to ordinary miscreants. Although some, like the Martyrs of Mantua in the 1850s, did contemplate violent means in pursuit of their political ends, the offences with which most were charged were non-violent ones.[3] These acts included publishing articles critical of the prevailing regime (the cases of Carlo Bini in Archducal Tuscany and Augusto Monti in Fascist Italy), belonging to

4   Sentences

political organizations a timorous government had declared illegal (the Carbonari for the occupying Austrians in the 1820s, the Communists and 'Giustizia e Libertà' members for the Fascists after 1926), or simply being out in the streets during times of social turbulence (Silvio Spaventa and Luigi Settembrini in 1848 Naples; Filippo Turati, Anna Kuliscioff, and Andrea Costa in Milan during the 1898 riots there). Many were incarcerated for acts that were not illegal in ordinary circumstances but had been declared such by a government-evoked state of emergency – in Austrian-ruled Lombardy and the Veneto in the 1820s, for example, or in Fascist Italy a century later.

Thrown into prison for activities they did not consider wrong, and then detained by forces whose legitimacy they did not always recognize, these authors did what they could, while in jail and afterwards, to promote the opinions they had always held and in this way continue to be who they were when arrested.[4] Many who wrote from or about prison during the nineteenth and twentieth centuries would thus agree with the opinion that people confined for political crimes are not prisoners at all but hostages in a social war of attrition.[5]

In addition to viewing them as unjust, most of the prisoners to be studied here considered their imprisonments temporary – maddening interruptions in a life of political, artistic, or intellectual commitment they were eager to resume when released. Many – including those sentenced to prison for the rest of their lives – were convinced they would not serve all of their terms. Since they had broken no serious laws, they reasoned, and since governments change more quickly than the legal measures they enforce, it was only necessary to wait for the collapse of the regime currently in power, or for an amnesty and return to civil society. As Giovanni Galletti wrote from a Roman prison in the 1840s, 'so long as his life is not threatened, a political prisoner can always hope for the passage of time.'[6] But while this optimism was well founded for Galletti, who was amnestied by a new pontiff after a relatively brief confinement, it would have been a cruelly inaccurate forecast for men like Silvio Spaventa and Luigi Settembrini, cell-mates for more than a decade on the island prison of Santo Stefano; or for Antonio Gramsci, who spent what proved a lethal decade in Fascist jails; or for Federico Confalonieri, imprisoned for more than fifteen years, much of it in the 'carcere duro' or 'hard-time jail' of the Spielberg; or for Umberto Terracini, who spent almost all of Fascism's twenty-year duration incarcerated or in forced internment. And while Terracini, Spaventa, and others emerged from prison relatively unscathed mentally and physically, this was not the case for other prisoners in this group. Gramsci, for example, exited prison an emotionally and physically broken man; even Pellico did little of significance after *Le mie prigioni*. And this is not to mention such even more tragic figures as Aldo Moro or the Mantua patriots, whose prison cells proved antechambers to execution.

In addition to being political prisoners, the writers whose works are discussed here were all intellectuals. Individuals able to analyse and historicize their experiences, they represent only a portion of the thousands of less articulate and now publicly unremembered people imprisoned for the same or similar reasons.[7] But of course it was intellectuals who considered their prison correspondence important enough to warrant subsequent publication or thought their confinement of sufficient interest to justify composing a retrospective memoir and it is these writers who have created the historical record examined here.

Separated, in most instances, from the common and historically voiceless criminals serving sentences elsewhere in the same institutions, these political dissidents lived their detentions as individuals rather than collectively. This is so even for those who did not suffer the long periods of solitary confinement endured by Luigi Pastro, Giovanni Galletti, Umberto Terracini, and Camilla Ravera, among others. For while some prisoners during the nineteenth and twentieth centuries were held in communal spaces like the 'stanzoni' in Mantua's Castel San Giorgio, the more usual practice was to confine them one to a cell. This procedure was dictated more by architectural than penological considerations. As the names Santa Margherita, San Vittore, and Regina Coeli indicate, the vast majority of the buildings where nineteenth- and twentieth-century political dissidents were confined are refurbished convents or monasteries. In these venerable edifices, cells intended for religious meditation were simply put to custodial use.[8] 'It's a curious twist of fate,' Sigismondo Castromediano mused about this in his prison memoir of the 1890s, 'how in all those localities where once there were monks, their places have been taken by criminals.'[9] But not only was the notion of prison as a kind of grim successor to the claustration of the convent or monastery strikingly apparent to many confined in such buildings, at least one inmate of a nineteenth-century convent – Enrichetta Caracciolo, whose writings are discussed in chapter 4 – applied the metaphor in the opposite direction. In her *Misteri del chiostro napoletano*, Caracciolo insisted that her religious claustration in mid-century Naples was no different from the life sentences being served by political prisoners elsewhere in King Ferdinand's domain. The convent as a prison, then, but also the prison as a convent: a place to confront one's self and then to depict that self in writing intended both as a means for psychological survival and as future testimony before the tribunal of popular consensus.

In many ways, the 1970s and 1980s have proved just such a tribunal. This period has seen a resurgence of interest in prison writing. Recent studies of the subject include the *Oxford History of the Prison* and Martha Grace Duncan's provocative *Romantic Outlaws, Beloved Prisons: The Unconscious Meaning of Crime and Punishment*, published in 1995 and 1996 respectively. Much of the reconsideration of the history and meaning of incarceration these two books propose was stimulated by Michel Foucault's *Discipline and Punish* of 1975. In this country, Foucault's book was followed by Victor Brombert's *The Romantic Prison* (1978), a seminal study of the prison theme in literature, especially in nineteenth-century France, and by Patricia O'Brien's *The Promise of Punishment* (1982), which further examines the work begun by Foucault. Mary Ann Frese Witt's *Existential Prisons: Captivity in Mid-Twentieth-Century French Literature* (1985), carries forward into the twentieth century the investigation of the prison theme in French literature begun by Brombert.[10]

In Italy, somewhat differently, interest in prisons and prisoners in this period was fanned not so much by Foucault and Italian critical responses to him (although there was, of course, some of that too),[11] as by such domestic events as the enormous and distressing wave of terrorism from both Right and Left that swept over the country in the 1970s, a phenomenon followed soon after by the equally disturbing political scandals of the 1980s that led to the dissolution of both the Christian Democrat and the Italian Communist parties. As part of these sensational events in Italian public life, a considerable number of ordinary Italians went to jail: students, professors, union functionaries, and political activists during the years of lead; industrialists, financiers, and politicians during the scandals of Tangentopoli. These individuals, most of whom had never been in trouble with the police before, were put into prison on what, to be sure, were criminal charges, but always in a thoroughly politicized context. Their dilemmas as the sometimes improbable detainees of a usually benign state apparatus further stimulated reconsideration of the meaning of prison and of writing about prison over the centuries in Italy.

During these same years, agitation for prison reform was also coming to a head as legislation on incarceration that had been devised during the Fascist period began to be replaced by more humane regulatory measures. These changes, it is now clear, have transformed the conditions of confinement in Italy. The descriptions of prison life in the pages to follow, therefore, should be understood as largely applicable to a period of Italian penological history that has now been superseded.

That the men and women studied below were political and not criminal prisoners, and historical rather than fictional figures, makes the writing they have left about their confinement somewhat different from that studied by most of the French and American scholars whose work has been reviewed above. Unlike the inmates Martha Grace Duncan writes about, for example, none of the Italian prisoners whose works I have studied found prison a 'nobler and more meaningful time and place' when compared to the 'mundane world-as-it-is.' Far from having their anxieties assuaged by the stoppage of time that prison imposes, these intellectuals and political activists found existence outside the normal flow of duration one of the most irksome aspects of their punishment. In contrast to the prisoners studied by Duncan, these Italian prisoners were not satisfied simply to 'do time,' but continued to struggle, even while in prison, to transform the times in which they were living. Although many of them already had fiction, poetry, or essays to their credit before they went to jail, the texts they produced about their confinements are not fiction as we usually understand it but testimonies of a historically situated physical and psychological struggle from which their authors either have emerged or hope to emerge victorious.

Prison, similarly, was never viewed by these writers as a welcome opportunity to study and reflect, free from the responsibilities of everyday life.[12] Over and over they insist – often in some surprise – how difficult it is for them to work in detention and how hateful they find their forced exclusion from normal social and intellectual exchange. Involuntary confinement, these writers underline, is dramatically different from the reclusion chosen by monks, nuns, or others who have chosen to withdraw from everyday life for the sake of spiritual growth. Though many of these prisoners do spend much of their time studying and writing, none found prison congenial for such work. Such an attitude is evident, I think, in Gramsci's impatient correcting of Tatiana's too sanguine description of his prison situation in the remarks quoted at the beginning of this book. If the caged bird of the proverb sings, it does not do so from love but from rage.

This sense of frustration at their confinement is often coupled for these prisoners with thoughts of the imminence of death. While only a few of the writers studied here were in danger of losing their lives while in prison (their positions in this regard unlike those of many of their counterparts in the United States today, for example), all of them lived their confinements on closer terms with their own mortality than they ever had before. Forced by the extreme situation of confinement to contemplate the ultimate significance of their existence, these authors of letters or memoirs considered their plights in a state of heightened teleological awareness in which such ultimate matters as the meaning and value of their lives and political commitments took on dramatically increased importance.

Since writing was of such supreme importance to these intellectually astute prisoners, they were willing to go to considerable trouble to write what they wanted without interference from the prison authorities. One characteristic of prison letters of the non-clandestine – that is, censored – sort is that while these documents treat matters of an intensely personal nature and deal with the ultimate issues in their authors' lives, they are always created within harsh and arbitrary externally enforced parameters. A common condition of detention not only in prisons but also in convents, mental hospitals, and other 'total institutions' is that communication from the inmates of these places is invariably monitored by institutional authorities.[13] At least since the Napoleonic era in Italy – and here Foucault's positing of an epistemic 'coupure' in social history between an ancient and a new regime seems accurate for Italy too – prison authorities have served as sole arbiters of the frequency, length, and content of all letters written by those they control.

Such control has led to some unusual collaborations. Nervous, for example, that Federico Confalonieri was continuing to plot insurrection through 'agreed-upon marks' in the handwriting itself of the notes he sent his family from Milan's Santa Margherita prison, the Austrian authorities there insisted that the count's correspondence be transcribed by a prison guard rather than written in his own hand.[14] In the letters she received from her husband, therefore, Teresa Casati Confalonieri was deprived of the 'inexpressible consolation' she had previously felt at the sight of her husband's handwriting (505). In the case of Confalonieri's correspondence, the censor not only participated in the physical creation of a text issuing from a place of detention, he was also able to project his hostile presence beyond the confines of the prison walls, penetrating into the boudoir or other private space where Teresa Confalonieri presumably read her husband's prison communications to her. While this is an example of an unusually conspicuous collaboration between censor and prison author (Confalonieri's letters of this period were signed by both the count and the amanuensis conscripted from among the prison guards), prison correspondence is always the result of an unwanted collaboration between bitter enemies. Even when the censor has not obliterated words, phrases, or paragraphs of a prisoner's letter, he (in all the instances I have studied the censor is male, even in women's prisons) is always there, a malevolent and powerful element in what is not a two- but a three-way process of communication.

In order to carry on a more meaningful exchange with their loved ones, many prisoners have had recourse to clandestine – as distinct from 'ostensible' – communication. Many of the clandestine messages these prisoners wrote were transcribed in 'inchiostro simpatico' or invisible ink, procured from such sources as starch extracted from prison meals, lemon or other acidic juices – even blood or other bodily fluids. Messages produced in this way were usually written between the lines of the writers' ostensible correspondence and became visible when the paper containing them was heated or appropriately treated. Sometimes, however, clandestine messages were written on other materials including cigarette papers rolled in a ball of wax and then transferred to a prison visitor during a goodbye kiss. Or they were scrawled in blood or other substances on the linen Risorgimento prisoners were able to send home for laundering and exchange. Despite the stringency of prison regulations, almost all the prisoners studied here were able to circumvent prison constraints by establishing some sort of clandestine link with the outside. Of modern prisoners, Antonio Gramsci is unusual in that he seems never to have communicated in this way with his comrades beyond the prison walls.

In addition to their indispensable role as links with a personal community of friends and relatives, prison writings also served as ties to history. Such ties were often strengthened by the physical circumstances of incarceration. During the Risorgimento, for example, Italian patriots were often both heartened and appalled to discover that the quarters assigned them had held patriots of an earlier era. Benedetto Croce, in his edition of Silvio Spaventa's writings from Santo Stefano, has recalled how Spaventa 'once spoke of the deep sense of comfort that he derived in that place by evoking the memories of the men of '99 – of Cirillo, of Pagano, of Russo – who had been held in those very same prisons.'[15] When Luigi Settembrini landed on the prison island of Santo Stefano, he was informed that the stronghold there had housed his own father a generation earlier.[16] And when Sandro Pertini disembarked on that same island in the 1930s, he was told by his prison guards that the cell he was allotted had once held Settembrini. 'I thought immediately,' the future president of the Italian republic wrote, 'about the connection between the struggle that we were carrying forward during the second Risorgimento and the struggle carried forward by the participants in the first Risorgimento. And I was proud, glad to be living in a cell in which there had once been such a man as Luigi Settembrini.'[17] Writing, then, served several functions for these prisoners. In addition to enabling them to articulate their own definitions of who they were and what their sacrifices meant, it also provided them with a means to reassert their connections with the flow of time and with history. But in order to establish truly meaningful definitions of themselves and to link their struggle with larger historical currents, almost all of them found it necessary to engage in some sort of clandestine communication.

At the same time, a surprising number of these writers seem to have felt dissatisfied with the accounts of imprisonment they ultimately produced. As will be seen more fully in a later chapter, one recurrent presence in the history of prison writing is the reiterated reference to secret, invisible, or otherwise unreadable texts. Such texts would seem more authentic than those the authors who refer to them have actually composed. In an account of his 1539 release from prison in Rome, Benvenuto Cellini noted how at the moment he regained his liberty, an angel wrote a secret message on his forehead. Admonished by this celestial being not to reveal the content of this message, the otherwise irrepressibly voluble goldsmith never did. Pellico, too, described a secret text that he scratched onto his writing table in the Piombi prison in Venice, a text that was in code, concealed beneath books and papers, and in the end erased with a broken piece of glass.

There are many additional examples of texts that were originally written in prison but later lost, destroyed, or in some other way rendered unreadable. The history of prison writing in the nineteenth century especially is filled with references not only to notes passed between prisoners that, as compromising infractions of prison regulations, were usually destroyed by their recipients, but to novels, poems, plays, devotional and other works composed with great difficulty in confinement only to be impounded, destroyed, misplaced, or lost. The persistence of this trope of an invisible prison text so secret, so clandestine – in Cellini's case perhaps even so sacred – that it cannot be read by anyone is an indication, I believe, of a widespread sense by these writers of the inadequacies of their own, surviving descriptions of their experiences.

The corpus, in this sense, of prison writing can be seen as a vague afterimage of the inexpressible texts of suffering and desire that these authors dreamed of from confinement but were never quite able to create, not in prison under the constraints of the authorities and not in recollection afterwards either. These writers from and about confinement, as we shall see, were prisoners not only of bricks and mortar, but also of the constraints intrinsic to textual creation, dissemination, and interpretation – by the conventions and limits of writing itself. Just how those limits and conventions shaped what they wrote and how they in turn shaped those conventions for their successors will be examined in the pages that follow.

1
Predecessors: Prison Writing before 1800

D'ogn'arte la prigion sa fare e tiene;
...
Poi l'ha in sè un certo naturale:
ti fa loquente, animoso e audace,
carco di bei pensieri in bene e in male.[1]

Benvenuto Cellini, Torquato Tasso, and Giacomo Casanova have long seemed figures more of myth than of history. As historical personages, however, none of them was a political prisoner in the usual sense of the term.[2] Cellini, imprisoned in Rome by papal mandate, was never charged with a specific crime and seems to have been the victim of court intrigue rather than guilty of the thefts with which he was charged; Tasso was imprisoned for purported madness rather than any criminal wrongdoing; and Casanova did not get in trouble for the kind of conduct associated with his name but because books on magic were found in his possession – in other words, because he too had enemies in positions of power.[3] While not criminals in the usual sense, or political subversives like the Risorgimento patriots or anti-Fascists who came later in the history of prison writing in Italy, all these men were transgressive enough in their behaviour for irritated ecclesiastical or civil authorities to decide they should go to jail. Culpable of offences against decorum or religious belief rather than attempts to subvert a government, these writers are precursors of later, more overtly political prisoners who were none the less also jailed for who they were and the ideas they held rather than because they had broken specific laws.

Predecessors: Prison Writing before 1800   13

It seems appropriate to begin a consideration of prison writing in modern Italy with Benvenuto Cellini – often considered the supreme representative of that country's Renaissance or early modern period. At least since Burckhardt, the impetuous, passionate, undisciplined goldsmith, writer, soldier, and lover has come to represent a moment in Italian history when that country's inhabitants were fashioning their lives into artifacts as aesthetically pleasing and widely admired as the Italian art and architecture that were the wonder of the western world.[4]

Cellini was born in Florence on 3 November 1500. After a turbulent adolescence punctuated by numerous scrapes with rivals and the law, he came under the protection of Pope Clement VII, serving during the invasion and sack of Rome as a 'bombardiere' who protected the Pope from the besieging forces of Hapsburg Emperor Charles V. But with Clement's death and the election of Paul III to the papal throne, Cellini lost his privileged position. At the new pope's court he was regarded with diffidence and hostility, especially by the Pope's son, Pier Luigi Farnese. Eager to find a more congenial patron, in 1537 Cellini left Rome for France and the service of King Francis I. When he returned the following fall, he was seized by the police, accused of having stolen papal jewellery during the siege, and clapped into prison in the same Castel Sant'Angelo he had helped defend a decade earlier. The incarceration, which was interrupted by an escape and recapture, lasted slightly more than a year. After release and a second sojourn in hospitable France, Cellini returned to Florence and the patronage of Cosimo de' Medici. During this period he cast the Perseus statue he considered his finest accomplishment in sculpture and wrote his *Vita di Benvenuto Cellini orefice e scultore fiorentino da lui medesimo scritta*. This work, which is sometimes considered the first European autobiography, was abandoned unfinished around 1566, and remained unpublished until 1728 when it appeared in Naples, edited by Antonio Cocchi.

Cellini's description of his life is significantly different from autobiographies written in the centuries to follow him. Unlike Rousseau, for example, the author of the *Vita* – an individual anything but shy about the more colourful aspects of his intimate life – is remarkably indifferent to the motives behind the deeds and adventures he describes. For the impatient and energetic Cellini, writing was not meant to be reflection or analysis but was instead surrogate action, a 'dire' or 'saying' on the same level as his more usual 'fare' or 'doing.' 'Since I have not been allowed to do anything,' is how he described writing about himself during a period of forced inactivity when commissions for sculpture and goldsmithing had temporarily fallen off, 'I have set myself to saying something.'[5]

Cellini's imprisonment lasted from 18 October 1538 to 24 December 1539. Although the accusation of stealing the Pope's jewels seems to have been a spurious one – the prisoner insisted to his judges that a glance at the court inventory would show no items missing – it was bolstered by the authority of Pier Luigi Farnese. And as Cellini well knew, it made no difference whether he had taken the jewels or not. Notwithstanding – or perhaps because of – his protection by the king of France, the Florentine artist was to be kept in prison until the Pope decided otherwise.

Cellini's incarceration was not unduly unpleasant in a physical sense, at least not at first. Thanks to the reputation that had preceded him into Castel Sant'Angelo, the Pope's prisoner was given free rein of the stronghold, allowed to receive mail and see his friends, even permitted to continue goldsmithing. When some of the material he was allowed for the latter activity was stolen from him by other prisoners planning an escape, Cellini persuaded the authorities that he had nothing to do with this plan and was thus able to keep his precious tools. But by this time he was making plans for his own flight from captivity, tearing up his accumulated bedlinen to make a ladder in a classic ploy that was used over and over by prisoners in the centuries to follow.

The disciplinary power at Castel Sant'Angelo during Cellini's stay was the *castellano* or prison warden. A fellow Florentine, Giorgio Ugolini seems to have been almost as bizarre a character as Cellini himself. The warden, moreover, suffered from what should – given his position – have been an incapacitating disease: 'a disorder,' as Cellini called it, that every year 'sent him mad' (199). In the grip of one of these dramatic fits, the warden would believe he had been bodily transformed into such things as an olive jar or a frog. During the time Cellini was with him, Ugolini was especially concerned he was about to change into a bat. When Ugolini told Cellini about his obsession, asking his distinguished prisoner whether he had ever thought of flying like a bat, Cellini responded as if to a challenge. Possibly because he knew of Leonardo da Vinci's earlier experiments in just this area – experiments that involved a remarkably bat-like piece of apparatus – the prisoner was eager to show his warden that he certainly could fly if he wanted to. 'I had tried to do and done all those things that men found most difficult,' he responded to his keeper, 'and as for flying, I said that the God of nature had endowed me with a body that was usually agile and capable of running and leaping exceptional distances, and that I would be able to make use of the little skill I had in my hands, and so I certainly had it in me to fly' (199). However brave one might consider this answer, it was the wrong response to a prison warden like Ugolini. As soon as Cellini's keeper realized what his prisoner's position was on this matter, he ordered him seized, securely tied, and guarded from then on 'with the most elaborate precautions' (200).

Treated in this fashion by the recipient of his confidence about flying, Cellini decided an earlier promise not to escape was now void and announced Houdini-like to his guards they should keep a very careful eye on him, 'because I would do all I can to escape' (200). By this time, in addition to the knotted ladder made from his sheets, Cellini's mattress contained a pair of pliers he had pilfered from castle workmen. Choosing a holiday for the occasion, he used these pliers to remove the nails from the metal supports on his cell door, replacing them with false nail heads he made from wax with his goldsmithing tools. Masking his progress in this way, Cellini was able to dismantle his entire cell door and then use his ladder to let himself down the castle wall. Once he reached the base of the keep, however, he was dismayed to discover he was not in the street but trapped instead in an adjacent courtyard. Thanks to a long beam he found nearby, however, the determined prisoner was able to scale the wall separating him from freedom. But by the time he reached the outer surface of the wall, Cellini was so exhausted from his efforts that he released his hold on his support much too early and plunged to the ground with enough force to knock him unconscious and break one of his legs.

Groggy from this mishap and in pain from the broken limb, Cellini could do little more than crawl to a nearby house, whose inhabitants provided him with informal asylum. By the next morning, news of the Pope's prisoner's escape had spread throughout a gossipy Rome and the celebrity Cellini was soon visited by 'all the nobility of Rome ... young and old, of every rank' (207). Even the pontiff, in Cellini's account, seemed eager to be part of the celebration of his prisoner's attempt, announcing to everyone that he too had once made his way out of captivity in Castel Sant'Angelo – though, as Cellini pointed out, the future Pope had done this the easy way by bribing the jailers – and had been sent to jail in the first place on a substantiated charge of forging documents. As Cellini clearly but somewhat undiplomatically put it, 'he was justly and I was wrongly arrested' (207).

Despite his moment of glory (or perhaps because of his too public basking in that glory), Cellini was soon back in confinement. This time, however, he was not dispatched to the relatively mild confines of Castel Sant'Angelo but held instead in the much grimmer and potentially lethal Torre di Nona, a prison from which few inmates had ever come out alive. Once again, however, Cellini was saved by the intercession of a powerful person – in this case the wife of his great enemy, Pier Luigi Farnese. But though Girolama Orsini was able to persuade her pontifical father-in-law to spare Cellini's life, when the goldsmith was returned to Castel Sant'Angelo, the warden there clapped him into a tiny cell 'down below the garden in ... a very dark, dank room full of tarantulas and noxious worms' (216).

At this point in the *Vita* the tone of the narration changes. Unable to escape physically from the nasty cell with its spiders and worms, Cellini, like many future prisoners, decides to seek refuge in an 'inner escape' of meditation and prayer. Even so, he is tormented by thoughts of suicide. However, when he tries to kill himself by causing a rock-powered booby trap of his own concoction to tumble on top of him, an 'invisible hand' intervenes and flings him – broken leg and all – to safety on the other side of his cell. Reflecting on this episode, Cellini concludes that the unseen force could only have been a 'divine power, my guardian angel.' This angel soon visits him 'in the form of a beautiful young man,' who berates his charge for the suicide attempt, exhorting him to have faith that his future will be a happy one. Encouraged by this encounter, Cellini is able to resuscitate his former and most authentic identity: that of artist. Writing in ink fabricated from brick dust mixed with his own urine, and using a wood splinter for a pen, he composes a sonnet that he inscribes on an empty page of his prison Bible. The subject of this poem is the brilliant future the angel has predicted for him. Thanks to the help of God and His angel, Cellini has conquered his earlier despair and regained both his aplomb and his true identity as artist rather than prisoner.

Before long Cellini finds some bits of charcoal with which he sketches on his prison wall images of 'God the Father, surrounded by angels, and ... the risen Christ in his triumph' (220). Then, on the morning of 3 October 1539, he has a miraculous vision. In this vision (which is remarkably similar to that described by Dante in the final cantos of the *Paradiso*) the Divinity appears to his faithful prisoner in the form of a bright sun the goldsmith can only describe as 'like a bath of the purest liquid gold' (224). For Cellini, this vision is a sign of the special favour he enjoys with the Divinity. 'God in his greatness has made me worthy to set eyes on His glory,' he says, 'on things perhaps never seen before by mortal eyes. So this proves my freedom, and my happiness, and my favour with God.' As for Cellini's enemies (presumably including the Pope, or at least his son Pier Luigi), they will never enjoy similar grace. 'While you, you villains,' he mocks them, 'you shall always be villains, unhappy and in disgrace with God' (224–5).

In the months between 3 October and his release from prison on 24 December, Cellini's enemies struck again, this time attempting to poison him with ground diamonds concealed in his food. But when his jailers stole the diamonds, substituting a 'a poor, cheap stone' (228) for the lethal dust, Cellini both thanked God and blessed the jailers' poverty, 'which although very often causing death this time was the real cause of my remaining alive' (228). In the end, Cardinal Ippolito d'Este was able to secure Cellini's release by detaining the Pope on his way to vomit during an eating orgy and not letting him relieve himself until he agreed to the cardinal's request. When, on Christmas Eve of 1539, Cellini was set free, he discovered that his shadow, especially when cast onto moist grass, was surrounded by an 'aura' or halo. He also had a 'terrible dream' in which 'words of the utmost importance' he was forbidden to reveal (and did not disclose in the *Vita* or anywhere else in his written works) were engraved on his forehead.

Cellini's two prison stints were spiritual and psychological struggles from both of which he emerged victorious, in the second case after divine confirmation of his special status as artist and human being. Confinement provided this early prisoner with an opportunity not only to see the glory of God but also to realize how favoured a person he truly was:

Chi vuol saper quant'è il valor de Dio,
e quant'un uomo a quel Ben si assomiglia,
convien che stie 'n prigione, al parer mio.
...
Sie tristo un, quant'e' può al mondo, in fama,
e stie 'n prigione in circa a due mal'anni,
e' n'esce santo e savio, e ogniun l'ama.[6]

Incarceration, in Cellini's account, has made him wiser, more pious, even more lovable than before. Far from diminishing his vital energy or destroying his identity, prison has strengthened Cellini's opinion of himself as a person uniquely favoured by God and too exceptional for any prison – even the Pope's – to hold. While few future prisoners will be able to match this Renaissance man's unflaggingly positive view of himself, the political prisoners who survive their ordeals in the centuries to follow often join Cellini in the assertion that confinement has not changed their basic identities or caused them to alter their views. However painful it might have been, and however broken it might have rendered them physically, prison, for these writers, was an experience from which they emerged vindicated.

Torquato Tasso (1544–95) belongs to the generation immediately following Cellini's. His experience of confinement was quite different from that of his slightly older contemporary. Best known today as author of the epic poem *Gerusalemme liberata*, Tasso, like his father Bernardo, was a courtier as well as a poet, though a courtier of the pen rather than of the sword or the diplomatic pouch. Much more a part of the literary establishment of his day than Cellini had been, Tasso was a brilliant, though sometimes uncomfortably volatile element in the glittering intellectual retinue gathered by Duke Alfonso II of Este (1533–97) at his Ferrara court in central Italy.

For in addition to being Tasso's patron, Alfonso was eventually forced to become the poet's jailer. Beginning at the time of his marriage to Margherita Gonzaga in 1579, the duke found it necessary to keep his court poet out of the public eye; for more than seven years Tasso was confined to house arrest in Ferrara's Ospedale di Sant'Anna. Whether his incarceration was punitive, a result of the duke's perception of an affront to his dignity and that of his court, or whether he was kept in custody as a preventive measure taken by a head of state worried the poet's ravings on the topic of religious orthodoxy would strain the delicate political relations between his duchy and Rome, Tasso, like Cellini, was imprisoned without trial or even a clear articulation of charges. Deemed mentally unhinged rather than criminally culpable, Tasso was held in Sant'Anna until it was decided he had regained, if not his sanity, at least some awareness of what constituted prudence at a court like Alfonso's.

The nearly five hundred letters Tasso wrote between 1579 and 1586 to a variety of correspondents throughout Italy were immediate responses to their author's trying circumstances; they were also potentially public communications. Just a few years before their author's imprisonment, Pietro Aretino had demonstrated with the successful publication of six volumes of his own letters how eager the Cinquecento reading public was to acquire collections of well-written texts of this sort by or involving famous contemporaries. Aware that anything issuing from his pen had commercial as well as personal value, Tasso viewed his prison letters as communication with a public larger than that of those missives' more immediate recipients.[7]

Despite their semi-public nature, Tasso's letters nevertheless differ from those of modern prison writers in that they are almost entirely free of signs of interference by the authorities detaining him. Not only was the duke's prisoner permitted to write as many letters as he liked, he was able to write to whomever he wanted and say whatever he wanted in them. Even if certain letters were impounded,[8] the letters that emerged from Tasso's place of confinement do not seem to have been censored. While Tasso does complain about 'lost letters' (310), and at one point ingenuously asks the duke to help 'facilitate the reception of the letters that he has written in the states of His Beautitude and of His Majesty and of other princes and republics, as well as of the responses they should have received' (67–8), on the whole he seems satisfied with how his correspondence has been transmitted.[9] And even if he sometimes protests that there are certain matters he would have liked to discuss 'more completely, except that I am not inclined to confide every sort of secret to a letter' (226), he seems to have spoken relatively freely in them.

The principal constraint Tasso felt on his writing while in confinement was not exercised by the prison authorities, but was an effect of confinement itself. In an early letter he described the physical humiliations of life in prison, what he called 'the indignities I must suffer plus the unkemptness of my beard and my hair and my clothing – the filth and the squalor.' Affronts such as these, however, were not nearly as distressing as the solitude to which this prisoner was subject. 'Above all,' he goes on in the same letter, 'I am afflicted by solitude, my cruel and natural enemy that has often bothered me even during better times' (61). Deprived now of any companionship but his own and always a person of extreme sensitivity, Tasso began to fear he was going mad. Encouraged, perhaps, by the ravings of other inmates of Sant'Anna – some of whom were genuinely crazy – or stimulated by the opium and other medications administered somewhat haphazardly to him, he began to experience hallucinations of a particularly vivid and bizarre sort. In a letter to Maurizio Cataneo of 30 December 1585, for example, Tasso describes hearing distressing noises like that of a wind-up clock, speaks of mice that seem preternaturally present, and says he sometimes feels as though a horse has fallen on top of him (479–80). Only once are these images encouraging. In the letter just quoted, the prisoner goes on to describe a vision he has had of the Madonna with the infant Jesus. But unlike

Cellini, whose similar experience with divine visions convinced him that God held him in special favour, Tasso was not encouraged but suspicious and distressed by what he saw. 'And although it might easily have been a fantasy,' he concluded, 'since I am jittery, and bothered incessantly by phantoms of various sort, and plunged in melancholy, none the less, by the grace of God, I am able at times to *cohibere assensum* [control my emotions]: an act that Cicero asserts is the mark of a wise man. For these reasons, I prefer to believe that what I saw was a miracle wrought by the Virgin' (480).

While this particular vision may have been a miracle, Tasso's hallucinations are usually the fruits of his imagination, a faculty he knows can be controlled by his reason. Although unsure if the forces badgering him are diabolical or human, Tasso knows he must trust in free will and his God-given intellect if he is to survive his psychological ordeal. 'And thus I am unable to defend anything from attacks by my enemies or the devil,' he says about this, 'except my will, thanks to which I would not agree to learn anything from him or his followers, nor to engage in any sort of familiarity with him or his wizards, the latter of which, as Ficino notes, though they can move one's imagination, have no force or authority without the consent of our reason, which derives directly from God' (478).[10] The principal danger of prison for Tasso is that his reason will not be strong enough to control the feelings and images that arise to beset him from the depths of his own imagination.

Although recent studies have documented how the sensory deprivation of prison itself is often enough by itself to produce terrifying apparitions,[11] Tasso's terrors seem to have besieged him even after he was moved to more comfortable, private accommodations and permitted visitors. The hallucinations, in addition, made it impossible for him to work. This, in turn, made him feel so overcome by an 'overpowering rage' that when he tried to write 'I often don't finish the letters but tear them up, and then begin to recopy them – as I have done with this one' (162). Whether Tasso was later able, as Giovanni Getto suggests, to make artistic use of his prison sufferings as 'experiences suited to give his poetry original nuances and enrich his poetic universe with unexplored provinces and continents,'[12] the jailed Tasso was sorely tried both as a man and as a writer. It is no wonder that when he finally emerged from prison he felt defeated by the experience. As he wrote in 1585 to Angelo Papio:

You must realize, therefore, that because of my sickness over these many years I am extremely forgetful and thus very unhappy. But it is not just this. I have other troubles too, any one of which – let alone all of them combined as I will describe and list them to you – would be enough to make a man unhappy. The first is my loss, after many years, of my employment and service. Then there is my poverty, the reason why I was put in this place and am still abiding here. Plus the infirmities of my faculties and my limbs in what is almost a premature old age. Plus confinement and consequent ignorance of what is going on in the world. And my loneliness, something more distressing and annoying than everything else, since it is based on the deprivation not just of people but of friends. In addition, there is the restlessness of many others nearby, people who constantly annoy me, unmasking themselves as enemies of my peace of mind. (398–9)

Loss of employment and consequent poverty, bodily and sensual debilitation, ignorance of what has been going on in the world outside his prison walls, above all his solitary condition far from his friends – this, plus resentment at his enemies' plotting, is the meaning of prison for Tasso.

One issue at the centre of all prison writing is that of the guilt or innocence of the prison author. Unlike most modern prisoners who, even if they concede their culpability under a prevailing legal system, frequently appeal to a higher authority for exculpation, Tasso admits he is guilty of whatever it is that has brought him to jail. 'Therefore, my lord,' he writes to the duke at the beginning of his prison term, 'rather than excuse, I accuse myself' (15), going on to explain that 'I am no longer seeking justice but asking for pardon and clemency' (43). Political prisoners of later years typically refused to solicit pardons, considering such a request both an act of cowardice and an inappropriate admission of guilt. Tasso, however, begged for mercy from Alfonso. 'Among transgressions toward one's neighbour,' he says, 'the most serious are those that offend the majesty of princes. Such acts are quite similar to those directed by pride and human impiousness at the greatness of God.' This is because, Tasso continues, 'earthly princes are the ministers of God, and the images and simulacra of his power' (9). When later in this same letter Tasso compares his sufferings to those of a parricide (10), it is clear he considers lese-majesty on a level with murdering one's father – an identification of the two crimes that will be invoked again in nineteenth-century Italy, though by civil government rather than by a prisoner.[13]

Even though he admits he is guilty, Tasso does not take sole responsibility for what he has done. His failings, in his view, are due 'partly to Fortune, partly to Nature, and partly also to the violence and treachery of my enemies, so that my own part is the least and the lightest.' Tasso's mistake 'if it must be considered such, must not be thought of as premeditated but is, rather, unpremeditated – an involuntary rather than a voluntary action' (481). Although towards the end of his imprisonment Tasso sings a somewhat different tune,[14] it is clear he wants Alfonso to grant him 'pardon for the false and ill-considered words for which I was imprisoned, and to bring about the pardon of all the errors of all my other ill-considered actions' (67). The Estensi, after all, have made him what he is. As he explains to Lucrezia D'Este, 'if I live, if I breathe, if I hope, if I write or think of writing poetry or prose that is not found unpleasing, this is thanks to your assent and special concession' (355–6). Tasso's very existence as man and writer has been granted him in the first place by the princely force that now has seen fit to send him to confinement.

The letters Tasso wrote from Sant'Anna were those of a political prisoner, if one defines such a person as someone whose views are deemed dangerous or otherwise unacceptable by a given regime. The themes he articulates in them – especially his fear of losing his mind, his surprise and irritation that prison is not such a good place for study and writing after all, and his realization that survival in prison will depend on his ability to exercise his free will and his intelligence successfully – recur in writings by political prisoners of subsequent centuries. But unlike Cellini, and unlike most later political prisoners, Tasso does not believe that he emerged from prison triumphant or vindicated. On the contrary, prison has been a terrifying experience he is relieved to have survived with his physical and mental faculties reasonably intact. While most of the prison authors considered in the pages to follow stress how their confinement left them unchanged, perhaps even 'santo e savio' as Cellini insisted, all of them were subject to the psychological torments described by Tasso, not least among them the realization that, as Tasso put it, 'when the body is imprisoned, it is unlikely that the pen be entirely free' (325). Or, as the vice-director of the Casa di Reclusione maschile at Rebibbia, Mariapia Frangeamore, commented in 1989, 'one commonly thinks that freedom of thought cannot be substantially impugned, but this is not true either. That a man is a psycho-physical unity is again confirmed and enhanced by the realization that depriving a person of his bodily liberty also deprives him of his liberty of spirit. Little by little, a person in jail loses the ability to think and to take care of himself independently and inevitably adopts the ways of thinking dominant in his peer group.'[15] Although his prison experience took place under very different conditions from those of Rebibbia today, Tasso too was aware of the paralysing effect prison could have on an inmate who was also a writer. His remarks on this subject are re-articulated centuries later not only by commentators such as Frangeamore but by such well-known prison writers as Antonio Gramsci in the 1930s.

One of the most extraordinary of all the Italian prison memoirs from the period before the French Revolution is *Les aventures de Joseph Pignata echappé des prisons de l'Inquisition de Rome*. Published, according to the title page, in Cologne by Pierre Marteau in 1725, Giuseppe Pignata's account of his escape from a Roman prison has been printed not only in this eighteenth-century French-language edition but in several Italian versions as well. The latest of these is *Le avventure di Giuseppe Pignata fuggito dalle carceri dell'Inquisizione di Roma*, published by Sellerio in 1980. In this edition, the translation from French into Italian is by Olindo Guerrini, and Pignata's text is accompanied by a historical essay on the writer and his times by Alessandro D'Ancona.[16] In the Sellerio as in the earlier French edition, Pignata's adventures are preceded by explanatory comments by the story's editor that address the extraordinary nature of the tale that is about to be told and explain why that tale is cast in the first person. 'It is so unusual and almost incredible,' Marteau says in 1725, 'that a man could escape on his own from the Roman prisons of the Inquisition, that I believed it would please the public to be informed how Joseph Pignata was successful in his attempt to escape from such a stronghold.'[17] Marteau then goes on to say that the story of Pignata's escape 'will be the word-for-word account that Joseph Pignata himself provided and that I will in fact present as if he himself were doing the telling' (4).

Thanks in part to the liveliness of the first-person narration that Marteau adopted, his presentation of Pignata's adventures was a resounding success, though it had to wait for translation into English until well into the twentieth century, when it was translated by Arthur Symonds in 1930.[18] In the years after 1725 Pignata's story became extremely popular throughout Europe – in Germany, for example, where annotated versions of it in French and Italian were utilized as texts for learning those Romance languages. Shortly after mid-century, moreover, as sometimes happened in this period of publishing history, Pignata's tale was issued in a contaminated version in which the story as it had appeared in 1725 was blended together with another tale: *L'Infortuné Napolitain ou les Aventures du Seigneur Rozelli* by the Abbé Olivier. In this German edition published at Augsberg in Italian in 1768, Pignata's story had become the

Avventure maravigliose ed interessanti del famoso Giuseppe Cafardo, nobile romano, date a luce da un suo amico fedelissimo colle annotazioni tedesche atte a portare in pro della gioventù di Germania, che brama d'inoltrarsi nella lingua italiana.[19] As the *British Library General Catalogue of Printed Books* points out (probably following D'Ancona), this Augsberg version destined in part for Italian language students is a translation of the French *Aventures*, but with Cafardo's name substituted for Pignata's, the dates altered, and new material added from *L'Infortuné Napolitain*. As this brief account of this text's publishing vicissitudes shows, then, the adventures of Pignata's book in the eighteenth-century publishing arena were nearly as varied, unpredictable, and cosmopolitan as those recounted in the story itself.

Leaving aside Giuseppe Cafardo, Seigneur Rozelli, and the Abbé Olivier, and turning instead to a consideration of the structure of Pignata's story as narrated by Marteau, it is immediately clear that the narrative material in *Les Aventures de Joseph Pignata* can be divided into two parts. The first of these centres on a description of the protagonist's imprisonment and escape, while the second features the fugitive's adventures travelling first south, then east and north across Italy and the Adriatic coast to Venice, Austria, and finally Amsterdam.

In the first several pages of his book, Pignata describes his imprisonment for suspected heresy, though he is careful not to specify the exact charges involved. As Marteau comments, his author 'was extremely reluctant to go into detail about the reasons for his detention,' in part because 'his fear of the Holy Office had been so strongly impressed on him that he still trembles when it is mentioned' (4–5). In regard to his life before prison, Pignata is equally reticent, though he does mention being in the service of several high churchmen before joining the retinue of the Roman Monsignor and 'protonotario apostolico' Pietro de' Gabrielli. He also notes that it was his presence in de' Gabrielli's household, in particular his association with the abbot Antonio Oliva there, that led to all three men's arrests, trials, and imprisonment. This is backed up by original documents D'Ancona says he has consulted, evidence that verifies how on 15 February 1692, de' Gabrielli made formal adjuration to Church authorities of his religious heterodoxy. On 15 March of that year, this record continues, Pignata's protector was sentenced to life imprisonment.[20] Something similar presumably happened to the *Aventures'* autobiographical hero.

In his book, however, Pignata has little to say about his difficulties with ecclesiastical authorities and concentrates instead on the story of his confinement. One of the first episodes in his story is an account of the unusual way this prisoner managed to write music in detention. When Pignata was not permitted the spinet piano he had hoped would be delivered to his prison cell, he turned instead to his writing table, which he managed to use as an imaginary keyboard, moving his fingers on it 'as if it were a harpsichord, imagining all the sounds of the strings just as if I were hearing them' (10). Working in silence in this way, he was able to 'set the Vespers of the Blessed Virgin, and compose some Airs – all to escape the distress of idleness' (10). As will be seen later, this set of silent musical texts composed on a writing desk in Pignata's Roman prison foreshadows the many lost, destroyed, invisible, or otherwise unreadable documents that appear in the writings of many Risorgimento and some later prisoners – 'virtual' texts whose significance is discussed in the chapters to follow.

After nearly two years of pre-trial confinement, Pignata was finally granted a day in court. Whatever happened during his hearing, the existence itself of his memoir is proof that he was not found guilty of heresy, since that crime was punished by excommunication and public burning. Instead of being led to the stake, it seems, Pignata and the others were sentenced to 'do penance by fasting and praying for a certain period, to make confession and take communion four times a year' – punishment that does not sound too severe until the narrator adds, almost as an afterthought: 'and they condemned us to life in prison' (46).

Pignata, however, was not ready to spend the rest of his days in confinement. Like Cellini, this later prisoner was an accomplished artist as well as a musician, and it was thanks in part to his artistic skills that he was able to obtain the tools he needed for his prison break. Noting that a number of the Inquisition's prisoners were making straw knick-knacks they then gave to the guards for sale or their own private use, Pignata too set to producing objects of this sort. His creations were so attractive, furthermore – possibly because he tried to give them 'a certain style that would strike the eye without revealing how they were made' (20) – that he was allowed first scissors, then a penknife, paints, and other materials. During this period the prisoner also pretended to be suffering from an abdominal hernia, simulating the malady so well that the prison doctor was fooled into providing him with a truss that contained a circular steel band Pignata was able to remove and fashion into a digging tool. This tool, plus two metal hinges from his cell door and the scissors and knife already mentioned, were all he needed to break out of his cell into the larger space of the prison proper.

Unlike Cellini and Tasso, Pignata had a cell mate, a certain Filippo

Alfonsi, whose historical existence D'Ancona has also documented. Inspired by a dream he later realized was of 'divine inspiration' (41), Pignata decided to use his improvised tools to breach not the walls but the less thick ceiling of his cell. Perched unsteadily on a scaffold made from all their furniture heaped up into a pile, Pignata and Alfonsi were able, in fact, to dig their way into the apartment directly over them, a space usually occupied by a prison official but that was fortunately empty at the time of their attempt. Once they reached the staging point of this apartment, which they did on the night of 9 November 1693, it was relatively easy for the duo to clamber down on knotted sheets into the street outside the prison. Alfonsi, however, like Cellini earlier, released his grip on the sheets prematurely and fell to the ground, breaking his leg in the tumble. When the more careful Pignata reached the bottom of the wall, he realized there was nothing he could do for his injured comrade and so escaped into the night without him. After several sensational adventures as he made his way out of papal into Neapolitan territory, then by boat up the Adriatic from Pescara to Venice, and then overland to Austria, the Inquisition's escapee finally reached safety in Protestant Holland.

As much a gentleman as Cellini with his earlier scruples about having given his word not to escape, Pignata took pains, before leaving his place of detention, to leave two notes, one to the Pope and the Holy Congregation, the other to the warden, in which he requested that masses be said in his name – a request that, given the circumstances, must have surprised this angry official. Though now a free man, however, Pignata – again like Cellini before him – soon discovered that his escape had made him a celebrity, a status that proved more liability than asset, since its principal result was to increase the zeal of his pursuers.

As depicted in the *Aventures*, Giuseppe Pignata is an immensely skilled and resourceful person. During his flight, he supports himself by giving music lessons, composing an opera, and – in a remarkable display of still another artistic skill – designing a house. He also manages to maintain his aplomb in what are often very trying circumstances. But if the hero of this account of a daring escape, with his unflagging self-confidence, formidable artistic skills, and ability to improvise, recalls the flamboyant and supremely self-assured Cellini of the *Vita*, Pignata's legal situation was somewhat different from Cellini's. Unlike Cellini, who was imprisoned as the result of the personal pique of a powerful cleric, Pignata was formally tried by an official arm of the Church and was thus a prisoner of this institution rather than of an individual. He also seems to have been tortured (37), something both Cellini and Tasso were spared.[21]

Both Cellini and Pignata escaped from prisons that belonged to the Catholic hierarchy, the earlier prisoner from the Castel San'Angelo, Pignata from the nearby Inquisition stronghold in St Peter's Square. Almost as if he had read Cellini's *Vita* (which in 1725 was still unpublished), Pignata was careful to make his break from a cell on the outside of the building and thus not end up in an inner courtyard as his unlucky predecessor had done. Like Cellini, he was able to obtain the tools necessary for escape because of his skills as an artist. Also like his predecessor, who used false nail heads made of wax to hide his escape preparations, Pignata concealed the hole he and Alfonsi were making in their cell's ceiling with a papier-mâché cover produced for this purpose in his tiny prison workshop.

But it is Pignata's account of his flight after his escape that differentiates his story the most from Cellini's. In this second part of the book, literary rather than historical influences come to dominate the narration. I think that it can be concluded, in fact, that despite D'Ancona's success in documenting the historical existence of de' Gabrielli, Alfonsi, and Pignata himself, as well as of his prison escape,[22] *Les Aventures de Joseph Pignata* is, finally, and especially in its longer, second part, too good to be true. To a striking degree, the story has all the characteristics of the popular picaresque novels of the day. Its first-person narration treats an outsider adrift in a world of danger who is quickly involved in a series of fast-moving episodes that take place in a markedly material social context – typical aspects of the picaresque as defined, for example, by Claudio Guillén.[23] The picaresque nature of Pignata's story is particularly evident in the fantastic adventures its hero has during his flight up the Adriatic to Venice, Austria, and Amsterdam. In this section of the book, Pignata is threatened first by bandits and then by a pack of wolves, is caught in a terrifying sea storm, and explores exotic and unfamiliar lands, some of whose inhabitants – women, for example, with breasts so long they suckle infants riding on their backs (186) – are clearly creatures more of fiction than of historical observation. Repeatedly rescued in the nick of time by surprise benefactors, his own quick wit, or just good luck, the fugitive is finally reunited with his brother and mother in an ending that also seems literarily contrived.

One episode at the beginning of the book is perhaps emblematic of Pignata's attitude to such artistic contrivance – to the relationship between melodies heard only in the imagination and those instead that are audible to all. During his knick-knack making period, Pignata was asked by a turnkey to do a portrait of this man's sweetheart. In response, he created a portrait so true to life that his delighted customer swore 'that it was his beloved in the flesh, and that it was impossible to imagine seeing a better likeness of her' (14–15). Whatever resemblances existed between this portrait and the jailer's girl friend were entirely fortuitous, however, since Pignata never saw the woman in question. But never mind. A composer of virtual music of an imagined rather than acoustically verifiable nature, Pignata seems to have been the creator of adventures that were unheard of as well, except in fiction.

Pignata's book, furthermore, is itself almost certainly a product – the cynical creation, even – of an individual who is himself a fictional concoction. In his *Imprimeurs imaginaires*, a study of eighteenth-century publishers' pseudonyms, Gustave Brunet says in regard to the Pierre Marteau who figures as the publisher of Pignata's book that 'there is no imaginary publisher whose name is used more often than his.' Brunet goes on to explain that 'especially during the second half of the reign of Louis XIV, presses in Holland increased the number of political writings, lampoons, and satires credited to him.' For this reason, Brunet continues, Marteau's name often 'appears on the frontispieces of many banned or bannable volumes destined to be sold clandestinely.'[24] Like other works of popular reading matter of the time,[25] the adventures of Giuseppe Pignata, I believe, were almost certainly fiction: the invention of an anonymous publisher, probably located in Holland (the country, it will be remembered, where Pignata's adventures reached a happy conclusion), eager to cash in on the vogue of prison writings during this period and along the way to do some Catholic-bashing of a sort he knew would please his Protestant readers in Germany and elsewhere.

The success of Marteau's – or, better, 'Marteau's' – book in German-speaking countries is thus explained. The positive reception of his rousing story in those latitudes seems to have been enhanced, furthermore, by the stereotypical nature of the book's principal character. In addition to being the innocent victim of a cruel and arbitrary Catholic church that by this time was an object of both mistrust and fascination in northern Europe, the Italian hero of the *Aventures* is also an exceptionally charming individual, much more so than the mostly dishonest beer-loving Northerners he meets outside Italy, individuals whose culinary and social habits frequently astonish and appal him. As is well known, this contrast between an engaging and educated but somewhat raffish Italian – especially in matters of religion – and stolid but honest northern Europeans is a recurrent theme in the literatures of northern Europe, a topos that reappears much later, for example, in the writings of Thomas Mann.

As an early example of the stereotypical Italian adventurer who lives by his wits and astounds the inhabitants of less favoured climes, 'Giuseppe Pignata' prefigures another famous Italian, the Giacomo Casanova whose name became eponymous for flamboyant seductions in the context of what can only be called his very catholic enthusiasm for women. Pignata's case also shows how much all writing from or about prison is itself captive to previous conceptualizations of similar ordeals. Giuseppe Pignata as he appears in Marteau's *Aventures* (or as Giuseppe Cafardo in the Augsberg *Avventure maravigliose*) derives in large part, I believe – especially if the date 'Marteau' gives his work is also false, and Pignata's *Aventures* were published after Cellini's *Vita* first saw the light in 1728 – from Cellini's autobiographical description of his similar prison break.[26] Although the prison writing of all the other authors considered here is not invented but based on what was often painful personal experience, the accounts presented in these texts could not help but be influenced by what previous prisoners – real or fictional – wrote about their analogous experiences. In addition to being prisoners of the state, the authors whose writings are treated in this book were also prisoners of preceding descriptions of the experiences they had of course lived through themselves but were none the less constrained to conceptualize in terms of what had been written by their predecessors. Pignata's fictional rather than historical status as a writer only underlines the inescapable nature of the intertextual dilemma with which all these individuals are forced to wrestle.

Giacomo Casanova (1725–98) was born in Venice the same year Pignata's *Aventures* were supposedly published for the first time. Thirty years later, on 25 July 1755, he was arrested in the city of his birth for possessing books on magic and imprisoned in the Piombi prison attached to the Ducal Palace in St Mark's Square. On the night of 31 October 1756, Casanova – like Cellini and Pignata before him – escaped from the stronghold confining him, in his case like Pignata's by making a hole in the ceiling of his cell, and climbing onto the palace roof. From there he was able to break into the adjoining complex of offices and meeting rooms, out of one of which he calmly (but briskly) walked the next morning. Some thirty years after these events, now resident at the court of Count Waldstein in Bohemia, Casanova wrote an account of his famous escape. He published this work in 1788, calling it the *Histoire de ma fuite des prisons de la République de Venise, qu'on appelle les Plombs, écrite à Dux en Bohéme 1787*, Leipzig (= Prague), 1788.[27] A few years later, still at Waldstein's court, Casanova incorporated the material of the *Histoire de ma fuite* into the fourth and fifth books of his *Histoire de ma vie*, the twelve-volume autobiography he wrote between 1790 and 1792 – a book whose publishing history is so unusual as to deserve a brief digression.

When Casanova died in 1798, the *Histoire de ma vie* was still in manuscript. Sold to the Leipzig publisher Brockhaus, Casanova's monumental autobiography was first printed in 1822–8 in a German adaptation by Wilhelm von Schütz. Although this German version did not always follow its author's manuscript faithfully, it was so successful that French translations pirated from von Schütz began to appear almost immediately. In response, Brockhaus decided to bring out Casanova's work in the original. Although its author's native language was Italian – more precisely Venetian – Casanova had reasoned that 'the French language is more widely known than mine,'[28] and composed both the *Histoire de ma fuite* and the *Histoire de ma vie* in that more widely read tongue.[29] But publishing Casanova's memoir in French turned out not to be a simple matter. Brockhaus, uneasy about the linguistic as well as the moral propriety of what Casanova had written, turned over the manuscript to Jacques Laforgue, professor of French at the University of Dresden, for editing. The version Laforgue produced was called (somewhat ironically, given what this editor did to it) *Mémoires de J. Casanova de Seingalt écrits par lui-même*. It was published in instalments, the first four volumes in 1826–7, volumes five to eight in Paris in 1832 (the same year as Pellico's *Le mie prigioni*), and the final four in Brussels in 1838.

Despite its title, the memoir that Laforgue published was no longer Casanova's. Not content with standardizing his author's occasionally Italianate French (among other things, Casanova had a very un-Gallic passion for the *passé simple*), Laforgue took it upon himself to correct his author's religious and political views as well. Laforgue's changes in both the substance and the style of the text entrusted him have been universally condemned by Casanova scholars, who have not hesitated to term him 'one of the crassest prigs in the annals of literature,' accusing Laforgue of 'all the crimes open to an adapter or translator, and some that go beyond those limitations.'[30] Even so, until well into this century, the Laforgue Casanova was the only French version of the adventurer's life in circulation and, as such, the principal source for critical opinion about Casanova and his writing.

Despite a rising tide of anti-Laforgue sentiment in the early decades of the twentieth century, Brockhaus refused to issue a more philologically accurate edition of the *Histoire de ma vie*, or even to permit access to the manuscript. It was only after the Second World War, during which the

Leipzig seat of the German publishing firm was bombed (the precious manuscript, according to one account, was saved by bicycle and U.S. Army truck), that Brockhaus gave in to the entreaties of the scholarly world. In 1960–2, more than a century and a half after Casanova finished writing it, an 'Édition intégrale' of the *Histoire de ma vie* was finally published by F.A. Brockhaus in Wiesbaden and the Librairie Plon in Paris – an occurrence hailed in some quarters as 'the literary event of the century.'[31] While Casanova's account of his adventures was not subject to censorship at the time of its composition, the story of his imprisonment and escape as contained in his autobiography was itself held hostage for more than two centuries after the events described in it.[32]

Casanova's point of view in his autobiography is perforce a retrospective one. The first volume, especially, presents the enthusiasms and activities of an inexperienced and often ingenuous young man as filtered through the sometimes defective and distorting memory of an old roué. As Casanova remarks in a preface, in the *Histoire de ma vie* he is content to 'jouir par réminiscence.'[33] The stories Casanova tells, however, are no more personal confessions than were Cellini's – much less 'Pignata's.' 'I would not give my history the title of confessions,' he says in the *Histoire de ma fuite*, 'for since an absurd person has soiled the word, I can no longer bear it.'[34] Unlike Rousseau and modern autobiographers who have followed his lead, Casanova, like Cellini before him, takes little interest in his hero's inner life and motivations. When looking back over his existence, moreover, he does not perceive that it has followed any special pattern. Although such other Italian memorialists of this period as Carlo Goldoni (1707–93) in his *Mémoires* (1787) or Vittorio Alfieri (1749–1803) in his *Vita* (1790–1803) saw their lives as the progressive realizations of their identities as playwrights,[35] when Casanova considers the years now behind him, all he can see is a non-purposive, almost random series of responses to invitations to seek pleasure and avoid pain – mostly the former. In his autobiography Casanova portrays his life as determined by his giving in to such impulses as hopping into the saddle of an unattended mount for the first horseback ride of his life, suddenly ordering a snappy military uniform of his own design, and of course (and above all) succumbing almost as if he cannot help himself to the blandishments of beautiful (or at least beautifully willing) women. 'The reader who likes to think,' he says about his helter-skelter approach to autobiography, 'will see in these memoirs that, since I never aimed at a set goal, the only system I followed, if system it may be called, was to let myself go wherever the wind which was blowing drove me' (1: 26). 'The reality that is transmitted by his pages,' an Italian critic has remarked, 'is thus substantially non-reflective – not transfigured, synthesized, or selected in light of a premeditated or preordained end, whether this be a self-apologetic or a didactic one.'[36]

For the narrator of the *Histoire de ma vie*, Casanova's imprisonment in the Piombi is another example of something that happened to him rather than something for which he was personally responsible. Although he could have taken the advice of his Venetian patron, Matteo Giovanni Bragadin, and have fled from the city when he realized he had come under official suspicion, Casanova let the State Inquisition arrest him almost without protest.[37] If he were to flee, he says, somewhat unconvincingly, 'I should be showing a fear which would declare me guilty, for an innocent person, having no remorse, can have no fears either' (4: 198). Even though he does not know exactly what he has been charged with, Casanova is sure there are several areas of his life and behaviour that might well have kindled the inquisitors' ire,[38] and it seems unlikely this famous scallywag, even in his own time, could have convinced anyone of his lack of culpability in regard to any number of escapades. None the less, during his detention – in this like Cellini and unlike Tasso – Casanova continues to protest his innocence, especially in the absence of a specific charge.

The French critic and psychoanalyst François Roustang has pointed out how in Casanova's book episodes of great happiness (or at least of very intense excitement) invariably alternate with passages of abysmal unhappiness. 'If the reader pays attention,' Roustang says, 'he will notice that the happy periods of love and power are followed by others during which the hero of the comedy descends into the most sordid depths of human experience. For Casanova, days of splendor and vanity are never far from those of misery and failure ... The whole of Casanova's autobiography could be read as an attempt to propose ever more complex montages so that he can hide from himself the abyss that constantly threatens to open under his feet.'[39] And it is true that in the *Histoire de ma vie*, Casanova's imprisonment in the Piombi comes right after one of the most spectacular erotic scenes in this author's work: a 'ménage' not 'à trois' but 'à quatre,' featuring one inexperienced and one thoroughly libertine nun, the voyeuristic French ambassador to the Venetian Republic, and an especially indefatigable and imaginative Casanova as star of the piece. Although there is no question of Casanova's suggesting, in some sort of Puritan economy of pleasure and retribution, that the cost of his exponentially augmented bliss in these encounters is his subsequent suffering in the Piombi's 'abyss,' the juxtaposition of these two episodes would none the less seem to support Roustang's theory.

It is not true, however, that the Piombi episode represents an 'abyss' in a spatial sense. After being taken to San Marco Square and escorted across the Bridge of Sighs to the prison in the Ducal Palace, Casanova was placed 'sotto i piombi,' that is, in a kind of attic beneath the lead-panelled roof of this famous building. At first he was held in solitary confinement, his only company some 'rats as big as rabbits' (4: 205) that terrified him almost as much as Tasso's mice had frightened him in Ferrara.[40] Unaware of the charges against him and excluded from the hearing eventually held about his case, Casanova felt like a cog in a malevolent machine. 'The only business of the Venetian tribunal,' he comments in a mechanistic metaphor typical of the imagination of his age, 'is to judge and to sentence; the guilty person is a machine that does not need to take any part in the business in order to co-operate in it; he is a nail which, to go into a plank, needs only to be hammered' (4: 217).

But though beaten down metaphorically like a nail into a plank, Casanova was in reality located high up rather than in a spatially subordinate position. Unlike Cellini, who after his escape from Castel Sant'Angelo was reincarcerated in a 'very dark, damp room' beneath the garden,[41] Casanova was successively confined in two different cells high above Venice, from the second of which he had a panoramic view of the city. Despite the heat rendering this location 'under the lead' almost unbearable in the summer, when compared to the 'pozzi' cells located at sea level (and sometimes below) at the bottom of the prison, the upper cells of the Ducal Palace were a kind of 'purgatoire' to the 'pozzi's' 'enfer,' (4: 262).[42] For Casanova, his physical position high above Venice is a figure for the moral and intellectual superiority he feels in regard to the jailers and other prisoners he meets during his stay there, individuals almost invariably described as 'sots,' 'bêtes,' 'animaux,' and 'monstres,' while he, on the contrary, is an 'homme d'esprit.'[43] When he makes his escape from the Piombi by clambering out onto the roof and then breaking into the Ducal Palace itself, Casanova has descended from the heroic world where he has risked his life but maintained his essential superiority, to a lower level of existence where, as he soon discovers, such commonplace essentials for flight as money, food, clothes, transportation, and a bed to sleep in become crucial.

But before this could happen and while still contemplating his escape from 'sotto i piombi,' Casanova came to an agreement with an accomplice, the Somascan monk Father Marin Balbi, who accompanied him on his prison break. He also became acquainted with an even more valuable confederate: the 'verrou' or door bolt he found abandoned in a hallway outside his cell and sharpened into an 'esponton' or pike that, during his escape, served him both as a digging tool and a potential weapon. Casanova also made astute use of the books he was supplied in prison. Permitted to purchase a folio Bible, he exploited the ample dimensions of this tome, hiding the 'esponton,' in its binding and then persuading the jailer to carry the volume to Father Balbi in an adjoining cell. To prevent the guard during this episode from seeing the tool's protruding ends, Casanova placed the Bible under a huge plate of gnocchi dripping with such an amount of butter that the jailer had to concentrate so hard on not spilling the butter onto the sacred book that he did not realize what he was really transporting. While the jailer here is the victim of his own prejudices (and possibly his gluttony as well), the Bible, for Casanova, is clearly a work of great utility.

The same is true for certain other books Casanova has read before his imprisonment – among them works by such Italian authors as Dante, Boccaccio, Ariosto, and Metastasio. Acting on one of his frequent whims, and protesting the while he does not believe in consulting verses chosen at random from the Bible or Virgil's *Aeneid* as a way of divining the future, the prisoner employs just this method of predicting his liberation by consulting Ariosto's *Orlando furioso*. Remarking about Ariosto that 'I worshipped his genius and I thought him far better suited than Vergil to foretell my good fortune' (4: 285), Casanova discovers in Ariosto that he is to regain his liberty 'between the end of October and the beginning of November' – that is, on Hallowe'en night, the date he does escape. 'The clarity of the verse and its appropriateness struck me as so amazing,' he says about this, 'that I will not say I had complete faith in it, but my reader will forgive me if, for my part, I prepared to do all that I could to help verify the oracle' (4: 285). There is nothing wrong with oracles, in other words, or with books either, as long as the person considering their messages knows how to use and not be used by them.

Another Italian author Casanova exploits while in jail is Boccaccio. Shortly before the date set for the break, Casanova realizes that unless he can manage to bully his new cell mate, the treacherous and cowardly Soradaci, into keeping quiet about his preparations, his plan is sure to fail. After Soradaci betrays him in another, less important matter that Casanova has arranged as a test, Casanova convinces this 'méchant sot animal' that the Madonna has come to him in a vision, has pardoned

Soradaci for his treachery, and intends to send an angel to release the two of them from prison. When Balbi, as prearranged, bursts through the ceiling of the two men's cell, the credulous Soradaci believes he is the Madonna's angelic messenger, though not 'en qualité d'ange mais en qualité d'homme' ('in the shape not of an angel but of a man'). This phrase is a tip-off that the entire episode has been lifted from Boccaccio's *Decameron*.[44] In making use of it, Casanova has again shown how a resourceful person must use literature rather than be used by it.[45]

For Casanova, self-reliance rather than passive trust in Providence is what is needed to escape from jail. After he finds the door bolt he will fashion into an 'esponton,' he notes how 'thus did God provide me with what I needed for an escape which was to be a wonder if not a miracle' (234). But while the workings of Providence are important in an individual's destiny, Casanova, like Tasso, is convinced that what really counts is the strength of one's will. Looking back at his escape at the end of the *Histoire de ma fuite*, he draws this conclusion: 'My tale will prove that we are all fools as long as we seek the causes for everything sinister that happens to us somewhere beyond ourselves. We will find these causes more readily within ourselves. But as we examine ourselves we must be careful not to flatter our vanity since this dims the divine light of reason, seduces and blinds us. We must make ourselves the judges not the advocates of who we are.'

Whether or not Casanova had read Cellini's *Vita* as well as the works by the other Italian authors he mentions in his two *histoires*,[46] his conclusions about why his escape was successful are very different from Cellini's. For Casanova, freedom from shackles of whatever sort – including those that come from incautious reading or from reliance on miracles – was crucial to success. As Roustang comments, 'what he tries to construct is a free man – not in the classical sense, but rather in the sense of freedom from any obligations or constraints' (3). Casanova himself had said in the first sentence of his memoirs, 'I begin by declaring to my reader that, by everything good or bad that I have done throughout my life, I am sure that I have earned merit or incurred guilt, and that hence I must consider myself a free agent.' In Casanova's life, prison is not just an episode, even a recurring one, but a symbol of all the constraints he struggled against throughout the course of his action-packed existence.[47]

Of the four writers considered in this chapter, three are famous for their escapes from prison, only Tasso for what he endured there. While Cellini and Tasso in particular became points of literary reference for many of the prison writers to follow, they were unlike Italian prisoners during the Risorgimento, who tended to be admired not because of dramatic flights from prison but for their ability to survive long ordeals in confinement without being brutalized or in other ways diminished by the experience. Unlike later prisoners, Cellini, Tasso, Pignata, and Casanova have little to say about the ultimate justness or injustice of their treatment. While all are outraged at confinements for reasons they find flimsy or arbitrary, none is surprised at what has happened to him. This lack, on their part, of appeal to a greater system of social justice makes them different from the more specifically political prisoners of centuries to follow.

That these writers could be clapped in jail on an individual whim or as part of someone's private vendetta also explains why confinement for them was a very personal experience, jail a highly individualized space. It is only later, when imprisonment begins to present itself as an institutional rather than an individual determination, that detention becomes a depersonalizing experience and prison writers begin to complain of being divested of their identities and reduced to a number or encapsulated in an often inapplicable and in any case perfunctory judiciary criminal category. Whatever else might have happened to them in confinement, Cellini, Tasso, Pignata, and Casanova never lost their unique identities.

As depicted in their own writings, these prisoners are determined to retain control over language and writing. When Cellini composes a poem in ink fashioned from his urine, then employs fragments of charcoal to make a drawing of God and the angels, he does so in order to assert his identity as an artist and an extraordinary individual. Tasso explains to Duke Alfonso that 'if I live, if I breathe, if I hope, if I write' he owes it all to his ducal patron, a stance important not so much for its obsequiousness to the duke as for its insistence that for the imprisoned Tasso living, breathing, hoping, and writing are existential equivalents.[48] For the virtual author Pignata, the equivalence between being alive and being alive in a written text is absolute. And for Casanova, finally, personal freedom, the goal of so much of his frenetic activity, was a condition he was able to realize thanks to his determination to control rather than be controlled, write rather than be written by his jailers or anyone else.

At the same time, and despite their efforts to dominate the discourse of captivity into which they were thrust, all four of these prisoners could not help but end up captives of the intertextual tradition of prison writing. If, as seems likely, the date of first publication of Pignata's book has been pushed forward and his story modelled on that of Cellini, the hero of the *Aventures de Joseph Pignata echappé des prisons de l'Inquisition de Rome* is more a reincarnation of the Florentine goldsmith than a product of the literary imagination of a member of the Cardinal de' Gabrielli's historical retinue. If Nino Borsellino is correct, furthermore, Casanova – or at least the Casanova of the escape from the Piombi – is also a Cellini epigone. Of the four prison writers, only Tasso seems unentangled in intertextual ties to his predecessors – though in the centuries since his death, he himself has become a fictionalized point of reference for all those who struggled to keep a grip on their reason in confinement and at the same time write meaningfully about their experiences. All these writers, then, were caught in the web of intertextuality that they, in turn, continued to spin for the authors who were to succeed them first in prison and then on the printed page.

2

The Spielberg: Concealment and Refutation

There is perhaps only one activity which small, despotic courts accomplish perfectly: that of guarding political prisoners.[1]

Giacomo Casanova and Silvio Pellico were both prisoners beneath the lead roof of Venice's Ducal Palace, and each wrote an account of his stay there. Such would seem – at first glance at least – to be the only tie linking the swashbuckling, free-thinking, eighteenth-century adventurer and the self-effacing Christian apologist of the Restoration. The apparent stodginess of Pellico and other patriots of the early Risorgimento, however, may be a notion fostered by conservative nineteenth-century historians intent on dissociating these founding fathers of modern Italy from the anarchist and socialist activists who went to prison for their beliefs at the time these historians were writing.[2]

No matter how radical, on the one hand, or conventional, on the other, one finds the prisoners of the 1820s and 1830s, these heroes in the struggle for Italian unification occupied an important position in their contemporaries' imaginations. So did the strongholds where they were confined. In *The Romantic Prison*, Victor Brombert has described the significance of the Bastille for the political, social, and literary imagination in France before and after 1789.[3] The equivalent structure for the Italian imagination was the Spielberg castle in the Moravian city of Brno, in what is today the Czech Republic but in Pellico's time was part of the Austrian empire.[4] All the prison writers treated in this chapter were either confined in the Spielberg or narrowly escaped being sent there.

The Spielberg: Concealment and Refutation   39

After the demise of Napoleon and the Congress of Vienna in 1815, the Restoration saw the return to power of states and statelets in Italy arranged more or less as they had been before the French invasion, though with Austria now a more dominant power in the northern part of the peninsula. In the period of government nervousness and reaction that followed 1815, many Italian intellectuals and professionals became involved in clandestine political activities – so much so that the entire peninsula could be said to be 'covered by a vast, dense network of secret associations.'[5] Many of the clandestine associations that sprang up after the Restoration borrowed their rituals and organizational structures from the Freemason movement. Unlike the Masons, however, the secret societies of the Risorgimento were unabashedly political rather than at least partly philosophical or theological in orientation.[6] But even though such associations proliferated widely throughout the country, membership in them was perilous – punishable by death, for example, in the parts of Italy controlled by Austria.[7]

Most of the members of such patriotic groups as the Carbonari were otherwise respectable members of society. Amateur subversives of patrician or middle-class origins unashamed of their political convictions, such part-time and sometimes bumbling conspirators were commonly discovered and arrested with ease by the authorities. Deprived of legal counsel while in pre-trial custody, unaware of the precise charges levelled against them, forbidden copies of the laws they were accused of breaking, once they were in the hands of skilled interrogators, almost all of them confessed to at least some of the activities of which they were accused.[8] Partly because they were such amateurs and the products of literary or journalistic environments, the writing these men produced about their detention is heavily marked by the conspiratorial nature of the activities in which they were involved. The changing character of identity, the instability and untrustworthiness of the written word, and an obsession with integrity, mutilation, and betrayal, together with concern for the accuracy of the written record of their acts are some of the issues that appear repeatedly in their writing from and about prison.

The prison writing produced during the early Risorgimento was an unusually collective affair. Especially after the extraordinary success of Pellico's *Le mie prigioni* of 1832, several additional accounts of confinement by Pellico's companions and others began to appear in Italy, France, and England. So great was the vogue for such memoirs that the principal

Austrian inquisitor himself, the astute and merciless Antonio Salvotti, contemplated publishing his own description of the conspiracy trials in which he had been involved.[9] As Salvotti's example suggests, while some of those who wrote prison memoirs might have been trying to cash in on *Le mie prigioni*'s commercial success, most of these prison authors seem to have been motivated as much by a desire to create an accurate and complete historical account of what had happened to them all.

Like that of Harriet Beecher Stowe's *Uncle Tom's Cabin* twenty years later, *Le mie prigioni*'s phenomenal success was due in part to extra-literary events. Though not fuelled by indignation at a system of slavery that would shortly be contested in a civil war of major proportions and lasting effect the way Stowe's work was, Pellico's book gave similar voice to widespread outrage at an antiquated and repressive political order that was already seething and that sixteen years later, in 1848, would explode in violent upheavals throughout Europe. This is largely because so many of the work's earliest readers took the message of *Le mie prigioni* to be a denunciation of Austrian tyranny and a plea for the liberation of oppressed Italy rather than an account of a religious crisis successfully overcome. Pellico, who had written his memoir at the urging of his confessor, had not entirely anticipated this. The book, a later critic has commented, 'led to a consequence that its author had not foreseen: rather than supporting the ethical-religious propaganda of the time, it functioned instead to support patriotic views, first in Italy and then abroad ... stirring up sympathy for Italy and hatred for the foreigner everywhere.'[10] Although Pellico's tract suggests that political struggle is ultimately futile – especially when compared to the more important issue of personal salvation – *Le mie prigioni* became such a powerful weapon in the struggle for independence that its effect on the Austrians has been described as the equivalent of a battle lost to the Italian forces.[11]

The son of a grocer, Silvio Pellico (1789–1854) was a member of a new generation of bourgeois writers in Italy. Unlike more sophisticated social commentators from an earlier period, such as Giuseppe Parini (1729–99) or Vittorio Alfieri, with their preference for high society and appreciation of what Casanova understood as 'esprit,' Pellico took a less superior attitude towards his social subject-matter, eschewing irony in his greatest work in favour of earnest autobiographical confession. In Italian theatre history, similarly, Pellico is important for his *Francesca da Rimini* (1815), a play that marks 'the transition from the court tragedy' in the manner of Alfieri and others 'to the drama of lower middle-class feeling' popular in the succeeding period.[12] In his memorialistic efforts as in his writing for the theatre, Pellico comes at the beginning of a tradition of bourgeois writing in Italy that stretches forward to such later apologists of middle-class life as Edmondo De Amicis (1846–1908) in the late-nineteenth and Carlo Cassola (1917–86) in the mid-twentieth century.

As its title indicates, Pellico's *Le mie prigioni* ('*My Prisons*') is an account of experiences in not just one but several jails. The institutions involved are the Santa Margherita prison in Milan, which at the end of Pellico's century would again house such politically suspect individuals as Filippo Turati, Andrea Costa, and Anna Kuliscioff; the attic cells 'under the lead' of the Venetian Ducal Palace, where Casanova too had been confined; and, finally, and for the longest part of his detention, the Spielberg. In his peregrinations through these gloomy fortresses, Pellico's autobiographical hero encounters several colourful characters, including a deaf-mute child; the thieves and degenerate women he meets in Milan; the libertine Giuliano and the jailer's daughter, Zanze, he encounters in Venice; and the rough-exteriored but golden-hearted jail-keeper Schiller of the Spielberg. This author's most significant encounter during his imprisonment, however, is with his Christian faith. His belief in God strengthened rather than weakened by his prison stay, Pellico emerges from his long and painful confinement more certain than ever of the consolatory power of his religion and the basic goodness of all people despite their sometimes questionable behaviour.

To a remarkable degree, *Le mie prigioni* is concerned with disguises and problems of identity. Freshly incarcerated in Milan, for example, Pellico's narrator notes with interest that one of the inscriptions on the prison walls has been taken from Pascal's *Pensées*. For Pascal in this reflection, the Christian God is Himself disguised, a *Deus absconditus* who has none the less left traces of His presence in the physical universe, signs that 'will be perceived by those who seek Him with all their heart.'[13] This inscription is a first example of many allusions to hidden presences and camouflaged identities in Pellico's book. Later on in *Le mie prigioni*, in a chapter that seems to have little function in the development of Pellico's story, the narrator comes into contact with a prisoner who claims to be the duke of Normandy – that is, Louis XVII, heir to the French throne – but who is almost certainly an impostor.[14] In chapters 33 to 41, similarly, the imprisoned Pellico engages in some forbidden correspondence with a libertine named Giuliano. Although Pellico rejects his correspondent's invitation to protract their exchange of messages, dismissing the other prisoner's notes as 'mostly obscenities' and the products of 'feverish erotic buffooneries,' Giuliano's real nature – is he an *agent provocateur* or a bizarre and corrupt *alter ego* meant to tempt Pellico's mental chastity? – is never disclosed and seems to be just as disguised as that of the 'faux Dauphin' or Pascal's *Deus absconditus*.

Even the police appear in disguise in Pellico's book. In chapter 22, the agents who take the narrator from Milan to Venice wear garments meant to conceal their real professions; so does the official who escorts the released prisoner back to Novara in the book's final chapter. Just as Pellico and the other conspirators are perceived by the Austrians to be criminals masquerading as patriots (while the Italians are convinced they are exactly the contrary), and just as the prisoners must disguise the real nature of their subversive activities from their interrogators, so the representatives of the Austrian state are constrained to camouflage their true identities in the problematic world they enter when leaving prison confines. In the same way, the interrogator Salvotti, an Italian working for the Austrians (and thus not a true Italian in the eyes of the patriots), must pretend to be the friend and confidant of those he questions when he is, in reality, their mortal enemy. In the world of Pellico's prisons, everyone has a secret identity that must be concealed – sometimes even at pain of death.

A similar secret shrouds the identity of Pellico's book itself. When *Le mie prigioni* was first published, some readers thought it a political tract disguised as a religious apology, while others found it just the opposite.[15] At the beginning of his text, Pellico declares there is nothing subversive in what he is writing, going on to defend his silence about political issues by describing himself as 'resembling a lover whose mistress has mistreated him' and who prefers to pout in dignified fashion ('dignitosamente risoluto di tenerle broncio') rather than confront the object of his desire directly. One result of this attitude is that the all-important motive for Pellico's imprisonment is itself concealed. Pellico's reader, a twentieth-century commentator has noted, 'will realize he is holding a book in which the politics that inspired it and suggested its title, must be sought between the lines or, especially, in silence.'[16] For many of Pellico's readers, in his own time and since, it was this silence that proclaimed the book's loudest message.

In his introduction, Pellico also draws a distinction between the generic nature of his book and that of other, apparently similar, autobiographical compositions. 'Have I composed these memoirs from pride in talking about myself?' he asks rhetorically before quickly answering, 'I hope that is not the case.' Motivated by considerations other than personal vanity, *Le mie prigioni* is thus a confutation of ordinary autobiography. As such, Pellico proposes, it should be read counter to these unnamed texts. Just as the Bible, as Pellico insists in a later chapter, must be read counter to ordinary writing if its true nature is to be grasped (chap. 25), so *Le mie prigioni* must be considered a countertext to such self-serving works as Alfieri's *Vita*.[17] As countertext rather than a text of the usual sort, *Le mie prigioni* is at once itself and the opposite of other, unnamed texts that define it by their absence.

Many other silent, hidden, or otherwise unreadable texts are alluded to in *Le mie prigioni*. When first confined in Santa Margherita, for example, the narrator describes two notes he sent his friend Piero Maroncelli, who at this time was being kept in another part of the prison. Although the external nature of these texts is described – one was written in Pellico's own blood, the other pricked out on paper with the point of a pin – the messages they bore are never disclosed.[18] Not that these notes were especially compromising. Since he knew the authorities were likely to intercept what he wrote, Pellico was careful to couch his communications to Maroncelli in ambiguous terms. Even so, exactly what he wrote to his friend is never specified in the account Pellico wrote of this episode after he had been released from prison.

Certain non-verbal texts in Pellico's narrative, however, can sometimes be read with ease. Zanze, for example, the adolescent daughter of the narrator's Venetian jailer, is said at one point to be able to decipher a dangerous message that she reads in Pellico's soul. In an episode just after the girl has been admonished to stop throwing her arms around the prisoner's neck, Pellico notes how 'she fixed her eyes upon my face, cast them down, blushed – though this was certainly the first time that she read the possibility in my soul of any weakness regarding her' (chap. 30). But here too, the precise nature of the message Zanze reads (or Pellico thinks she reads) is one that neither the sender nor the recipient of this message can quite acknowledge. Like that of his notes to Maroncelli, the content of the message in Pellico's soul is something that must not be articulated.

In another episode with Zanze, Pellico again conceals the meaning of a text he and the girl are examining together. During her visits to his cell, Zanze has made a habit of opening the prisoner's Latin Bible at random, kissing the book wherever the pages fall open, and then insisting Pellico translate the passage she has just kissed. When the book opens to the Song of Songs, the embarrassed prisoner refuses to translate all the words before him, preferring instead to equivocate. 'I took advantage,' he says in regard to his eager interlocutor, 'of her ignorance of Latin, and employed phrases in which both the sanctity of that volume and her own innocence could be preserved' (chap. 31). Though both the Bible and Zanze's presumed innocence fill him with 'the highest veneration,' Pellico – the author of a very successful stage treatment of the story of Francesca da Rimini and thus aware of the perils of close reading in certain situations – masks the text before him, though not without signalling to the reader as to the true nature of what he has concealed.[19]

Of all the hidden texts in *Le mie prigioni*, the most remarkable is that described in chapter 27. After some time in the Piombi, Pellico has finally been permitted writing materials and is scribbling furiously. Not only is he composing plays and other 'literary matters' on the numbered pages officially supplied him, he is also scratching another text onto the wooden surface of his cell's writing table. Though Pellico claims what he is scratching into the table's surface are nothing more than autobiographical 'meditations on the duties of men and of myself in particular,' he takes great pains to keep the text he is producing hidden, not only from his jailers but from his subsequent readers too.[20] Pellico's writing on the Piombi table is not only disguised under a tablecloth, inkpot, and his 'legal block of paper,' it is also in code. 'I wrote in code,' he explains, 'that is to say with letters transposed and abbreviations, something to which I was quite accustomed.' Further, when there is so much coded, hidden text inscribed on the table that its surface can hold no more, Pellico carefully erases what he has created by scraping the wood with a sharp piece of glass he has concealed for that purpose.

Why this elaborate concealment? And, above all, what was the text Pellico was composing in this way? He will tell us only that what he inscribed on the table was a history of his inner life that he composed in a style very different from that of *Le mie prigioni*. Unlike the published account of his captivity, with its measured linear progression in brief 'capitoletti' or small chapters, the erased text is 'slowed down constantly by every kind of digression, analysis, or metaphysical, moral, political, or religious argumentation.' Pellico's hidden text, then, not only treats politics, philosophy, and religion, it is based on free association of the sort that a little more than half a century later would be employed as a standard psychoanalytic technique.[21] Writing on the desk, Pellico can say whatever he wants about his otherwise concealed inner life. But no one must see the text that results – not at the time of its composition, not ever. Like the female figure of politics evoked (but never seen) at the beginning of *Le mie prigioni*, the notes to Maroncelli, or the meaning of the biblical verses Zanze chooses for translation, these 'meditations' of a 'rather biographical character' must be concealed from the curious just as the piece of furniture on which he has written them must be restored to what is literally *tabula rasa*.

It is also startling to realize that, in flagrant violation of prison regulations, Pellico is concealing a sharp piece of glass in his cell. More immediately dangerous than anything a prisoner might write in confinement, this sharp object could easily serve as the ultimate eraser not only of an illicit text but of the life of such a text's author. As Pellico well knew, in another Venetian prison in these same years, Felice Foresti had used broken glass in an attempt to do just this.[22] In his evocation of this deadly sliver, Pellico has established an equivalence between text and erasure on the one hand, human existence and death on the other. Pellico's secret writing on his desk in the Piombi is part of a network of references to writing and erasure – true and false identity, hidden and ostensible messages, good- and bad-faith communications, prison solidarity and betrayal, determination to survive and suicidal fantasies – that runs throughout his book. Unlike Casanova, who was proud of his ability to manipulate written works both in the physical sense (the Bible, for example, containing the pike he sent Balbi beneath the plate of gnocchi) and in regard to their content (his hilarious recycling of Boccaccio's story of Frate Alberto), Pellico cannot or will not look directly at the texts he encounters in prison. Or if he does manage to peek at them, he refuses to reveal what he has seen.[23]

Pellico's fellow inmates at the Spielberg must have sensed that his description of his personal prison ordeal, while in many ways admirable, was an inadequate account of their shared experiences. For no sooner was *Le mie prigioni* published than responses, revisions, and rewritings of Pellico's story began to appear. The first and most explicitly corrective of these was by Piero Maroncelli, Pellico's friend and artistic collaborator from his pre-prison days as well as his Spielberg cell mate. Maroncelli's 'Biographical Introduction' and 'Additions to *Mie prigioni*' began to be added to published editions of his friend's book beginning with that published in Paris by Antoine De Latour in 1833.

Maroncelli, who is perhaps best known for an episode in *Le mie prigioni* where he demonstrates extraordinary courage during the amputation of his leg, was born in 1795 in Forlì, a city in the Romagna that in his day was under papal rule. Like his later compatriots Galletti and Frignani – two subjects of the Pope from central Italy whose prison writings are examined in chapter 3 – Maroncelli was passionately opposed to Roman suzerainty and in 1817 spent several months in prison for anti-government agitation. A musician as well as a writer, after release from the Spielberg in 1830 he went to Paris and married a German singer with whom he eventually emigrated to the United States, where he ended his life penniless and mentally deranged in 1846.[24]

Before their arrests as Carbonari, Maroncelli and Pellico frequented the same artistic circles in Milan and were in love with two actresses who were also cousins: Maroncelli with Carlotta Marchionni and Pellico with Teresa Bartolozzi. The two men even wrote a musical farce for Carlotta and Teresa, Pellico providing the book and Maroncelli the music. But though the two were thus comrades in both love and art, Maroncelli was also the unwitting cause of Pellico's imprisonment. An inept conspirator, he was so careless with compromising documents as to spur not only Pellico's arrest but also the uncovering of the Carbonari circle to which the two men belonged. When interrogated by Salvotti, to make matters worse, Maroncelli supplied way too much information about his former activities, supposing that what he said would not incriminate others. Like Pellico, he was found guilty of treason and sentenced to twenty years in the Spielberg, five years more than those specified in the sentence handed down to his friend.

In 1832, when *Le mie prigioni* was first published, two years had elapsed since Pellico and Maroncelli's release from prison. Thanks to his book, Pellico was suddenly famous, a living symbol of the consolatory power of the Christian faith and of Italy's determination to obtain political autonomy. Acutely aware of his friend's success and short of both money and prospects, even though he considered himself 'one of the principal actors in the historical drama sketched in the book of memoirs, *Le mie prigioni*,'[25] Maroncelli decided to publish his own account of the Italian patriots' detention. His *Notes et éclaircissements historiques* for De Latour's 1833 edition of the French translation of Pellico's book, as well as his *Alle 'Mie Prigioni' di Silvio Pellico, Addizioni di Piero Maroncelli*, are further commentary by him in both French and Italian about what happened in the Spielberg.[26]

Maroncelli's additions contain a number of mostly minor corrections to Pellico's narrative. But one of the topics that he treated was of great significance for the future of *Le mie prigioni* and for the two men's friendship. While Pellico had been extremely circumspect about how one of the priests assigned to the Italians in the Austrian prison had been instructed to ferret out what he could about the prisoners' political beliefs and activities, Maroncelli spoke openly and indignantly of such attempts by the Dalmatian cleric Stefan Pavlovich.[27] Because they were deemed anticlerical, these revelations were enough to cause Pellico's book, whenever printed with Maroncelli's introduction and additions, to be placed on the *Index*. Once again, Maroncelli had unwittingly played Austria's game: although Metternich had earlier attempted to have *Le mie prigioni* banned by Catholic authorities, it was only when it was printed with Maroncelli's addenda that this step was actually taken.[28]

In addition to his remarks on Pavlovich, Maroncelli made other comments that Pellico must have found personally offensive – revealing, for example, how Pellico was not completely weaned until he was more than seven years old and reopening the old sore of his friend Odoardo Briche's suicide, a troubling episode in Pellico's past treated only obliquely in his own prison memoir.[29] Pellico responded to his friend's comments with the twelve 'Capitoli aggiunti' or 'additional chapters' that appear at the end of most editions of *Le mie prigioni* after 1843. In the ninth of these, Pellico notes sadly how even though his old friend did not intend 'to try consciously to hurt me and to fail me in any manner,' none the less, 'the addition that my friend the unfortunate Piero Maroncelli made to *Le mie prigioni*' had in fact wounded him deeply.[30]

That Maroncelli found it necessary to publish additions to Pellico's account cannot help but suggest that he believed his friend's memoir to be inadequate, his truth incomplete – mutilated, so to speak, by self-censorship or a failure of political nerve. From Pellico's point of view, Maroncelli, by correcting his text in this unwanted fashion, was questioning his authority as an author and attempting to maim his reputation. When Maroncelli, in a letter of 1833 about his imprisonment, describes the decade he spent in prison as 'a century of horrible suffering, from which I have emerged mutilated,'[31] the issue of mutilation versus integrity is made explicit. Unable to replace the leg amputated in prison, with the prosthetic additions he proposed for Pellico's book Maroncelli was attempting to ensure that the corpus of testimony about the Spielberg would not reach the world similarly incomplete.

Interestingly, textual emendations and amputations are also at issue in regard to Pellico's letters, whether in collections of his own writing of this sort or in the correspondence of others. In 1839, when Nicomede Bianchi, who was preparing an edition of letters by Ugo Foscolo, sought permission to include documents by Pellico in such a volume, Pellico refused, instructing Bianchi that any material concerning him be omitted from the projected collection.[32] In 1853, when another edition of Foscolo's letters was being prepared, this time by Silvio Orlandini, Pellico again requested that Orlandini omit any references to him in the work he was about to publish, saying it was 'better to keep silent about matters that are now futile and irritating. Insert an ellipsis, therefore, and then resume.'[33] More than a century later, Mario Scotti, in the course of his preparation of what was this time an edition of Pellico's own early letters, was stunned to discover that Pellico himself had already tendentiously edited them for posterity. The cuts and other changes made by the author of *Le mie prigioni* in his early letters, for Scotti at least, were 'cancellations so dense and so careful that they were almost the equal of those made on prisoners' letters by the Austrian censor that irreparably destroyed the texts.'[34] In some of the letters examined by Scotti, for example, Pellico changed what were originally gibes against *religione* or 'religion' to make them seem directed against *ragione* or 'reason' – just the opposite of his earlier intent. Free from the constraints of the Spielberg and its regulations, in his later years Pellico chose to become a censor himself by amputating offending passages from the corpus of his own writing – an act of surgery that was perhaps both more radical and more serious than that lamented by his friend Maroncelli.

The aristocratic Count Federico Confalonieri (1785–1846) was unlike the bourgeois writers Pellico and Maroncelli in several ways. Although Pellico's was certainly the voice that made the plight of the Spielberg prisoners known throughout the world, the most politically important of the conspirators arrested in the 1820s was without any question Confalonieri.[35] If Pellico and Maroncelli were relatively minor Carbonari, Confalonieri was a pivotal figure in the struggle for Italian self-determination. A leader of a federation of Italian patriots in Lombardy,[36] the count had been part of an 1814 Italian delegation to Paris that debated the situation in his native region with such powerful figures of the time as Britain's Lord Castlereagh, Czar Alexander I of Russia, and Austria's Emperor Francis I. After conviction in 1823 of having urged Charles Albert of Savoy to invade Lombardy in an attempt to unite that region with Piedmont, Confalonieri was not dispatched directly to prison in Moravia but routed instead through Vienna. In the Austrian capital he was interviewed by Prince Klemens von Metternich (1773–1859), the Imperial Chancellor and Austrian Minister of Foreign Affairs, who wanted to discuss the Italian situation with his now disabled adversary face to face.

In the Spielberg afterwards, but before either *Le mie prigioni* or Maroncelli's *Addizioni* were published, Confalonieri wrote an account of his life. His *Memorie*, together with the letters, both ostensible and clandestine, that he managed to send his family from confinement, can be seen from today's perspective as additional rewritings (though, in his case, *avant la lettre* since Pellico's book was not available to him at the time of this writing) of *Le mie prigioni*. How Confalonieri felt about Pellico once he read his friend's account of their collective imprisonment is evident in a comment the count made about *Le mie prigioni* in a letter to Gino Capponi while en route to America, his prison sentence having been commuted to deportation. In this 1837 letter, Confalonieri confides to Capponi that 'it can suffice to say to anyone who has read Pellico that everything that he says is the *absolute truth* – though it would go too far to assert that all the truth has been said – said, that is, by him.'[37] Though vastly different from him in political importance, Confalonieri would seem to be of the same opinion as Maroncelli in regard to Pellico's account of the conspirators' life in the Spielberg.

Confalonieri's own prison memoirs were written not for publication but for private consumption by his wife, Teresa Confalonieri Casati. Although probably composed before *Le mie prigioni*, they were not made public until 1889 – well after the deaths of Teresa and Federico Confalonieri, in 1830 and 1846 respectively, as well as nearly thirty years after the Unification of Italy. Though written primarily for consumption by his family, it is clear from their focus on the legality of Confalonieri's interrogation and sentencing that Confalonieri's *Memorie* were also composed with at least one eye cocked at the tribunal of history. His editor D'Ancona, in this regard, finds the work 'more than an organized narration of the facts ... almost a legal brief.'[38] The pages on this topic that Confalonieri wrote in prison have been preserved for posterity thanks to one of his prison guards. 'We owe the preservation of these memoirs,' the count's grand-nephew Gabrio Casati explains, 'to the care and sharp-sightedness of a compassionate jailer ... who began in 1829, it seems, to furnish the prisoner with paper, one sheet at a time, that he would take back as soon as it was full and add to the others. By so doing, he was able in 1836 to consign the entire fascicle to its author upon his liberation from prison.'[39] Although the manuscript of *Memorie* in fact arrived in Milan well before its author's release in 1836, and Confalonieri was probably provided with paper for somewhat more venal reasons than those suggested, his memoirs are unlike those of his prison comrades in that they were composed in a prison cell rather than after their author's release from confinement.[40]

The first portions of Confalonieri's book deal with their author's arrest, interrogation, detention in Milan, and his Vienna interview with Metternich. As is clear from both his letters and *Memorie*, Confalonieri was strongly opposed to social 'disorder,' 'anarchy,' or 'mad democracy' (108–9). 'Only mild, progressive means were dear to me, violent ones never,' he declared in *Memorie*, 'for I was ever suspicious, instead, of such highly imprudent or immature methods. Never a partisan of revolutions or disorders, I opposed them instead as long as I could and knew how' (118). But it was precisely because of these moderate, not to say conservative, views that Metternich considered Confalonieri the most dangerous of the Spielberg prisoners. In Confalonieri's account of their meeting, the Austrian minister points out to his guest that while radical thinkers 'can accomplish everything during activity and disorder ... they can do nothing during times of tranquillity' when their opinions are found so 'revolting' and 'discredited' that 'the preaching of such cannibals is no longer cause for our alarm.' In all but the most exceptional of times, in fact, it is the opinions of the liberals that 'come to be listened to, that gradually insinuate themselves, that seduce, persuade, and corrupt even those who would abhor ideas of a revolutionary nature' (174). For Metternich, Confalonieri was much more dangerous than a whole jail full of radicals. For this reason, throughout the Italian count's confinement, the Austrian authorities continued to pressure him to reveal what he knew about patriotic activities in northern Italy.

After describing his stay in Vienna, Confalonieri goes on in his memoir to provide details about his life in the Spielberg, noting among other things how difficult it was for him to write in confinement. 'It was not possible,' he explains, 'except in bits and pieces and over long intervals of time, among privations and difficulties of every kind, to slowly add one line of writing to another' (16). Finding proper writing materials was difficult too. How Confalonieri managed can be seen from the description he gives of contraband objects taken from the prisoners' cells during a search. These included 'a few miserable bits of writing, done with herb juice or colouring extracted from various medicines scratched onto rough grey paper provided us for unmentionable purposes – writing done with little sticks with a bit of fingernail to be used as pens stuck onto them' (206–7).[41] But even under such conditions and with these materials, Confalonieri managed to produce an extensive account of his arrest and confinement.

In the portions of the *Memorie* concerning his arrest and interrogation, Confalonieri makes no attempt to keep the 'beautiful mistress' of politics hidden. Unlike Pellico's, his account reverberates with indignation at the arbitrary nature of his treatment by the Austrians. *Memorie* also contains information on a number of other subjects left undescribed by both Pellico and Maroncelli. Confalonieri notes, for example, that in the Spielberg political prisoners were treated more harshly than criminal convicts in that they were not permitted to earn money they could use to pay for better food and living quarters. Nor were they allowed to read or write to their families the way the count had been able to write Teresa while awaiting trial in Milan (198). Unlike the perpetually charitable Pellico, moreover, he is sharply critical of the prison staff, characterizing one guard as a 'man neither good nor bad, but filled with the fear of proving insufficiently vigilant' (146), others as 'crude, both because of their lengthy experience of servitude, the stick, and living among slaves, and because debased, and even if able, then depraved guardians ... arbiters, though scarcely definitive ones, of our more or less difficult existence' (245). As an aristocrat, Confalonieri was particularly irritated at being made subservient to men he considered his social, intellectual, and moral inferiors.

Confalonieri, in addition, in part because he was not writing for immediate publication, is more explicit than either Pellico or Maroncelli had been about the spying priest, Pavlovich. 'How is it possible,' he asks angrily about this ethically equivocal figure, 'under a Sovereign who appears so pious and religious that such a dangerous, not to say abusive, contamination of religious and political interests is adopted with us?' (226–7). Confalonieri was so angry at Pavlovich's spying that in 1826 he decided to abstain altogether from attending confession, a protest so scandalous it led to a prison visit from the bishop of Brno (225).

Part of Confalonieri's *Memorie* contains a self-portrait of the author that he claims he copied from a report to the emperor written by Pavlovich that had somehow found its way into this prisoner's hands. In Confalonieri's retracing of Pavlovich's description of him in this document, the author of the *Memorie* is a man 'of great intelligence, highly clever; politically savvy, covert, masked, dangerous and more to be feared than any of the others.' Despite poor health, moreover, the count is none the less master of his situation. 'His conversation tends,' the report included in the *Memorie* continues, 'to draw out others without contributing anything of his own; his words always have an additional agenda, and no one is able to read what is in his heart.' Confalonieri's religious beliefs, however, as least as far as Pavlovich is concerned, are insincere. 'One should not be deceived by the repentance and religious sentiments he professes,' the priest continues. 'Your Majesty and I know very well that this is little more than a pretence aimed, thanks to the Sovereign's compassion, at causing some improvement in his condition.' Pavlovich's description concludes with the following warning: 'Be very careful with him; watch how you speak because he is very clever and learned and if he can catch you up he will try to compromise you just as he has not failed to do with me' (233). While Pavlovich himself was not seriously compromised by anything Confalonieri did to him – in fact, he was awarded a bishopric for his efforts with the Italian prisoners – he was clearly intimidated by a prisoner able to maintain his inner dignity by concealing his deepest self from observation. Because he is, as Pavlovich puts it, 'coperto' or 'covert' and 'mascherato' or 'masked,' the unrepentant count is especially dangerous. That Confalonieri was pleased by his arch-enemy Pavlovich's view of him is evident from his having copied the priest's description into his memoir. Rather than rewriting another prisoner's account of confinement, as Maroncelli had done for Pellico, Confalonieri simply puts forward his enemy Pavlovich's portrait of himself in vindication of his prison conduct.

The surviving letters documenting Confalonieri's imprisonment include texts sent to Teresa from Santa Margherita that were dispatched through official censored channels, as well as clandestine letters Federico smuggled out of first Santa Margherita and then the Spielberg.[42] It is the Spielberg letters, written in invisible ink, from Confalonieri to Teresa and, later, to Camillo Casati, however, that are Confalonieri's most interesting prison correspondence.[43] Partly because some of the texts in this correspondence were not legible even to their recipients at the time of their delivery and are even more difficult to decipher today, Gallavresi gives only a sample of them in his edition of Confalonieri's correspondence. The sample is enough, however, for some observations to be made about these communications. In his clandestine messages back to Lombardy, Confalonieri calls his wife 'Carolina,' while he himself is 'Tasso.' But unlike such other clandestine prison writing in invisible ink as the letters by Camilla Ravera or Umberto Terracini in the 1930s, and also unlike Confalonieri's own letters smuggled earlier out of Santa Margherita, these clandestine Spielberg communications deal almost exclusively in what can only be called banalities. Although in this uncensored correspondence Confalonieri was free to say whatever he pleased, the content of most of these letters is surprisingly similar to that of earlier missives sent through the censor in Milan.

One letter in this group, however, is different from the rest. Writing to his wife on 3 September 1830, during a time when the countess was herself mortally ill, Federico describes what seems to have been a religious conversion. In this letter he sounds for the first time like his friend Pellico, even defending his new-found beliefs in similar terms from possible charges of bigotry. 'Don't think that I have become a bigot,' the prisoner urges his wife in Milan, before going on to complain about the limits of written communication. 'You have seen me too different a person,' he says, 'for a piece of writing to be enough for you to recognize the nature and limits of the change that has taken place in me' (651). Something seems to have altered Confalonieri's beliefs significantly. Contrary to everything he has maintained earlier, he now asserts that, as far as the emperor is concerned, his own 'religious feelings are by now known to him and he recognizes that they are sincere ones,' stating further that the emperor (who in this regard must have ignored the advice contained in Pavlovich's report) is aware that 'a Christian cannot do other than be a loyal subject' (652). This change in Confalonieri's attitude, coming at the same time his wife was gravely ill in Milan, may have been brought on by his reading of religious works by Pascal and St Augustine, which he was able to consult illicitly in prison,[44] or it might have represented a last attempt by the prisoner to reassure his wife there is nothing he will not do in order to hold her in his arms again.[45]

In all he wrote in any form from prison, Confalonieri presented himself as superior to the conditions of his environment even when he himself was in such poor health it did not seem likely he would survive his prison sojourn. Aimed from the beginning at a restricted, private audience rather than the large, international public Pellico's writings in fact reached and Maroncelli's hoped to, Confalonieri's prison writings, whether letters or memoirs, are those of someone anxious to maintain his dignity and preserve his reputation in the eyes of both his contemporaries and posterity. Unsuccessful in his efforts to bring about the independence of his native region from Austria, gravely ill, and pushed to the limits of his physical endurance by his prison ordeal, Confalonieri insists he is none the less the master of his own soul, though of course not without the help of God. Perceived by Pavlovich as dangerous because so adept at dissembling his true feelings and in this way masking his real identity, Confalonieri seems in many respects a less problematic narrator of his prison experience than many of his comrades in the Spielberg. Like them, he too feels the need to add his account to the collective description of what happened there.

Another nobleman caught up in the Carbonari trials of the 1820s was Count Giovanni Arrivabene (1787–1881). A Lombard like Confalonieri, Arrivabene was from Mantua, though he spent much of his early life in exile. Arrested in May of 1821, Arrivabene was imprisoned in Venice's Piombi prison and then on the island of San Michele near Murano, where his cell mate was Piero Maroncelli. On 10 December, after detention of more than six months, he was found innocent of concealing his knowledge that Pellico was a Carbonaro. This was a serious accusation, since Austrian subjects like Pellico and Arrivabene were not only forbidden to belong to secret societies, they were obliged to report those they knew to be members. Found innocent, however, of this charge, and released from San Michele, Arrivabene thought it likely he would soon be arrested again, this time on charges more difficult to evade, and for this reason he decided to emigrate. After brief periods in Switzerland, France, and England, he settled in Belgium, where he became a prominent economist and an official in the Belgian government. Named senator when Italy was unified, Arrivabene lived to be more than ninety years old, witnessing not only the Unification all the Risorgimento patriots had dreamed of and struggled for, but such later political events as the democratic shift of power from Right to Left and the beginnings of Italian socialism.[46] Although Arrivabene's prison memoirs were written in Brussels in 1838, they were not published until 1860, when they appeared in Turin as *Intorno a un'epoca della mia vita*. An English edition, *An Epoch of My Life*, was published in London in 1862, one year after French and German versions had also appeared.

In his brief account of his prison experiences, Arrivabene, like Confalonieri before him, stresses the importance of his identity as an aristocrat. When the police come to Mantua to arrest him, for example, far from resisting, he immediately offers his guests refreshments. 'Whether this was from an exaggerated sentiment of the duties of hospitality, or the vanity of showing myself superior to any vicissitudes, or from the pleasure of making my conduct contrast with the office they filled, or perhaps a little of all these feelings combined ... I treated them rather as guests than as instruments of misfortune.'[47] Similarly, when freshly released from prison on San Michele where a number of his comrades were still confined, Arrivabene returned to the island for a last meal with them before leaving for Venice and liberty. After all – as he pointed out at his trial – it was because of his respect for the laws of hospitality that he did not denounce Pellico to the authorities when he learned, during a visit by Pellico to Arrivabene's country estate, of his guest's secret political affiliations (39). The count's return to prison for a final meal was only confirmation of his belief in the supreme importance of proper manners and *noblesse oblige*.

Although Arrivabene's memoirs do not contribute much that is new to prison writing in this period, they are remarkable for their references to mysterious texts of undisclosed content. In confinement, Arrivabene, like Pellico in his text scratched on his table in the Piombi, 'wrote letters which were never to be sent, and put down on paper thoughts which were never to be communicated to any one' (49). Although he says nothing further about these texts, what Arrivabene does say about this 'epoch of his life' undoubtedly contributed to the myth of the dashing patrician patriot who dines with countesses and princesses the night after his release from prison – but not before joining his companions in misfortune for a final visit – and meditates the wisdom of a flight into exile while in his usual box at the opera (83 ff). Detained for a matter of months rather than years the way many others were, Arrivabene, like Confalonieri, was able to survive the experience by clinging to his social identity. While in prison, as in his memoirs, his mask of aristocratic insouciance proved his best defence against any attempts by the police or his jailors to redefine him as a dangerous criminal rather than the distinguished member of a noble family that he was convinced he continued to be.

Like Confalonieri, Arrivabene wrote primarily for the historical record and without concern for financial gain. The same cannot be said with equal conviction for the next prison writer to be considered here. Author of one of the most widely read descriptions of the trials and imprisonments of the 1820s, Alexandre-Philippe Andryane (1797–1863) was a French citizen who, through contacts in Switzerland with the exiled Italian revolutionary Filippo Buonarotti (1761–1837), had become peripherally involved in the struggle for Italian independence. Andryane's four-volume *Mémoires d'un prisonnier d'état au Spielberg par A. Andryane, compagnon de captivité de l'illustre Comte Confalonieri* was written in 1834 and published in Paris by Ladvocat in 1837–8. The work is dedicated to Teresa Confalonieri Casati.

In a note near the end of his memoir, Andryane sounds very much like Pellico in the introduction to *Le mie prigioni*. Just as Pellico had done earlier, Andryane insists that what he has written was not composed out of what he calls 'the mad presumption of talking about myself' but because of his dedication to 'a more noble motive' – that of the truth. 'I alone, among all the prisoners of the Spielberg,' he explains in an allusion to his French citizenship, 'was able to make the entire truth known without calling down the Austrian government's rigours upon my family or friends.' For this reason, 'I have thus believed and continue to believe that it is my duty, now that my companions in misfortune have been liberated, to break the silence that the Italians *are obliged by circumstances to respect.*'[48] Unlike Italian prisoners of the Austrians, who were subject to reprisals if they described what really happened in the Spielberg, Andryane, in this view, was uniquely positioned to tell the complete and unmutilated truth about the events he had witnessed there.

As a prisoner of the Austrians, Andryane, of course, had not always enjoyed this freedom of expression. While in Milan awaiting trial and then transfer to Moravia, he describes the repugnance he felt at the thought that his correspondence was going to be censored, and the consequent 'constraint I was obliged to impose on myself while writing.' 'What a lot of things,' he continues, 'I was forced to pass over in silence! How many impressions I had to conceal!' (I: 345). In his later memoirs, by contrast, the once invisible text of his earlier self-censored reactions and repressed feelings can finally be revealed in its entirety.

Partly because his book was written in the principal language of intellectual communication in the Europe of the time, but also because Andryane tells his story with élan and a deft sense of drama, the *Mémoires d'un prisonnier d'état* were well received by his early readers.[49] Many passages in Andryane's book provide explicit revelations of what was only hinted at in other Spielberg writings. In the *Mémoires*, for example, Father Pavlovich is an even more unrestrainedly reactionary figure than he was in Pellico's cautious or Confalonieri's indignant (but clandestine) depiction. 'It is in thinking that the abusive behavior lies,' the obscurantist Dalmatian priest says in Andryane's book; 'this is what fosters the pride and rebellions of both the evil angels and our own ancestors. To hinder such audacious attempts, discoveries, and dangerous exertions of the human spirit is to do no more than render homage to God and work for the eternal happiness of all those made in His image' (IV: 67). For Pavlovich, in Andryane's account, it was the unauthorized exercise of reason that led, first, the rebellious angels, then Adam and Eve, and now the impudent Italian patriots to disobedience and inevitable punishment.

In addition to unmasking Pavlovich, Andryane provides additional revelations about Confalonieri's 'secret means of corresponding' (II: 233) between Moravia and Lombardy. For the wealthy count, Andryane points out in his cell mate's own words, 'the gates of the Spielberg will be no more unbreachable than were those of prison in Milan' (II: 240). Andryane further reveals that the person who provided the imprisoned Confalonieri with the necessary materials for his forbidden correspondence was none other than the Swiss guard Schiller who, in *Le mie prigioni*, is invariably presented as a model not only of compassion but also of moral probity (III: 258). Andryane's portrait of Schiller is thus an unmasking of this individual as depicted by Pellico and a rewriting of this portion of his comrades' accounts.

Andryane's *Mémoires* also reveals that two attempts were made by Teresa Confalonieri and others to break Confalonieri out of the Spielberg. 'Bear in mind,' the count himself reportedly commented about this to his companion, 'that nothing is impossible for the love of a woman and the devotion of a friend!' (II: 328). But both a first (III: 305–28) and a second attempt at a prison break were aborted, in the second instance, according to Andryane, because the count refused to regain his own freedom if his prison mates – especially, Andryane underlines, himself – had to be left behind (IV: 195–6).

There are other revelatory details in Andryane about forbidden activities by the Spielberg prisoners, the ways they exchanged messages in confinement, for example. One means for doing this was through whistling, the employment, that is, of what Andryane calls an 'inarticulate language none the less so melodious, so rhythmical that no words could equal its penetrating force' (II: 46). Another was the 'langage mural' of wall tapping, which at first Andryane could not understand, since he was expecting the message to be in the French rather than the Italian alphabet. When he realized his mistake, he compared his discovery to that of another Frenchman of the era. 'I wonder,' Andryane exults, 'whether Champollion would have felt more delight at his first deciphering of the hieroglyphs of Egypt than I felt at making this discovery.'[50]

But there was also a much simpler way of communicating in prison. Even though none of them chose to reveal this in their own memoirs, the Italian prisoners clearly managed to bribe or otherwise persuade Spielberg trustees to carry written messages through the prison for them. The texts of such messages, Andryane notes, were sometimes produced with materials like those mentioned by Confalonieri: pens made from bits of straw or wood (III: 44, 210), stationery fashioned from toilet paper (III: 207), and soot (III: 91–2) or liquids including blood used as ink. Blood, in fact, was the writing substance for one of the most extraordinary texts described by Andryane in his memoir, a lengthy religious poem he claims he composed in the Spielberg. This poem, he claims, was admired so unreservedly by Silvio Pellico that Pellico offered to donate his own blood to its author if this would hasten the completion of its composition. 'It is with my own blood that I am writing to you,' Andryane describes Pellico communicating with him in a note apparently carried by a trustee. 'It is with my own blood that I beg you to complete your work – so much so that I would give you all that is left in my veins, my good young man, in order for you to raise to the glory of God one of those long, solemn hymns that so profoundly teach humans to seek their happiness in the practice of virtue and the adoration of the Lord!' (III: 234).

Given this enthusiastic advance notice, one might well wonder about the content of the text Andryane was preparing at such sacrifice on Pellico's part. But although its author tells us his manuscript was both extremely long and the repository of 'all my thoughts' (III: 232), Andryane's religious poem is another example of a prison text that has disappeared. Like the autobiographical writings scratched by Pellico on his writing table or the 'thoughts which were never to be communicated to any one' that Arrivabene wrote down in prison, Andryane's *magnum opus* too has been lost, burned in a prison stove, its author reports, by a guard fearful of its discovery during a surprise requisition and search of the prisoners' belongings (III: 290–2).

There are other references as well in the *Mémoires d'un prisonnier d'état* to texts that were produced by unusual means. While in Milan, Andryane preserved his secret thoughts by scratching them with a pin in the margins of his English edition of Ugo Foscolo's *Ultime lettere di Jacopo Ortis* (final edition 1816). 'Notwithstanding my fear of its being read,' he says of this activity, 'I used the point of a pin to trace in the margins of Jacopo Ortis characters and entire lines hardly visible to the naked eye. In them I gave voice to the regrets, anxieties, and bitterness with which my heart so often overflowed in this gloomy situation!' (I: 230). In the Spielberg Andryane again used a pin to scratch a German-French dictionary on the walls of his cell (II: 331), later adding another tally of all the English words he could remember (III: 388). Texts written in the blood of a loving companion, texts burned to prevent punishment by the authorities, texts inscribed with a pin in the margins of Foscolo's novel of political and amorous despair, texts scratched onto the walls of a prison cell – Andryane's memoir is filled with allusions to writings of an unusual physical nature but whose precise message can no longer be deciphered.

What the *Mémoires* do make plain is their author's sense of his own heroism. Although the 'illustrious Count Confalonieri' is mentioned prominently in the title of Andryane's book, it soon becomes clear that the work's real hero is its autobiographical protagonist himself. In his memoir Andryane is depicted as an exceptionally heroic individual who is able to endure his ordeal without revealing the political secrets he knows. His resistance to all attempts to make him confess – resistance that must be considered fictitious since historians have a different view of Andryane's behaviour under pressure – is a principal theme.[51]

Despite his avowed devotion to 'the language of moderation and conscientious truth' (I: 12–13), Andryane's memoir was considered by those who had shared prison with him to have unacceptably blurred the line between historical testimony and fiction. In an 'Avant-propos' to the third volume of his *Mémoires*, Andryane admits that Confalonieri was not pleased with the way he was represented in the work's first two volumes and had asked that there be no references to him in future instalments. Andryane, however, decided to disregard his old cell mate's entreaty. 'I have had to overcome the pain that I felt at his refusal,' he explains, 'in order to respect truth and gratitude' (III: iii). The count, however, was not persuaded by this appeal. After making clear to Andryane 'my absolute insistence that he not speak about me or anything concerning me,' Confalonieri had no recourse but to 'break off those ties between us that the brotherhood of prison had made sacred, and that nothing on my side except a powerful obligation would have loosened.'[52] Pellico had similar reservations.[53] The diffidence that Pellico, Confalonieri, and others felt towards Andryane's memoirs was not due merely to their feeling that he was intruding in affairs that were more properly the business of Italians. Whether or not they realized how much he had confessed to the Austrians, Andryane's old prison comrades were intent on repudiating what they called 'the novel' he had written about their common calvary.[54]

One aspect of the *Mémoires d'un prisonnier d'état* found especially irksome by Andryane's fellow-prisoners was the portrait he drew in it of Giorgio Pallavicino. In a letter to Confalonieri in 1837, Pellico noted how 'a matter that has caused me some pain in the second volume is where the miseries of Pallavicini are described with such vivid merriment.'[55] Pellico also knew that Pallavicino was preparing a response to Andryane's depiction of him and was concerned that public bickering was about to break out among the ex-prisoners. 'After all of our pain,' he wrote later, 'a war among those who bore the same leg irons would be ugly.'[56]

The principal belligerents in the post-prison hostilities among the Spielberg veterans were in fact Andryane and Pallavicino. In the second volume of his memoirs Andryane had described not only how Pallavicino had broken down completely under questioning, but also how he had feigned madness in a humiliating but vain attempt to retract his earlier revelations. Andryane's description of Pallavicino's pretending he was a blackbird and the emotionless reaction of Salvotti to this comedy – 'Bring him some birdseed!' he is reputed to have said when he learned of his prisoner's new avian identity (II: 349) – is vividly but not very tactfully drawn. It is no wonder Pallavicino was distressed by it.

Before confinement a major figure among the Lombard conspirators who had Confalonieri at their centre, the Marchese Giorgio Guido Pallavicino Trivulzio (1796–1878) made significant contributions to his country's political welfare after release from prison and the house arrest in Prague that followed. By his own account a person of 'volcanic temper,'[57] in another dramatic figure of speech involving the blood of an ex-prisoner, Pallavicino declared to King Vittorio Emmanuele that he was prepared to give 'the last escudo in my purse and the last drop of my blood ... for the independence of Italy' (xvii). After prison, exile, and return to Italy in 1840, Pallavicino fought in the War of 1848–9, participated in the 'Five Days of Milan,' and served as both 'prodittatore' of Naples and prefect of Palermo. In 1861 he was named a Senator of the Realm.

Pallavicino published two accounts of his imprisonment. In 1856, more than twenty years after the first wave of Spielberg writing, his *Spilbergo e Gradisca*, a sprightly third-person description of confinement in the two prisons mentioned in the title, was published in Turin. At the beginning of this book, the elderly Pallavicino warns his readers that they are not beginning a conventional narrative. 'Even though I am old,' he says in a passage that gives the flavour of his work and a sense of the man, 'and also a bit senile ... I intend in this last period of my life to pester my neighbour incessantly with my chatter – an ancient habit of old age.' Although the book's 'chatter' may be tiresome, Pallavicino's readers should bear in mind, he goes on, that 'the catechism teaches us how meritorious an action it is to hear out bothersome people patiently,' and that reading this author's possibly tedious book should thus ease their paths to Paradise (1). Throughout the rest of his memoir Pallavicino manages in similar ways to avoid undue solemnity.

In 1895, almost two decades after this patriot's death in 1878, Pallavicino's widow published three volumes of her late husband's memoirs. These *Memorie* include letters from the 1820s plus extracts from a journal Pallavicino kept during his confinement in Prague. The passages in it that treat prison experiences are drawn from the earlier account in *Spilbergo e Gradisca*, though now in the first rather than the third person, with Pallavicino's account bolstered by supporting commentary from a number of other writers, including Pellico, Confalonieri, Andryane, and the non-prisoner Niccolò Tommaseo.[58] Pallavicino's memoir, as edited by his wife, is thus a further example of the collective and reiterative nature of prison writing about the Spielberg as well as a rewriting of his own and his comrades' contributions to this tradition.

One difference between Pallavicino's book and other prison memoirs of this period is that his *Memorie* contain not just allusions to texts he composed in prison but excerpts from them. In 'Canto del prigioniero' ('The Prisoner's Song') (70–7), for example, Pallavicino compares the Austrian emperor to famous tyrants from Russian history. This sample of his poetic abilities, however, makes it clear that the marchese was fortunate to have been a wealthy aristocrat and man of action who did not have to rely on his pen for a living.

The principal intent of both *Spilbergo e Gradisca* and the *Memorie*, as well as the impetus for their composition, was to discredit Andryane's *Mémoires d'un prisonnier d'état*. No other text by a Spielberg prisoner displays such a powerful determination to refute another competing account as Pallavicino's does Andryane's. As justification for his rewriting of Andryane, Pallavicino insists that since neither Pellico nor Andryane was a professional historian, there is little reason to consider their descriptions of confinement definitive. While conceding that 'it would be a good thing if Italy were to have a history of 1821 and of the matters that we are discussing,' Pallavicino wants it clear that in the respective cases of Pellico and Andryane 'the one wrote a poem, the other a novel.'[59] In his opinion, moreover, Andryane's work is not just fiction but a 'mendacious work' (22) in which the Frenchman 'attempts to diminish Pallavicino by making fun of him and comparing him to Confalonieri' (25). Although Pellico might have counselled turning the other cheek in circumstances such as these, the 'volcanic' Pallavicino is not accustomed to forgiving slights of this sort:

The good Silvio might have wanted me to allow myself to be slapped in the face by Andryane without responding since, according to him, a war between those who bore the same leg irons would be ugly. On the contrary, I would add, it would be extremely ugly! Except that, in such cases, the fault does not lie in defending oneself by refusing to accept such slander but resides instead with the one who is doing the provoking, mocking, and slandering. And who would dare to deny me the sacred right to reject unjust imputations! I have no pretensions to becoming a saint. When insulted I respond, no matter who it is who is insulting me. (*Memorie*, 37)

Pallavicino, after all, is an aristocrat, not a saint in training. His book is his response to Andryane for the slurs the latter has made on his honour, the literary equivalent of accepting a challenge to a duel.

In defence of his own position and rebuttal of Andryane's, in his *Memorie* Pallavicino reprints an 1857 review of *Spilbergo e Gradisca* by Tommaseo. In this article, Tommaseo says of Andryane's *Mémoirs*: 'I do not question whether these things are true, I question whether they are told in such a way for them to be understood as true' (43). While not impugning the historical basis for Andryane's descriptions, Tommaseo is critical of Andryane's presentation of the matter. For this literary critic, prison writing is a 'narration like that of history, of law, and of the theatre.' A successful author of such work, therefore, must be a 'chronicler,' a 'witness,' and an 'author and actor who presents a picture as well as renders men's words and emotions' (41). Even if such a writer is extremely able, distortions can occur – to such an extent that 'the truth, although sought out and cherished, cannot be or seem truly articulated due to shortcoming either in the writer's mind or his heart or his style, or even because of some excellence in this regard' (41). Writers, then, because they are able to write effectively, can produce a representation that does not correspond to the truth. In Tommaseo's view, Andryane has succumbed too often to the temptation to produce a well-written as distinct from an accurate description of his experiences in the Spielberg.

In his own remarks on his fellow-prisoner's memoir, Pallavicino is less restrained than Tommaseo. He devotes an entire chapter of his *Memorie* to a scathing critique of Andryane's book, announcing that he will show 'in a few words what Signor Andryane tells or does not tell you speaking incessantly of himself in four fat volumes' (62). The chapter that follows (chapter 9) is a bilingual one, apparently written initially in French and then translated into Italian, as if to prove Pallavicino could write just as well in Andryane's native tongue as in his own; it even includes some verses that rhyme perfectly in both French and Italian.

Pallavicino's raising of his uniquely individual voice in the chorus of Spielberg writing shows again how intertextual all of this writing was. His *Spilbergo e Gradisca*, first, and his *Memorie*, later, rewrite a book,

The Spielberg: Concealment and Refutation   63

Andryane's, that was itself a rewriting of a best-seller, Pellico's *Le mie prigioni*, which had also been rewritten by the public additions made by Maroncelli and the private ones by Confalonieri, among others. In his contribution to this tradition, Pallavicino justifies his position by bringing in additional documentation and appealing to the literary authority of Tommaseo. Attempting to confute what he insists is Andryane's tendentious and insulting account, Pallavicino feels honour-bound to correct his one-time comrade's unacceptable description of the Spielberg prisoners' common plight.

The final prison writer to be considered in this chapter has been dubbed an 'anti-Pellico' and proposed as the antithesis of the author of *Le mie prigioni*.[60] Gabriele Rosa (1812–97) from Iseo, a small town on the lake of the same name near Bergamo, was born to a numerous and 'extremely poor family' that, after his mother's death, he helped support by working as a baker.[61] Rosa, who was eight years old when Pellico and Maroncelli were arrested, was from both a different social class and a younger generation than his predecessors at Brno.

Unlike other Spielberg prisoners, Rosa was not a Carbonaro but a member of the 'Young Italy' group founded by Giuseppe Mazzini (1805–72) in 1831, an association of republican-minded individuals that has been characterized as the 'first organized Italian political party.'[62] Following his term in prison, Rosa became 'provveditore agli studi' or district school superintendent in Bergamo. Later in life he displayed a striking talent as a polygraph, ranging widely over such disparate fields as history, linguistics, agriculture, and geography.[63] Rosa is also the author of a biographical sketch of Federico Confalonieri, whose term in the Moravian prison just overlapped his own.[64]

Like Confalonieri's, Rosa's account of his imprisonment was written with his family in mind rather than for publication.[65] The portions of Rosa's text that concern his prison sentence were apparently composed between September and October of 1863 – that is, when the ex-prisoner was about fifty years old. Some six decades later, more than a century after its composition, the memoir was republished along with Pellico's *Le mie prigioni* under the collective title, *Due patrioti allo Spielberg*, edited by Ugoberto Alfassio Grimaldi.

Even without Grimaldi's prompting in the introduction, the intertextual links between Rosa's memoir and Pellico's are evident. Writing just after the triumph of Unification, Rosa looks back with a certain condescension on such earlier Spielberg writers as Pellico and Andryane – the latter, in his view, someone whose 'povertà d'arte' ('lack of style') was 'aggravated by a certain personal and Gallic vanity' (85). In regard to *Le mie prigioni*, which had just been published at the time of his arrest, Rosa notes that before going to prison he 'had not read that book, though those among us who had been able to see it before their incarceration drew compassion from it for the prisoner, hatred towards the persecutor, as well as fear – though no encouragement to imitate the martyr and become patriotically militant.' Far from being worth a battle won against the Austrians, Rosa deemed Pellico's 'a book of resignation, which moved the sensitive hearts of a great multitude throughout Europe but inspired no conspirators or martyrs for national freedom' (84). On a more human level, Rosa is also critical of Pellico for breaking the pact with his prison comrades not to publish anything about the Spielberg until all the prisoners confined there had been released.[66]

Rosa's account of his own imprisonment is very different from Pellico's. While awaiting trial in Santa Margherita in 1835, this young man from the provinces was thrust into a picaresque world of crime and criminals unlike anything he had seen in Iseo. 'One can see,' he says excitedly about Santa Margherita, 'prostitutes in for their medical examinations, pimps, pickpockets, thieves, and spies, arrested for common crimes. Policemen in disguise, Italian, French, and German high commissioners passing through or in consultation, theatre people involved in disagreements or for solicitation, spies of every sort and class. There are monks, priests, travellers in elegant clothes, female adventurers, clerks, and zealous bloodhound-like informers' (59). Far from being repelled – or being only repelled – by the 'degraded women' and others he saw at Santa Margherita, Rosa was fascinated by the Hogarthian scene unfolding before him.

Rosa's motto in the Spielberg might well be his astute (if not entirely original) observation that 'necessity sharpens one's wits' – especially in prison (75). An enthusiastic participant in the prison 'langage mural' that gave Andryane so much trouble until he realized it was based on the Italian rather than the French writing system, Rosa was able in this way to communicate freely with his comrades, even organizing checkers tournaments between prisoners in contiguous cells (69). His youthful ardour undampened by the circumstances of confinement, he managed to charm the prison's assistant cook into sneaking him special portions from the prison refectory (72) and attracted the attention of the warden's daughter (and Spielberg goose-girl), who was inspired enough by his interest to learn some Italian and thus be able to provide this captivating prisoner with support and encouragement (72). Not only does the resourceful dandy Rosa manage to re-tailor his prison garb for the sake of appearing 'less of a mess' to the assistant cook, the goose-girl, and whomever else he may encounter (75), he and his comrades cope with the hated chore of knitting socks by rolling the wool provided into balls they then employ in improvised *bocce* tournaments (72).

Rosa is also so adept in the contributions he makes to the collective oral novel the prisoners compose for their evenings' amusement that when it is his turn to continue the story even the guards gather to listen (74). And when a pipe and other forbidden materials are discovered in the prisoners' possession, these same guards are so afraid of being compromised by the discovery that they let the infraction pass unreported. His wits sharpened indeed by the exigencies of prison, handsome and endlessly resourceful, Rosa almost seems a Giuseppe Pignata brought back to life and once again dazzling all those about him.

Certainly this is a very different picture of existence in the Spielberg than that depicted by the prisoners of the 1820s. Some of this is because Rosa knew he had to serve only a three-year term – a long enough segment in a life, but dramatically shorter than the twenty-and-more-year sentences meted out to Maroncelli, Pellico, and Confalonieri. Moreover, at the time of his confinement Rosa was still, as he puts it, 'in the April of his life, filled with hope, beguiled by illusions, excited by a need for pure love, whose sweetness he had just begun to taste' (52), and prison did not seem to have dimmed any of these sparkling emotions. Most important of all, it is also clear that when he wrote his memoir, Rosa was looking back on events whose painful features were by then attenuated by the passage of time. As a result, he described his prison stay as more of a lark than it probably was. Even so, Rosa's account demonstrates that there were other ways, if not of enduring prison, at least of looking back on it than those championed in *Le mie prigioni*. Whether or not Gabriele Rosa himself can or should be considered the 'anti-Pellico,' his description of his stay in the Spielberg is certainly the converse, in many ways, of that contained in Pellico's book. Whatever Rosa might have been concealing about the reality of his prison internment, his is a triumphalist rewriting of Pellico and other writers of his school.

Though its author was old enough that his sentence coincided in part with that of Confalonieri, Gabriele Rosa's account of his imprisonment in the Spielberg seems a deliberate refutation of the memoirs of earlier inmates of that same institution, especially Pellico. Try as they might, however, to restore what they believed had been excised from Pellico's account of 'his prisons,' all those who contributed to prison literature after *Le mie prigioni* must be deemed captives not only of the Austrian government but also of Pellico's extremely successful memorial text.

But the imperative later writers felt to rectify Pellico's testimony was more than an urge to set the historical record straight. One meaning, perhaps, of the many references to lost, burnt, stolen, hidden, erased, or otherwise invisible texts in *Le mie prigioni* and the other works studied here is their shared conviction that beyond anything written about the collective experience of imprisonment lay another text of inexpressible emotion. This ineffable master-text encapsulated the real nature of an experience that none who had endured it could quite disclose or perhaps even clearly perceive but certainly did not recognize in accounts by others. Due, perhaps, to the guilt these patriots felt at the confessions most of them rendered under interrogation, there is a sense in all their writing of something unsaid and perhaps unsayable that lurks beneath their otherwise earnest testimony. Although united first as participants in a common misery and then as veterans of a shared nightmare, the Spielberg prisoners could never free themselves from suspicions about even those comrades with whom they had shared their most intimate moments and most terrible suffering. These suspicions explain their repeated attempts to unmask one another, their obsessions with hidden identities and invisible texts, and the squabbles in which they became entangled after prison. The intensity of their bickering plus the rewriting, refutation, and repudiation of one another (and sometimes themselves) that characterizes the Spielberg texts indicates how crucial these writers believed their experiences had been in defining not only a period of their lives but the whole span of their existences. This intensity of emotion further reveals how deeply the Spielberg prisoners wanted their experiences to be inscribed correctly into the historical record, even if for many of them the true nature of their prison experience would always remain unutterable.

3
Bodies Politic

... if my letters show a certain warmth, it is a feverish warmth. I write them with my heart, and the heart has nothing to do with the mind. My heart is still young and robust and I still love forcefully. But I do not want to discuss this with you further because doing so is useless and in fact hurtful to you.[1]

Although the patriots sent to the Spielberg following the trials of the 1820s were arguably the most famous prison writers of the Risorgimento, they were by no means the only ones. In the Archduchy of Tuscany and the States of the Church in central Italy, in the Kingdom of Two Sicilies in the south, and in such northern cities as Mantua during the 1830s, 1840s, and 1850s, hundreds of Italians went to prison for their political beliefs. Less obsessed, for the most part, than the Spielberg prisoners with correcting the record of their sufferings that would be transmitted to posterity, these later authors clung tightly in their writings to what they felt were consoling ties to such institutions as the family, a social milieu, the Italian cultural tradition, or humankind itself. Such extramural and institutionalized communities tended to provide these prison authors with a sense of self and of personal value while they were in confinement. In the pages that follow, these mid-nineteenth century writers – authors who include lawyers, doctors, writers, a priest, a university professor, and a student, but only one aristocrat – are grouped according to the regions where they lived, with prisoners in what were in many ways the anomalous States of the Church treated last.

The poet and journalist Carlo Bini (1806–42) is one of two Tuscan writers to be considered in this section. The son of a wholesale grain dealer in the seaport city of Livorno, Bini in Tuscany, like Pellico and Confalonieri in Lombardy, began his career by contributing articles to a politically progressive periodical, the *Indicatore livornese*.[2] The Forte della Stella prison on the island of Elba where Bini was held as a precautionary measure for a brief period in 1833, however, was nothing like the 'carcere durissimo' his opposite numbers from Lombardy came to know in the Spielberg. In a letter to his father, Bini described his island cell as the classic 'gilded cage.'[3] But although the young journalist was imprisoned for only a dozen weeks or so, his confinement on the island of Elba was a turning-point in his life. Instead of devoting his time there to the translations and articles that had been his accustomed fare in Livorno, Bini directed his attention to consideration of broader social and existential issues. The work that issued from his reflections was entitled *Manoscritto di un prigioniero*.[4] For Bini, as he put it in lines appended to that text: 'La prigione è una lima sì sottile / Che aguzzando il pensier ne fa uno stile[5] [A stay in prison is such a fine file / It sharpens your thought and provides it with style].

The style Bini derived from his prison-honed thought sought to avoid the 'rhetorical' and the 'heroic' this writer deemed 'truly insufferable in a century such as ours' (70). Instead, Bini took a nonconformist approach to writing by adopting a style meant to emulate that of England's Laurence Sterne (1713–68), some of whose work the Italian author had translated for the *Indicatore*.[6] But Bini was also influenced – negatively this time – by more recent memoirs. 'Oh Silvio Pellico!' he exclaimed in a passage in the *Manoscritto* that demonstrates again how pervasive *Le mie prigioni* was for all who wrote prison memoirs after 1832, 'I ask only that you teach me where your ten-year store of patience came from – even if this means risking my producing a facsimile of *Le mie prigioni*, an account and an experience that I do not envy you.'[7] In Bini's work, the beautiful mistress of politics Pellico had relegated to a position away from the core of his narrative is instead at centre stage.

What most distinguishes the *Manoscritto di un prigioniero* from Pellico's memoir is the position it takes on the class struggle. Unlike his friend Guerrazzi, whose prison writing I consider next, Bini was more a thinker than a man of action, an idealist who dreamed of 'a form of society in which every individual, when doing so will not harm his neighbour, is guaranteed the right to move freely and in complete security anywhere within the sphere of activity that is determined by his own nature' (112). Perhaps because he had grown up in mercantile Livorno rather than the still partly feudal Lombardy of Confalonieri, Arrivabene, and Pallavicino,

Bini was convinced that all people deserved equal treatment before the law.[8] But in confinement he quickly learned that, when imprisoned, the rich are treated differently from the poor. When a rich man is sent to the Forte della Stella, Bini discovered, he is permitted to buy more comfortable living quarters and is allowed to read and write as much as he wants – his jailer, on occasion, even carrying billets-doux to his mistress. An imprisoned businessman, for this and other reasons is considered 'to be made of metal' and thus retains 'value even if a minimum one,' while a jailed poor man, by contrast, 'is money made from mud' (36). The labouring classes, while of use for their ability to produce value, are little more than inert elements of exchange – creatures of dirt rather than of precious metal.

As long as such notions prevail, Bini believed, class conflict and, eventually, revolution will be inevitable. 'The time is perhaps not far off,' he writes in the *Manoscritto*, 'when a society somewhere on the globe will become engaged in a universal chaos from which a more harmoniously organized world will emerge' (117). Although uncertain when or where this transformation of social disorder into harmony will occur, Bini does know which side will be victorious in the coming struggle. 'I do not know when this battle will take place,' he continues, 'though the battle is inevitable and will be fought to the end – a battle of the disinherited against the usurpers. Everyone, these days, expects a greater or lesser share of the patrimony Nature has granted to all of us but that the few have seized for themselves' (117). Sooner or later the pain of the disinherited will be followed by the violent redistribution of the earth's wealth. But however inevitable such combat may be, Bini does not think that the revolution can be hastened by artificial midwifery. 'Rivers move by themselves,' he insists, 'and if you leap into their midst and splash about to hurry them along, you may muddy the waters but you will not accelerate the speed of their flow' (136).

Convinced that the disenfranchised are already preparing for the coming upheaval, Bini makes a final plea not for revolution but for tolerance. In words reminiscent of those of Giacomo Leopardi in that poet's testamentary poem, 'La ginestra,' he sounds a call for increased human solidarity and an end to internecine wrangling. In terms that foreshadow those of the *Communist Manifesto* fifteen years later he proclaims:

Men of all countries and beliefs, why do we insist on bloodying one another? The earth is large enough and fertile enough to bury and to feed each one of us. If Love were our god and the world his altar, it would be worth it to live forever, and there would be little cause for tears. But given that love is in short supply and we need to save it for ourselves, let us take what remains and share it with one another, attempting, for the rest, to practise a little tolerance since being tolerant is what it means for humans to be wise. (122)

For this idealistic writer, a society that ignores the basic equality of rich and poor is 'false, unjust, rotten to the core,' and for this reason 'must be born again in a more suitable form' (117). Our allegiances, according to Bini, should be with all humanity rather than restricted to a single social class. In addition to articulating his political beliefs, by reaffirming his membership in this larger body of individuals Bini is able, while in prison, to conserve his identity as a man and as champion of social equality.

Bini's companion in Forte della Stella jail, Francesco Domenico Guerrazzi (1804–73), did not share his friend's belief in tolerance. Notorious for his atrabilious nature, Guerrazzi was born two years earlier than Bini and outlived him by three decades. While Bini was neither a commercially successful nor an especially copious writer, Guerrazzi was one of the best-known and most prolific literary figures of his day.[9] Although his fiction is not highly valued today – a standard reference notes the 'impression of coldness and insincerity that is the fundamental defect of all of Guerrazzi's work'[10] – his writings at one time occupied what seemed a secure position in Italy's literary canon.[11]

The posthumous plummet of Guerrazzi's literary fortunes mirrored the ups and downs to which his political life was also subject. After serving with Mazzini and Giuseppe Montanelli as one of the ruling triumvirate of Tuscany in 1849, and then as sole 'Dittatore' (Dictator) of the region after the triumvirate dissolved, Guerrazzi was promptly arrested when the archduke and the old order returned. Following a lengthy pre-trial detention, he was convicted of lese-majesty and exiled to Corsica. After escaping from confinement there, he was able to return to Italy where, in 1860, he was elected to the country's first Parliament, remaining a member of that body until 1870.

During the four years of his pre-trial incarceration in Tuscan prisons, Guerrazzi wrote many letters, an *Apologia della vita politica di F.D. Guerrazzi*, and several literary works, among them his play, *Beatrice Cenci*. It is his prison letters, however, that critics today have found this prolific writer's most enduring contribution to the literature of his country.[12]

Despite the brave bluster of much of what he wrote from confinement, the gregarious Guerrazzi found prison to be torture. 'For a writer, a poet,' he says about his solitude in an outburst that is echoed by many later prison writers, including Bartolomeo Vanzetti in distant Massachusetts, 'lengthy detention is putting your very soul on the rack: a man becomes broken both in body and in spirit.'[13] 'Your intelligence loses its elasticity,' he complains elsewhere, 'your thoughts, like pools of stagnant water, lie there inert and turn putrid, your blood and your spirit turn to lead' (124). In his current situation Guerrazzi finds that all ambition has deserted him. 'My apathy has arrived at such a point,' he writes, 'that if I had to climb a flight of only eight steps to attain the governorship of the world ... I wouldn't climb them' (142–3).

Guerrazzi's greatest frustration in confinement was at his inability to provide needed guidance to the person he loved most in the world: his nephew, ward, and future adopted son, Franceschino Michele Guerrazzi – or Cecchino as he affectionately called him. 'I am never so cruelly aware that I am in prison,' he writes this young man early in his detention, 'as I am when I receive a letter from you. If they only knew the damage and hurt that I feel at the sight of your inexperienced youth left without guidance and advice! ... I want you to know that my heart has been irreparably pierced, and that reasons for grieving increase with each passing day' (171). In this and his other letters to Cecchino, Guerrazzi frequently reveals a heartfelt capacity for affection that is largely absent in more public writing such as his novels. Sometimes, however, his attempts to advise his nephew make him appear a latter-day Polonius to Cecchino's impatient Laertes.[14] For instance, Guerrazzi recommends that Cecchino imitate Napoleon, who at age 26 had already conquered Italy (68), or, if inclined towards a commercial career, at least read Benjamin Franklin (325, 329, etc.). Cecchino, however, was far from a Napoleon or a Franklin, as his uncle eventually realized. From his jail cell Guerrazzi could do little more than rail at his charge's errors in spelling (133 and elsewhere) and his sometimes shaky Italian, a language he feared Cecchino was in danger of forgetting while at school in French-speaking Piedmont (157–8). While Cecchino does not – to his uncle's vast relief – become engaged to a girl the older man thinks unsuitable (185–6), the boy is so unsuccessful in his studies that the prisoner, furious, threatens to disinherit him (263). Later, however, he arranges for Cecchino to travel to America, and later still makes preparations to include him on an expedition to a Genovese trading outpost near the port of Taganrog on the Sea of Azov (336). 'I have your portrait,' the doting uncle writes in another letter, 'and I kiss it often: it is cold but I warm it with my breath. If only I could take you into my arms sometime soon!' (168). Throughout his frustrating period of confinement, Guerrazzi's love for Cecchino never flags.

It is a striking paradox that this notoriously thorny writer, known for his unbridled outbursts of personal pique, could compose such tender letters to his nephew. Unlike Bini, whose writings from prison deal with the more abstract topic of social justice and whose point of reference is always mankind in general, Guerrazzi, in his private communications with his nephew, discovered a powerful vein of familial affection. Thanks to the blood ties he felt with Cecchino, this once popular author has transmitted a very different image of himself to posterity than he might have had he never been made to undergo the psychic torture of incarceration.

For generosity of spirit of the sort Guerrazzi was urging on his nephew and perhaps discovering within himself while in prison, few prison writers of the Italian Risorgimento can equal the eleven patriots known as the Martyrs of Mantua, or of Belfiore after the locality where they were put to death by the Austrians. Unlike others studied so far, the patriots in this group did not return triumphantly to freedom after prison but proceeded instead to death on the scaffold. The letters they wrote before being hanged are contributions both to the history of prison writing in Italy and to the melancholy tradition of testamentary writing or 'last words' before execution.[15] In what follows, I turn first to the work of Luigi Pastro, who, though not himself a Martyr, was imprisoned with the Mantua group, and then consider the writings of Carlo Poma and Enrico Tazzoli, two of the Mantua eleven executed at Belfiore.

Luigi Pastro (1822–1915) was a Treviso physician and later senator who, despite the physical trials of his imprisonment, lived to be over ninety. His *Ricordi di prigione dell'unico superstite dei condannati di Mantova dal 1851 al 1853* were not published until 1907, more than half a century after his 1856 release from Austrian confinement. Although his book may seem to belong to the tradition of *Le mie prigioni*, Pastro, like Bini before him, is determined that his description of his ordeal not be confused with that of Silvio Pellico. If Pellico made his peace, while in prison, not only with God but also with the political forces oppressing him, Pastro never wavered in his defiance of the Austrians or in his adherence to his political principles. This, indeed, was why he avoided the fate of the Martyrs, all of whom seem to have been unaware that Austrian law forbade execution of an accused in the absence of a confession.[16] While Pastro's silence about the charges levelled against him saved his life, his obstinacy in this matter also led to extremely harsh handling by his captors, treatment so severe he almost died from the lack of nourishment and medical attention he was made to endure while in prison.

Although he was a physician and not a writer by profession, poetry – or at least verse – was one of the weapons Pastro used to counter his captors' efforts to control his will and imagination. By composing verse, especially sonnets, in jail, this early patriot was able to repudiate his jailers' definition of their captive as little more than a fomenter of revolution and exponent of a discredited national culture. Through the Italian poetry he composed in captivity, Pastro strengthened his sense of identity as a representative of a vigorous cultural tradition both older and richer than that of politically dominant Austria. Because Pastro was held mostly in solitary confinement, where he was forbidden all reading and writing materials, the prison sonnets he composed were initially merely mental compositions that came to be written down only after their author's release. Some of these poems are acrostics, complex texts that in addition to their overt content bear clandestine meanings hidden in the initial letters (for the four-level acrostics, in the initial four letters) of each of their traditional fourteen lines. The creation of such stylistically demanding works in painful circumstances and without writing materials obviously required both extraordinary verbal dexterity and a prodigious memory as well as unflagging determination.

While still in Austrian captivity, Pastro managed to have one of these sonnets smuggled out of jail and published in nearby Padua.[17] When the first four letters of each line of this 'Sonetto per laurea' (Graduation Sonnet) for the prisoner's friend Count Giuseppe Avogaro are read in isolation from the rest of the text, the following message emerges: 'T'attien al canon / il serto posponi / ve, i prodi mai son / [abbastanza] a smuover i troni.'[18] In this clandestine message Pastro is advising Avogaro to postpone further medical studies and stick (literally!: T'attien al canon) to his guns until the 'prodi' (brave) young men like himself succeed in overturning the thrones of the oppressors, which for the moment are only wobbling but which clearly will topple soon. By writing and then publishing this poem purportedly dealing with his friend's university graduation but in reality bearing a subversive message urging continued struggle against the common oppressor, Pastro is attesting to the continued viability of the Italian literary and cultural tradition as well as demonstrating how the fight for Italian liberty can be carried forward even from a prison cell.

Pastro was determined in other ways, too, to demonstrate that prison could not diminish him as a man. Despite the solitary confinement in which he was held for much of his detention, he none the less managed to meet, fall in love with, and even dream of marrying a woman he encountered in a Mantua prison. All of his communication with Giuseppina Perlasca Bonizzoni, an important Risorgimento figure in her own right, took place through tapping on the prison wall in the same 'langage mural' that had so intrigued Andryane in the Spielberg. Undeterred by the obvious physical impediments to consummation of his love (and without much consideration either for whatever views on the matter his correspondent on the other side of the wall may have held), Pastro began to fashion an image of the child he fancied he and Giuseppina would one day produce. He even conceived a name for this infant: 'Santo Lucio Barnaba,' an anagram for 'Nato in barba a Culos' (born to spite Culos' face) – Culos (more correctly Culoz) being the surname of the Austrian general in command of the city where the two lovers were held. Although this anagrammatically subversive child was never born in a biological sense, and Pastro went on to marry a woman he met elsewhere in the Austrian penal system, the real offspring of this patriot's prison desire was not a son but the poetry he produced in confinement: the sonnets he conceived parthenogenetically 'in barba a Culos.' Through his writing of this sort, Pastro succeeded in reasserting in the imagined body of his son both the importance of Italian culture and his own biological individuality.

Writing of all sorts was also crucial for the Mantua conspirators Enrico Tazzoli (1812–52) and Carlo Poma (1823–52).[19] Tazzoli the priest and Poma the physician in many ways represent middle-class Risorgimento idealism at its finest. Tazzoli was a person of considerable learning and energy who taught philosophy at the Mantua seminary. He was also regional treasurer for Mazzini's 'prestito nazionale' (national loan), Young Italy's project to finance the struggle for unification through the sale of patriotic bonds. Perhaps because he was unaccustomed to activity of this kind, Tazzoli was unusually scrupulous about his stewardship of the monies he had gathered and kept a coded ledger listing the amounts and names of contributors to the fund. Raising money for the sake of Italian unity, however, was a criminal act under Austrian law. When Tazzoli's ledger was discovered and decoded, those whose names figured in it were arrested and the young priest was convicted of treason and sentenced to death. Catholic Austria, however, was reluctant to hang a man of the cloth. For this reason, before being taken to the scaffold, Tazzoli and another convicted clergyman, Bartolomeo Grazioli, were made to undergo the humiliating experience of ecclesiastical degradation and ritual defrocking. During this ceremony, Tazzoli's vestments were taken off him and his hands scraped with a penknife in symbolic removal of their anointing at his investiture, an erasure on his body itself of the status now officially denied the doomed patriot.[20]

Unlike Pastro, Tazzoli was allowed to write in prison while awaiting sentencing and then execution. The texts he composed in these circumstances included works both aimed at the general public and directed to close friends. Among the former were nineteen sermons, all of which are now lost, and an open letter *Al General Culoz sulle cause della congiura del 1850* (To General Culoz on the Reasons for the 1850 Plot), which has survived.[21] In this tract – often considered Tazzoli's final testament and message to posterity – the patriot priest ringingly justifies his political past in a long and detailed list of Austria's abuses during that country's occupation of his homeland.

In addition to this public statement – disseminated throughout the region after he let it drop from his carriage during a prison transfer – Tazzoli also authored a *Gazzettino* or prison newspaper that was read by his fellow inmates until such time as this publication's editor himself, as Luzio wryly puts it, 'was suppressed by the authorities.'[22] In this prison paper as in his open letter to Culoz, Tazzoli, like his fellow conspirator Pastro, was attempting to carry on the political struggle while in prison, directing his comments both to his fellow prisoners and to the Italian community at large.

Tazzoli's prison poetry is of a more personal nature. It includes two epithalamiums for a cousin, Marianna Arrivabene, a series of 'decasillabi,' or verses of ten syllables each, for the same relative, and a ballad on a bird glimpsed from his prison window whose freedom the confined writer envies – a trope that appears in the writings of many prison authors.[23] Tazzoli's own estimate of his prowess as a poet was a modest one. As he admitted in lines about this written to his brother Silvio:

> Silvio mio, tu lo sai; non son poeta.
> Ma allor che prepotente ferve in petto
> Soävemente ricambiato affetto,
> Perfin all'asin di cantar chi vieta?
> Soffri dunque che metta quattro versi
> Quand'anche andar si dean per l'aer spersi.[24]

Though he is no more a poet, in his own view, than a donkey is a singer,

Tazzoli must respond to the emotion that is burning in his heart. The prison verse he produces in this way enables Tazzoli, like Pastro, to assert his individuality as an Italian and tighten his bonds with the linguistic and social communities that provide him with personal identity.

In addition to the ostensible letters he sent home from prison, Tazzoli managed to communicate clandestinely with his family as well. Some of his writings of this sort were directed to his aunt, Teresa Giacomelli Arrivabene, or 'Gege' as he called her, the widow of Tazzoli's uncle, who after the death of the priest's own mother became a kind of second parent to him. Tazzoli's letters to Gege were written in both normal ink and 'inchiostro simpatico' fashioned from lemon juice or other acids with which the prisoner traced communications to her between the lines of his usual and permitted correspondence.[25] When the paper on which messages written in this way was then heated, the clandestine words became legible. Communicating through these non-censored channels, Tazzoli and his aunt were able to discuss matters they might not have broached in other circumstances. Surprisingly, these matters – at least in the documents that have survived – concern neither politics nor Tazzoli's internment, but are dominated instead by expressions of affection, sometimes of such an intense nature that the young priest himself has cause to wonder if the two participants in this correspondence are not behaving like 'two fifteen-year-olds.'

In his own account, however, the passion Tazzoli feels for Gege is not a carnal but a spiritual emotion of universal rather than individual scope. This emotion is located in his burning heart. 'Indeed, my dear,' he explains, 'this heart of mine is such a furnace that it attaches itself to everyone. Even loving my enemies is not my doing. And I hope that God will punish even my gravest shortcomings because of the amount that I love.' In this universalist context Tazzoli does not hesitate to include his aunt's body in the circle of his love. 'I love your soul and nothing else,' he says to her, 'and I love your body because it is yours.' As for Gege, in return, she is fortunate in Tazzoli's view not to be in love with her nephew's body since 'there is nothing lovable about it' in the first place, and in the second, 'it will soon cease to exist.'[26] In Tazzoli's passionately uninhibited articulation of the feelings raging in his heart, his clandestine communications with his aunt are invested with subversive power as a counter-discourse opposed to official prison discipline. Tazzoli's heart has in this way metaphorically melted the prison bars constraining him.

Perhaps the most interesting prison texts written by this Mantuan priest are those he inscribed in his own blood. Shortly before his arrest,

Tazzoli fell from a carriage, in the accident injuring his leg. While in prison, he was permitted to send the dressings for this wound to his family for laundering and replacement. On these bandages, using the blood and other discharges from his injury as writing fluid and the 'pezzuoli' or cloth strips themselves as paper, Tazzoli wrote additional letters about his confinement. In them another Tazzoli emerges, a figure unlike the affectionate nephew of the letters to Gege, the cheerfully conventional poet of the light-hearted prison verse, or the measured but indignant patriot of the letter to Culoz. In perhaps the most famous of the messages written in this way – one inscribed on a bandage that is now lost but was purportedly scrawled 'with the bloody pus oozing from a wound in his leg' (62) – Tazzoli described his incensed reaction to accusations of betrayal levelled at him by his prison comrade and fellow priest Ferdinando Bosio. The prisoner's response to charges of treachery by Bosio, an individual he characterized elsewhere as a 'wicked person who turned out to be extremely cowardly,' (332–3) was straightforward and instinctive. 'I spat,' he wrote on the bandage describing this scene, 'in Bosio's face' (62). In this text, bodily fluids – blood and pus in the one case, saliva in the other – constitute both the medium of communication and the principal element of the message. The unconventional material nature of the text plus its extraordinary content endow the message scrawled on this 'pezzuolo' with singular intensity and bestow an unusual aura of incontrovertibility on the entire communication.

Unlike Pastro in his retrospective *Ricordi di prigione*, Tazzoli was not remembering the past in his prison writings but communicating from the centre of a maelstrom of vindictive violence that would soon suck him down to destruction. For this reason his writing from prison has a special immediacy. Most obviously in the public letter to Culoz, but in his other prison writing as well, Tazzoli was determined to demonstrate his innocence in the context of a larger scheme of justice than that encompassed by Austrian law, in this way asserting his true identity as an Italian patriot rather than a traitor to both Austria and the church. Despite the message to that effect inscribed on his body during the degradation ceremony, by writing from the incandescent alembic of his heart, and on some occasions using as ink fluids emanating from that same body, Tazzoli was able to communicate in effective fashion with the world that would eventually transform him into a martyr.

Of all the Mantua patriots, Tazzoli's friend Carlo Poma had the most developed literary interests.[27] Poma was also among the conspirators with the most sophisticated political ideas and, as his collaboration with Tito Speri in the ultimately aborted plot to assassinate Police Commissar Rossi suggests, the person in the Mantua group who came closest to embracing violence as an instrument for political change.[28] Because of these intellectual and cultural interests, Poma lived his imprisonment in exceptionally literary, – that is, given the era in which he lived – Romantic terms. In a letter describing his prison experience to his mother, the twenty-nine-year-old medical doctor, like Tazzoli and others in this group of mid-century patriots, also refers to the state of his heart when he explains how during his confinement 'my heart has become more sensitive; I would say, in fact, that previously my reason alone guided my actions and inspired my thoughts but that prison has now led me to discover my heart.'[29] Because incarceration sharpens the ability not only to write better, as Bini had said, but to feel deeply too, Poma can exult in the solitude he has found in the Mainolda prison. 'I still long from time to time for my cell in the Mainolda,' he confesses to his mother after being moved from solitary confinement in that prison to collective custody in the nearby San Giorgio castle, 'where, though all alone, I could be with you and my brothers in my thoughts. While I was there, I thought too much, here I think too little' (123). For Poma, prison was an opportunity for reflection and renewed contact with what he believed was his most authentic self. If the Forte della Stella had provided Bini with a style, in the Mainolda Poma had found a precious reservoir of feeling.

Poma was sometimes able to read as well as write in prison, while in the Mainolda earlier he was not permitted any reading material. But in a gesture of both familial and Italian solidarity, Poma's relatives managed to smuggle poetry by Dante and other Italian writers into the prisoner's cell. Texts by these authors were transcribed, on some occasions, onto small strips of paper that were then concealed in the seams of Poma's laundry. Other times, whole pages from an inexpensive edition of Dante's poem were used to wrap objects sent to the prisoner through unsuspecting and in any case illiterate guards.[30] Poma, whose preferred canticle of Dante's poem in this situation was, understandably, the *Purgatorio*, also received passages of this poetry copied onto the clean shirts returned to him from home.[31]

Poma's laundry also served as a means for him to communicate with his family through messages to his relatives that were either inscribed on his soiled linen or entrusted to small slips of paper hidden in the seams of clothing and other linen sent home for laundering.[32] Like the communications in his own blood written in prison by Tazzoli, Poma's prison messages were powerfully valorized by their linkage to the garments that had earlier enclosed his suffering body and that in this way testified to the veracity of the accompanying text.[33]

Carlo Poma's principal correspondent from prison was his mother, Anna Filippini Poma, with whom he exchanged both letters and poetry.[34] A sonnet written on his mother's name-day is an example of Poma's prison poetry that has been highly enough considered by posterity to have been reprinted in anthologies of Italian poetry from the period:

> Tale dolcezza madre nel tuo nome
> Io trovo che null'altro lo somiglia,
> E nel gran duol che all'alma aimè! s'appiglia,
> T'invoco qual di Dio benedizione.
> Per te trovo riposo e si compone
> La tempesta che l'alma mi scompiglia;
> Il seren mi ritorna sulle ciglia
> E aspetto con ardir l'aspra tenzone.
> In quest'orribil carcere, quand'io
> Teco favello, abbenchè in vista nulla,
> Pur ti sento vicina come viva.
> Così nei primi dì del viver mio,
> Se tacita movevi alla mia culla,
> Io sorridea dormendo e ti sentiva.[35]

This is clearly a different kind of composition than either Pastro's coded acrostics or Tazzoli's humorous and self-deprecatory verse to his brother. By reassuring his mother that she is as close to him now as she was when he was a baby, Poma uses the image of his own childish body to evoke an imaginative palliative for both his own and his mother's anguish.

In these verses on his mother's name-day, Poma the author has himself become a literary character, much as he will be in the poetry Anna Poma wrote about him after her son's execution.[36] After Carlo's death, Anna Poma kept a lock of her martyred son's hair and a handful of dirt from Belfiore as precious mementoes of her lost offspring. This fetishization of Poma and the other Mantua patriots, a process that began with the images they constructed of themselves in their autobiographical prison writings, was perpetuated in more public fashion after Unification when streets and squares throughout Italy were renamed for one or another of the Mantua eleven. Stigmatized by the Austrians as subversives, Poma, Tazzoli, and their comrades were thus metamorphosed into secular icons in the Italian cultural tradition they had clung to with such determination in prison, their identities thus transmitted to posterity long after the suffering bodies that had helped attest to the nature of their martyrdom had been consigned to the earth at Belfiore.

While prisoners in the north of Italy during the 1850s were frequently able to establish more or less tenuous epistolary relations with their families outside prison, the situation in the south was very different. Those incarcerated for political reasons in this region fell into one of two extremes where writing privileges were concerned. Either they were completely forbidden to write to anyone, or they were able – though by clandestine means – to correspond as much as they liked with whomever they wanted. In the section that follows, prison writing from the south of Italy at mid-century is represented by three writers who spent long terms in Bourbon prisons. The first is Sigismondo Castromediano (1811–95), whose *Carceri e galere politiche* are memoirs of his confinement in several southern institutions where writing, for the most part, was forbidden. The others are Luigi Settembrini (1813–76) and Silvio Spaventa (1823–93), both sentenced to life imprisonment on the island of Santo Stefano, from which, however, they were able to correspond freely with friends and supporters on the Neapolitan mainland and elsewhere in Europe.

Even before the Risorgimento, the south of Italy had produced a number of authors who created enduring works from political confinement. Among them was the social historian, Pietro Giannone (1676–1748), whose *Vita scritta da lui medesimo* was composed in the Piedmont prison where he spent the final thirteen years of his existence. Like Giannone, a critic in the eighteenth century of the temporal power exercised by the Catholic church, the nineteenth-century patriots interned by the Bourbons were intent on reforming the civic life and institutions of their homeland. Unlike their frequently republican counterparts in the north, most of these southern patriots were monarchists who did not want to do away with the traditional system of government in the Kingdom of Two Sicilies but were seeking instead to provide that system with a more rational and less arbitrary foundation in the form of a 'Statuto' or constitution. Despite their critical views, all these writers were ardent nationalists who, while not opposed to limited help in their struggles from the British, for example, were opposed to massive interference in their country's affairs by foreign powers. 'Those who hope for independence through the efforts of foreigners,' one of them wrote from his prison cell, 'are parricides, villains, like naughty sons trying to get even for a wicked father's injury to them by joining with strangers to do him harm.' Though he might prefer that King Ferdinand II 'were just, reasonable, and worthy of trust,' Luigi Settembrini did not want his sovereign 'trampled and derided,' since, 'like it or not, he is the head of state: disrespect for him is disrespect for the entire nation.'[37]

In the final years of Bourbon Naples, political criticism was so widespread and so extensively repressed that, as one historian has put it, 'whoever, in the South, represented political ideas, intelligence, industriousness, or culture was subject to police harassment, put in jail or hounded into exile.'[38] The number of intellectuals, in fact, who were imprisoned during the last years of the Kingdom of Two Sicilies has been estimated to have been as high as thirty thousand or one of every three hundred of the king's subjects.[39] These mostly middle-class patriots were typically confined with bandits, members of the Camorra, and other common criminals, a class of people from which their counterparts in the north had usually been segregated.

A nobleman whose title and Germanic first name reflect the antiquity of his family origins in once-Norman Puglia, Duke Sigismondo Castromediano from Cavallino near Lecce was certainly not a political radical. Though described by a zealous *intendente* to the Minister of the Interior as determined to 'topple thrones' and 'destroy Religion,' in a headlong 'rush to Communism,'[40] in reality, the 'White Duke'[41] had scant sympathy for 'the new ideas of socialism' and considered the more radical positions of his times 'political and philosophical madness' (II: 128–9). Castromediano's mistrust of the government was partly that of a feudal lord whose family had struggled for centuries against the Neapolitan and other distant governments ruling his region. His social views, moreover, were so conservative, according to one account, that he opposed attempts by the local Jesuits to 'open the minds' of their students in the schools they wished to establish in the area.[42]

Despite his position as a nobleman and his conservative social views, Castromediano was enough of a political reformer to be found guilty of sedition against the crown and condemned to thirty years in jail. He served more than eleven years of this sentence in places of confinement that included two jails in Lecce, the Carmine prison at Naples, another on the island of Procida, and the grim strongholds for political dissidents at Montefusco and Montesarchio in the Neapolitan interior. Castromediano's release in 1859 was the result of an unsuccessful attempt to deport him and other critics of the regime to America, an attempt that ended unhappily for these men's adversaries when the deportees managed to jump ship in Ireland and from there make their way back to Italy. After Unification, Castromediano, like Pastro in Lombardy and Guerrazzi in Tuscany, was elected to the Italian parliament, where from 1861 to 1865 he represented his region and the centre-right.[43]

Castromediano's *Carceri e galere politiche: Memorie del Duca Sigismondo Castromediano* was written well after the ex-prisoner's retirement from public service and published at the end of his life, the second volume posthumously. The book is dedicated to its author's admired friend and one-time fellow prisoner Carlo Poerio (1803–67) – a significant figure in Neapolitan and national politics in the first years of Italian unity – as well as to 'all the others living or dead who suffered shackles and pains with me – Health to the living; peace to the dead!' First appearing more than three decades after the experiences it describes, Castromediano's account of his sufferings under the Bourbons is thus a discharge of the deep obligation he continued to feel after his release towards his comrades in captivity. 'From the first moment I set foot in the Lecce prison,' he says in a preface, 'the idea of writing these memoirs was born, and I promised my companions then and there that I would be the historian of their grief.'

Looking back as they do at events from a much earlier period in their author's life, Castromediano's memoirs should be viewed, he suggests, as the 'worn and broken relics of what was a glorious time [but that now are appearing] in the midst of the idle gossip that currently inundates us so violently' (II: 205). The events Castromediano describes took place in a political climate dramatically different from that prevailing at the time of the work's composition, a moment in Italian history when the country had ceased to be 'the land of heroism and sacrifice' and had become instead 'a filthy mire for the moronic and the greedy.'[44] By 1895, clearly, the buoyant idealism of the Risorgimento had given way to disappointment and cynicism on the part of many.

Like other memorialists of the period, Castromediano knew that his account of his prison experiences would be compared to *Le mie prigioni*. Recalling his first night in confinement, he admits that he could not help but compare his feelings of apprehension and dismay at that time with those of Pellico in a similar situation a quarter of a century earlier (I: 36). Castromediano's sense of solidarity with his famous predecessor was attenuated, however, by his awareness of how, on a visit to Naples in 1852, the author of *Le mie prigioni* had refused to speak out in support of King Ferdinand's political prisoners, limiting himself instead to invoking

'God's help' on their behalf (I: 254). In the journey Castromediano makes through 'his prisons,' furthermore, the White Duke tends to direct his gaze not so much inward to an examination of his soul, in the manner of Pellico, as outward onto the astonishing social reality he witnesses while a prisoner of the king.

Castromediano's description of his odyssey through several of the most dangerous places of incarceration in Bourbon Italy has much the same fascination for the reader as the earlier, fictional *Aventures de Joseph Pignata*. Like Pignata in his flight from prison, the imprisoned Castromediano is plunged into a 'new world definitely different from the common one' (I: 200), a frightening universe of strange individuals and bizarre practices.[45] His forced cohabitation with people sequestered from society for reasons of collective security rather than political expediency was an important part of this experience. 'Austrian prisons,' a Castromediano biographer has commented about the different attitudes to confinement taken by the authorities in the north and the south of Italy, 'tortured the body but, by leaving him alone in his cell, respected a political prisoner's soul. Neapolitan prisons, by contrast, tore at the prisoner's soul and his body by mixing him in with thieves and parricides' (II: 226). If the Austrian government in its persecution of such patriots as Pellico, Confalonieri, or the Mantua eleven was able to distinguish between purported acts of sedition on the one hand and parricide on the other, the paternalistic Bourbon regime held instead that murdering a father and rebelling against the king were analogous enough that those convicted of such deeds should be punished together.[46]

As a result, Castromediano, unlike Pellico or Bini, Cellini or Tasso, all of whom lived in a kind of monastic solitude in confinement, seems never to have been alone in prison. When Pellico, for example, in chapter 12 of *Le mie prigioni*, described a raucous and distressing encounter at the Santa Margherita prison with a group of coarse and uncomprehending thieves, he was writing about an unusual moment of social contact in what was otherwise mostly solitary penance. And when Luigi Pastro was suddenly forced at Theresienstadt to share a cell with another inmate serving time on criminal rather than political charges, his indignant and alarmed protests to the prison authorities indicate that dangerous promiscuity of this sort was unusual for him too. Castromediano, by contrast, spent almost all eleven years of his imprisonment in intimate contact with criminals of all sorts; during prison transfers he was often connected physically to such individuals by a length of prison chain.[47]

The other convicts Castromediano meets in prison exemplify in often colourful ways the social ills endemic to the Bourbon regime. At Lecce, for example, where the prison warden was a drunkard and the gendarme in charge of records illiterate, the duke shared his captivity with the self-styled tyrant of Torchiaolo. A grotesque figure of muddled but intensely felt anarchist convictions who took as his watchword 'Liberty for all' (I: 32), this 'king of the republic of Torchaiolo' (who was in fact the politically powerless pharmacist in that small municipality) was a parody of the reigning sovereign. At Lecce Castromediano also met the public executioner (I: 58 ff), a person scarcely distinguishable in temperament or experience from the miscreants he dispatched from life with unconcealed glee. That the political system in which he lived was based on arbitrary rather than rational principles distressed Castromediano deeply. Speaking of the king's *intendente* for his native city, Castromediano notes that this individual's very name had become synonymous with 'l'arbitrio' as well as with 'bullying and a filthy soul' (I: 77); in the duke's descriptions of conditions elsewhere the term 'arbitrio' (arbitrariness) recurs frequently in regard to the interpretation and enforcement of the laws.

After transfer from Lecce to Naples, Castromediano came into contact with inmates who were members of the Camorra, the criminal association that dominated much of life in the capital (I: 168). The organizational structure and day-to-day operation of the Camorra fascinated him, so much so that he devoted an entire chapter of his memoirs to a description of it ('Camorra e camorristi,' I: 229–46). Like the Torchiaolo pharmacist who functions in Castromediano's narrative as a counter-image of King Ferdinand, the Camorra is in some ways similar to the king's own justice system. While administered in theory according to certain 'maxims remembered by heart and handed down orally from one generation of the wicked to another,' in the Camorra too 'the arbitrary will of the strongest ended up prevailing over reason, over custom, and over precedent' (I: 233). Concerning the financial structure of this extortion-based society, however, Castromediano notes how, unlike those of the Kingdom of Two Sicilies in regard to the citizens of that realm, the Camorra's accounts are at least open to the scrutiny of its members. 'If only this were the case in our own public budgets!' (I: 237), he exclaims.

On Procida, Castromediano discovers still more sinister aspects of the Camorra. At that island prison, an institution governed by the strongest among its inmates rather than by its appointed administrators, convicts' lives are wholly dependent on the decisions of the Camorra. In this prison several executions are organized by this de facto ruling organization rather than by prison authorities (I: 222), and in at least one instance this event is preceded by a public announcement crudely sketched on the prison wall (I: 242ff). If the Camorra members are at the top of the prison hierarchy at Procida, the bottom of the scale there is occupied by the 'naked' and the 'desperate.' These are individuals who have sold their clothes and all else they possess for drink or other favours and now sleep naked on the naked ground, disgraced and repugnant in the eyes of everyone (I: 220). As Castromediano quickly discovers and as the case of these desperate individuals confirms, in prison too, honour is important. Castromediano, in fact, thanks to his status as a nobleman and the spiritual ascendency he is able to maintain, belongs to the upper echelon of society even in this Camorra-run stronghold.

There are also brigands on Procida, one of whom lectures the duke on the futility of political idealism, arguing that true liberty can be attained only in the mountains, rifle in hand. 'Courage and disdain for life are more valuable than virtue and understanding,' this man declares, proclaiming as well that except for the outlaw life, 'all other occupations, all other aspirations are suitable only for the weak and deluded.'[48] On Procida, as elsewhere within and without the Bourbon prison system, liberty is a supreme value, but one that can only be enjoyed by the strong.

From Procida Castromediano and his comrades are transferred to the prison of Montefusco on the mainland, a 'galera eccezionale' (special prison) (I: 299) for prisoners guilty of political misdeeds. On their way to this location, the group of convicts that includes the duke is mocked by a beggar who prophesies to them that the king's enemies are unlikely ever to emerge from prison confines alive.[49] And when they arrive at this prison, Castromediano and the others are treated to a harangue by a warden who announces fiercely that those unhappy at their situation are free to find remedy for their plight by hastening to cut one another's throats (I: 302). This official, it is clear, shares his king's dislike for the 'pennaruli' (intellectuals) of the realm. 'Damn writing pens,' he explodes in terms that recall Pavlovich's purported outburst to Andryane in the Spielberg, 'paper, ink, and all the books in the world! These are the things that confuse the mind. But I, their capital enemy, from this moment forward forbid you ever to own or to ask about owning such things.'[50] Deprived of the privileges to read and write extended to them on Procida, the Montefusco prisoners are subject to a system intended to 'kill their intellects' (I: 304) if not their bodies, a policy Castromediano describes as one 'that chafed us more than our chains did, was darker in intention than our cave, and that had been designed to encourage a hatred for life and to transform us into brutal beings denied any hope of ever returning to what we had been' (I: 304).

The last of the prisons where Castromediano stayed was that of the castle of Montesarchio. Although it too was a special prison of particularly forbidding aspect, the duke's fortunes began to take a turn for the better there. Perched high on an isolated peak in the midst of rugged mountains, the Montesarchio castle was not without Romantic overtones that in turn seemed to encourage those housed within its walls to persevere in their resistance (II: 72–3). When he is summoned to Naples from his cell in this ruined castle, therefore, and urged by the authorities to request the pardon that would permit him to regain his freedom, Castromediano refuses to bend to these requests in a show of strength that makes it clear his spirit has not been broken.

Throughout his sojourns in King Ferdinand's terrifying and demeaning jails, Castromediano clings to his identity as an aristocrat and a gentleman. Beginning with his initial arrest by 'a single gendarme' (I: 26) from whom he could easily have escaped had he been willing to break his word not to make such an attempt, the White Duke is careful never to act in ways discordant with his personal honour. Even though prison, as he noted while still at Lecce, is certainly one of the rare locations where a gentleman may be insulted with impunity (I: 28), the Lecce nobleman was determined never to behave in undignified fashion, much less to sink to the level of the mere bodily existence of the 'nudi e disperati' he encountered on Procida. His unyielding and aristocratic attitude, in turn, earned him the respect of even the most depraved of his fellow convicts. When, for example, the duke learned in the Carmine of an escape plot by the prisoners there, he was able to persuade the dangerous Camorristi that, while he would not join them in their attempt, they could also trust him not to reveal their plans (I: 182). Similarly, in his interview with the authorities in Naples, Castromediano bluntly refused to ask for pardon in exchange for information about other conspirators, stating simply that 'I do not beg' and 'I denounce no one' (II: 56). On Procida, in addition – in a classic case of *noblesse oblige* – he even organized a charitable 'emergency fund' for his poorer companions (I: 262). 'The duke is without doubt the sort of man,' a contemporary said of him, 'who by nobility of birth, education, and rectitude of his spirit was not destined for imprisonment.'[51] By maintaining these personal qualities in prison Sigismondo Castromediano was able to survive the rigours of a very difficult and dangerous confinement.

In an observation echoed by anti-Fascist prisoners of later years, Castromediano insisted that the prisons in which he was being held were little more than a synecdoche for the oppressive society of which those prisons were a part. For this writer, the anarchy, cruelty, and injustice that reigned in King Ferdinand's prisons were examples in small of the 'malgoverno' at large in a kingdom where one could see 'the rise exclusively of the evil, the reactionary, the turncoats, and professional connivers in search of power, prizes, and jobs – the ascendency of corruption, spying, and false testimony,' a place where 'rectitude has been lost and all that is left is a paucity of virtue and an abundance of vice' (I: 87).

The master story of the White Duke's *Carceri e galere politiche* is its tale of a voyage through a realm of corruption and evil in which the book's hero is forced to immerse himself but from which he finally emerges uncontaminated. Because he has remained a man of honour, Castromediano is able at the conclusion of his memoir to persuade the naval doctors who attend him at Montefusco to come over to the patriots' side. 'I was a reactionary when I arrived here,' one of them says to him in admiration, 'but your moral excellence and your honesty have cured me of this vicious illness. I thank my stars for this and I thank you as well. Henceforth you will have in me not a friend but a brother ready to leap into fire for you' (II: 37). Although during his imprisonment, Castromediano has been reduced to a more purely biological integer than ever before in his life, his allegiance to a basically feudal code of conduct and his capacity for civic indignation are what have enabled him, in both his own eyes and those of his contemporaries – be these members of the Camorra or the king's own medical staff – to exit his long imprisonment the same honourable person he was when first arrested.

Luigi Settembrini (1813–76) was a product of metropolitan Naples rather than the provinces like Castromediano, and a bourgeois rather than a nobleman. A university professor of Italian literature, he is the author of both the widely read *Ricordanze della mia vita* (Memories of My Life) (1879) and *Lezioni di letteratura italiana* (Lectures on Italian Literature) (1866–72), the standard guide to this subject until displaced in 1882 by fellow Neapolitan Francesco De Sanctis's *Storia della letteratura italiana* (Naples, 1881–2).[52] Selections from Settembrini's *Ricordanze* were at one time obligatory reading in the nation's schools and in this way contributed to a definition of the Risorgimento for the generations of Italians succeeding him.[53] The fame that Settembrini achieved as a political martyr rather than a literary historian, however, left the Neapolitan professor with mixed feelings. 'I made so bold,' he said in his *Ricordanze* about a prayer to God he had made as a young man, 'to ask Him for what all wise men want: fame. And fame I had – though while I wanted to attain it for work of great genius, God decided I should attain it for great suffering'

(354). Today, indeed, it is the *Ricordanze* rather than the *Lezioni* that is the most widely read of Settembrini's writings. In terms of the history of prison writing in Italy, however, the nearly four hundred letters Settembrini wrote in confinement are of even greater interest than his *Ricordanze*. This is largely because of what a critic has called the 'very unpretentious and human image' that emerges from them, a portrait of their author most readers find preferable to what the same critic characterizes as the 'respectable daguerreotype' of the *Ricordanze*'s 'delayed and ironic autobiographical recollection.'[54]

Although not as conservative as Castromediano, Settembrini was a political moderate. Nevertheless, he too had been confined for political reasons even before the 1848 Naples uprising that led to his eventual imprisonment on Santo Stefano. In 1839, while a young schoolteacher in Catanzaro, Settembrini was 'accused, along with others, of having been a member of Young Italy and, taken to Naples, was thrown into prison where I remained for twenty-six months with no other company than my misfortunes and those of my poor family,' an adventure he later described as 'three and a half years of undeserved imprisonment, including fifteen months after being found not guilty.'[55] Unfazed by this experience, Settembrini continued to agitate for social reform. In 1849, he was again arrested, found guilty of subversion,[56] and condemned to death, a sentence commuted to life imprisonment on Santo Stefano – by a happy or unhappy coincidence the same island where his father had been incarcerated for political reasons half a century earlier.[57]

Prison life at the Santo Stefano 'Ergastolo' (the word means a place of incarceration for convicts serving life sentences) was strikingly different from that at other places of confinement in nineteenth-century Italy.[58] A panoptical, rationally organized place of detention that grouped the most dangerous of its inmates on the lowest and the least dangerous on the uppermost level of its three-story structure, the Santo Stefano prison could be efficiently monitored by a single, unseen surveillant.[59] Because this prison was believed escape-proof, its inmates, while subject to the usual prison discipline, lived in relative comfort and enjoyed a modicum of personal liberty. The 'ergastolani' housed on the island, for example (though not the prisoners serving term sentences), were exempt from wearing the painful leg irons dragged about by prisoners elsewhere. The vigorous winds, moreover, that gusted across the tiny bit of ocean-bound land bore air to the prisoners that was fresh and clean, a striking contrast from the 'pestilential' exhalations Castromediano and others were forced to breathe at other institutions. On Santo Stefano, in addition, political prisoners were not required to consume the scanty and often revolting prison fare typical in other institutions but could purchase food from their guards or have it imported from the mainland. Given the abundance of fresh air, the ready food supply, and the lack of compulsory physical exercise, some convicts even grew fat during their detention on Santo Stefano.[60] They were further spared the humiliation of the prison costumes described with loathing by such other nineteenth-century prisoners as those confined to the Spielberg. Most important of all, prisoners on Santo Stefano could read and write as much as they pleased, though Settembrini was not sure whether this was due to 'the contempt and the oblivion in which we are being held, plus the ignorance or should I also say the good-naturedness of those who have us in their custody.'[61]

In addition to receiving food, clothes, and reading materials from the mainland, the Santo Stefano prisoners were also permitted to exchange gifts with their families in Naples. The items Settembrini and Spaventa dispatched home with the couriers who plied back and forth through the gulf were usually agricultural products such as tomatoes and preserved fish, but on occasion included such more suggestive indications of their plights as cages of turtle-doves and of quail (which their families then ate) and a miniature Ergastolo modelled for this purpose by a fellow convict.[62] The prisoners were also allowed family visits. In 1855, for example, Settembrini's wife, Gigia, and daughter, Giulia, spent six days on an island sojourn that included a harpsichord recital by Giulia for her delighted father and the prison warden. This visit seems to have been prolonged beyond the normal limit partly because of rough seas and a consequent lack of immediate transportation, partly because Settembrini was able to bribe the authorities (with, of all things, fish!) to arrange the delay (405–7). In addition, the prison guards at Santo Stefano were unlike their often ferocious counterparts elsewhere, tending instead, as Elena Croce put it, to be 'either subservient or amenable to bribes or both,'[63] the Crusoe-like environment in which they lived contributing, no doubt, to the relatively humane relations that prevailed between them and their charges.

The laissez-faire attitude of prison life on Santo Stefano was particularly evident during holidays, which were celebrated with remarkable verve. Christmas of 1851, for example, featured a torchlight procession and gifts from the warden to the political prisoners that included bottles of wine, nuts and figs, different kinds of Neapolitan sweets, pickled peppers, and a brace of octopus arms ('un coppo di noci, un altro di nocelle, un altro di fichi secchi, un altro con un *susamiello*, un altro con dei struffoli, un altro con dei peperoni in aceto, un altro con due branche di polipo' – *Lettere*, 70–1). During one carnival season the convicts dressed in masquerade costumes and observed the holiday by drinking, laughing, and – leg irons notwithstanding in the case of the term prisoners – dancing. On that occasion the *comandante*, either in response to the carnival spirit, or as a demonstration of his power, or both, 'brought the whipping bench and the whips into the courtyard so that whoever did the least thing out of line was immediately punished,' a gesture, however, that was evidently welcomed by the merry-makers since Settembrini reports that in response they danced madly 'around the bench like a horde of demons around a coffin.'[64]

During his confinement in this sometimes strangely permissive prison, Settembrini's contacts with the mainland, if never as rapid or dependable as he might have liked, were remarkably free from anything more than perfunctory surveillance. Not only was he able to engage in such activities as playing the Naples lottery (*Lettere*, 138) and even – in an act of *noblesse oblige* that recalls a similar gesture by Castromediano – permitted to take up a collection for earthquake victims elsewhere in the Bourbon kingdom,[65] he also maintained an assiduous correspondence with his family, and through his family with political comrades in Naples and elsewhere, including England. 'He was able to correspond in secret with his wife and friends, even English friends,' writes the astonished Castromediano about his fellow patriot, 'who not only comforted him with noble thoughts and encouragement but even made plans to remove him from that terrible place.'[66] Although the 1855–6 rescue attempts masterminded by the British Museum's Antonio Panizzi, Garibaldi, and other supporters of the Naples patriots were ultimately unsuccessful, that Settembrini could take part in their planning from prison is further indication of the looseness of the Bourbon leash on Santo Stefano.

Life at the Ergastolo was none the less psychologically oppressive, and Settembrini was deeply worried that sharing his life with the criminal inhabitants of the island would lead to a spiritual 'contamination' worse than death. 'Will I emerge alive?' he asks in his diary, 'and, if so, when? This is the thought that makes me uneasy. Though what makes me more uneasy still is whether I will emerge pure, the way I was when I went in. Oh, cruel men who torture the body and contaminate the soul! Why commit such an outrage on a soul that has been created by God, is the spirit of God, part of God?' (354). Even though he was never treated badly by Santo Stefano's criminal inmates – 'all of these unhappy men in prison for life,' he said of them, 'are courteous to us and would like to make us feel better. They tell us that they know we are here because we were working for the welfare of everyone, including the welfare of prisoners' (329) – he feared moral warping from his contacts with them, even seeing an image of such deformation in the twisted limbs of the caged quail and turtle-doves he sent home to Gigia. 'Alas! what happened to the tiny bodies of these birds is happening too to the souls of those incarcerated! I pray God to preserve my soul from this filth,' he wrote her in alarm about his situation (*Lettere*, 35). In order to keep busy and as a kind of 'opium that puts me to sleep' (209), Settembrini spent many hours of his confinement translating the Greek writer Lucian of Samothrace. Inspired, apparently, by this translation project, he also wrote an erotic work about homosexual love in ancient Greece titled *I neoplatonici* (The Neoplatonics). This 'Milesian fable' of the youth and loves of Doro and Callicle, while known to an inner circle of Settembrini scholars for many years, was not published until 1977. It reveals still another aspect of this prisoner's life on the island and may very well be a clue to the reasons for Settembrini's concerns about his purity in confinement.[67]

In addition to being concerned about these issues of contamination and purity, Settembrini was also afraid his mental capacities were deteriorating. 'What saddens me deeply,' he wrote Gigia in a letter composed after several years on Santo Stefano, 'is that every day I lose strength of mind and am rendered more stupid. If I read, I understand little; if I write, I can no longer collect and marshall my ideas.' For this professor of literature, the Bourbon Ergastolo was a kind of Circe's isle – an idea strengthened in his mind by scholarly speculations to the effect that Homer's witch's abode was located somewhere in the Pontine chain that included Santo Stefano – and he feared its brutalizing effects. 'This is the air that destroys men's intelligence,' he wrote Gigia about his place of detention, 'this is the ancient isle of Circe who transformed men into animals. And I can sense that I have been changed and completely transformed' (*Lettere*, 351). What most alarmed Settembrini was the danger to his ethical principles he believed was posed by life on Santo Stefano. 'This world is a forest inhabited by savage beasts,' he said in another letter, 'where those who have stronger teeth and sharper claws are the most respected, where using tooth and claw is considered a virtue, justice is dispensed with tooth and claw, and Providence lies in the power to adopt tooth and claw.' In such circumstances, intellectuals too were subject to a demeaning bestialization. Even 'the speech that we men have,' he goes on, 'and of which we are so proud is nothing more than a bit of hair and feathers covering our claws – one more way of betraying one another and rendering this isolation more cruel' (*Lettere*, 212).

Despite these bouts of despair, Settembrini managed, he says, to avoid the spiritual degradation he feared in prison. If Silvio Pellico was sustained in confinement by his religious faith, Settembrini had his wife, Gigia, and his children, Giulia and Raffaele. He was not only able to cling for support to these people, he was also aware that they needed his support as much as he needed theirs.[68] 'My soul no longer resides in me,' he writes Gigia about this; 'it lives in you and in them so that I feel there are four hearts who endure all that you who are so dear to me endure' (*Lettere*, 414). Of these four hearts, the most important for Settembrini was that of his wife. 'When I compare you to other women,' he writes Gigia, 'I see others who know how to sing, play a musical instrument, speak foreign languages, or know how to draw: but they do not have your heart, that heart which, like a hard, glistening diamond, lends so much force and so much radiance to your entire person' (532). Settembrini has been saved from despair not because of his religious or political beliefs but thanks to Gigia's extraordinary devotion. While his body might have been menaced by the appetites that threatened to contaminate and pervert him, he did not return to his family brutalized in spirit, but victorious in his struggle with what he saw as the beguiling and dangerous wiles of an island not dissimilar from that of Circe as described by the ancient writers.

Another celebrated political prisoner on Santo Stefano was Settembrini's cell mate, Silvio Spaventa (1823–93). Spaventa too was much concerned with matters of the heart while in jail. This prisoner, whose given name was selected by his parents in honour of the author of *Le mie prigioni*, was the younger brother of the philosopher Bertrando Spaventa (1817–83) and uncle of the philosopher and historian Benedetto Croce (1866–1952).[69] A journalist and political activist in Naples before his confinement, after prison Spaventa had a distinguished career of public service, first as Neapolitan police commissioner and then in positions nationally, including a stint as Minister of Public Works in the Minghetti cabinet. 'When D'Azeglio announced that with Italy created, what was needed next was Italians,' Castromediano wrote, 'I would have liked to present him with the example of Silvio Spaventa. Just as his character is upright and unbending, so too his mind is lofty, his heart generous and honest.'[70] While never the philosopher his brother, Bertrando, was, Spaventa spent many of his prison hours reading the works of Hegel, Spinoza, Descartes, Kant, and other writers on ethics and metaphysics.

Unlike Settembrini, whose family responsibilities kept him busy and made him feel needed even in confinement, Silvio Spaventa was unmarried during his stay on Santo Stefano, though he did have deep emotional ties with his brother, Bertrando. In the Ergastolo cell he shared with Settembrini, as Guerrazzi had done with Cecchino's portrait, Spaventa kept an image of his brother over his bed that he would talk to 'under his breath as if to a person actually present.'[71] For his part, Bertrando was able, though living in exile and poverty himself, to provide Silvio with both moral and financial support while he was in prison.[72]

Silvio Spaventa's unusually warm feelings for his brother are evident in his many letters to Bertrando. In one, he declares that all his sufferings are of minor importance compared to his lack of news from his sibling. 'What does this lengthy and interminable imprisonment matter,' he wrote from Naples where he was awaiting trial, 'or my ill health, the isolation cells, the fortresses, the Vicaria, hateful poverty, and even the horror of the utterly dishonest trial I have been involved in?' For Silvio, the thought of his brother remains 'the only sentiment in which my heart can take pleasure and feel at rest. This is all I care about in the future, all that I can believe and understand of myself as part of a being at once unlike and identical with myself.'[73] The extraordinary warmth of this letter, though perhaps less unusual in mid-nineteenth-century Naples than in English-speaking countries today, is testimony of a fraternal affection as profound as Settembrini's love for his Gigia and recalls similar expressions of affection for family members in the prison letters of Tazzoli, Poma, and Guerrazzi.

Despite the interest Spaventa's correspondence with his brother holds for a later reader, the most fascinating texts this prisoner wrote from confinement are the more than two hundred letters dispatched to his cousin, Felicetta Ulisse. The epistolary relationship Spaventa had with this woman lasted from the beginning of his stay on Santo Stefano until after his arrival in Ireland in 1859. Like Settembrini's *Lettere dall'ergastolo*, Spaventa's *Lettere a Felicetta* provide a day-by-day account of life in cell number 5 of the Santo Stefano Ergastolo. In the history of prison writing, these texts are remarkable for the clearly discernible plot they present to the reader – a dramatic story with a beginning, middle, and end – though whether this tale has a comic or a tragic form depends on whether the story is considered from Silvio's or from Felicetta's perspective. Their epistolary love affair is a striking example of a prison correspondent's construction of a recipient who is perhaps more the reflection of his deepest desires than an independent entity.

In the early stages of his correspondence with Felicetta Ulisse, Spaventa worried that his feelings for his cousin would come into conflict with those for Bertrando. Writing to her in 1854, he describes the effect of their relationship on him, declaring that his love for his cousin has provided him with 'two lives, two hearts, and two minds fused into a single unity.' 'I am living,' he continues, 'in another, I am living in you while still living within myself.'[74] The dual existence that Silvio enjoyed with both his brother and his cousin, however, threatened to develop not into the parallelogram he is hopefully tracing here but into a triangle of potentially damaging jealous forces.

From the beginning of his correspondence with Felicetta Ulisse, Spaventa insisted he was hiding nothing from her. Even so, in his early letters, he found it difficult to call his correspondent 'tu' and when he finally does so it is in French and at the closing of a letter in which she is otherwise 'voi' (67). By October of 1853, however, he declares that he loves her – or rather that he 'reciprocates her love' (36). For the philosophically minded Spaventa, the affection he felt for his cousin entailed both freedom and moral exaltation. As he wrote in a prison essay composed during this same period that treated the responsibilities that existed between citizen and state, 'freedom is objective and subjective at the same time ... I am free if I will and do what is reasonable. Freedom, for me, consists of doing what you ought to do and willing to do what you are doing.'[75] Far from having his autonomy curtailed by the state, the citizen described in Spaventa's essay discovers that his civic obligations are the basis for his individual freedom. In the same way, the prisoner at first believed, his love for Felicetta Ulisse was at once a personal responsibility and the externalization of his freedom.

By March of 1855, Spaventa's letters make explicit mention of marriage (172). By November he is addressing his cousin as 'my dear wife' (220). But even though it would now seem that Silvio and Felicetta are in effect man and wife, he will not permit her to join him in the exile that seems to be looming. 'How could you imagine,' he asks her in a letter of 1856, 'that it would be easy for me, in exile, to marry you and for us to keep up even a very modest household?' (258). Some days later he is even clearer, warning her that 'if you persist with the thought of going with me to America, I intend to remain in prison' (301). Although he sticks to his position that they should not marry and then be separated when he must leave her for exile, poverty, and an uncertain future (336), Spaventa insists to the end that his love for his cousin has been the spark that has kept his ideals alive in prison.

Once liberated and plunged again into the world of politics, however,

Spaventa quickly abandoned all thoughts of marriage. 'You must comprehend my present circumstances,' he tries to explain in one of the last of the letters to his correspondent. 'I have obligations towards you that should not brook any further delay. But how to discharge them? How could we set up a household, provide ourselves a living, protect and maintain a respectable life in the face of the lack of interest I feel for everything, for every task – plus my invincible repugnance for favours from anyone' (462). Although he has emerged from prison with his ideals intact, Spaventa claims that he has lost the enthusiasm for life necessary for him to be a good husband. The most responsible course for him to follow, he says, is to break off relations with his former correspondent.

Thanks to the water cure he underwent in confinement, the exercise regime he devised for himself, and the nourishing food and fresh air available on Santo Stefano, Spaventa left prison in excellent physical health. From this point of view, at least, he does not seem to have been especially incapacitated for marriage.[76] But politics and public service had always been the principal passion in Spaventa's life. Although it was due in part to the debate with himself about Felicetta Ulisse that he had conducted in prison that Spaventa was able to endure that ordeal, once this was over, the ex-prisoner found himself morally exhausted. In the end, his passion for public service prevailed over that for his cousin. Constrained to move out of the realm of his imagination and confront the real object of his desire, Spaventa found that what really stirred his blood was the seductive visage not of marriage but of politics.

The last two writers to be considered in this chapter were incarcerated several years before those that have been discussed so far. They are treated at the end of this geographically arranged chapter because their imprisonments – though they date from the 1820s and the 1840s and thus come before those of the patriots from both Mantua and Naples – were at the hands of a political antagonist like no other in nineteenth-century Italy. Giuseppe Galletti from Bologna and Angelo Frignani of Ravenna were jailed and threatened with death not by a nervous imperial power or a colonizing regime, but by a totally indigenous (if also international) state: that of the Roman Catholic Church. Both *La mia prigionia* (My Imprisonment) by Giuseppe Galletti and *La mia pazzia* (My Madness) by Angelo Frignani have titles that recall *Le mie prigioni*; both books were meant, however, as refutations of the attitudes taken towards politics and the clergy by Pellico in his famous memoir.[77]

Giuseppe Galletti, who lived between 1798 and 1873, was a lawyer of some prominence in his native Bologna. Accused of conspiracy and transported to Rome for his trial, Galletti was outraged at the treatment that he, a respectable member of society, received during this transfer at the hands of a clerical government. 'In this obscene and shameful fashion the government of priests forcibly transports an honoured citizen and member of the most cultured part of society into Rome in the middle of the day,' he exclaims in a description of his shackled arrival in the capital, 'a man mature in age, the father of five children, a man suspected of a political crime but who so far has not been found guilty or even brought to trial.'[78] Like Guerrazzi, another lawyer who suddenly found himself on the wrong side of prison bars, Galletti was indignant at the more than fifteen months of preventative detention he was compelled to serve without a hearing in the appalling conditions of Rome's Carcere Nuovo.[79] One of the purposes of this detention, as Galletti knew well, was to get him to reveal what he knew about the charges on which he stood accused. But although hardly innocent of seditious activities (arms and ammunition had indeed been concealed at his house at the time of his arrest), he managed to keep silent about these preparations (89–90).

Following a trial whose outcome seems to have been predictable to everyone but the unhappy defendant, Galletti was transferred out of solitary to detention 'alla larga' in Castel Sant'Angelo. It was while he was detained in this ancient stronghold that the Bolognese lawyer learned of his amnesty on the occasion of the election of Pius IX. In later years, partly thanks to this amnesty, the ex-prisoner felt sufficiently reconciled with Pius's regime to serve four times in the pontiff's cabinet and to act as Minister of the Interior and general of the papal carabineers.[80]

In his preface to his prison memoir, Galletti explains that he has written *La mia prigionia* out of disappointment and disgust at the anti-liberal character of the Pope's regime. Although Pius's reign began with hopes of reform, at the time Galletti is writing the glory of his native region has taken a topple 'into the mud' – to such an extent that the patriotic author feels compelled to 'make ever better known' to his readers 'what the government of the Popes used to be and unfortunately still is' (3–4). Working from notes composed in prison by writing with a fish bone dipped in wine (140–1), in his memoir Galletti exposes the failings of an 'ill-prepared and disorganized government' regulated by 'the most absolute despotism.' In his own case, for example, any court other than the hyper-suspicious papal tribunal would have quickly exonerated him. 'For the pontifical government,' however, 'and in a political case, mere suspicion sufficed' (99). Although for this respectable lawyer and future valued public servant, prison was an opportunity to testify to 'the rights of man and the duties incumbent on all members of the great human family' (186), during his confinement Galletti contracted a nearly fatal illness that marked his body afterwards. 'The dangerous and lengthy illness from which I suffered,' he writes in reference to the prison malady (smallpox? diphtheria?) that nearly killed him, 'left such marks and reminders on my body as to disfigure me' (227–8). These marks, however, like Galletti's prison pallor, also work to authenticate the sacrifice he has made on behalf of the human family. Although the law that prevails in the Pope's dominions is a text interpreted in ways that are too often careless or malicious, the signs inscribed on Galletti's body demonstrate the depth of his commitment to real justice.[81] Because Galletti's post-pardon existence was little more, by his own account, than 'a path filled with thorns, suffering, loss, and such anguish that I began to think longingly of returning to the other prison's isolation cells' (273), his confinement came at a crucial moment in his life. Marked both internally and externally by this experience, Galletti is now a 'martyr for freedom' (271), able to consider his past ordeal a moral and physical test that he has faced and overcome. The signs left on his body by the experience are thus badges of a victory he is proud to display.

The extravagant, inventive, mischievous, and perhaps slightly mad Angelo Frignani (1802–78) was very unlike the earnest and conventional Galletti. As already noted, the title of Frignani's *La mia pazzia*, like that of Galletti's *La mia prigionia*, is an obvious reference to Pellico's *Le mie prigioni*. The first edition of Frignani's book appeared in Paris in 1839, moreover, 'after he had seen the immense success of Silvio Pellico's *Le mie prigioni*, which came out in 1831 [sic], and was immediately translated in France, and indeed published by the same publisher who accepted the memoirs of our author.'[82] Like Pellico's, Frignani's memoir was soon being read all over Europe.[83] The first publication of the book in Italy, however, came only many years later when the historian and later Minister of Education Luigi Rava published his *Angelo Frignani e il suo libro 'La mia pazzia nelle carceri.' Memorie autobiografiche di un patriotto romagnolo per la prima volta pubblicate in Italia*. Rava's book, which has extensive notes and a long essay on 'the papal restoration in the Romagna and Angelo Frignani' is otherwise a reprint of the Paris edition of 1839.

Like Galletti, who was four years his senior, Frignani too was imprisoned by papal authority, though in the 1820s rather than the 1840s. In the years just before 1831 – a time of insurrections throughout central Italy –

anti-government feeling ran high in Frignani's native Ravenna. Reasons for such sentiment are not difficult to find. Rava, for example, cites examples of despotic behaviour in the region that include the 1820 death sentence in Ravenna of a Jew who had converted to Catholicism and then reverted to his original religion, and the routine Friday searching in Cesena of the baskets of those suspected of preparing to eat meat on that fast day (xiv, xvi). In such circumstances, many Romagnoli were said to have announced their preference for a 'government by the Turk rather than the Pope' (xiii).

When arrested in 1827, Angelo Frignani was twenty-five years old and a student of law at the University of Bologna. Detained first in the monastery attached to Ravenna's historic San Vitale church, he was later transferred to the mental hospital in Faenza. For in order to avoid what he believed would be execution by the authorities, Frignani – like Pallavicino as prisoner of the Austrians a few years earlier – decided to feign insanity. He arrived at this decision, however, after a certain amount of soul searching (31ff). As the idealistic young man saw the matter, while pretending to be crazy 'to preserve one's own honour plus the freedom and lives of other people is sometimes excusable,' simulating 'from fear of dying, even in a good cause' was, by contrast, 'cowardice' (32). In the end, however, bolstered by examples he was able to remember of biblical and classical heroes who had behaved in similar fashion, Frignani concluded it was also 'cowardice to die if you can live with honour' (32).

Accordingly, and before he received a definitive sentence, Frignani proceeded to 'mentally create the character that I had decided to represent.' His plan was to fabricate such an individual according to 'the circumstances of my notion, the dominant ideas of the day likely to have influenced my spirit, the passions that I knew best, the kind of education I had received, my activities earlier – plus the example of some real maniacs' (36). The theatrical creation concocted with these ingredients was a Moses-like individual able to converse directly with God, a favoured disciple of the great Tommasini of the University of Bologna, and the only person in the entire Romagna able to say what everyone knew: that the emperor (that is, papal government) was in fact naked – cruel, incompetent, corrupt, and, for these reasons, flagrantly un-Christian. For the duration of his confinement, Frignani denounced Church rule of the Romagna in terms no other subject of the Pope dared employ, all this to the undoubted 'delight of the liberals,' he notes gleefully, 'who indeed envied me such a privilege' (148).

Frignani's choice of Giacomo Tommasini for a supporting role in his theatrical fiction was an astute one. A distinguished physiologist and pathologist in both Parma and Bologna whose complete works were published in the latter city in 1833–8, Tommasini had given lectures Frignani had attended as a student (243). In the ex-student and now prisoner's mad tirades, this able and respected scientist was transformed into a Mesmer- or Frankenstein-like genius dedicated to the creation of a new race of people.[84] Frignani, for his part, served as the 'right eye of the Divine Tommasini, himself a near God to whom nature, men, and beasts would bow in homage' (40). In making Tommasini a central character in his histrionic performances, Frignani was substituting a scientific authority for the religious ones that had proved so dramatically unworthy of his trust, transforming his old professor into a secular anti-Pope legitimized by science rather than theology.

Unlike other nineteenth-century detainees who spent their prison hours in study or meditation, Frignani, by way of the flamboyant alternative *personaggio* he had constructed for himself, acted the part not just of a scholar but of a warrior and a statesman as well. In the latter capacity, he felt obliged to devise regulations for a new kind of political system the precise opposite of the cruel and corrupt structure under which he was currently living. In order for this new state to flourish, it was necessary, he believed, to 'organize the militia, promulgate laws,' and – above all – 'to establish religion' (77).

Whatever religion Frignani may have had in mind for his utopian construction, the representatives of the still-prevailing Roman Catholicism holding him in jail seemed not to have known what to do with their impossible prisoner. Frignani's own comments on their dilemma sound like dialogue in the plays by Luigi Pirandello (1867–1936), which would not be written until a century later. In the times in which he is living, Frignani asserts, a person is considered crazy if 'he flings the naked truth directly into the tyrant's face: for if Christ himself were to reveal it this way, the Pharisees would insist he was mad' (45). As if to validate this extravagant notion, when a doctor selected by the authorities examined the prisoner and declared him sane, Frignani's guards were convinced that their charge was indeed mad. In this, Frignani explains, they were 'perhaps led in this way to make this mistake: since Signor Lorenzo [the doctor in question] had for many years been rumoured to be truly mad, and the mad believe among themselves that they are sane and the sane mad ... the soldiers assumed that since he was mad and believed himself sane, he had to consider me, who was mad, to be sane' (52). Here again this barely post-Napoleonic figure seems projected forward into the world of Pirandello, in which madness and sanity, fiction and reality, truth and falsehood swap logical places with head-spinning rapidity. Like Pirandello, Frignani too would seem to suggest that when the traditional guardians of order – in this case the examining doctor but in a larger sense the entire governmental system – cannot be relied on for either probity or accuracy, an entire cognitive and ethical system is plunged into chaos.

The ecclesiastical authorities responsible for Frignani, however, could scarcely adopt the paradoxical reasoning that Pirandello has suggested is sometimes necessary to understand the true nature of madness and sanity. Instead, Frignani tells us, the people who decided his case were forced to embrace one of two suppositions: either their prisoner had been truly touched by the Holy Spirit – something these sceptical and not particularly pious clerics were convinced was beyond human experience as they knew it – or he was mad. 'And though at first they wondered if some trick was involved and were suspicious of being fooled,' Frignani says of the papal commission, 'in the end they none the less tumbled blindly right into it – not opening their eyes until I had already made it to safety' (41).

But before this happened, as part of his plan to persuade his captors that he was indeed mad, Frignani staged a number of 'maniacal acts' for their benefit. In the first of these he acted the part of a priest saying Mass (46), a gesture that in the States of the Papacy was a blasphemy so outrageous that only the truly mad would dare commit it. But for Frignani, another meaning of his performance was to suggest that the real priests saying Mass in such conditions of political tyranny were the true parodies of religion. Another extremely dramatic gesture by Frignani of a medical rather than a religious nature was his successful curing of a fellow mental patient. Through sympathetic and rational argument Frignani managed to convince this woman to abandon excessive feelings of remorse over what in reality were little more than normal human failings and in this way be able to leave the hospital and return to her husband (114–18). But although successful with this patient, when Frignani tried to repeat his success with another inmate, he failed spectacularly; this man, a person obsessed with the desire to eliminate the devil from the world, left the hospital only to murder the baby of a peasant he believed was demonically possessed (142).

Frignani's plan to hoodwink the authorities succeeded in part because of the support he received from the head of the Faenza hospital, the liberal doctor Paolo Anderlini. When Frignani first met Anderlini, he was astute enough to address him sanely, reasoning that 'if I had taken to speaking and acting like a madman about everything, this would have been reason for them to suspect that I was simulating. This is because those who fake madness (I mean the not very smart ones) are careful never to speak or answer correctly in any situation' (84). The truly mad, in other words, have inevitable intervals of sanity while those who seem always and irrevocably crazy probably are dissembling. For this reason, 'I frequently repeated that I was not mad, and attempted to prove this with arguments. To do such a thing, in the view of many, constituted obvious proof of the craziest craziness, even if some idiot or other might perhaps judge it otherwise' (106).

Was Frignani mad or not? Is *La mia pazzia* a retrospective justification of what really was a slipping of mental restraints in a young man terrified by the thought of being executed? To confuse the issue even more, when this book's author died in France in 1878, he did so, in Rava's words, 'the victim, by a strange and painful coincidence, of the terrible illness that half a century earlier he had faked for so long to fool his executioners' (lxviii). Though Frignani's mother is reputed (but only by Frignani's own account) never to have doubted that her son was simulating – 'my Angelo knows what he is doing. I know what a brave person he is and what a person with his intelligence can do' (96) – in a medical report of 1828, Doctor Anderlini only says 'I have no hesitation in asserting that just as it would be hasty to judge this detainee a false madman, by the same token it would be equally hasty to declare him genuinely mad' (256–61). Whatever the final state of his psyche, Angelo Frignani, like Giuseppe Galletti, whose devotion to political ideals could be read in the marks inscribed on his body, was willing to risk the complete dissolution of his physical constitution in the harsh reagent of insanity if by doing so he could continue his denunciation of a corrupt regime.

The writers treated in this chapter lived in different regions of the Italian peninsula as the dissatisfied subjects of governments large and small, both foreign and domestic. Most (the exceptions are the two prisoners of the Pope) were part of the generation succeeding that of the Spielberg prisoners of the 1820s; with the same exceptions, they went to prison after the pivotal year for European history of 1848. Although none was a peasant or industrial worker, with the exception of Castromediano, all of them came from a different layer of the population than did their predecessors – clear indication that Risorgimento idealism was percolating down from the aristocratic and intellectual circles where it held sway earlier in the century into what by mid-century were the increasingly mobilized professional and middle classes.

Confined, then, in different kinds of institutions and treated with greater or lesser severity as determined by the more or less oppressive regimes detaining them, the authors whose works have been analysed in this chapter were subject to punishments that ranged from Bini's few months to the life sentences meted out (though not served in their entirety) to Castromediano, Settembrini, and Spaventa. For some – the Martyrs of Mantua are a celebrated example – their stays in prison were terminal rather than provisional episodes in their lives. But whether they survived their confinements or not, all these men were witnesses while in prison to an astonishing variety of experiences – from writing in bizarre mediums including human blood, to chilling encounters with the Camorra and other dangerous outlaws, to the merry festivals, theatrical productions, and harpsichord recitals that enlivened life on Santo Stefano, to the avant-la-lettre Pirandellian relationships that blurred the boundaries between mad and sane, custodians and inmates, authority and its adversaries at the Faenza mental hospital.

With the exception of the nobleman Castromediano, the political positions these mostly middle-class individuals assumed were more radical than those held by the Spielberg group. Unlike their anti-Austrian predecessors, whose goal was the moderate one of putting an end to the colonial status of their native regions, these later patriots were in favour of additional, institutional reforms. Although they shared no common vision of what these reforms might consist of, Carlo Bini, Sigismondo Castromediano, and Giuseppe Galletti – to choose three very different patriots of this period – were agreed that the government under which they lived was in fact a 'malgoverno' that should be replaced by a more rational and less arbitrary system of rule. For many of them, what this meant was nothing more (though also nothing less) than the inauguration of a monarchy or other one-person government that would be respondent, however, not to a ruler's whim but to previously established constitutional restraints.

About half the writers considered in this chapter are known to us through letters rather than memoirs. Guerrazzi, Tazzoli, Poma, and Spaventa left writing of this sort about their confinement, while Bini, Pastro, Castromediano, Galletti, and Frignani composed memoirs, and Settembrini left both kinds of writings.[85] Unlike similar writings by the more highly ideological activists jailed later in the century, or by anti-

Fascists during the 1930s, the letters that these individuals wrote from imprisonment have been transmitted to us largely unmarred by censorial mutilation. Guerrazzi's communications from the Murate, for example, do not seem to have had any words or phrases obliterated by prison authorities the way those of Turati, Monti, or Rossi did later. And a striking characteristic of at least some of Poma's and Tazzoli's clandestine correspondence is the similarity between their letters of this forbidden sort and the same authors' authorized, ostensible communications. At the same time, though Settembrini's and Spaventa's letters eluded what censorship there was supposed to be on Santo Stefano, the printed texts of their writings have been mediated subsequently by family members and editors who have not always elected to transmit every word of what has been entrusted to them. None the less, the letters written by the prisoners of this period are much more frank, even uninhibited in character than the corresponding texts by such captives of a later, more totalitarian regime as the anti-Fascists Gramsci, Monti, or Morandi.

The prison letters from this group, moreover, were addressed to real, historical personages (usually the writer's relatives) without, it would seem, much consideration for posterity. Such an authorial stance distinguishes these writers from such market-directed prison memorialists as, if not Pellico, then at least Maroncelli and Andryane. Although such politically prominent (in their pre-jail lives) later prisoners as Costa, Turati, Gramsci, and Ravera at least suspected that what they wrote in their prison letters would one day reach readers beyond the circle of their immediate acquaintances, those writing to their relatives from Santo Stefano, the Murate, or the Mainolda in the 1850s do not seem especially attentive to the possibility that their communications with their relatives would one day be studied by large numbers of strangers, let alone become part of their country's scholastic curriculum and thus defining elements in a consensus definition of the meaning of the Risorgimento.

A principal purpose of the prison correspondence produced by these men was, instead, to maintain precious links with the communities from which they derived their sense of personal identity – whether the community involved was middle-class Mantuan society as in the cases of Tazzoli and Poma, that of a patriarchal Neapolitan family in the case of Settembrini, or of conventional bourgeois marriage suitors in the case of Spaventa. All of the letter writers studied here were intent in their prison writings to reassure their loved ones they were surviving prison 'uncorrupted' (to use Settembrini's term) by the experience. In order to do so they found themselves constrained to construct the recipients to which their texts were addressed and were attentive to regulate the authorial voice employed in them. Tazzoli, for example, was determined, during his confinement and subsequent death-watch, not to show any signs of physical weakness in his letters; Settembrini struggled to appear psychically strong in the midst of the impurity that he felt surrounded him; Guerrazzi attempted in his letters to create an image of himself as benevolent uncle and tutor; while in the case of Spaventa and his Felicetta an erotic relationship that in the end turned out to have been more wishful thinking than reality was carefully, and with what seemed to have been varying degrees of good and bad faith on both sides, fabricated.

Throughout the writings examined in this chapter, whether letters or memoirs, one can note the intrusion of the body into the scene of confinement, and not only in the descriptions Frignani provides of the extravagant physical behavior he indulged in at Faenza. This issue had never been absent from prison writing. Cellini in Castel Sant'Angelo wrote the poetry signalling his recovery of his identity as artist in ink made from his own urine; Tasso in Sant'Anna was at times in such physical distress he said he felt as though a horse had fallen on him; in the Spielberg Andryane claimed that Pellico had invited him to inscribe the text of his lost devotional masterpiece in his admiring friend's blood, while one of *Le mie prigioni*'s most celebrated chapters is a description of the amputation of Maroncelli's leg. Even so, in the writings of the prisoners examined in this chapter, the body is a more insistent presence than ever. Tazzoli writes messages in the pus and blood oozing from a sore on his leg. Poma's clandestine letters are inscribed on underclothes that have previously enclosed his suffering limbs. Another figure from Mantua not discussed above, Luigi Castellazzo, who was compelled by beatings to confess what he knew about subversive activities at the time of the Martyrs, later made a dramatic display of his scarred buttocks to sceptical fellow military officers as evidence of the torture that had preceded his apostasy.[86] Galletti, moreover, was convinced that the marks left on his face and body by his prison ordeal were a more trustworthy indication of his patriotic probity than even the Pope's official pardon. In all these cases the body has been made to speak, to act as a witness of a prisoner's ordeal, in this way not only supplanting the legal texts adduced by these prisoners' adversaries as proof of their guilt but proposing its own indelible testimony of indisputable martyrdom. In succeeding decades, however, the notion of political martyrdom and of the suffering body as testimony of that martyrdom was to give way to a more reasoned and at the same time more radical assault on the institutions of society by activists who, while perfectly prepared to endure suffering and prison for the sake of their ideals, focused more intently not so much on their individual sacrifices as on the need to continue the struggle to achieve the political goals for whose sake they had suffered prison and attendant indignities.

4
Authority, Desire, and Dissent: Serving the Revolution

The authorities, lacking the courage and the trust to persecute them because they profess humanitarian ideas, have recourse to hypocrisy in treating them like vagabonds, subjecting them to official warnings and forced residence. And if these methods do not work, they hold them in jail for months and even years accused of supposed conspiracies, releasing them afterwards without proceeding forward to a trial ...[1]

I detest that man every bit as much as a prisoner of state detests the person responsible for his confinement. Is he not the one who by brute force is holding me against my will in this situation?[2]

During the night of 29–30 March 1856, the political activist Felice Orsini broke through the window of his prison cell in Austrian-occupied Mantua and clambered down the exterior wall of the same San Giorgio Castle where a few months earlier the Martyrs of Mantua had spent their last days before execution. Unlike his companions in confinement at San Giorgio, however, men who in most cases had interrupted careers in medicine, the clergy, or commerce to become part-time conspirators, Orsini had devoted all of his life and energy to political subversion. From his youthful days in the Romagna, when he founded the 'Congiura italiana dei figli della morte' (Italian Conjuration of the Sons of Death),[3] through his experiences as a military leader – first in the service of the Roman Republic of 1849 and then at the Battle of Venice during the Wars of Italian Independence – right up to his death on the guillotine in France for his part in an unsuccessful attempt on the life of that country's emperor, Orsini lived a life of violent political contention; everything else, including his wife and daughters, took second place. 'The redemption of my country,' he had vowed as a young man, 'is my cause: I live for its sake and have dedicated everything in my power to it.'[4]

A contemporary of Bakunin, Proudhon, Marx, and Mazzini, Orsini was born in 1819 at Meldola near Forlì; he was not quite forty when he ascended the Paris scaffold after the attempt on Napoleon III. The three accounts this dashing and controversial figure published of his imprisonment and escape from San Giorgio were read almost as avidly throughout Europe as Silvio Pellico's prison memoir a quarter century earlier. But while Pellico had been careful to avoid all mention of politics in his pious tract, Orsini's work was meant from the beginning as political protest. The product of an activist rather than a theoretical imagination like that of his early mentor, Giuseppe Mazzini, Orsini's prison writing was intended to stir anti-Austrian opinion and rally support for the Italian cause. And while Pellico's autobiographical hero had accepted his imprisonment with resignation and trust in God, even in prison Orsini never slackened his defiance of the oppressor. 'I knew,' he wrote about his confinement in San Giorgio, 'that I could never content myself with training a spider or with feeding ants. No! curses on Austria! I must escape, if only to repay her a thousandfold all the moral and physical sufferings to which she had subjected me, in common with my countrymen.'[5]

Two of Orsini's prison memoirs were originally published in English. In August 1856, just four months after he had shinnied down San Giorgio's wall into the muddy moat below, *Austrian Dungeons in Italy: A Narrative of Fifteen Months' Imprisonment and Final Escape from the Fortress of S. Giorgio* was published by G. Routledge in London. The translator was Jessie Meriton White, later Jessie White Mario – herself a figure of some consequence in Risorgimento history.[6] Appearing as it did only months after the events described in it, *Austrian Dungeons* has nothing of the retrospective slant of the memoirs of Pastro or Castromediano, writers contemporary with Orsini whose accounts of their imprisonment did not become available, however, until decades later. Orsini's work, instead, had a much more immediate impact. Because of the censorship prevailing in much of Italy in Orsini's day, his was the first widely read description of prison under the Austrians since those by Pellico and the other Spielberg inmates some twenty years earlier. For all these reasons, Orsini's book was a rousing commercial success, selling more than 35,000 copies in the first year of its publication.[7]

Though the financially strapped Orsini was gratified that *Austrian Dungeons* had made him some money, he was less pleased with Jessie White's treatment of his story. An intelligent and literate woman – but also an enthusiastic disciple of Mazzini, from whom Orsini had increasingly distanced himself by the time of his Mantua imprisonment – White had not only added a stirringly anti-papist introduction to Orsini's memoir, she had also and on her own initiative deleted all unfavourable references to her adored Prophet.[8] When Orsini decided to bring out a second edition of his work, therefore, he turned to a different translator, and when the expanded *Memoirs and Adventures of Felice Orsini* appeared the following year, the translation was by the 'much more faithful interpreter of Orsini's thought,' George Carbonel.[9] This second version of Orsini's story of his imprisonment and escape contained additional information about the author's early life and included an appendix documenting papal misgovernment in the Romagna. In the 1857 account of his adventures, Orsini also revealed the role played in his escape by an accomplice: the strong-minded and sharp-witted German bluestocking Emma Herwegh, who had become a staunch supporter before Orsini's apprehension and afterwards was able from Switzerland to supply him in Mantua with money, materials, and encouragement.[10]

In 1858, a still fuller, final account of Orsini's life was published in Turin by Ausonio Franchi. This Turin edition of the *Memorie politiche di Felice Orsini* was dedicated to the 'youth of Italy,' in whom the author had placed his hope for his country's future. Appearing for the first time while Orsini was on trial for his life, the *Memorie politiche* has been reprinted frequently since.[11] A more forceful call for revolution than the English-language accounts, the Italian *Memorie* had originally contained instructions, in a section titled 'How to Be a Revolutionary,' on the best ways to strangle one's jailer – directives, however, that Franchi found too 'hair-raising' to include in his published text.[12]

All three of Orsini's accounts of his imprisonment and flight from San Giorgio are in the tradition of Cellini, Pignata, and Casanova – writers whose escape narratives the later writer may or may not have read.[13] Like his predecessors, the imprisoned Orsini made meticulous preparations for his flight, sawing through the bars on his window a little at a time and concealing what he had done by smearing wax over the cuts. Unlike Pignata, with his digging tool fashioned from the hernia truss, or Casanova with his celebrated 'esponton,' Orsini was able to make use of the latest in escape technology in the form of two English saws smuggled in to him by Emma Herwegh. The redoubtable Herwegh had also provided her prisoner with a supply of soporifics – first opium, then morphine – for the prison staff Orsini had planned to render unconscious before leading a mass exodus of all San Giorgio's prisoners out the castle door. When put to the proof, however, San Giorgio's hard-drinking guards turned out to be impervious to the opiates. Disappointed but not daunted, Orsini decided to make his break at a later date, alone, and without knocking out the guards first.

In letting himself down the castle wall on a rope fashioned from prison linen, Orsini unfortunately followed Cellini's precedent too well, letting go of his support when he was much too high on the wall, and seriously injuring his leg – even if he didn't break it, as both Cellini and Pignata's confederate Alfonsi had – in the subsequent fall. Also like Cellini, who after his descent found himself temporarily trapped in a Castel Sant'Angelo courtyard, when Orsini bumped (or splashed) to the ground outside San Giorgio, he found he was in the building's moat rather than on the encircling terra firma. But thanks to some help from a passing fisherman, the Italian fugitive was able to clamber out of the mire, conceal himself in some reeds bordering the lake at the city's edge and later slip out of Austrian-held territories to Switzerland and eventually London.

While he was imprisoned in San Giorgio, writing was important for Orsini, though in different ways than for earlier prisoners held in that stronghold. Instead of reinforcing personal ties with a beloved personal social milieu – ties that Orsini had by this time severed – the messages in invisible ink Orsini sent Emma Herwegh focused on such practical matters as obtaining the saws, opiates, money, and maps crucial for his pending escape. Orsini's letters to Emma, moreover, were not his only writing project from detention – or at least so he told his guards. When first sent to Mantua from Vienna after his arrest in Hermannstadt, Orsini had managed to persuade his keepers to consign him to a *segreta*, a solitary confinement cell in the castle instead of the *camerone*, the prison common room. The reason for this preference, he told his guards, was that he needed the solitude such a cell provided so that he could finish a historical novel he was writing. But although Orsini seems to have spent some of his time in his *segreta* working on a fictional composition purportedly titled *Di Spiliberto e d'Altavilla*,[14] while protected from the authorities' surveillance he was really busying himself with plans for his escape.

Given the true nature of Orsini's writing activities, we can imagine his reaction when the castle chaplain – the same Father Martini who had comforted the Martyrs and later published their prison letters and other memorabilia – recommended that he 'go on and write a good deal, put down all the ideas that come to him, without worrying about the disorder in which they present themselves but employing Horace's *lima* or file to them afterwards, at which point everything will be well-done and in good order.'[15] Once the priest left his cell, however, it was not Horace's figurative file for polishing his prose that Orsini turned to, but Emma Herwegh's far from metaphorical saws.[16] Despite the reports by later historians of a 'ms. of a historical romance' written in Orsini's cell and then lost in the moat during his escape, what Orsini was really composing in San Giorgio was another dramatic episode in his life as activist and adventurer, an existence that even one of his jailers could not help but wonderingly describe as 'a novel from beginning to end.'[17]

If Orsini's life seemed to him every bit as dramatic as the historical novels that crowded the market during this period of Italian literary history,[18] the hero of the narrative Orsini was creating in his prison cell differed from the leading characters of such earlier escape stories as those by the more individualistic Cellini, Pignata, and Casanova. For Orsini, revolutions were not the result of heroic gestures by individuals nor even of philosophical ideas, but the product of mass discontent. 'It is not philosophers,' he explained in a long and – given the topic – rather surprising conversation with a Mantua jailer, 'who make revolutions, but the people's needs; revolutions are born if these are left unsatisfied.'[19] Without the support, furthermore, of not just 'a few individuals' but of 'whole masses,'[20] Orsini believed he would never have escaped from San Giorgio. In the *Memorie* he makes it clear that by these masses he meant Italian working people chafing under Austrian rule. These would include individuals like the fisherman Tofin who helped pluck him from the moat, and the peasants and other country folk who helped him make his escape afterwards – and not, he emphasizes, the landowners allied with the occupying powers, the shopkeepers intent only on profits, and the foolish young people indifferent to 'the tears of working-class people' (199). The historical novel in which Orsini figured as protagonist and hero was not his creation alone but that of the entire Italian people. The book of his life that he added to in San Giorgio was only a part of the collective epos of revolution being written everywhere in Europe in the years following 1848.

In his concern for the labouring masses, Orsini was anticipating changes in his country's political sensibilities. By the second half of the century, the idealistic doctrines of Mazzinian liberalism that had earlier inspired Gabriele Rosa and Orsini himself were giving way to different notions of how best to achieve social justice. This was particularly true for Italy's working classes. 'If Mazzini's doctrines were still able to excite a certain consensus among the lower middle classes and city artisans,' a modern historian has commented about this period, 'their impact was slight, not to say non-existent, on the urban proletariat and the multitudes in the countryside.'[21] In the years following Unification, it was the doctrines first of Bakunian anarchism and later of Marxist socialism and not Mazzini's populist humanitarianism that inspired new generations of activists. Like their predecessors, virtually all the political militants of this period spent time in jail, and many left written records of that experience. The voices these men and women raised as part of this new chorus of prison writing were no longer those of aristocrats, intellectuals, or middle-class gentlemen intent on freeing their country from foreign domination or establishing a constitutional basis for more modernized monarchies. This time the voices were being lifted by internationally minded revolutionaries determined to replace what they considered the archaic social and economic structures of their now-united country with new and more equitable social configurations in which representatives of the old regimes would have little or no roles to play.

Some of the most powerful writing from confinement in later nineteenth-century Italy was produced by three political prisoners who were also major figures in the political activism of the period: Anna Kuliscioff (1854–1925), Andrea Costa (1851–1910), and Filippo Turati (1857–1932). These three writers form a curious triangle, if only because Kuliscioff was the companion first of Costa, and then of Turati – almost as if changes in her alliances of affection were mirroring transformations in the Italian workers' movement as the freewheeling anarchism of the 1870s and 1880s evolved into the scientific socialism of the end of the century.

The letters Kuliscioff exchanged with Andrea Costa in the 1880s were collected and published in 1976 with notes and an introduction by Pietro Albonetti under the title *Lettere d'amore a Andrea Costa, 1880–1909*. Kuliscioff's other important prison correspondence – that with Filippo Turati in 1898 – comes, by contrast, from a different period in both her life and Italian social history. By the end of the nineteenth century, the workers' movement in which Kuliscioff had participated first with Costa and then with Turati had abandoned much of its earlier anarchist tendencies and become a parliamentary force committed to legalitarian tactics similar, as such, to socialist groups elsewhere in Europe.[22] On a more personal level, by the century's end Kuliscioff had become a mother and settled into a stable relationship with her new companion, Turati.

Unlike Orsini's memoirs, which were aimed from the beginning at a large, international audience, the letters exchanged between Kuliscioff and Costa and then between Kuliscioff and Turati were largely private communications, even if they perforce reflected the changes in public sensibility that have just been mentioned. As Albonetti notes, the epistolary exchange between Costa and Kuliscioff, 'not only provides us with a better understanding of the inner lives of the individuals writing, it allows us to take the pulse of a specific epoch in regard to certain issues among the socialist avant-garde, allowing us to uncover numerous contradictions in interpersonal areas that are usually left unexplored.'[23] Costa and Kuliscioff were not unaware of the 'trans-private' nature of their feelings. As Costa commented to his companion, 'when you have the poor luck to have the character that we have, love is not only made up of the life we give one another but irradiates around us to clarify and warm.' For Costa, the couple's emotional commitment to each other was 'a redoubled life force that makes us love with intensity, leaving us unable to tear ourselves from each other's arms ... to satisfy what is best within us and is what impels us to love as we do' (215). Unlike Silvio Spaventa and Felicetta Ulisse's slightly earlier love affair, which crumbled when public life was once again an option for the ex-ergastolano Spaventa, the private emotions shared by Costa and Kuliscioff were a powerful stimulus in the political struggle to which they had committed themselves.

From the beginning of his career, Costa had known that jail and separation would be an 'obligatory step' in his life.[24] This does not mean, however, that he welcomed – much less enjoyed – imprisonment. In 1880 we find him glumly recording in a letter to Kuliscioff how 'by now I have spent nearly five years in prison – and I am only twenty-nine!' (205). Costa, in fact, was arrested so frequently and incarcerated so consistently that the *Corriere della sera* disapprovingly dubbed him the nation's 'arrestato perpetuo' (perpetual arrestee) (190).

Kuliscioff, too, had had brushes with the police even before her arrival in Italy. Born Anna Rosenstein in Russia in 1854,[25] the future first lady of

Italian socialism had abandoned her birth-name about the same time she terminated the university studies she was pursuing in Switzerland and decided to devote her life to revolution. By the time of her death in 1925, Kuliscioff had become a legend. A collaborator with Bakunin, Kropotkin,[26] and Vera Zasulich, and a correspondent from Italy with Friedrich Engels, Kulisciof was a socialist and a feminist in the formative years of both movements. One of the first women to graduate from an Italian university, she succeeded in becoming a physician and social worker when few of her sex were active in either of those fields. Throughout her career she campaigned energetically for universal suffrage and women's rights, even though these positions were not shared by most of those in her party. Not only a socialist activist, writer, lecturer, and editor, she was also a warm-hearted companion and an affectionate and loyal mother. 'In Milan,' Antonio Labriola wrote Engels in 1893 about the political scene in Italy, 'there is one man – and she, on the contrary, is a woman, Anna Kulisciof.'[27]

For the history of prison writing in Italy that is being traced here, there are two important periods in Anna Kulisciof's life. The first is that of the ten weeks from 31 October 1880 to 15 January 1881, when Costa was in prison in Perugia, and Kulisciof, banned from Italy, was confined to what she considered the equally harsh even if only metaphorical prison of separation from him in Switzerland. 'I would prefer,' she wrote Costa about her plight in Lugano, 'to be in jail, for that matter I am in jail so that now this unhappy existence does not seem so hard for me: we are living the same life.'[28] The second period came nearly two decades later, in the spring of 1898, when Kulisciof and her new lover, Filippo Turati, were both incarcerated in Milan following the agitation there that resulted in the massacre of scores of civilians by Italian troops under the command of General Bava Beccaris.[29] Convicted of instigating civil war for their purported roles in this uprising, Kulisciof and Turati were both given long terms in prison, she two years, he twelve.[30]

The first theme that emerges from Anna Kulisciof's first letters to Andrea Costa – those from the earlier period of her life – is that of her frantic desire to be reunited with her lover in Italy. Costa, too, was distraught at the meagre news he was receiving from the distant Kulisciof, whom he now missed as never before. 'I don't know to what I should attribute it, my dear,' the 'perpetual prisoner' wrote from Perugia, 'but prison has never weighed down and unnerved me as much as this before. Perhaps this is because my arrest this time was so illegal and unexpected; perhaps it is because my letters don't reach you and I receive yours after such long delays; perhaps it is because the future is so uncertain.'[31] For her part, although physically safe in Lugano, Kuliscioff was so profoundly upset at separation from her partner that she had become physically ill. 'As you know,' this future medical student and then physician describes her condition, 'strictly speaking I am not really sick; my nervous upset comes only from the intense and unsatisfied activity of my brain and emotions, an unhealthy and abnormal activity that even people who hardly know me recognize. I miss you, that's my illness, and as soon as you are restored to me, as soon as I can live and be with you all through the day, an hour will be enough to transform and cure me' (199–200). Although prison was nothing new for either of these political activists, their present sacrifice of their personal passions for the sake of the public cause was especially painful. 'Do you remember the letter I wrote you from Paris the day after being sentenced *to two years in prison*?' Costa writes contrasting their present dilemma with that of an earlier period. 'With what enthusiasm, with what fullness of life – with what abandon I wrote, and how certain I was of being able to console you single-handed! Now, by contrast, though I don't know why, I am deeply and desperately hurting: is it that I used to love you less then – or was it that I didn't realize what I was losing?' (221). Although their love for each other was a source of strength in the political struggle to which this couple was committed, their separation at this point in their liaison was almost too much for either to bear.

In the course of his relationship with Kuliscioff, Costa learned a certain amount of Russian, and the couple frequently employed words in that language in their prison letters. 'If you only knew,' Kuliscioff writes from Lugano in a passage where the italics indicate expressions originally in Russian, 'how much I *desire* you, how much your absence makes me suffer, how I want to be together with you, hug you *in my arms* and disappear in you. Oh *dear love*, my beautiful life, my everything, I want to have my physical life joined completely to yours and for us to be not only one mind but *one body*. If that were the case, I wouldn't be in this cursed Lugano any longer, I wouldn't be far away from you but I would be living in you as you would be living in me – we would be like one being, all one being. Kiss me, love me, write me, I beg you, and *I adore you*' (218). Just as the poetry the Martyrs of Mantua wrote in Italian or read in Italian texts smuggled into prison provided a textual barrier protecting them from Austrian definitions of who they were, so the Russian terms inserted in these letters placed Costa and Kuliscioff's passion beyond the reach of the authorities confining them – this even though the meanings of the foreign words in this letter could not have been especially difficult for the prison censor to imagine.[32]

Even though it was Costa in Perugia and not Kuliscioff in Lugano who was standing trial, in Switzerland Kuliscioff began to have nightmares about going before an imaginary tribunal herself. As Kuliscioff knew, during the time she was in Lugano, the jealous Costa had become suspicious of the attentions paid his partner by the flamboyant and wealthy anarchist Carlo Cafiero, who was also living in the Swiss city.[33] Stung by Costa's lack of faith in her probity, but apparently sympathizing with his suspicions on at least some subconscious level, Kuliscioff began to have bad dreams of grotesque trials in which she was 'sentenced to death' and forced to imagine 'the execution in all its details.' Even though, as she wrote to Costa, in such circumstances 'what makes me suffer the most is the thought of being taken from this life without having seen you,' what caused Kuliscioff the deepest pain was that in these dreams it was Costa himself who was sitting in judgment on her case. In still another letter Kuliscioff imagines dying with Costa in a complex *liebestod* in which she now expires by his side, now is strangled by him, now instead is his executioner. 'Hug me tight against your chest,' she writes, 'I want to die at your side. Life is unbearable. I want you to strangle me. Oh, to become intoxicated and lose all consciousness of existence. Kiss me, bite me, I would like to kill you' (219). In this passage, it might be said, the Russian revolutionary is behaving more like Mascagni's Santuzza in that composer's 1889 *Cavalleria Rusticana* than the well-organized, determined, and successful advocate of women's rights and of Socialist coherence she later became. In this remarkable exchange one can see the limits of Kuliscioff's social emancipation, at least at this point in her still young life.

In 1898, nearly twenty years after the letters that have just been examined, Kuliscioff was again writing and receiving letters from prison. By this time she had been the steady companion of the Socialist leader Filippo Turati for more than a decade. Although Kuliscioff's relationship with Turati was never as stormy as her earlier liaison with Costa, her forced separation from her lover following the riots in Milan was none the less painful for both of them.[34] Commenting later on the first days of her arrest in the spring of 1898, Kuliscioff described the 'terrible days' she spent in 'a dark, filthy, damp, and smelly cell' and the 'sense of being truly buried' that she experienced there. She also remembered how when she caught sight of Turati in a courtyard, she shouted at him 'with all my strength' until 'carabinieri, officers, soldiers, and policemen jumped on me, threatening who knows what consequences if I were to continue.'[35]

As this passage shows, Kuliscioff was able, in her later years, to view imprisonment with greater detachment than she could muster as a young woman in Lugano. 'There was something terrible,' she went on mischievously to describe a prison transfer early in her 1898 detention, 'in that parading past all those bayonets and revolvers pointed at that terrible criminal [that is, Kuliscioff herself], but at the same time there was something so comical that it was all I could do to suppress a smile' (611–12). Kuliscioff's capacity to perceive the ridiculous as well as the tragic aspects of her situation is evident in much of her prison correspondence with Turati. If the theatrical equivalent of the Costa/Kuliscioff epistolary exchange of the early 1880s was the grand opera of Mascagni, that of the Turati/Kuliscioff correspondence at the end of the century might be a sophisticated comedy of manners by Scribe, Sardou, Wilde, or Shaw.

Kuliscioff, none the less, took her imprisonment seriously and was intensely aware of its symbolic political value. Because she knew her actions were being watched by many both in and out of prison, the forty-four-year-old prisoner made clear to captors and friends alike that she neither demanded nor would expect special favours because of her sex, her social status, or what was in fact her precarious health. 'I beg you with my hands clasped,' she wrote Camillo Prampolini, 'to oppose any step anyone might make to obtain my freedom with a personal pardon or a special reduction of my sentence,' going on to explain that 'if I were forced to regain my freedom at such a price I would be so ashamed, so diminished, and so degraded that freedom would be worthless, as would the affection of my loved ones, the affection of my friends.'[36] Kuliscioff's refusal to accept either pardon or special treatment from authorities she believed had acted illegally in arresting her in the first place would be shared by many later prisoners in Italy. At the same time, her position would have been incomprehensible to Cellini, Tasso, Casanova – or, for that matter, Orsini – for all of whom what mattered most was to get out of jail as promptly as possible.

Anna Kuliscioff's is the first female voice in the chorus of prison writing traced in this study. Although other women were important in the struggle for Italian freedom – from Emma Herwegh and Jessie White Mario to Teresa Confalonieri and Matilde Dembowski – the Russian-born Socialist is the first woman to make a significant contribution to the history of prison writing in Italy.[37] In the letters she wrote Andrea Costa while still in her twenties, the young student and activist seems to have been dominated by morbid and erotic fantasies of an unusually powerful sort. In a later letter to Turati, by contrast, the by now important Socialist leader describes her correspondence with her companion as 'conversation at a distance' in which 'ideas, feelings, and projects meet, as though the abyss dividing us had been eliminated, as though we shared a single brain, a single soul' (II: 552) A bridge of tender affection uniting the correspondents rather than a desperate cry of pain torn from her by an almost unbearable separation, Kuliscioff's letters to Turati were almost the opposites in tone and content of her earlier communications of the same sort with Costa. For Kuliscioff, writing at the end of the nineteenth century, prison letters had become a means to overcome rather than to give vent to emotional pain. Her private emotions now much more disciplined for the sake of the political cause to which she and Turati had devoted their lives, in these later writings Anna Kuliscioff was able not only to endure her privations but to accept them with serenity, dignity, and even a sense of humour. Such discipline was necessary, she believed, if the revolution to which she had devoted both her pen and her physical existence was to succeed.

Andrea Costa, Anna Kuliscioff's companion from 1877 to 1885, the father of her child Andreina, and her fitful correspondent until his death in 1910, is often considered the father of Italian Socialism. Born in Imola in 1851, the son of servants in the same Orso Orsini household where Orso's nephew, Felice, had also grown up, Costa maintained ties to his native city throughout his career as labour organizer and first Socialist member of the Italian Parliament – though it was Ravenna and not Imola that sent him to that legislative body in 1882. Thanks in part to Costa, Imola and the surrounding eastern Po valley, where Italian agricultural workers first organized in imposing enough numbers to become a significant labour force, have become landmarks in the history of Italian Socialism.[38]

As a young man, Costa studied at the University of Bologna, where his professor of Italian literature was the philologist and poet Giosue Carducci, whose comments as editor of Guerrazzi's letters have been referred to earlier. Although he never graduated from Bologna, Costa benefited enough from his university studies to become an excellent public speaker. During his lifetime, he also learned a number of foreign languages, among them German, Russian, and English, and was adept enough in French to be imprisoned by French police for his organizing successes with workers in that country. Throughout his career, language, literature, and rhetoric were essential components of this public figure's many conspicuous political successes and of his private writing as well.[39]

In addition to the letters he exchanged with Anna Kuliscioff while incarcerated in Perugia, Costa composed several other works during the several long periods he spent in jail. These include his *Annotazioni autobiografiche per servire alle Memorie della vita* (Autobiographical Notes to Be Used in the Memoirs of His Life) written in Milan in 1898.[40] While in his letters to Kuliscioff, Costa had stressed how painful it was for him to be separated from the woman he loved, in these 1898 jottings he quotes Stendhal's famous dictum that 'the worst discomfort while in prison is not being able to lock the door' (317). Although Costa could study and absorb information while in confinement, he found it difficult to produce truly creative work there, since for a prisoner, 'you concentrate, you work, you even dream; but your dreams hang as if suspended here, in the air of the cell, and don't seem able to move on, can't find their way out, cannot manage to rise very high' (341). During this later period of Costa's life, prison was, as he put it, an intellectual bell-jar (325) – a reaction to confinement similar to comments by many later prisoners, including Antonio Gramsci, who also lamented the lack of significant – that is, dialectic – human exchange while in confinement.

During his earlier stays in prison, Costa, like Poma and Tazzoli earlier, gave vent to his feelings in verse. One poem, for example, which was originally composed in Paris and quoted later in a letter from Perugia to Kuliscioff, describes prison life as follows:

> Oh come triste fra le sbarre ferree
> Penetra nella cella il dì invernal!
> Oh come meste gemono le passere
> Come parmi il silenzio sepolcral.
> E che fantasmi dalla nebbia assidua
> Sorgono e passan qui d'inanzi a me!
> Quali strani fantasmi! E come l'anima
> Oppressa anela confortarsi in te!
> E tu, con un sorriso ecco t'approssimi;
> Fiorir sotto ai tuoi passi io veggo il suol.
> Le nebbie, al raggio dei tuoi occhi, sfumano
> Azzurro si fa il ciel e splende il sol![41]

In this brief text, the vocabulary adopted, the rhymes, and the situation could all have figured in poems by Costa's Bologna professor Carducci; the oppositions of sun to darkness and the beloved woman to the poet's melancholy are also familiar parts of the older poet's repertoire. A prisoner of the French police, the amateur poet Costa is also the captive of a poetic tradition he had no doubt learned to admire as a student in Bologna and could not help but draw on later.

In his prison letters to Anna Kuliscioff, Costa's prose, too, is filled with rhetorical devices of the sort popular at the time. Just as his poetry is derivative in character, with Carducci its obvious model, his prose also follows common oratorical patterns. In a letter to Kuliscioff of December 1880, the repeated direct address, reiterations, excited exclamations, and recurrent exhortations are typical of the public-speaking style that the activist Costa had made his own:

Let's not fool ourselves, my Nina: life is sad; and everything works to suffocate the best part of us! Society today crushes us beneath its iron foot both in prison and outside; and it is already something if we sometimes manage to stick out our head and breathe! It is this and nothing else, my Nina, that makes me melancholy when in everyone else's view everything should be smiling at me. It is my instinctive desire to struggle against this monstrous oppression that has torn me from your arms and flung me into the whirlpool that is bearing me from you. (208)

In this letter Costa's relationship with his partner is part of a larger political struggle, while the terms he uses to describe that relationship are those he is accustomed to employing in his public harangues on social topics.

As is evident from the passage just quoted, Costa is aware that his detention, however painful, is not without a dramatic, heroic side. 'Oh, how many dramas, Nina, how many sublime and terrible dramas in this cell – within these four walls, on this cold bed – while the wind outside rages and the sentinels shout *Who goes there!*' he exclaims in another letter from this same period (221). For Costa, however, the tragedy he is living has not been caused by some illogical concatenation of the stars but is the result of a badly arranged political system that contributes to the suffering of everyone, oppressors and oppressed alike. 'I am unfortunately aware,' he says in another place, 'that the violence and brutality that we endure cannot be attributed to this or that but to a whole order of things that numbers among its victims our persecutors too. When I think about this whole matter of causes and effects making up a kind of Gordian knot that would strangle humanity if from time to time a people's Alexander didn't cut right through it ... But enough of this. Let's continue to struggle and to move forward. We are young and in love' (147). In the dramatic struggle in which they are both participating, Costa hopes to take up the role of a Socialist Alexander who can cut the Gordian knot of injustice that is impeding progress in his country and victimizing even his oppressors. Cultural history has provided this populist figure with the literary metaphor necessary if he is to imagine himself a political leader.

Whatever effect Costa's periods in prison may have had on his famous decision to lead his party into less illegal forms of political activity, his stay in Perugia in 1880–1 certainly deepened, if only temporarily, his passionate feelings for Anna Kuliscioff. Soon after Costa's trial and release, she was able to rejoin him clandestinely from Switzerland, and shortly afterwards bore him a child. Costa's liberation from the Perugia prison was also followed by his decision to run for Parliament and, when elected – in an unprecedented move – to take the oath of fealty to the crown and thus remain a member of that deliberative body rather than stand down from it in protest as his radical predecessors had invariably done. This public gesture by the new deputy from Ravenna marked the entry not just of Costa but of the Italian Socialist Party into the Italian government system.

Once in Parliament, however, Costa seems to have had less time for personal matters; after 1882, the ties binding him to his companion and their daughter loosened dramatically. After that time, the heroic period of Costa's liaison with Kuliscioff (and perhaps with the Socialist movement too) was finished. In the sparse letters he exchanged with Kuliscioff in later years – many of which are given over to practical matters involving the couple's daughter, Andreina – the impassioned rhetoric of Costa's earlier communications noticeably dims as public concerns take precedence over what had earlier been his self-nourishing passion for both Anna and revolutionary activism. For Costa, as for the Italian Socialist movement, a dramatic moment in the history of Italian Socialism – a moment in which he configured himself as a leading actor and at least potential hero – had come to an end.

Filippo Turati – who was born in 1857, three years later than Kuliscioff, and died in 1932, seven years after his companion – could not have been more different temperamentally from Andrea Costa. His attitude towards his existence, both personal and public, contrasts sharply with Costa's heroic conception of his mission. Though he began his career writing poetry, Turati was a man, if not of prose, certainly of reason and moderation. In his public life he was thus very much at his ease during what have often been described as the gray or prosaic decades of the Giolitti period (circa 1890–1910) in Italian political history.

Cautious by temperament, or perhaps just more prudent politically than the volatile Costa, Turati as a young man considered himself 'the most neurotic man in all of Europe,' going so far as to consult a leading Paris expert, Jean-Martin Charcot, for treatment of his acute neurasthenia.[42] Turati's mental problems during the first part of his detention recall Torquato Tasso's similar ailments more than three hundred years earlier. 'I am living here as though in constant terror,' the later prisoner wrote from his cell at the Pallanza prison at Lago Maggiore. 'I burst into tears at any moment, cry out all alone in my cell, each sensation is sinister and lacerating for me, and I think and feel that it is all too much for me and that I am too worn out.' His prison ordeal is so painful, Turati continues, that 'the death penalty would be charity compared to this terrible, atrocious confinement, where everything is horrible, everything a knife plunged into my heart.'[43] In addition, during the first days of his imprisonment, Turati was beset and nearly overwhelmed by a plethora of physical ailments, among them asthma, 'petit mal,' and the inability to digest 'even as little as one hundred grams of any sort of wheat product.'[44] Over the long run, however, the story Turati's prison letters tell is one of victory over his psychological and physical weaknesses – an unexpected emotional triumph for 'the most neurotic man in all of Europe.'

The son of a Piedmontese police official, Filippo Turati, like Anna Kuliscioff, was of middle-class origin, and it was possibly the shared contradiction between their similarly comfortable economic origins and their passion for social justice that made the couple such a congenial pair.[45] A proponent of compromise and reform from within the parliamentary system, Turati was likewise a flexible and understanding partner for the frequently fiery Russian-born activist – much more so than the politically more radical but socially more conservative Costa.[46]

Written as they perforce were on official, prison-supplied stationery, the letters Turati sent out of the Milan and Pallanza prisons are all very brief. Turati himself was aware of this artificial dimension of his correspondence. Ending a letter to his mother with an ironic comment meant for both her and the censor, he remarks wryly that if he had his way, 'I would never leave you, but the regulations forbid prolix love' (33). The gentle defiance implicit in this and other similar phrases in Turati's letters was his way of resisting the levelling effect the prison regime was meant to have on him.

A more subtle and witty letter writer than the expert public speaker Costa, Turati was well aware that the rules of censorship (rules apparently more rigidly applied in his case than they seem to have been for Costa earlier) compelled him to 'make an effort to render our letters as bland as possible.' But he urged his loved ones to keep writing him anyway, even banalities, since the letters he received in prison 'function as a physical springboard thanks to which, we can obviously intuit each other's thoughts and heartbeats' (8). Beneath the commonplace communication imposed on the correspondents by prison regulations, a careful reader could perceive a hidden, invisible message of affectionate heartbeats and unexpressed thoughts: a secret text of prison writing of a different sort than that discussed in regard to the Spielberg prisoners, since what is communicated in the Turati-Kuliscioff letters is unexpressed affection rather than unutterable pain.

Turati believed the history of his imprisonment could be divided into three dialectical phases, which he playfully compared to the sequence proposed by Auguste Comte for the progression of history: phases of depression, convalescence, and recovery corresponding to the theological, metaphysical, and scientific ages in Comte's system (404). 'Depression,' however, is too mild a term for the despair verging on uncontrollable panic Turati experienced when first locked up. In another letter from the early part of his confinement, he describes his situation in these terms:

It is now three months since I have slept even an hour without sleeping pills, my digestion upside down, my heart a constant torment, day and night, first running on and beating like mad, then lying torpid within me so that the blood seems immobile, then making me think I am about to have a heart attack. Three months with my breathing frequently laboured and asthmatic; assailed at night by nightmares and convulsions; my legs barely able to hold me up, deprived because of my nervous condition of the immense comfort reading and study provided (61).

But even in circumstances such as these, Turati was able to predict that 'it seems that no one dies from nerves, and if I were to get out, I would recover right away' (106). Unlike Gramsci, whose letters from the 1930s about his physical ailments over the course of a long and ultimately fatal prison term contain similarly despairing descriptions, Turati did recover from his maladies, going on after release from confinement to live another thirty, relatively happy years,[47] and in later life he in fact made two parliamentary addresses on the subject, which were later published as *Carceri. Repressione dei tumulti e fondi segreti* in 1906 and *Il cimitero dei vivi* in 1911.[48]

During the first part of his imprisonment Turati seems to have wondered whether a stay in jail might not even have enduringly positive effects on his life. 'I have already mentioned to you,' he exclaimed to Kuliscioff in an early letter, 'how this sad and unexpected episode is going to constitute a *turn* in my life,' going on to say that 'I am almost grateful for this brusque bump that has forever broken the somewhat grey routine of that life and that will force us to appreciate a hundred times over the joy of our loving one another' (8). After additional time in jail, however, Turati realized it was a mistake to confuse prison with a health cure or a religious retreat (177). At one point he even entertained the idea of madness as a means of escaping his torments, suggesting that 'perhaps madness would bring peace.' No sooner had he formulated this thought, however, than he rejected it: 'maybe ... but no it wouldn't: the number of those who leave confinement mad is extremely large, but they suffer for the most part from terrible paranoia. And then, poor Mother, I don't want to go mad! Where would they send me? To an institution for the criminally insane, maybe, certainly somewhere far from you, where I would go insane and die hydrophobic and still in prison. No, no, no, my poor adored saintly Mother!' (116) Not threatened, after all, with imminent execution, there was no need for Turati to adopt the solution Angelo Frignani had found so bizarrely congenial some eighty years earlier. On the contrary, it was essential for him to hold on to his sanity by refusing to yield to the pressure exerted on his mental well-being by his confinement.

Fortunately, while in prison Turati received a large number of letters from political supporters. Several communications came from people he had never met, some of whom, he noted to his mother, 'scarcely know how to write and ... trace lines on the paper so as to write straight' (217). Expressions of solidarity from such individuals, Turati later observed with understandable satisfaction, 'are the most moving ones, and make us think about what we have accomplished, afterwards, to deserve such affection' (220). Even in the confines of his prison cell, Turati was still remembered as a respected public figure.

Of all the letters Turati received, however, the most important were the more private communications from his mother, the 'talismans of health' (182) that the remarkable Adelaide Turati regularly sent her imprisoned son. Describing the value of these missives in another passage from the early part of his correspondence, Turati notes how 'my gastroenteritis is getting better, my diarrhea seems over and will certainly be over. I hope to see some improvements in my diet,' then concludes 'but it's the news from outside that matters the most' (121). Whatever his health, it was this vital linguistic link to the outside world as mediated by a loving mother that mattered most to this inveterate activist.

Once the news – especially the political news – began to filter through to Turati through the *filo* (thread) for clandestine communication Adelaide Turati established for him (apparently by simply bribing a jail attendant), Turati adapted so thoroughly to prison life that 'it's almost the case of the opposite worry from that I suffered from earlier: the worry that I am adapting too much' – a notion so compelling he began to wonder 'if I weren't born to go to jail?' (174; cf. also 177). By this time, then, Turati's attitude towards his imprisonment had changed completely. From the moment he began to enjoy the benefits of the *filo*, the tone of Turati's correspondence becomes witty rather than desperate. Speaking, for example, of his feigned engagement to Anna Kuliscioff – a step the couple felt should be taken to prevent Kuliscioff's possible deportation as an undesirable alien[49] – Turati makes a somewhat clownish formal proposal of marriage, begins to call his longtime companion 'my dearest wife' (602), and good-humouredly describes how during their engagement, thanks to the vigilance of the Italian state, she can be sure of his unswerving faithfulness. 'It is already plenty,' he goes on in mock complaint, 'that, during our engagement, I cannot keep an eye on you all the time, as would only be my right, while you, in regard to my constancy, have magnificent guarantees. Just so your mind will be at rest, the entire government administration plus several sentinels with loaded rifles are standing guard' (603). Turati and Kuliscioff had never been a conventional couple: that the state was now chaperoning his fidelity to her seemed too delicious an irony not to share with his companion (and of course tease the censor with as well).

In the history of prison writing, Turati's letters are distinguished for this irony at the expense of both the censor and the prisoner himself, his wit and intelligence triumphing over his physical frailty. In the long run, in fact, prison improved rather than worsened Turati's health. Like Luigi Settembrini earlier, he was released from confinement plumper and in better health than when he went in. And also like Settembrini, Turati's bonds with his family were strengthened rather than frayed by the time he spent incarcerated – a tribute to the constancy and intelligence of Adelaide Turati and Anna Kuliscioff as well as to the courage of Turati himself. As a result, after initial moments of deep desperation, Turati was able to rise above the circumstances of his confinement, progressing like the phases of Comte's history from depression through convalescence to triumphant recovery. Like social history itself according to the 'scientific socialism' of the period, Turati's life and writing too had proved themselves subject to a dialectical analysis in which the stress and storm of a previous period have given way to a more measured and reasonable assessment of his existence.

When at mid-century Antonio Panizzi, Giuseppe Garibaldi, and other Italian exiles in London were scheming to rescue Luigi Settembrini and Silvio Spaventa from the Bourbon ergastolo where they were being held in the Gulf of Naples, the code name they used for their imprisoned comrades was *le monache* (the nuns), while the Santo Stefano prison where they were incarcerated was *il convento*.[50] At the same moment when these plans were being made in London to rescue the 'nuns' Spaventa and Settembrini from their 'convent' in the Gulf of Naples, a real nun in a real convent in Naples itself was wondering bitterly if the life sentence of her personal 'ergastolo' would ever be terminated short of her death.[51] Enrichetta Caracciolo belongs to an earlier period in the history of prison writing in Italy than those of Kuliscioff, Costa, and Turati. Caracciolo's writing is examined after that of the more strictly political prisoners who came later in the century because of the similarities between the Neapolitan nun's beliefs in the need for reform and those of the later Socialist activists whose distaste for oppressive authority she also shared.

Enrichetta Caracciolo was born in 1821 and died in 1901 – her life thus coinciding for about four decades with that of Anna Kuliscioff. Like Kuliscioff and Turati, Caracciolo came from comfortable – or at least socially prominent – circumstances. The daughter of a military commander and a direct descendent of the Francesco Caracciolo (1752–99) hanged by Lord Nelson at the time of the Parthenopean Republic, she belonged to an impoverished branch of a distinguished Neapolitan family. Urged to do so by her closest relatives, apparently, rather than in response to a genuine sense of vocation, Caracciolo entered the convent of San Gregorio Armeno on 4 January 1840, taking her vows in the same institution two years later. Although initially reassured that her claustration would be temporary, in the end Caracciolo lived twelve years an unwilling prisoner of religious institutions and was not released from her vows definitively until the fall of the Bourbon regime in 1860. For the last period of her confinement, moreover, the unwilling prisoner was held in 'absolute sequestration' in the *ricovero* or shelter of Mondragone, a situation that for this reluctant nun was as much the equivalent of an 'ergastolo' as Santo Stefano was for Settembrini and Spaventa.

First published in 1864 by Barbera in Florence as *Misteri del chiostro napoletano*, Caracciolo's memoirs were issued at a time when anti-Catholic feeling was running high throughout Europe. Partly for this reason, her book was a huge success, first in Italy and then abroad where French, English, and German editions appeared in quick succession.[52]

At the very beginning of her memoir Caracciolo states unequivocally that convents, in her view, are 'prisons inaccessible to any social progress, any word of humanity' (5). In response to the possible objection that San Gregorio Armeno was in reality a 'gentle imprisonment' (85) akin, perhaps, to Carlo Bini's 'golden cage' on the island of Elba, she retorts that the cloister she has come to know best is 'a place whose inactive and stupid confinement' is 'more insufferable than prison itself' (62). Her principal adversary, similarly, in her later attempts to regain her freedom, Riario Sforza, Cardinal of Naples, is detested by his virtual captive 'every bit as much as a prisoner of state detests the person responsible for his confinement' (189).

Paradoxically, however, and in a trope that will also be employed by such later, anti-Fascist prisoners as Ernesto Rossi and Augusto Monti, Caracciolo was able to find comfort in her suffering by recalling how all of Italy was similarly held in what could be considered an analogous confinement. 'What are my sufferings,' she exclaims in a mixture of dejection and patriotic fervour, 'compared to those of the nation to which I belong? If all of Italy is languishing under the double yoke of spiritual and secular tyranny, how can I, a tiny atom, I alone among so many millions of the oppressed, pretend to consume my life in pleasures and prosperity?' (65). For this Risorgimento nun, the cloister was both the source of her personal oppression and a figure of her country's more general humiliation. As was the case for the prison correspondence of Costa and Kuliscioff, here too the personal and the political reflect and intensify each other.

Given her highly critical views of the institution where she was confined, it is not surprising that the other nuns at San Gregorio Armeno considered Caracciolo a dangerous 'revolutionary' (193). Her political attitudes, in fact, were as pointed and passionately held as her views on religious claustration. 'At the noisy awakening of populations, the tremendous roar of revolutions, the clamours at the barricade, the toppling of thrones that contrasted so vividly with the sepulchral silence on my prison,' she writes, describing her reaction to the widespread uprisings of 1848, 'I felt a satisfaction, a strange happiness that sent me into rapture' (194). If only she can be released from her vows, she continues, she is ready in person to join the ranks of the patriots fighting for Italy in Lombardy (195).

Estranged emotionally from her fellow nuns, Caracciolo found the forced intimacy of the convent one of its most repellent features. Like many prisoners in secular institutions, she was convinced that even in confinement she might have been happy with her books, her meditations, and occasional visits from her relatives, 'if the nuns with their silly chatter and their vulgar jealousies had not made my confinement irksome' – that is, in effect, if only she could lock her door from the inside (113). Believing as she does that 'I had sacrificed my body but not my reason to the community' (122), Caracciolo wants most of all to protect her private identity from the buffeting of institutional levelling.

Despite the harshly critical language she sometimes uses to describe the personnel and institutions of the Catholic Church, it should not be imagined that Enrichetta Caracciolo was a person of tepid or wavering faith. In moments of difficulty she turns unhesitatingly to God for assistance – to help her with the illicit erotic attraction she feels, for example, for a prison doctor. Extremely candid in this as in all other matters, Caracciolo seeks 'help from God' when she becomes aware of her feeling for this man. 'And God' in turn, we are laconically informed, 'smothered the sparks' (165). For this woman of enthusiastic passions, true piety does not lie in blind obedience to earthly authority but must be founded on 'that supreme harmony known as *love for one's neighbour*' (204). Caracciolo, the nonconformist nun, is thus a 'Christian of that rite that will encourage civility, well being, and the liberty of all people,' a proponent of that belief 'that must be the faith of the future' (253) when a new social order will be proclaimed.

Convents for Caracciolo have become inhuman places because their inhabitants are saturated with repressed desire that is quickly transformed into pestilential jealousy. This is especially evident when one considers 'the frenzied passion of the nuns for monks and priests.' Sealed off from and thus no longer subject to ordinary social restraints, the nuns Caracciolo meets in the convent enjoy a freedom they would never have had in the secular Neapolitan society of the day. 'They are made especially fond of their prison,' she says about them, 'by the limitless freedom they enjoy to see and write to those they are in love with. This freedom,' she continues, 'localizes, incorporates, and identifies them with the cloister to such a degree that they are unhappy when, because of some serious illness or before taking the veil, they are forced to spend a month or two in the bosoms of their families' (90). As was the case for certain criminal prisoners at the Spielberg, the nuns Caracciolo meets in Naples have become so attached to their place of confinement – in this case because of the paradoxical freedom they enjoy there in expressing feelings they could not articulate in secular life – that they come to view the world outside their convent walls as inferior to the cloister. Although Caracciolo understood that writing for these nuns was one of the few things they could do in absolute freedom, she was scandalized at the content and the tone of what they wrote their confessors – 'a courtesan would have used more moderate turns of phrase,' she comments in regard to certain expressions in one letter (91).

Like Pellico, Turati, Tasso, and a host of others, Caracciolo feared that the rigours of her detention would eventually cause her to lose her mind. In a long chapter concerning 'the mad women' she encountered at San Gregorio Armeno, she identifies another link between convent and prison life when she notes how 'one third' of the inhabitants of the convent are either 'completely crazy or fixated on something' and that 'this malady, provoked by the same conditions, has also long been noted too in penitentiaries organized in cellular fashion' (135). For Caracciolo as for such inmates of similar places of claustration as Torquato Tasso in Ferrara, madness is the ultimate incarceration and a threat she must parry if she is to survive her ordeal.

Unlike that other prisoner of the Church, Angelo Frignani – who insisted throughout *La mia pazzia* that his insanity was strictly simulation and a mere expedient he was employing to avoid the scaffold – Caracciolo admits that at one point at Mondragone she really did become mentally unhinged. 'The more I tried,' she says of this painful period in her life, 'to hold on to the tiller of my reason that was slipping from my grasp, the more I realized that I was no longer in charge as before: my reason weak, my memories confused, my senses rattled, all my faculties were upside down' (239). In this state of confusion, Caracciolo even attempted to commit suicide with a knife. But like Cellini in a similar attempt, the Risorgimento nun was prevented from completing this imprudent act – not by a guardian angel of the sort that rushed to Cellini's aid, but because of the whalebone corset she seems to have been wearing in further defiance of convent regulations (248).

Clearly some of what Caracciolo suffered were, as Maria Rosa Cutrufelli states in her introduction to the Neapolitan nun's writings, 'special adventures of a "feminine" kind (v). 'If only I were a man!' Caracciolo in fact exclaims in frustration at one point in her narrative. 'I would be able to struggle with inexorable destiny in quite a different way! But as a woman ...' (220). Later she says that 'to be a man and not a woman (even if for only a few days), to find myself in London, Paris, or America, in a free country, owning nothing more than a pen and a few sheets of paper, would have been enough for me to renounce, I won't say my existence since no one except He who has created that can dispose of it, but certainly a throne, if one were at my disposal' (238). Like Kuliscioff later, Caracciolo is struggling not just with a retrograde political order but with a sexually tyrannical society as well. Her dilemma was that of how to remain a woman and still control the conditions of her life the way a man could. The later publication of her memoir of convent life was thus an affirmation that she had regained control of her personal autonomy. By seizing the *penna* or (pen), she had now become *padrona* or (mistress) of her destiny. For Caracciolo, writing was a deeply revolutionary act at once intensely personal and a contribution to the collective struggle of all women, whether cloistered by conventional convent walls or not.

The periods of confinement described by the writers examined in this chapter date in two cases – those of Orsini and Caracciolo – from shortly before Unification, and in the others – those of Costa, Kuliscioff, and Turati – from the 1880s and 1890s. Despite these differences in the dates of their detentions, all five writers were life-long social agitators, Caracciolo going on after release from her vows to devote the succeeding decades of her existence to feminist issues and a career in journalism.[53] Though all of them were of middle-class or, in Caracciolo's case, impoverished aristocratic origins, they conducted their lives outside the parameters of the dominant social codes to a much greater extent than had been true for earlier Risorgimento patriots. While in later years Costa, Kuliscioff, and Turati all became part of the left-wing political establishment, for the early portions of their careers the trio were considered dangerous subversives who even as late as 1898 were sent to jail on the clearly spurious charge of incitement to civil war. Because, perhaps, of their marginalized social positions, Orsini, Costa, Kuliscioff, Turati, and Caracciolo bring a sense of energy to prison writing absent from it since the time of Cellini.

In the writings of these individuals the imprisoned body is once again at issue – but the body in question is now depicted as energized by desire. Costa's and Kuliscioff's letters from prison are unabashedly erotic. Caracciolo speaks candidly of her attraction to the convent doctor and describes a bout of genuine madness resulting from attempts to suppress her identity as a woman. The powerfully charismatic Orsini escaped from

Mantua thanks to the help of a devoted female confederate.[54] And while the more reserved Turati may seem odd man out in this group, his warmly affectionate though often ironic prison writings were, after all, addressed to two women who served as mediators with the world for him and to whom he was attached by the most tender of ties. For all these writers, the sexual and the political, the private and the public have become powerfully intertwined. For all of them, prison, however inevitable given the careers they had chosen, maddeningly impeded their freedom as both sexual beings and proponents of collective struggle. 'Curses on Austria, I must escape!' Orsini exclaimed; 'I must live, live, live!'

As partisans of unpopular ideas they were convinced would one day triumph, the authors studied in this chapter knew they were the exponents of historical forces whose development would one day be scrutinized by their spiritual descendants. That his life was considered a work of fiction even by his enemies was a source of wonder, though not surprise, to Felice Orsini who considered his personal romance only one episode in the larger saga of struggle for independence on the part of the Italian masses. Andrea Costa lived his relationship with Kuliscioff in the same passionately rhetorical terms he used to confront the public issues of his day. As leaders of the Socialist movement in turn-of-the-century Italy, Turati and Kuliscioff must have known that even their most intimate feelings as expressed in their letters from prison were not theirs alone. And Caracciolo was willing to confess intimate, even shameful episodes from her private life because she was convinced her testimony would be of value to others determined to carry her struggle forward. The writings of all of these individuals thus look ahead to a future whose direction their sacrifices – first of their freedom through imprisonment, then of their privacy in the dissemination of the literary texts they produced from or about that confinement – would help to forge. For these political activists in the age of Marx (and in Italy of Bakunin, too), their prison writing was not just their contribution to the historical record; it was meant to influence what the history to follow them would be, literature, to be sure, but literature of deeply felt personal and political commitment.

5
Answering Gramsci: The Anti-Fascists

Who will be drawing breaths in these cells a century from now?

In the first chapter of *Le mie prigioni*, while reflecting on a confinement in Santa Margherita that was still new to him, Silvio Pellico asked himself who might occupy the surrounding cells a hundred years later. A century after Pellico's stay in the Milan prison, it and similar institutions throughout Italy were again filled with Italians protesting government oppression. The power imprisoning these men and women now, however, was not a foreign one like that of Austria in Risorgimento Lombardy or of extra-Italian origin like that of the Bourbons in Naples during the same period. Though an entirely indigenous regime, the Fascist government that ruled Italy from 28 October 1922 until 25 July 1943 incarcerated so many political dissidents that the situation in the country during those twenty years can be compared to that of Lombardy in the 1820s or of Naples in the 1840s and 1850s.[1] In addition, many of the prison writers of this period, like their Risorgimento forebears, were intellectuals rather than professional revolutionaries – schoolteachers, scholars, novelists, and artists so outraged by prevailing conditions they had set aside their usual activities to devote themselves to working for political change.

These men and women, furthermore, were frequently arrested for acts that had not been crimes in pre-Fascist Italy. Some, as duly elected members of the Italian Parliament, should have been protected from prosecution by the immunity guaranteed members of that body. Legal niceties such as these, however, were swept aside by the special tribunals for crimes against the state that, starting in 1926, began to try those accused of anti-government activities. So that even if Ernesto Rossi chose to argue in 1932 that the very existence of special courts and laws showed how much progress there had been in Italy since the beginning of the century, most observers took a darker view of the situation, maintaining that the application of special statutes by special courts staffed by special military judges was a clear indication of the disintegration of rule by law in their country.[2]

If nineteenth-century prison writing in Italy has for many come to be summed up by the writing of Silvio Pellico, for the Fascist era this same kind of literature can be epitomized by the prison writing, and especially the prison letters, of Antonio Gramsci (1891–1937). Because, obviously, no prison texts by political dissidents could be published in Italy as long as Fascism was in power, the documents discussed in this chapter reached the reading public only after the end of the war and the collapse of Mussolini's regime. All of these texts, whether proposed in corroboration of his testimonial or meant as alternatives to his account of prison life, should be seen, I believe, as responses to Gramsci's epoch-making *Lettere dal carcere* as first published in 1947. As has been noted by Barbara Allason – herself briefly imprisoned by the Fascists for her political activities, and whose comprehensive biography of Silvio Pellico has been cited earlier – for Italian readers of the postwar period, Gramsci's letters were 'the most unique and unforgettable work produced under Fascist oppression,' in the same way that Pellico's book of 1832 was considered 'the most unique and imperishable work produced under Hapsburg oppression.'[3]

In the dramatically altered intellectual climate after the end of the war in Italy, Gramsci's account of his long imprisonment found a large and receptive body of readers, whose enthusiastic interest in his prison testimony can be considered analogous to that felt during the 1830s for Pellico's account in *Le mie prigioni* or in the 1850s for Orsini's descriptions in his *Austrian Dungeons*. When first published in 1947 – ten years, that is, after its author's death – in an abridged edition by Felice Platone and Palmiro Togliatti, Gramsci's book won the Viareggio Prize for nonfiction and was favourably reviewed everywhere, in some instances by critics who had earlier been its author's political adversaries. Benedetto Croce, for instance, in a review of the letters published in his journal *La critica*, lauded Gramsci as 'one of ours,' a fellow intellectual who – whatever his differences with the anti-Marxist Croce – shared the Neapolitan philosopher's commitment to cultural progress in their common homeland.[4]

Nearly two decades later, in a 1964 introduction to a reissue of *Il sentiero*

Answering Gramsci: The Anti-Fascists 133

dei nidi di ragno, a novel first published the same year as the *Lettere dal carcere*, Italo Calvino (1923–85) described the 'literary explosion' that took place at that moment in Italy's literary history, a period he characterized as a time when everyone seemed bursting to describe the extraordinary experiences they had just lived through and were free to talk and write about for the first time.[5] Because so many testimonials about experiences in Fascist prisons have appeared in Italy since 1947, I have chosen to focus the remarks that follow on prison letters alone, excluding from consideration the memoirs that have been part of my analysis in previous chapters as well as the many fictional and semi-fictional accounts of resistance and imprisonment from this period. The survey of prison writing by anti-Fascists that follows, furthermore, concentrates on letters written by prisoners of the government and does not deal with writings by prisoners of the German occupying forces or letters by anti-Fascists in exile or internment or held in detention camps.[6] The letters I treat have all been drawn from published work by individual authors rather than taken from anthologies or unpublished sources; they are grouped, for the most part, according to their authors' political affiliations.[7]

Mine is forced segregation rather than a voluntarily monastic life ... I am simply taking advantage of this ... government hermitage to practise some lofty spiritual gymnastics.[8]

If Gabriele Rosa in his posthumous *Autobiografia* of 1912 can be considered a kind of anti-Pellico, the Italian politician and Catholic leader Alcide De Gasperi (1881–1954) can be viewed, similarly, as an anti-Gramsci. His *Lettere dalla prigione, 1927–1928* (Letters from Prison, 1927–1928) of 1955 can be seen as a Catholic alternative (by a member of what in that year was the party of the relative majority) to the *Lettere dal carcere* by the atheist, minority party member Gramsci. When De Gasperi's prison writings appeared posthumously one year after their author's death, De Gasperi was among the best known and most respected public figures of his day. Prime Minister from 1945 to 1953, he helped found and then led the Christian Democrat Party that was to dominate Italian politics from the end of the war until the Party's dissolution in 1992. De Gasperi had begun his public life as an Austrian citizen in the border region of the Trentino. In 1904, more than twenty years before his imprisonment by Mussolini, he spent nineteen days in an Innsbruck prison for pro-Italian agitation.[9] A member of the Austrian Parliament before the First World

War, De Gasperi continued his career as an Italian citizen after his native region became part of Italy in 1919. But whether as an Austrian or an Italian, for this patriotic and religious man, politics was a mission. 'There are many people,' he wrote in one of his prison letters, 'who take a small excursion, like that of amateurs, into politics. Then there are others who consider politics, since that is what it is for them, an accessory of secondary importance. But for me, ever since boyhood, politics has been my career – better yet, my mission' (73–4).

In the early days of Fascism, De Gasperi was not nearly as intransigent in his opposition to Mussolini as some of his fellow deputies further left on the political spectrum. As a leader of the Popular Party in the years before the founding of the Democrazia Cristiana in 1942, he did not oppose a 1923 coalition between his group and the Fascists.[10] In addition, De Gasperi supported the Acerbo election law of 1924 – widely known as *la legge truffa* (swindle-law) – that granted the party gaining a plurality (in this case the Fascists) a two-thirds majority in the Italian Parliament, though the Christian Democrat leader proposed that the required plurality be raised from 25 to 40 per cent.[11] In general, from the end of the First World War to 1924, De Gasperi was inclined to make the best of a bad situation rather than rupture relations with the surging Fascists. After the assassination of the Socialist Deputy Giacomo Matteotti in 1924, however, he joined other anti-Fascists in the mass withdrawal from Parliament known as the Aventine Succession, a protest meant to signify how impossible it was not only to share power with Mussolini's followers but even to continue in the same legislative chamber with them.

At the time of his arrest in 1927, then, De Gasperi was a forty-six-year-old political veteran. Found guilty of the relatively mild transgression of attempting to cross into Yugoslavia with improper papers, he was assessed a large fine and sentenced to four years in prison, though highly placed Church officials soon arranged a royal pardon that provided a reduced sentence.[12] De Gasperi spent the first part of his confinement in the Regina Coeli prison in Rome. But after three and a half months in that stronghold, he was moved to the nearby Ciancarelli Clinic, a transfer that seems to have been due more to the prisoner's political stature than to the state of his health.[13] After release from the clinic, De Gasperi was at first unable to find a job. Soon, however, and thanks again to highly placed friends, a position was found for him at the Vatican, where he remained until the liberation of Rome in 1944.

Alcide De Gasperi's *Lettere dalla prigione, 1927–28* was published by his widow one year after the author's death and eight years after the first edition of Gramsci's similarly titled collection. The book is dedicated to the couple's daughters, 'to enable them to appreciate better his Christian spirit and great faith that never wavered, not even in the saddest moments of his life.' The narrative presented by the letters is in some ways similar to those of other prison collections. At the beginning of his confinement the letter writer is deeply depressed, though later, after his transfer from Regina Coeli to the clinic, De Gasperi, like Turati and others before him, is able to view his situation with more calm and equanimity. 'My feelings have become strangely sensitized,' De Gasperi wrote his wife in the first part of his confinement, 'and I am unable to turn my thoughts to you, to the girls, or to their grandfather, without crying' (24). In this initial period of spiritual anguish, even the name of the former convent where he is held is a source of pain to this pious prisoner. 'I have always known how to sing "Regina Coeli, laetare, alleluia, [Queen of Heaven, rejoice, Hallelujah]"' De Gasperi muses, 'though Regina Coeli, at present, is a synonym for bitterness' (42). Once safe in the clinic, moreover, the prisoner is terrified he will be forced to return to his former abode, a fear that deepens when he has a nightmare in which a malevolent spirit exults to him:

You belong to me and I am going to carry you off! I am going to plunge you into that stagnant air beneath that grey sky again. This will not be today, this will [not] be tomorrow, though the day will come soon when I will seal you off behind the clanging iron door in that degrading and vulgar setting in which the refined spirit, hypersensitive mind, and ardent imagination that have sustained you for all of your life will be exchanged for an extremely painful martyrdom and your heart once filled with generous aspirations will be wrung out like a laundered rag. (73)

In this frightening, Gothic vision of abduction by a diabolical creature, Regina Coeli has nothing to do with the Queen of Heaven, but becomes a site of humiliation and suffering, where the prisoner's generous impulses and nobility of spirit face both humiliation and destruction.

Even so, De Gasperi does not regret the decisions that have brought him to this pass. Like Pellico a hundred years before him (but unlike such more secularly minded prisoners as Turati, Costa, Kuliscioff, or, of course, Gramsci), De Gasperi drew sustenance in prison from his religious convictions, from the outset viewing his prison stay as a 'period of testing and mortification' (17) that would end only when God saw fit. Once this occurred, De Gasperi believed that he and his wife would be requited for their present suffering. 'Oh, my wife, my friend, my sister,' he exclaims in a letter to her, 'how the pain I have involuntarily caused you hurts me; how your tears run down into my heart, which, like a vessel of bitterness, receives them all. One day the Lord will recompense you, and I ask His grace to be able to live and work until such time when they will all be transformed into pearls of joy' (26).

If he can no longer engage in an active political life, furthermore, the prisoner himself must bear some responsibility for what has happened – though not because he has chosen his political affiliation unwisely. 'During these months of confinement I have reflected a good deal about the past,' he notes towards the end of his imprisonment, 'and I have concluded that there is much that I have to do penance for; though not, as some might want to make me believe, because that life was on the wrong track. It is rather because I was unable to walk upright and briskly enough on that path, which was the right one' (108). Far from blaming his political adversaries for his plight (something impossible in a censored letter anyway), De Gasperi insists that his own behaviour has not always been 'upright and brisk' enough for the circumstances.

Towards the end of his stay in prison, De Gasperi constructed the following extended metaphor to sum up the emotional trajectory he had just traversed:

> In the beginning, I stood at the centre with everything else on the circumference: God, my family, my friends. God? Why had He allowed me to be treated in that way? My family, what were they going to do without me? My friends, what were they going to say about me? This was still viewing things the way we usually do in life, that is from the centres of our own ego, from our personal points of view ... Later, slowly, and with great effort, moaning and sighing beneath the weight of the experience, the centre moved. Now it was God Who was at the centre and I on the periphery, with all the rest of the world a grain of dust in an unfathomable vortex. (153)

Once he recognized his own unimportance in God's greater plan, De Gasperi was able to overcome his egocentrism and accept his suffering. At the same time, he continued to be distressed that his confinement prevented him from using his talents for the benefit of his family and country. 'It makes me sick at heart,' he complains at one point, 'to think how I, a person who for many years has done so much for so many, is unable today to do anything for those who are closest to me' (81).

Like many other political prisoners, De Gasperi was aware of the intertextual ties binding his prison ordeal to those of his predecessors, especially Christian ones.[14] Among these forebears, he especially cherished Silvio Pellico, and *Le mie prigioni* seems to have been, along with the Bible and Dante's *Commedia*, one of the books he consulted frequently. Pellico even served as a model of conduct for his own prison behaviour. 'Last evening,' the later prisoner writes in February 1928, 'I had become irritated because I could not leave my room and gossip for five minutes ... but later, reading Pellico's description of the mosquitoes that tortured him so horribly when he was beneath the lead and his determination to bear it like a man, I was ashamed of my impatience in such a futile matter' (112–13).

A latter-day Pellico in his own eyes, De Gasperi felt demeaned by a confinement that prevented him from accomplishing his political mission. But he also believed that this confinement provided him with the occasion to testify to the strength of his faith. Like Pellico's, De Gasperi's prison writing is that of a political dissident who is not a religious rebel but a humble believer doing his best to endure prison as a necessary part of a divine plan, which for the moment is inscrutable but which he believes will one day provide a more than adequate recompense for all he has suffered. Prison, meanwhile, is an opportunity for religious reflection and possible expiation of previous sins. But in terms of the history of anti-Fascist prison literature of the 1920s and 1930s, De Gasperi was in a minority. These are not topics that appear in the writings of the more secularly oriented anti-Fascist prison authors of this period. Nor are they among the themes of Gramsci's letters where the notions, especially, of prison as expiation or a hoped-for recompense for current suffering are not part of the prison writer's repertory. If De Gasperi can be seen – and he was, I believe, proposed as such by those publishing his letters in 1955 – as the anti-Gramsci, then Gramsci is also the anti-De Gasperi.

And good for me, if my entire life will render me worthy of a gravestone on which is inscribed: he didn't change flag![15]

While some of those incarcerated by the Fascists were Catholic militants like De Gasperi, many more were inspired by more materialistic – though perhaps not less visionary – ideals. The most important of these prisoners were without question the Communists. By its very institution, the special tribunal was designed to crush this newly formed wing of the international Socialist movement. One sure way for the Fascist state to disable this most formidable of its opponents was to lock up all the Communists it could lay its hands on. With the tightening of Fascism's grip on political power after the murder of Matteotti, most Italian Communist leaders were soon in jail or in exile. Among those caught up in the initial round of arrests in 1926 and tried in the *processone* (mega-trial) that followed was Francesco Lo Sardo, a Sicilian lawyer and member of the PCI's legal committee.[16]

Lo Sardo, who was born in Messina in 1871 and died in prison in 1931, came from the opposite end of Italy from De Gasperi both geographically and ideologically. The first Sicilian Communist deputy, Lo Sardo was fifty-five when arrested – nine years older than De Gasperi in the same circumstances. His *Epistolario dal carcere (1926–1931)* consists, in the second edition of 1988, of 378 letters.[17] Presented there just as they were received by his family, Lo Sardo's letters are more repetitive than those in more extensively edited collections. Because they are less severely abridged, however, his letters depict the oppressive boredom of prison life in particularly effective fashion.

Not a member of the working and peasant classes on whose behalf he laboured so diligently, Lo Sardo was a well-to-do lawyer and landowner rather than an intellectual. Describing his political views with a certain modesty in the 'Memoriale' presented at his trial, he none the less noted that 'if in terms of intelligence and culture my communism might be inferior to that of other comrades, it is certainly not such in terms of its intensity and sincerity, in its informed desire to persist in those beliefs that you, gentlemen of the court, might consider erroneous or even criminal, but that I believe and consider, today more than ever, an honest political and civic duty' (188). Neither as given to abstract thought as Turati or Gramsci, nor a member of a social class particularly oppressed by the Fascist regime, Lo Sardo seems to have become a Communist for reasons that were primarily instinctual and ethical.

Perhaps because he was less interested in the life of the mind than other political prisoners of this and the preceding period, Lo Sardo did not devise and carry out a plan for systematic study during his confinement the way that Gramsci, for example, did. Instead, he asked his wife for reading that would help him 'to kill time' (76). His letters from prison, by the same token, are not characterized by philosophical or cultural reflections but focus instead on the prisoner's family and business affairs. In his own way a 'grande borghese' of traditional stamp, Lo Sardo himself recognized that, had he held slightly different political views, he might well have found himself on the opposite side of the political barricades.

'You know,' he writes his wife, Teresina, 'that the Fascists from Messina and elsewhere would have received me with open arms if I had only wanted them to and that today I would perhaps be filling one of the highest positions.' But even considering this, he continues, compared to life as a Fascist, 'I love prison more while you yourself ... understand completely that my imprisonment is worth more than any sort of honour associated with power and position' (68). For Lo Sardo, sticking to his political convictions in the face of adversity is a way for him to demonstrate his commitment to his personal honour.

A recurrent theme in Lo Sardo's prison correspondence, and one that reveals his conservative social views is his traditional attitude towards his family and his wife. A woman without much formal education, Teresina Lo Sardo was not qualified, in her husband's view, to make important decisions independently. From prison her husband provided Teresina with detailed instructions not only about how to deal with business matters, but also about exactly which trains she should take on her visits to him and how she should be sure to retain an older servant since the young maid who was also in the family's service must not be permitted to walk the streets of Messina alone (299). In the same spirit, when he became seriously ill, he concealed the gravity of his condition from his wife, confiding how sick he really was only to his brother Giovannino.

The tie that bound the Lo Sardos most tightly was the couple's profound grief for their son Ciccino, a victim at fifteen of the 1908 earthquake that killed sixty thousand inhabitants of Messina. Perhaps the most important point of reference for both Lo Sardo and his wife in the long years of the Communist deputy's confinement was the anniversary of their son's death. On these occasions the prisoner never failed to remind his wife that she should visit their son's grave and honour his memory suitably.

Just as Ciccino Lo Sardo's death seems never to have been far from either of his parents' minds, so too readers of these prison letters are constantly aware that another death hangs heavily over the texts they are perusing. In the very first letter of the collection, Lo Sardo points out – tragically incorrectly in this context – that prisoners, unlike soldiers, always return to their loved ones once their sentences have been served. As readers of his letters know, however, Lo Sardo never completed his stint in prison. Somewhat later, therefore, when he notes hopefully that his health has deteriorated to such an extent that release must surely be imminent, the reader again knows how deluded Lo Sardo is about this matter and cannot help but read these lines with a sense of bitter irony.[18]

Though by no means a religious man the way De Gasperi was, Lo Sardo believed that his suffering was part of a larger plan, in his case a secular one of social redemption. 'Just as believers accept adversities with resignation because they are hoping for paradise,' he writes, 'so too I am bearing this imprisonment with patience and resignation, certain that it will advance the cause I have been fighting for' (431). Even when he was extremely sick, Lo Sardo's faith in the rightness of his actions did not waver. Aware that 'it would be a great piece of luck for me to be taken care of by my wife,' Lo Sardo also believed that 'if I had to buy this piece of luck at the price of either an explicit or an implied denial of my politics, I would prefer to die in prison' (488). For this deputy from provincial Sicily, neither his political faith nor his sense of personal honour were matters subject to compromise. Progressive in his political if not his social views, Lo Sardo preserved his dignity and thus his identity while in prison by clinging to traditional notions of faith and honour. A martyr to the secular cause he believed in and sometimes conceived of in parareligious terms, Lo Sardo, like Gramsci, paid the price of his political intransigence with his life. As a writer of prison letters, however, he was unlike Gramsci, who was opposed, mostly for tactical reasons, to assuming the mantle of a martyr and was not persuaded that his death at the hands of the Fascists would necessarily favour the cause that he continued, like Lo Sardo, to espouse from prison.

Because for us, in the fruitless nothingness of our days, the party means the carrying forward of our work, our absence notwithstanding: with each day that passes we feel more and more connected with its name, its idea, its strength, its struggle.[19]

Unlike Lo Sardo, whose contributions to the history of the Italian Communist Party are measured today in mostly regional terms, Umberto Terracini (1895–1983) was a Communist leader of national and international stature. A founder, with Gramsci, Palmiro Togliatti, and Angelo Tasca, of the radical Turinese periodical, *Ordine nuovo* (New Order), Terracini was among those who in 1921 broke with the Italian Socialist party to form what would eventually become the largest Communist party in Europe. Though he was expelled from the party during his internment on Ventotene, where he was sent after prison, Terracini's expulsion was never ratified at the national level and is probably best considered the result of local squabbles rather than an official party decision. Restored in any case to good standing by the central hierarchy after 1943, in 1976 Terracini could assert that 'there is no one, comrade or not, who doesn't feel that I, despite some implications to the contrary, am a Communist down to the last scrap of thought and action.'[20]

After the war Terracini continued his political career by serving on the Constituent Assembly responsible for drawing up the new Italian constitution. He was later a senator of the republic. But under Fascism Terracini spent more than eighteen years in jail, by far the longest term of any Italian prison writer considered here – including Pellico and his comrades in the Spielberg. One of the many remarkable aspects of this physically durable and tough-minded man is that he was able to emerge from a confinement that lasted almost as long as Fascism itself with his mental and physical faculties intact and sharp.[21]

From prison Terracini was secretly in touch with his party's Central Committee in Paris, the party's home after it and other opposition parties were declared illegal in 1926. In 1975, twenty-three of the clandestine communications he exchanged with the party in the years from 1930 to 1932 were made public, primarily to document this still active politician's earlier position on the famous *svolta* (shift of direction) taken by the PCI in response to pressure from Stalin and the Communist International in the early 1930s.[22] Terracini's communications with the party on this and related matters were written in invisible ink between the lines of the letters he sent from prison to his Russian wife, Alma Lex, who then forwarded the prisoner's announcement of his position to the party leadership.[23] The writing medium for these communications was the starch the prisoner was able to extract from the bread, rice, and pasta he was fed in prison, the messages becoming legible when brought into contact with iodine or a similar reagent.[24] Messages from the party to Terracini were sent into prison by the same method, the communications in this instance inscribed in the margins and on the blank pages of books and other printed material his comrades were able to send him in jail. Fortunately, Terracini seems to have had access while in prison to an unlimited supply of iodine.[25]

Unlike most clandestine prison communications – those written in blood by Enrico Tazzoli, for example – which tend to be cryptic and telegraphic, Terracini's secret communications with the party are often quite lengthy and detailed. One of them, written in instalments while he was being held in solitary confinement, occupies some thirteen pages in the 1975 printed volume.[26] In this secret document to the Central Committee, Terracini stressed that, whatever Togliatti and the others might have thought, conditions in Italy were not ripe for revolution. 'To talk today about setting up defence groups,' he wrote in unequivocal terms, 'that is, to posit in practical terms the problem of the arming of the proletariat, in other words of the highest form of organizing, while the most elementary forms of organization are lacking, is pure demagoguery, destined to stir up extremist tendencies that can translate into episodes of terrorism and banditry, or else lead to discouragement due to the obvious impossibility of success' (33). In addition to disagreeing with the party (and with Stalin behind the party) about the wisdom of fomenting an armed revolt at a time when Fascism was so firmly entrenched in Italy, Terracini also opposed – or at least needed to know more about – what seemed to him the hasty and arbitrary expulsion of three members of the Party's Central Committee: Paolo Ravezzoli, Pietro Tresso, and Alfonso Leonetti.[27]

It is not the purpose of this study to discuss the political implications of Terracini's position on the *svolta* of 1930 or of his questions about the expulsion of the dissident Communists. What should be noted is how, in this and the other letters Terracini sent the party from confinement, he was able to influence – or at least to believe he was influencing – Party thinking on the most important issues of the day. It should also be noted that the only prison writings by Terracini available to the public today are the clandestine letters on *la svolta* as published in 1975. The letters to Alma Lex that passed through the censor and served as the medium for the clandestine messages have not been released to the general reader. For this reason, what at the time was Terracini's hidden agenda is now a part of the public record, while the ostensible (if more private) communications he sent his wife from prison have not been divulged.

What is unique, then, about Terracini's published prison correspondence is that, with the exception of a few paragraphs, his prison letters deal *only* with those matters that never appear in such other collections as those by his comrades Lo Sardo or Gramsci. Conversely, the expressions of boredom, concern for family members, even despair at the thought of ever being released that characterize much of these other prisoners' correspondence are absent in the more pragmatic and essential communications that we have from Terracini.

As he himself saw very clearly, Terracini in prison was succeeding in doing exactly what jail was meant to prevent him from accomplishing: carrying on with his plans for the revolution, even if he disagreed with party leaders in Paris about when it was likely this event would take place. Terracini's prison activities, as he emphasized in a postwar interview with *Belfagor*, enabled him to express 'my refusal to acquiesce supinely in that sort of half vegetative and half contemplative life to which Fascism, our common enemy, had humiliatingly constrained me.' For this reason, 'my reactions that were sent to the Centre, my comments, my opinions about what lay on the horizon (no matter how limited from such a vantage-point!) were, in addition and more than anything else, a source of satisfaction that I was able to give to my thinking that demonstrated to those to whom I sent them that my intellectual vigour had not been unduly debilitated by the cruel life regime to which I had been subject for so long.'[28]

What is more, if Terracini was able to communicate his views regarding policy to the party while in prison, on a more immediate level he was also able to carry on his activities as an organizer. We thus see him soliciting economic subsidies from Soccorso Rosso for the families of his fellow prisoners (54, 82–4), and on another occasion verifying the identity of a spy to be disciplined by his comrades outside prison (67). Without activity of this sort, Terracini believed, his confinement would have been – in a phrase similar to one that Gramsci used about his own detention – 'a prison within prison: a huge isolation cell, where not even the slightest news from the outside could get in' (86).

While the traditionalist Lo Sardo was concerned with maintaining his sense of honour while in prison, the pragmatist Terracini was intent on keeping his rational powers sharp and effective by exercising them in preparation for his release. At one point in the *processone* of Gramsci and the others, public prosecutor Isgrò vowed that the long prison sentences about to be meted out would stop Communist General Secretary Gramsci's 'brain from functioning for the next twenty years.'[29] In Terracini's case, at least, during the eighteen years that he spent in jail, his vital mental functions do not seem to have been impaired at all. Although Gramsci was finally broken by his prison experience, first physically, and then in spirit, Terracini was not. Unlike Gramsci, he emerged from captivity ready to carry on with the revolutionary work that had led to his imprisonment.

I have the impression that the day I emerge into the open air again, I will immediately feel any sense of these years of prison, of this interruption, disappear. It will be as though I were reconnecting and continuing my life of yesterday. This is because I have always lived with all my heart on the outside: with you and among the things that are dear to me. Prison, in this sense, may wear out the body but it leaves no traces on the spirit, which, because it has been granted the opportunity for thinking deeply and at length, emerges amplified and even stronger.[30]

With her friend Terracini, Camilla Ravera (1889–1988) was a leader of the Italian Communist Party from its foundation. A member of the editorial board of *Ordine nuovo*, in 1922 she was a delegate to the Fourth Convention of the Communist International in Moscow. A year later she became a member of the Italian party's Central Committee. When the PCI was declared illegal in 1926, Ravera continued her militancy, first in Paris and Switzerland, then underground in Italy, where by 1930 she was responsible for the direction of all party activities, including military ones. Convicted *in absentia* in 1927 of plotting against the state, she was arrested three years later and sentenced to fifteen years in confinement. Ravera served most of this term at two women's prisons – at Trani on the Puglia seacoast north of Bari, and at Perugia in central Italy. Afterwards she was sent to internment in the small southern towns of Montalbano Jonico and San Giorgio Lucano and then to penal colonies on the islands of Ponza and Ventotene. In all, Ravera spent more than thirteen years in prison and forced residence (*confino*). Like Terracini, she too had been expelled from the party by the Ventotene collective; and like him, she was rehabilitated after the war and able to resume her leadership position. In 1981 she was named an honorary senator of the republic, the first woman chosen for that office.

The letters from prison collected in Ravera's *Lettere al Partito e alla famiglia* provide an interesting, 'feminine' counterpoint to Gramsci's *Lettere dal carcere*. Dating, for the most part, from the first five years of her confinement, the period she spent at Trani and Perugia,[31] Ravera's prison letters in all but one case are 'ostensible' texts written for the censor as well as for their named recipients. As such, they contrast strikingly with the exclusively clandestine letters by Terracini that have just been examined. None the less, Ravera, like Terracini but unlike Gramsci, was able in her prison writings to communicate extensively with her supporters on the outside.

Because the Trani and Perugia prisons were staffed by members of female religious orders under the supervision of a lay, male director, Ravera's prison writing can be seen as part of a long tradition of communication from claustration in an almost entirely female environment that stretches back to Enrichetta Caracciolo and beyond.[32] What is more, like many similar institutions for men in Italy, the prison at Trani where Ravera stayed had once been a convent. Upon arrival there, the Communist leader admitted that she was unable to avoid 'the feeling of having entered a convent' and of living 'among novices.'[33] In this spirit, Ravera did not view the nuns assigned to guard her as antagonists, believing them victims instead of the same class and gender oppression she had spent much of her life combatting. Although some of the nuns at Trani and Perugia were openly hostile, Ravera was able to establish more cordial relations with others – so much so that her description of one of her first surveillants is reminiscent of that of the good jailer Schiller in *Le mie prigioni*.[34] Despite her profession of an ideology that was certainly anathema to her religious guardians, this advocate of the violent overthrow of the bourgeois state and such allied institutions as the Catholic Church seems in prison to have won the respect and in some cases the confidence of those responsible for monitoring her confinement.[35] None the less, as a leader of the most powerful anti-Fascist political group in Italy, Ravera was considered extremely dangerous. Despite her innocuous appearance, this bespectacled, forty-year-old ex-schoolteacher of middle-class origins was kept under close security throughout her imprisonment. 'For no one else,' Ada Gobetti remarks about Ravera's prison stay, 'was there total isolation ever applied all the way to the end of her sentence; for no one else was such constant surveillance put in place by the OVRA.'[36]

If the conditions of her confinement were significantly different from those of most of the other prisoners who have been studied here, so too Camilla Ravera's prison correspondence is of a very special sort. As already mentioned, the prison texts by Ravera later printed as *Lettere al Partito e alla famiglia* (Letters to the Party and to Her Family) were with one exception sent out of prison by ordinary channels. In the cases of what she called her 'magical letters,' however, these ostensible letters were replete with double meanings apparent to their recipients and through them to the party – though not, apparently, to Ravera's prison censor. In these communications Ravera was able not only to keep her comrades informed about her state of mind but also to make suggestions about the party policies they were formulating.

That Ravera was something more than the doting aunt and loving relative she pretended to be in the letters she wrote from prison to her relatives is immediately clear when these ostensible prison writings are compared to the uncensored messages she sent the party before being apprehended and, in one case, afterwards – texts that are also included in the *Lettere al Partito e alla famiglia*. Instead of the apparent prattle that fills her censored letters, these uncensored communications are full of common-sense directives that show their author to have been an efficient organizer and a tough and uncompromising revolutionary with little patience for small talk or equivocation. Careful consideration of these texts makes it clear, moreover, that the title of Ravera's book, *Lettere al Partito e alla famiglia*, in so far as it refers to her prison compositions, should not be understood as meaning 'letters to the party' on the one hand, and 'to her family' on the other. Every letter Camilla Ravera wrote from jail was meant for both recipients.

As published in the *Lettere al Partito e alla famiglia*, only one of Ravera's 'magical letters' is furnished with a key to its hidden meaning. The letter in question is an important one. In it Ravera identifies the person who had betrayed her to the Fascist police and thus caused her capture. Once this information reached the party in Paris, her comrades there sentenced the individual in question, a certain Eros Vecchi, to execution – a procedure, however, that was not carried out successfully.[37] In the letter she wrote about Vecchi to her brother Cesare in Paris, Ravera described this renegade Communist as a 'pedagogue' who should be kept at a distance from Cesare's infant son. 'Now that he is beginning to speak and to imitate,' she writes, 'you should not be in a rush to teach him too many things! Above all, keep him distant from that so-called illustrious pedagogue' (93). What must be borne in mind to understand the rest of Ravera's letters, I believe, is not just this characterization of Vecchi as a 'so-called illustrious pedagogue,' but also Ravera's description of the fledgling Communist party as a 'bambino.' Throughout the rest of her correspondence, Ravera's frequent references to infant relatives are almost always allusions to the party, its problems, and solutions to those problems as she sees them.

From the very beginning of their party association and while still out of jail, Ravera and Terracini had established 'a constant exchange of coded letters with comrades from the directorship who found themselves in prison.'[38] Examination of this sort of communication from Ravera's underground period casts considerable light on her later prison letters. In some of these earlier communications, Ravera is already using 'magical language' when she refers to Antonio Gigante as 'the man who is not a dwarf' and Felice Platone as 'the Philosopher' – obvious plays on these men's surnames.[39] In her *Diario di trent'anni*, moreover, Ravera confirms that at a meeting with her sisters shortly after her arrest, the women agreed that they would continue to use 'previous agreements regarding the exchange in the new situation of news and information.'[40] The editorial disclaimer, therefore, in the *Lettere al Partito e alla famiglia* that 'the meaning of the letters, especially those to the family, is not always perfectly clear' seems disingenuous, especially since this note goes on to say that 'there is also the difficulty with Ravera's letters of coded writing: what she and her family members called "magical letters"' (17).

While in prison Ravera also received 'news of male and female comrades in confinement,' including information about 'Gramsci, Terracini, Amoretti, and others.'[41] As was the case for Terracini, this information seems to have been sent her in messages written in books and other permitted reading materials. Ravera alludes, I think, to the flow of such information when she writes at one point: 'I am now expecting the books you have prepared for me and that I very much want' (117), and when she complains that she has not had much recent news about the 'bambino, for even if, by some unhappy chance, there have been incidents of difficulties small or grand, it is always better to write me about them than to leave me so long like this without news!' (120).

Clearly, Ravera's first concern while in prison was to keep abreast of party affairs and not be forgotten by the leadership. Thus she writes to her brother Cesare that 'the detailed news about the bambino that you sent me makes me feel much better. Keep it up and work if you can in such a way ... that the bambino doesn't forget me.' (85) Later, when plans were evidently already under way for the Party's Fourth Congress in Germany, she writes approvingly about the decision to hold the meeting outdoors: 'Good for you to take the bambino into the woods! Take advantage of these last weeks of good weather to get him to breathe plenty of clean air: it's the very best thing' (89). When, moreover, she writes in regard to 'il bambino' that 'I feel every scrap of good inside me constantly flowing toward him, I think of him continually and try to imagine what he looks like' (91), this is additional indication that she is talking about the party and not her nephew. So are her frequent references to how the 'bambino' becomes even 'redder' when things are going well for him. 'Do you remember how he learned, in just that way, to walk?' she writes in what would seem a reference to the first years of the PCI. 'All of a sudden, letting go of a chair [the Italian Socialists?], he walked all alone across the room, completely red from pride and trepidation though well aware, with that triumphant smile of his, of our joy and enthusiasm?'[42]

From prison Ravera was in touch not only with party headquarters in Paris but, through the party, though tenuously, with her fellow prisoners.

A letter of 18 September 1930, for example, contains a reference to the 'mondo grande e terribile' (immense and terrible world), a favourite phrase of Gramsci's; immediately afterwards Ravera asks about the health of 'Antonio.'[43] Other letters contain references to the imprisoned Terracini and to Piero Sraffa in Cambridge, whose forwarded letters and other information about Gramsci Ravera had certainly read in Paris before her return to Italy.[44]

To a limited extent, the imprisoned Ravera also expressed her opinions on party policy through remarks in her letters on family matters. Often, I believe, these allusions masqueraded as advice to her sister Elena about the problems Elena was having teaching school. Writing in the spring of 1931, for example, Ravera urges, 'My dear Elena, don't worry too much about the fact that you have to flunk three of your students: if that is how things stand, your class has enjoyed what seems to me excellent success.'[45] In my opinion, the three naughty students indicated here are almost certainly the famous 'three' – Pietro Tresso, Paolo Ravezzoli, and Alfonso Leonetti – whose expulsion from the party became the *cause célèbre* already mentioned in the section of this chapter devoted to Terracini.[46]

Another way Ravera expressed opinions on party personnel decisions, I believe, was through the comments she made about possible first names for her brother's second baby – the names involved being those of party members under consideration for leadership positions (143, 151, 153). In addition to expressing her ideas on these practical matters, Ravera was able to voice more generalized views on such issues as the perennial problem of the extent to which the leadership should maintain contact with the masses. In a letter ostensibly about her brother Carlo's painting, Ravera warns Carlo that 'artists today live so isolated from the masses of people (for whom, at bottom, these artists either are or should be working in so far as they are artists – in the real and largest sense of the word) that they end up finding themselves virtually isolated with their work. And people are so obsessed with the difficulties and the questions of the material problems of everyday life that they pay no attention to either the artists or their works' (131). That Ravera believed continuing contact with the masses was essential for party success is evident also in her uncensored pre-prison writings included in the *Lettere al Partito e alla famiglia*.

Through the allusive language of her 'magical letters' Ravera was even able to say something about her hatred of the Fascists and her conviction that the Communists would one day triumph. In a purported description of geese preening in the courtyard outside her prison window, she seems to be referring to another kind of goose-steppers. 'The geese,' she says in this letter, 'lengthening and stretching their necks as if they were not necks but upraised arms [apparently the Fascist 'Roman' salute] have started to cackle at the tops of their voices, and are getting more and more excited, clumsily hopping and flapping around.' Rather than see other 'goslings' grow up to be geese, Ravera would like to take the 'lovely white duckling' that a fellow inmate has made from paper and turn it over to 'il bambino,' who, she is sure, 'would have fun with it at least for the time necessary to destroy it' (127).

In another letter Ravera spoke almost openly of her faith in the coming Communist Revolution. 'Today's great events,' she says, 'although variable and sometimes extraordinary, have this in common: all of them can be reduced to that which in a sick person are the various and perhaps unexpected manifestations of a single illness [certainly capitalism]. All of them give the sensation of sparks that at any moment now can ignite a fire – a fire that one senses is there ready and in waiting!' Just in case her recipients do not get the message, she writes just after this passage, 'but let's leave aside the big issues, for they do not belong on these little sheets of paper!' (225).

Ravera's strategy is to embrace her political convictions even more tightly while in jail and to defy the censor by expressing them to others. 'Even in prison,' she writes about her continued militancy, 'women Communists are obliged to abstain from all acts and attitudes that might discredit a Communist woman and thus the p[arty] and to give proof of consistency and control of themselves' (262). Or, as she put it in retrospect in her *Diario di trent'anni* of 1973, 'the reasons that got us to prison remained alive and operative even in solitary confinement; they continued to give a sense to existence ... Even in prison the Resistance was ripening.'[47]

Despite the apparent candour that characterizes Ravera's postwar writing about herself, especially that aimed at a mass audience that appeared after she was named senator, Camilla Ravera was not always the person she appeared to be. When she was director of the underground party in Italy, many of her comrades were unaware of her true identity and position. 'It sometimes happened,' Gobetti writes about this, 'that, in a meeting, comrades would ask her to tell certain things to Micheli [Ravera's underground pseudonym], that is, to herself. So innocent was she that it did not cross anyone's mind to identify the mysterious character who was directing the party in all its branches with that little woman with such clear eyes and a sweet voice' (48–9). As consideration of her 'magical letters' from detention makes clear, Camilla Ravera was by no means the kindly relative she pretended to be to the prison censor or the sweet old lady smiling up from the books printed about her when she became an honorary senator, but was instead an astute and alert organizer who took pleasure in carrying on her revolutionary work in defiance of her enemies. Watched over in prison every bit as closely as Gramsci was, she was able to a much greater degree than her Sardinian comrade to carry on with the practical work of Communist militancy through her astute employment of such 'feminine' and apparently innocent topics as the raising of infants, the education of children, and the spectacle of geese at liberty in a courtyard: all occasions for her to work her clandestine political 'magic' and in this way outwit and defy her captors.

In considering the history of modern times, humanity seems a giant that is fumbling in a cave looking for the way out: after slipping and stopping he has managed so far to move towards a strip of light that he sees in the distance. But the earth at any moment can give way beneath his feet and he can tumble into a hole. It is up to us, those who understand the value of the civilization in which our intelligence has been formed, to struggle to prevent this from happening.[48]

The Communists were of course not the only anti-Fascist group to be persecuted by the special tribunal. Although not nearly as disciplined as the members of the PCI, the intellectuals who banded together under the motto of Giustizia e Libertà (Justice and Liberty) were just as firmly opposed to Fascism and just as ready to face exile or jail for their beliefs. A loosely connected group of like-minded individuals rather than a disciplined political party, the 'Giellisti' opposed Fascism for reasons that were primarily ethical. The group has been described as anti-monarchical, anti-clerical, and anti-Communist – though otherwise thoroughly pragmatic.[49] In contrast to the Communists with their 'scientific' Marxism, the Giellisti were proud of their unabashedly 'utopian' social views. For many of them, as Carlo Rosselli put it, 'partial socialistization is a guarantee of freedom, universal socialistization is the origin of slavery.'[50] Although the movement went to pieces after the fall of Fascism, during the darkest years of the 1930s the Giellisti in Italy and in exile were rare spots of light in the political gloom. Of all the writings by anti-Fascist political prisoners in the 1920s and 1930s, those by Ernesto Rossi and Augusto Monti from the Justice and Liberty movement are among the most remarkable for the firmness of mind and warmth of spirit they exhibit in the midst of suffering.

Ernesto Rossi, who lived from 1897 to 1967, grew up in Florence. He fought in the army in the First World War, a conflict in which his brother died and Rossi himself was wounded nearly fatally.[51] When arrested in 1930, Rossi was a teacher of economics at an Istituto Tecnico in the Lombard city of Bergamo, not too far from the Iseo of that earlier nonconformist political activist, Gabriele Rosa. Convicted of crimes against the state, Rossi spent more than thirteen years in prison and internment, not regaining his freedom until 1943. Although his health was severely tried by prison life, in internment later on Ventotene Rossi was able – like Silvio Spaventa nearly a century earlier – to regain much of his physical strength through exercise and exposure to the sea air. Recurrent health problems, however, made it impossible for him to participate in the Resistance, which he sat out reluctantly in Switzerland.[52] After the war, Rossi served in the Parri government as under-secretary for reconstruction.[53] He was also active in the Partito d'Azione and later in the Partito Radicale. A proponent of a federated, united states of Europe, in the postwar period Rossi wrote several widely read books dealing with the need for political reform, among them *Settimio non rubare* (Don't Steal Settimio, 1951), *Il malgoverno* (Misgovernment, 1954), and a best-seller, *I padroni del vapore* (The Lords of Steam, 1954). During this same period he was a regular contributor to Mario Pannunzio's *Il mondo*, through whose pages he reached a wide audience of intellectuals and others.[54]

Ernesto Rossi is represented in the history of prison writing by two collections of letters: his own *Elogio della galera. Lettere 1930/1943*, and a companion work, the *Lettere ad Ernesto*, written by his mother, Elide Rossi.[55] Elide Rossi was such an exceptional correspondent with her imprisoned son that, even though she was not herself a prisoner of the Fascists in any but a metaphorical sense, her contribution to the tradition of prison writing deserves comment here, if only to restore the missing other voice that has always been part of prison discourse and is usually a female one.[56] Confined to a convent for seven and a half years as a young girl, Rossi had herself lived through a period of painful claustration, an experience that led to her definitive break with organized religion. 'I refused,' she stated in later remarks about these years, 'to go to church and, little by little, thanks to considerable reading about the Catholic religion, I have arrived at old age happy to renounce all of Holy Mother Church's superstitions, hypocrisies, and legends.'[57] The survivor of an unhappy and violent marriage who had lost one son in the war and another to political exile, and two of whose daughters had committed suicide, Elide Rossi was certainly not unacquainted with grief. Partly for this reason, perhaps, she was able to provide her son with exceptionally credible psychological support while he was in prison. In her first letter to Ernesto, none the less, she does not conceal how much her son's arrest has hurt her. 'The blow stings,' she writes, 'but by this time I am accustomed to destiny's cruelties: it has persecuted me for years without any signs of let-up.' Despite her pain, Rossi is quick to assure the prisoner that 'your mother will always know how to remain strong and calm, you should have no doubt about this,' going on to specify that 'I have known pain at much too close hand – despair, however, never' (3, 5).

Elide Rossi, it should be clear, was not an unflaggingly upbeat correspondent. But she was never bitter or ashamed about what her son had done. 'I know that you would never be able to commit an act at odds with your ideals of justice and decency,' she writes him (18), and in a later letter, 'you have done well to sacrifice yourself for a cause whose decency you are well acquainted with: if nothing else, you remain at peace with yourself' (129). For Elide as for Ernesto, it is better to be in jail than to compromise with a corrupt social system. 'If I compare you to the great preponderance of profiteers, *nouveaux riches*, and the many who exist through lies and compromises,' she writes in 1937, 'I consider myself proud to be your mother. Thanks to you, I would not exchange my painful motherhood with that of any other woman' (140).

While Ernesto was in prison, Elide read a number of books by famous Italian prisoners in the past, among them Benvenuto Cellini, Felice Orsini, Luigi Settembrini, and Silvio Pellico (69, 66, 83, and 85). In regard to the last of these she concludes that 'the figure that Pellico cuts is really a miserable one. He found himself involved by chance in a struggle that was not adapted either to his character or to his modest temperament, and if he endured so much suffering with resignation, this was not due to strength of character but because of the fervid Catholicism that promised to reward him with the joys of Paradise' (79). For the anti-clerical Elide, her son will survive prison not because he hopes for compensation for his suffering at some later date, but thanks to his 'strength of character' – a quality he has obviously acquired from her.

For his part, prevented as he was for much of the time he spent in prison from writing anything but letters home, Rossi used his correspondence as a repository for ideas on a number of topics he was unable to develop in writing of other kinds.[58] These comments on a variety of economic and political subjects give Rossi's letters a scholarly cast that makes them quite different from those of such other prisoners as the less reflective Francesco Lo Sardo or the more activist Terracini and Ravera.

During his confinement, Rossi, like so many others, read several works by earlier prisoners. Among these were Felice Orsini, whom he finds 'one of the figures from our marvellous Risorgimento who stands out the most for the sincerity of his faith and the manliness of his character,' though he also notes that 'he must have had several screws loose in his cranium' (401); Luigi Settembrini (183); Alexandre-Philippe Andryane (69, 200); and Giovanni Arrivabene, whom he admires for his lunatic character, concluding that 'whoever is unable to understand the truth of this judgment, doesn't, in my opinion, understand anything about the Risorgimento and is crediting the wise for having reaped what was sowed by madmen' (524). For Rossi, in a more serious vein, intellectuals have the obligation to try to imagine a decent society and then work for that image's realization. 'Just as a good cobbler is a man who makes solid shoes that don't let in the water,' he says, 'so people who belong to the ruling class should try to understand the needs and potential of the environment in which they live, and try to improve that environment, while always maintaining in every way what they see as the truth' (12). Rossi later goes on to note that 'we are a privileged group because we are *intellectuals*. In order not to be ashamed of this privilege when compared to the masses *who are forced to live like animals*, it is appropriate for us to be worthy of our position, for each one of us at every moment to reaffirm his status as an intellectual, to seek the truth disinterestedly and whatever it might be, to make it known.'[59]

Because he believes that in a tyrannical society the place for a free man may very well be prison, Rossi can write about his confinement with irony and even merriment, pointing out, for example, that when after his release he needs to use a public urinal he will probably walk back and forth several times in it, thinking he is once again in the 'air' of the prison exercise space (108). Unlike some other political prisoners, Rossi never denied that he was guilty of the crimes imputed him. 'In all conscience,' he writes about his twenty-year sentence, 'I really earned these twenty years, much more so than those who gave them to me realized' (89). His conviction of the rightness of his actions plus the fierce and unflinching support of his extraordinary mother enabled Rossi to endure a long and difficult imprisonment and to emerge from this confinement with his political principles strengthened rather than diminished. Meanwhile, he was able to make his prison correspondence into a record of his political and ethical reflections in the same way that Gramsci did in his *Quaderni del carcere*.[60]

But then, you see, Luisa, there is another thing, one more important for me than all the others. You know that 'to live' for me means 'to love,' and 'to love' means 'to have compassion' in the very precise sense of 'to suffer together.'[61]

Augusto Monti was also associated with Giustizia e Libertà. In fact, his only crime – and the one for which he was sentenced to five years in jail – was to have written some articles for the organization's Paris newsletter.[62] Monti's letters were written to his daughter rather than to his mother, wife, or sweetheart. First published in 1977 in an edition annotated by both the letters' original recipient and their author, the *Lettere a Luisotta* were later also published in an abridged version for Italian middle-school readers, a suitable fate for the prison writings of an anti-Fascist who was first and above all an educator.

Augusto Monti was born in 1881, imprisoned between 1936 and 1939, and lived until 1966. For much of his life a professor of Greek and Latin at Turin's Massimo D'Azeglio high school, he was also a successful fiction writer, his best-known work the trilogy, *I sansôssí* (The Nonchalant), *Quel Quarantotto!* (What a Mess!), and *L'iniqua mercede* (Iniquitous Grace), collected in a single volume in 1949 as *Tradimento e fedeltà* (Faithfulness and Betrayal), and again in 1963 as *I sansôssí*. During the 1915–18 war, Monti served in the military, spending two years as a prisoner of war before cessation of the hostilities.[63] His later imprisonment under the Fascists lasted three years, a relatively brief ordeal when compared to the prison sojourns of Rossi, Terracini, Ravera, or Gramsci – though trying enough for the elderly schoolteacher. After 1943, Monti, who was then over sixty, participated in the Resistance; at seventy he married a twenty-five-year-old woman and lived to the age of eighty-five.

Although Monti was arrested on the basis of very slender evidence, his captors' perception that he was a serious threat to the regime was correct. Monti's classes at the D'Azeglio were attended by several young men who would later play significant roles in the life of their country, first in the Resistance, then in the formulation of an anti-Fascist Italian culture in the years after the war. This group of young Italians included, among many others, Cesare Pavese (1908–50), Leone Ginzburg (1909–44), Giancarlo Pajetta (born 1911), Vittorio Foa (born 1910), Massimo Mila (1910–88), and Giulio Einaudi (1912–99). The extent of Monti's influence on this new generation of intellectuals may be seen in the dedication to him of the first poem of Pavese's ground-breaking and implicitly subversive 1936 volume of neo-realist poetry, *Lavorare stanca*, a gesture that the collection's American translator has called 'a homage in the deepest sense of the word: literary, political, cultural, personal.'[64]

Like Ernesto Rossi, Monti was not ashamed to be in prison for his beliefs. Refusing to flee the country when informed his arrest was pending, he also refused to hire a lawyer for his trial, reasoning that defending himself in this way was tantamount to an admission of guilt.[65] Found guilty of 'fomenting an armed insurrection ... and of provoking civil war,' Monti was sentenced to the same penitentiary at Civitavecchia where Terracini was also resident.[66]

Despite his age and precarious health, Monti refused to ask for a pardon, standing firm even when Senator Giovanni Agnelli intervened with Mussolini on his behalf (46–7). 'A person who is guilty,' Monti wrote his daughter about this, 'is the one who asks for pardon. What have I done? Nothing. Nothing that even according to their criteria could appear to be a crime: so what pardon is it I should seek?' (44). For Monti, Italy under Fascism was nothing more than one vast prison anyway. In a phrase censored from his original letter of 1936 but whose substance Monti was able to supply in the postwar, annotated edition of his prison writings, he commented that 'to return home because of a partial amnesty or a new hearing ... meant nothing more than being decanted from a smaller into a bigger prison ... what would be wonderful would be to come home at the restoration of everyone's freedom everywhere' (49).

The graceful, witty tone Monti employed in his letters had the twofold function of keeping up his family's spirits and minimizing illusions on his captors' part that they had succeeded in making him suffer. In this vein, Monti insists in an early letter that prison is in fact a very pleasant place, since for those so confined there is 'no one who comes to call and nothing to disturb you,' a situation that offers a busy man 'nirvana; the bliss allowed me by solitude and my ability to do I please' (43).

Going to prison, for Augusto Monti, was a more serious way for him to express his solidarity with all of Fascism's other victims. In the continuation of the passage quoted as the epigraph to this section, he explains to his daughter that prison has provided him the opportunity to share in his people's common suffering and thus to demonstrate his love for his fellow citizens:

My lack of participation in everyone's suffering finally became unsupportable for me. Very well, for the past seventeen days everything is different. I suffer too. I am deprived of many things too. I am upset too. I, too, in short, am part of the greater circle of pain, including physical pain. I 'show compassion' for my people and for their sake demonstrate 'love' for them as best I can and know how ... Believe me, Luisa, when I ponder this issue as deeply as I can, I find at bottom it is solely and utterly this: my taking part in Italy's pain, my conscious satisfaction at being a person who suffers and feels pain in the midst of all my people's pain and suffering. You shake your head no? You're not persuaded? You feel 'compassion' for me in another sense. But you *do* understand me. You're my daughter. Ciau. Papà. (16)

However pervasive prison may be for everyone living under the Fascist regime, however, this does not mean that all of life – as Pavese had suggested – is prison. Writing to Luisa in words he knew would be forwarded to Pavese about the latter's poem, 'Semplicità' (Simplicity), Monti says:

It is not true that all of life is a prison. Because prison is a place, state, or condition where you are against your will. But such a place or condition or state does not exist. You have only what you have chosen to have. If I am in Regina Coeli, I am there because *I wanted* to be there and because I did *not* want *not* to be there. I am therefore not there because of external coercion. And thus I am free. And thus I am happy. And thus I am not attempting to escape. Not even in my dreams. This is my catharsis, my poem. (119)[67]

For Monti, prison was not a constraint on his freedom but the consequence of a freely chosen moral position that continued to provide him with both ethical and aesthetic satisfaction. This remarkable attitude, which he was able to maintain for most of the relatively short period of his detention, was not shared by his long-term comrades in confinement. Gramsci, for example, while also noting that his imprisonment was the result of a consciously chosen political position, did not hesitate in his prison letters to express his hatred of a confinement he did not consider an opportunity to express his solidarity with all the others who were suffering in his country or an occasion for satisfaction at the moral stand he had taken.

I have before my eyes the image of a sumptuous and extremely solid building, which has been torn from top to bottom by an explosive that has rained down from the sky and which must be demolished right to the ground. In reality, it is one of the many war photographs that are published today. But in my mind it has assumed the value of a symbol. A large building of imposing majesty that today is being struck by fate, knocked to the ground while apparently in the full vigour of its strength.[68]

The prison writers to be treated next – Carlo Levi (1902–75), Rodolfo Morandi (1902–55), Giorgio Bassani (born 1916), and Mario Alicata (1918–66) – made their most significant contributions to Italian cultural life after the war and the fall of Fascism.[69] When Gramsci was arrested in 1926, Levi and Morandi were in their mid-twenties, Bassani was ten and Alicata eight years old. All these writers were intellectuals first and political agitators only in response to the extraordinary circumstances in which they were living. Even Alicata, who became a leader of the Communist Party in the 1950s, at the time of his arrest in 1942 was most active in the areas of Italian literature and the cinema. By his own account, it was only through the experience of prison that revolutionary politics became a priority for him.[70]

The writing these four men did in prison was published, with the exception of Morandi's, well after the first wave of anti-Fascist prison writing had appeared in the postwar years. Bassani's fragmentary prison letters came out when their author was nearly seventy; Morandi's, Alicata's, and Levi's collections were all published posthumously. Put before the general reader, then, at different moments in Italy's history – Morandi's in 1959, Alicata's in 1977, Bassani's in 1984, and Levi's in 1983 and 1991 – and at late points in or after the end of their authors' careers, the writings from confinement by these men were addenda to what for each of them was an already distinguished record of intellectual accomplishment. Their contributions were none the less significant within the genre of anti-Fascist prison testimony begun by the 1947 *Lettere dal carcere*.

Carlo Levi was imprisoned twice for anti-Fascist activities: in 1934 for a little more than seven weeks and in 1935 for about the same length of time. Following his second incarceration, he was not restored to freedom but dispatched instead to internment in Lucania. This episode inspired *Cristo si è fermato ad Eboli* (*Christ Stopped at Eboli*), Levi's autobiographical description of his discovery of the underdeveloped South, which is usually considered his literary masterpiece. A skilled painter as well as a writer, before his arrest Levi had shown his work at the Venice Biennale. In fact, the record he has left of his two incarcerations is in the form not only of letters and other writings but also of drawings, the latter confiscated while Levi was a prisoner but rediscovered later in police archives and eventually published as *Disegni dal carcere 1934. Materiali per una storia* (Drawings from Prison, 1934: Material for a History). In 1991, the letters to his family that Levi wrote during his prison stays were also made public as *E' questo il 'carcer tetro'? Lettere dal carcere 1934–35* (Is This the "Dreary Prison"? Letters from Prison 1934–35).

With Monti, Pavese, Mila, and other Turinese intellectuals, Levi was associated in the 1930s with Giustizia e Libertà. After the war, he joined the Action Party and in the 1960s was twice elected to the Italian Senate, both times as an independent on the Communist ticket. Throughout the postwar period Levi continued to paint, write, and participate in public debates on political and cultural topics. The forty-two letters that make up *E' questo il 'carcer tetro'?* are clearly the work of a cosmopolitan intellectual. In them Levi mentions his prison reading of works by Dante, Petrarch, Nievo, and D'Azeglio among the Italians; Tolstoy, Gorki, Goethe, Diderot, Kipling, Macaulay, Sand, Huxley, Romains, and George Eliot among foreign novelists; Caesar, Cicero, and Horace among the Latin classics; and the philosophers Augustine, Longinus, Spinoza, Bergson, Leibniz, Kant, and Fichte. His prison experience is mediated in his imagination by accounts of similar events in the lives not only of Pellico and Cellini (who as a painter was of particular interest), but also of Tasso, Defoe, Campanella, Cervantes, and even Giovita Scalvini (1791–1843), who translated Goethe's *Faust* into Italian while in prison.[71]

Despite the solidarity he felt with these illustrious predecessors, for the intellectually restless Levi, prison marked an unwelcome halt in the flow of his creative life, which for him meant the complete cessation of time. 'These imprisonments,' he wrote his mother, 'are truly quite unnatural things, real ruptures in the flow of time: the idea of time itself ends up interrupted in a certain way, as if through the intervention of an element foreign to thought. A single day in prison,' he continues, 'is something unmeasurable, the equivalent of a century or an eternity – an empty century, a non-existent eternity' (112).[72] Part of the trouble was that Levi was forbidden to paint while in prison, though he did manage, in 1934, to make use of found materials, including a mixture of methylene blue and glycerine supplied him for a supposed throat infection. The clandestine blue-washed drawings that he created with these substances enabled him not only to reenter lived time but also to reaffirm his identity as an artist, much as Cellini had done centuries earlier. Like Cellini, Levi also wrote poetry during his incarceration, using the empty spaces in the letters he received from home for its transcription. As it had been for such earlier prisoners as Poma, Tazzoli, and Pastro in the 1850s and for Costa a little later, writing poetry for Levi was another way of resisting the debilitating effects of confinement and of defying his captors.

The letters Levi wrote home from prison were also a means of combatting that confinement. By creating a series of metaphors in these letters that compared his detention to a variety of other experiences, he was able to obliterate the oppressive specificity of his situation. In these metaphors, prison is consecutively a voyage (29), a monastery (30), an anachronism (31), an infantile regression (31), convalescence (50), a sleepy country town (57), a place for detailed 'minute analysis,' (68, and see 128, where he again says that prison offers a break from life's usual routine), a test (75), and the opposite of painting, which is freedom (113). In addition, given his innocence (or so he claimed: Levi was in fact guilty of the charges levelled against him), Levi the prisoner was only an abstraction and an erroneous one at that: a statistical mistake rather than a genuinely confined human being. Unlike Monti, who was unwilling even to think about being anywhere else than confinement and accepted his imprisonment as an occasion for demonstrating his solidarity with all the others oppressed by Fascism, Levi preferred to retire into the world of the imagination he had long considered his principal abode, and in this way escape the oppressive conditions of his confinement.

It has been suggested that two major sources of inspiration for Levi's figural imagination while in prison were the contrasting ones of sustaining memory on the one hand and a painful present on the other.[73] In his letters from prison published in the miscellaneous collection, *Di là dal cuore* (Beyond the Heart) of 1984, Giorgio Bassani seems influenced by these same two forces. Born in 1916, Bassani grew up under Fascism. Like Levi, Morandi, and Alicata, he later participated in the Resistance. Although he does not indicate in *Di là dal cuore* exactly when the fourteen undated and fragmentary letters printed there were first written, they seem to come from 1939 when their author was twenty-six.[74]

Not unlike Levi, for whom the worst thing about prison was not being allowed to paint, Bassani found that the worst aspect of prison life was not being allowed to write more than brief notes home. Many of the themes that appear in his communications from prison, however, are similar to those that became constants of his mature fiction. Expressing gratitude, for example, for food sent by his family, Bassani notes how 'home cooking that has, moreover, been prepared with loving care, seems extraordinary, way beyond its physical value. You can see from this how in the depths of misery the comforts and pleasures of life, in themselves vain and transitory, can acquire a spiritual value of their own. But how could the things I receive not have such a meaning since they remind me of home and of my loved ones?'[75] Because it recalls the comforting ritual of the family meal, the food Bassani receives in prison is a source of spiritual as well as physical nourishment. Although he terms this delight 'vain and transitory' like so many other pleasures of the flesh, the prisoner recognizes that his family's providing sustenance for him is a gesture powerful enough to have breached the walls separating him from the community that he relied on for a sense of identity.[76] The rituals and transitory pleasures of middle-class and urban life; the walls that separate the individual from the community; loneliness and the need for affection – all these are themes that Bassani will treat over and over again in his fiction of the 1950s and 1960s. Addenda to be sure to his major production as a writer, Bassani's fragmentary prison letters are also early hints of what will become the major motifs of his mature fiction; as such they indicate how much his reaction to prison was that of a writer who saw his confinement as paradigmatic of other existential concerns.

At the time of Bassani's imprisonment in 1939, Rodolfo Morandi (1902–55) was already an established scholar. One of the books Gramsci read at Turi in the early 1930s was Morandi's *Storia della grande industria in Italia* (The History of Heavy Industry in Italy).[77] It is not with this book, however, but with his *Lettere al fratello, 1937–1943* (Letters to his Brother, 1937–1943) that Morandi enters the history of prison writing. First published by Einaudi as volume three of this author's opera omnia, Morandi's *Lettere al fratello* documents a crucial phase in his reflections on the social and intellectual history of his country.

Unlike Levi or Bassani, who spent only a few months in prison, Morandi – who was also associated with Giustizia e Libertà and later became a leader of the Socialist party – was confined for the six years from 1937 until 1943. Freed at the end of the war, he played a major role in the Resistance, serving as President of the Committee of National Liberation for Northern Italy (CLNAI). In the postwar period he was appointed Minister for Industry and Commerce and contributed to such initiatives of those years as the establishment of the Istituto per lo Sviluppo del Mezzogiorno. Morandi's other scholarly writings, all of which were published by Einaudi, include *La democrazia del socialismo (1923–1937)* (The Democracy of Socialism [1923–1937]), *Lotta di popolo (1937–1945)*

(The People's Struggle [1937–1945]), *Democrazia diretta e ricostruzione capitalistica (1945–1948)* (Direct Democracy and Capitalist Reconstruction [1945–1948]), and *Il Partito e la classe (1948–1955)* (The Party and Class [1948–1955]).

Perhaps because they are written to his brother rather than to a mother, wife, daughter, or sweetheart, Morandi's prison *Lettere al fratello* contain little of an intimate nature. Apprehensive, perhaps, about the power of the censor to mutilate or stop his correspondence, in his letters Morandi is careful to avoid controversial topics. He does take fire, however, when describing the Crocean philosophy that dominated Italian intellectual life in his pre-prison years, a school of thought he now finds not only passé but pernicious. 'These virtuous contemporary currents that are the miserable drippings of the great systematic philosophies that flowered within the bosom of German culture during the last century,' he says in regard to the Italian idealist school, which included Fascist Party member Giovanni Gentile (1875–1944) as well as Croce, 'find it easy to throw dust in a neophyte's eyes thanks to their universalistic sententiousness. Lacking any restraints of their own, in their immodesty they depress rather than stimulate a thinker's critical sense and dissolve cosmic reality into their formulas, emptying it of any concrete content and depriving it of any positive determination.'[78]

Even from prison Morandi could see that the end not only of Croceanism but of the war and of Fascism was fast approaching. In the passage quoted at the beginning of this section, he describes the old political, social, and philosophical structures as a building ready to collapse. 'But you see,' he writes his brother in an apocalyptic vein spurred by the events of July 1940, 'upheavals and extreme situations are necessary; it is necessary to experience disaster to the limit and maintain a firm point of view – at least if we are to persevere in such dispositions – to find the energy necessary to free us from a state made possible initially by a too frequent lack of control and introspective vigilance and that laziness later allowed to put down roots' (120). Although Morandi is not an elegant prose stylist in the manner of Monti, Levi, or Bassani, this passage indicates how clearly he and other members of his generation perceived that a new order was dawning, one that would require new men and women for its implementation. For Morandi, prison has been a decisive moment both politically and intellectually, a moment of secular conversion.

This theme of conversion while in prison, with its repudiation of an old life and embrace of a new one, is central to the letters of Mario Alicata.

Born in 1918, Alicata is the youngest of the prison writers treated here. Incarcerated in Rome from 29 December 1942, until the city's liberation in August 1943, he spent much less time in prison than did Morandi, though under more dangerous circumstances. What confinement meant to Alicata can be summed up in a phrase he wrote in a clandestine letter to his wife from Regina Coeli. In this letter the young prisoner proclaims that 'while imprisoned here I have *truly* become a *Communist: humanly, morally* above all – something that I had yet to accomplish earlier.'[79] Just as was the case for prisoners more than a century earlier in the Spielberg, prison, for Alicata, has been a life-changing spiritual experience.

Alicata's stay in Regina Coeli involved considerable physical danger. This is a new element in prison writing that should probably be ascribed to the wartime circumstances of his incarceration. For the first time since the days of the Martyrs of Mantua, in the texts themselves of Alicata's letters there is evidence of beatings, extra-textual activities whose existence is deducible, as his editor points out, 'not only from the context, but also from the handwriting of the original, which is different from usual and very confused' (43).

Of admirable clarity when not written after physical abuse, Alicata's prison texts are little given to the flashes of humour that enliven much of Carlo Levi's and Augusto Monti's prison writing. In confinement, this student of Italian literature and contemporary cinema spent much of his time meditating on what seemed to him life's most significant values. In a phrase that echoes Anna Kuliscioff's metaphor of imprisonment as 'a great washing out of the soul done in solitude,' he maintains that confinement has involved him in a 'intimate cleansing' (27).[80] There was nothing mystical or confessional about Alicata's mental exercises, however. 'I less and less understand the many illustrious individuals who let themselves be overwhelmed in prison by "crises" of renunciatory mysticism,' he writes about his own mental progress, 'who when they found themselves in the same or almost the same position as the anchorites of the Thebaid, felt compelled to make the same vow of self-denial. For me, by contrast, each day in prison gives rise to an increase in my joyous faith in life – a faith that is limpid, solid, and concrete; and makes me believe more and more in a "humanity" that involves working and constructing with hope and faith in oneself and in others' (56). For Alicata, the cleansing his soul has received in prison has readied him not for further contemplation but for action. The story Alicata tells in his *Lettere e taccuini di Regina Coeli* is the old one of conversion and the convert's arrival at a new and superior emotional status. The commitment this prisoner has made, however, is not to a confessional faith of the usual sort but to the cause of revolutionary Communism. In this way his book reiterates the story of *Le mie prigioni* but in the spirit of Gramsci's *Lettere dal carcere*.

In the letters of each of these four intellectuals, especially when read after they had become well-known figures on the postwar Italian cultural scene, prison seems, however prolonged as in the case of Morandi, or painful, as it was for Alicata, an almost obligatory stopping-point on the way to a position of cultural prominence. In Levi's writing one thus finds a portrait of a polymath for whom painting is of supreme importance, in Bassani's the themes that will later be part of his fiction, in Morandi's a break with outmoded philosophical interests, and in Alicata's a description of his definitive embrace of a revolutionary political cause. For none of these writers, with the possible exception of Morandi, did prison function as the excruciating test of one's personal strength and intellectual commitments to the extent that it did for Gramsci who, none the less and after the fact, was part of the inspiration for the publication if not the writing of these documents.

> It seems to me that all of life is a struggle to adapt to the environment but also and especially to dominate it and not let it crush you. [81]

The best-known and most widely read today of any Italian prison writing including Pellico's, as well as the catalyst for the many anti-Fascist prison testimonials that followed, Antonio Gramsci's *Lettere dal carcere* are a moving account of a physically frail but morally strong individual's gradual annihilation by overwhelming material circumstances. Despite the lethal consequences of Fascist jail for Gramsci, however, it must be said that his imprisonment itself was not as objectively harsh as that endured, for example, by Pellico, Maroncelli, Confalonieri, and the others in the Spielberg's 'carcere duro.' Not only was he not chained to the wall or to other convicts during his imprisonment, the institution where the Communist leader spent most of his confinement boasted a doctor and an infirmary. Compared to the black bread and foul soup provided in Moravia a century earlier, the diet at Turi was reasonably nourishing and could be supplemented with purchases from the prison commissary. Italian prisoners of the 1920s and 1930s, moreover, were allowed both to write and to receive letters, a privilege, as has been seen, that was available to the Spielberg inmates only in special, administratively defined, emergencies. Furthermore, while in prison Gramsci was allowed to receive books and journals and to take notes on his reading. The Communist deputy, however, although only thirty-five years old when arrested, simply did not have a physical constitution robust enough to survive what in his case were the extremely trying and ultimately fatal conditions in which he served his sentence. During his confinement Gramsci suffered from several serious ailments that received virtually no medical attention but instead were exacerbated by the prison environment. If Mussolini's purpose in incarcerating his political opponent was to keep Gramsci's mind from functioning, as Isgrò had said, the Duce succeeded only by breaking his body first. Gramsci's struggle to prevent his spirit from snapping while his fragile nervous system slowly crumbled is a central theme of the *Lettere dal carcere*, a constant preoccupation of this prisoner from the beginning to the tragic end of his correspondence.

When the Fascist police arrested newly elected member of parliament Antonio Gramsci on 8 November 1926, they knew they had collared a dangerous adversary. Although Gramsci was born in extremely straitened economic and cultural circumstances in provincial Sardinia, his native intelligence, determination, and the broader experiences he gleaned in the more sophisticated political and intellectual circles of turn-of-the-century Turin had helped him mature into a powerful and original thinker respected both in Italy and abroad. A founder of *Ordine nuovo* and one of the instigators of the breakaway from the Italian Socialist Party that led to the establishment of the Italian Communist Party in 1921, by the following year Gramsci was a delegate to the Fourth Congress of the Communist International and a member of that organization's executive committee. In 1924, when he was elected to the Italian Parliament, he was made general secretary of the party.

After his arrest, Gramsci was held in the same Regina Coeli prison in the capital city that in later years would house De Gasperi, Alicata, and other anti-Fascists. Tried in Rome with other opponents of the regime including fellow Communists Lo Sardo and Terracini, Gramsci, notwithstanding his parliamentary immunity, was sentenced by the special tribunal to twenty years, four months, and five days in prison. Most of this sentence was served at the same Turi institution for prisoners in poor health where Lo Sardo was also confined. While at Turi Gramsci suffered from chronic uremia, persistent insomnia, and a number of other ailments, including Pott's disease afflicting his spine. In 1934, when he was finally transferred to a clinic after some eight years in painful confinement, it was too late. On 25 April 1937, the ex-prisoner suffered a stroke his wasted organism was too weak to withstand; he died two days later.

Although Gramsci had played a crucial role in formulating policy and establishing strategy for the party before 1926, his imprisonment prevented him from taking part in any further activities of this sort.[82] His absence from the political fray came at a crucial time for the Communist movement throughout the world. The years Gramsci spent in confinement were those not only of the Wall Street crash and Great Depression, but also of the Stalin-inspired *svolta* in party policy mentioned in the section of this chapter concerning Terracini. This change in policy, as has already been noted, involved abandoning cooperation with other anti-Fascist forces, condemning the Socialists as 'Social Fascists,' and proclaiming – despite all signs to the contrary, at least in Italy – that a worldwide revolution was at hand. What views Gramsci held in prison about these matters – or what opinions he might have formulated had he not been confined and, consequently, how Italian Communist policy might have been different had Gramsci spent these crucial years in Paris, say, rather than in Turi – all this has been a matter for considerable conjecture.[83] What is clear is that during the years of Stalin's domination of the Comintern, Gramsci's forced silence made his position very different not only from that of his comrades in Paris but also from that of either Terracini or Ravera, both of whom were able, even though in the very limited ways described above, to express their political views to the party's Central Committee in exile.

Like many of the other political prisoners whose writings have been studied here, Gramsci struggled in confinement to continue to engage in the activities that had always defined him as a person and a political militant. Though he soon discovered it was more difficult than he had anticipated to read and write effectively in confinement, Gramsci was just as determined to keep his brain functioning as the Fascists were to shut down that organ's operations. For Gramsci, therefore, it was essential that he continue the analysis of contemporary history and its antecedents that had always been at the centre of his intellectual activities. Although masked for his jailers as idle erudition or benign literary speculation without apparent political significance,[84] Gramsci's prison studies continued to focus on such issues as the relations between intellectuals and power and the influence of political domination on cultural production, considerations that since his time have proved extremely fruitful in Marxist thought everywhere. Like Luigi Pastro worrying over his acrostic sonnets nearly a century earlier in Mantua, Gramsci was determined to thwart and defy the forces that were imprisoning him. Unlike Pastro, however, he was not able to publish what he wrote while he was still in confinement, his immensely influential writings reaching their eventual audience only well after their author's death.

While Gramsci's prison writings, the thirty-two notebooks of the *Quaderni del carcere* in particular, can be adduced as proof of his posthumous triumph over the forces imprisoning him, the story told by his nearly five hundred prison letters is a much more sombre one.[85] 'Taken all together, in the rhythm of captivity that they mark,' an Italian historian has commented about these writings, 'they are a story whose tragic nature slowly takes shape and then culminates in a kind of farewell to life that is noticeable in the rapid, solemn notes sent to his distant sons in 1936. The reader enters a tunnel and, the more he proceeds into it, the weaker the light at the end becomes until it finally is extinguished.'[86] Unlike most of the prison writing that has been considered in this study, Gramsci's letters tell a story that does not culminate in the happy dénouement of their author's liberation.[87] In their requiem-like final pages, instead, the ineluctability of their author's approaching demise becomes apparent as the writing voice weakens and the author too begins to acknowledge what his posthumous readers have known all along: at the end of this volume lies not freedom but death.

To a greater degree than for those of any other prisoner examined in this study, the letters Gramsci wrote in confinement were read even in the first instances by an unusually large and heterogeneous audience. Principal among Gramsci's first readers was, of course, the prison censor.[88] The censor intervened into Gramsci's correspondence in two ways. In addition to obliterating whatever he deemed offensive or forbidden – and, compared to those of other prisoners, Gramsci's letters contained relatively little material of this sort – the censor also made copies of these prison missives that he then forwarded to Rome for further scrutiny. There, according to one account, Gramsci's mail was not only regularly monitored by the OVRA, but read with interest by Mussolini himself.[89] The very first readers of Gramsci's prison letters were thus not the acknowledged, loving recipients to whom they were addressed, nor the often ignorant and sometimes bored prison functionaries who typically reviewed other prisoners' correspondence, but attentive representatives of the forces Gramsci had spent his life combatting, who were now determined to maintain their psychological as well as their physical ascendancy over him.

In compliance with prison regulations of this period, all of Gramsci's correspondence in or out of prison was exclusively with family members. The principal recipient of his letters was not his wife, mother, or other immediate relative but his sister-in-law, Tatiana Schucht. A Soviet citizen temporarily resident in Italy while the rest of her family, including Gramsci's wife, Giulia, were living in the Soviet Union, Tatiana was a faithful intermediary between Giulia and her imprisoned brother-in-law. Besides writing hundreds of letters and postcards to him, paying him visits when she could, and seeing generally to his needs, Tatiana also forwarded Gramsci's mail to her sister in Moscow. Just as the censor had done for different purposes, Tatiana too made copies of Gramsci's letters. She sent these copies to England, where Piero Sraffa, an economist who had been a friend of Gramsci's from *Ordine nuovo* days, held a position at King's College, Cambridge. Sraffa, who had been nominated to his Cambridge post by John Maynard Keynes, shared many of Gramsci's intellectual interests and political convictions.[90] In Cambridge he was able to serve as intermediary between Gramsci and the party's Central Committee in Paris. In addition to supplying Togliatti and the others in that city with Tatiana's copies of Gramsci's letters, Sraffa made frequent stops in the French capital on his way to and from Italy; during these sojourns he was able to consult directly with the party hierarchy about his imprisoned friend.[91]

Gramsci's letters, then, were read both in Rome by the Fascist police and in Paris by his Communist comrades. His letters to Moscow, in addition, were almost certainly monitored by political police in that city.[92] In Moscow, Giulia Schucht's letters to her husband, in turn, were posted in at least some cases at what their author described as a 'certain office' – presumably that of the Soviet police – and upon arrival in Italy were read again by Italian authorities before being consigned to their eventual recipient. It is only when we turn to the letters that Gramsci wrote his family in Sardinia that we find documents that seem to have followed a relatively linear trajectory – though here again, for convenience's sake, many of these were sent through Tatiana, duly copied for Sraffa, and so on. And these letters, too, were of course read by the Italian prison authorities and forwarded to higher authorities in Rome.

The recipients of Gramsci's letters, then, included people their author trusted (though less and less as his sentence wore on, his health worsened, and his nerves became more and more frayed), others such as the OVRA and Mussolini that he detested, and still others such as the PCI and the forces in Moscow he was not always sure were on his side or not. In all the letters he wrote in prison, Gramsci was acutely aware of the many different readers he was addressing and as a result was extremely circumspect about what he said and how he expressed himself. Furthermore, while some of this prisoner's correspondents – Sraffa and the party intellectuals in Paris, for example – shared Gramsci's intellectual and political outlook, others – his mother and other family members, sometimes Tatiana, certainly Giulia – were much less culturally and politically sophisticated. For such readers, even while seeking to unburden himself of his feelings, Gramsci was careful to do so in terms his correspondents would understand. In all of his prison communications, Gramsci was an unusually self-conscious writer and, in more senses than one, an exceptionally guarded correspondent.

Gramsci's mother was perhaps the easiest person for him to write to: the one he knew best and trusted most. At the same time, Peppina Gramsci did not share or comprehend Gramsci's political views to nearly the degree Elide Rossi or Adelaide Turati did those of their sons. In one of the first communications Gramsci wrote from prison, for example, he is at pains to reassure his mother that his arrest and confinement are not a dishonour for him or his relatives. 'My honour and my rectitude are not at all in question,' he explains in a gesture that Filippo Turati or Ernesto Rossi would have found unnecessary, 'I'm in prison for political reasons, not for reasons of honour' (I: 90). Like such other anti-Fascist prisoners as Augusto Monti, Gramsci considered prison the result of a conscious choice, resulting from a line of action he had elected to follow, rather than something imposed on him from without; he was not ashamed of where he was, though at the same time he was not proud of it either. He worried, furthermore, about the suffering he might be causing his family. 'I would really like to embrace you and hold you tight,' he writes his mother in a passage in which notions of personal honour similar to those articulated by Lo Sardo are evoked as the prisoner describes 'the sorrow that I've caused you,' then explains that 'I could not have acted otherwise.' 'Life is like that, very hard,' Gramsci goes on, 'and sometimes sons must be the cause of great sorrow for their mothers if they wish to preserve their honour and their dignity as men' (I: 206). For Gramsci, Peppina had always been the steel against which his own flinty nature could strike sparks of comprehension. 'As with flint,' he writes her, 'only the sharp impact of steel can draw sparks from me. But you, along with very few other people, certainly have this steel-like power: I give you a warm embrace' (I: 191). Even if this writer and his mother did not share a common political or ideological perspective, at a deeper level they were as much a pair as flint and steel.

The affinity Gramsci felt for Piero Sraffa was of a different sort. One of the few among Gramsci's correspondents who might be considered his intellectual equal, Sraffa did all he could to support his imprisoned friend, setting up an open-ended account for him with a Milanese bookseller, writing him through Tatiana (as a non-relative, Sraffa was not permitted to write Gramsci directly), and struggling generally to keep the prisoner mentally alive. In 1932, for example, Sraffa suggested that Gramsci write a review of the freshly published *Storia d'Europa nel secolo XIX* (*History of Europe in the Nineteenth Century*) by Benedetto Croce. Earlier he had urged him to develop his thoughts about interpretations of canto 10 of Dante's *Inferno* for another paper that might be published from prison.[93] A number of the topics that are treated in Gramsci's letters to Tatiana – that of anti-Semitism in contemporary Italy, for example – were in reality debates at one remove with Sraffa, who Gramsci knew was receiving copies of what he wrote his sister-in-law. Sraffa's role in his correspondence with Gramsci, in fact, may be compared to that of a therapist who moves the arms and legs of a coma-stricken patient in order to keep the sick person's essential functions operating – except that in Gramsci's case it was his intellect and critical imagination that were in danger of atrophying.[94]

Unlike Sraffa, and for reasons that are still mysterious, Giulia Schucht Gramsci was unable to provide her imprisoned husband with much support of either an intellectual or an emotional sort. Her surviving letters to her husband are few, brief, and fragmentary.[95] While at least some of what she wrote to her husband has been lost or is otherwise unavailable,[96] Giulia Schucht's letters, it must be said, stand up poorly when compared to what other prisoners received in confinement from their closest relatives. Perhaps Giulia was so inhibited by the malicious scrutiny she knew her correspondence with her husband was receiving that she was too emotionally frozen to send even the most banal news through such a complex and hostile gauntlet. Certainly she was herself in poor health during the years of her husband's incarceration.[97] 'If Giulia doesn't write,' her father in Moscow told Tatiana in a communication he knew would be passed on to the prisoner, 'it means that she finds it difficult to do so, it means that she is unable to write.'[98]

But with Giulia unable for whatever reasons to write freely, Gramsci found it increasingly difficult, as he put it, 'to cast stones into the darkness' in futile attempts to communicate. 'Ordinarily,' he explained to Tatiana in 1930, 'I need to set out from a dialogical or dialectical standpoint, otherwise I don't experience any intellectual stimulation ... in my family relations too I wish to carry on dialogues, otherwise it would seem to me that I'm writing a novel in epistolary form, who knows what, that

I'm turning out bad literature' (I: 369). Without a true correspondent, without some sort of dialectical relationship between their author and a recipient, Gramsci was afraid his letters would become little more than outpourings of his own self-absorbed emotions – the equivalent of 'bad literature.' For this Marxist thinker, love too needed to be grounded in what he called 'praxis' – the concrete struggle for human betterment without which all ideas must founder in sterile emotionality.[99]

As suggested earlier, the one correspondent with whom Gramsci had a practical, everyday relationship was Tatiana. As had been the case of Felicetta Ulisse for Silvio Spaventa, Tatiana Schucht was not someone Gramsci knew well before his confinement. During his years in prison, however, she gave up most of her private life in order to look after him. Schucht's sacrifice for the sake of her brother-in-law has led one critic to characterize her as an Antigone to Gramsci's Polyneices (with Mussolini the presumed Creon). Like Antigone, Tatiana Schucht succeeded in seeing that her loved one was buried with suitable honours – the honours in this case being her rescue of the manuscripts of Gramsci's notebooks from the hands of the Fascist police after their author's death in 1937.[100] 'Without her,' Aldo Natoli sums up his view of Tatiana, 'Gramsci would not have lasted ten years in prison.'[101]

But having Tatiana as his principal contact with the world created additional problems for the prisoner. In particular, Gramsci was concerned that his sister-in-law not become a surrogate for his wife, especially in her own mind. 'But these,' he warns in 1932 about issues that had arisen in the course of their epistolary relationship, 'are not matters where one person can replace another and what's more, the matter is very very complicated and difficult to explain completely (also because of the walls that are not metaphorical)' (I: 331). Not only was it necessary for Gramsci to control what he called the 'epistolary Pirandelloism' of this situation (I: 220), he needed to do so in such a way as not to provide the censor and his other enemies an opportunity to gloat at his predicament. In addition, while Gramsci's frequent outbursts of exasperation with Tatiana were no doubt part of his general frustration and the result of his physically and emotionally draining maladies, there were also fundamental differences in intellectual outlook and character between the two.[102]

Gramsci, then, was not only physically isolated from the family members he corresponded with from prison; he was isolated from them emotionally as well. With none of them could he communicate with the ease and familiarity of Andrea Costa in his letters to Anna Kuliscioff or of

Filippo Turati or Ernesto Rossi in their correspondence with their mothers – though none of these writings, admittedly, had to pass through the hostile and complex monitoring system to which Gramsci's prison texts were subject. Although he tried to maintain a serene tone in all that he wrote from his prison cell, as his term wore on Gramsci became increasingly irritated with his correspondents. Some of this had to do with the difficulties he experienced in accomplishing scholarly projects in prison. Even at the beginning of his confinement Gramsci had noted how 'it is very difficult for me to become completely absorbed in a train of thought or subject and delve into it alone, as one does when one studies seriously, so as to grasp all possible relationships and connect them harmoniously' (I: 112). In later years this sense of dissatisfaction with his work grew; as it did, Gramsci felt diminished as a man. In an attempt in 1932 to describe his condition, he compared himself to a Prometheus unable to struggle with the other gods on Olympus because he was tied down by Lilliputians – a Gulliver whose liver is devoured by ants instead of by an eagle the way his classical counterpart's had been. Such a figure, Gramsci notes, is risible rather than tragic. 'Jove,' he concludes about the difference between Prometheus' ancient torture and the more sophisticated procedures used on modern prisoners, 'in his day was not very intelligent; the technique for getting rid of one's opponents was not yet very developed' (II: 129).

Fairly or unfairly, Gramsci attributed some of the powerlessness he felt in prison to the maladroit efforts of his friends to support him there. He was particularly irritated when they did not respect his explicit requests or injunctions. 'I'm subject to various prison regimes,' he told Tatiana sternly. 'There is the prison regime constituted by the four walls, the bars on the window, the spy hole on the door, etc. etc.; this had already been taken into account by me and as a subordinate probability, because the primary probability from 1921 to November 1926 was not prison but losing my life. What had not been included in my evaluation was the other prison, which is added to the first and is constituted by being cut off not only from social life but also from family life etc. etc.' (I: 331). The 'prison within a prison' that Terracini had worried about during his captivity[103] had become a reality for Gramsci.

From the beginning, Gramsci was sharply aware of the effects of prison constraint on the way he expressed himself from confinement. In an early letter written on the island of Ustica, where he had been sent before being consigned to prison proper, Gramsci complained already in a burst of self-irony that his epistolary style had become that of a 'bureaucrat' or a 'sacristan' (I: 40). Later he notes that while he might have liked to write passion-filled letters to his wife, it was simply impossible for him to do so. 'I could of course write them in all sincerity,' he says about letters of this sort, 'but I don't want to; my letters are "public," not restricted to the two of us, and the awareness of this inevitably forces me to curb the explosion of my feelings insofar as they are expressed by the words written in these letters' (II: 111). For Gramsci, as for many other prisoners whose work has been reviewed here, beneath the ostensible message of what he writes from prison lies a hidden text of inexpressible desire that the conditions of his confinement prevent him from articulating. And unlike many of the other prisoners whose work has been studied here, Gramsci wrote nothing clandestine from prison.

Especially towards the end of his ordeal, Gramsci found it difficult to write to anyone, especially Giulia. 'Every one of my letters,' he explained to Tatiana, 'is the result of a complex series of efforts of the will and acts of self-control that cannot help but come together in a form that seems ridiculous even to me' (II: 241). For this one-time student of linguistics, the gap between what he wanted to say and the words he was able to produce had become unbridgeable. 'I'm always obsessed by the thought of being reduced to conventional epistolography,' he wrote about this in 1927, 'and, what is worse than conventionality, to a conventionally prison epistolography' (I: 109).[104] Although Gramsci was determined not to be trapped by the commonplaces of the tradition of prison writing as it had developed over the centuries, he found that language itself had become a prison for him. 'It seems to me that if I were to express all that I wish,' he wrote Giulia in 1929, 'I would be unable to go beyond a certain conventionalism and a certain melodramatic tone, which is almost incorporated in traditional language. The selfsame professional study that I've made of the technical forms of language obsesses me, setting before me again all my utterances in fossilized and ossified forms that arouse my repugnance' (I: 247). Gramsci's letters, despite their author's own misgivings about them, are frequently considered models of clarity, admirable for their delicacy of expression. Gramsci, however, was disgusted by their conventionality and convinced of their inadequacy as a vehicle for his thoughts and emotions.

Nowhere is Gramsci's sense of language's shortcomings more acute than in the communications with his sons that appear in the final pages of his prison correspondence. Just as this prisoner was determined while in jail to maintain his identity as a revolutionary intellectual, so too he wanted to remain a father – even though this meant he would have to invent a relationship with his children by means of letters dispatched to them across immense barriers of time, space, and cultural and linguistic difference. During what he called 'a phase of my life that without exaggeration I can define as catastrophic' (II: 270), Gramsci wrote Tatiana in 1933, 'I assure you that what still gives me a bit of strength is the thought that I have certain responsibilities toward Julca and the children: otherwise I wouldn't even put up a fight, living has become so burdensome and odious to me' (II: 270–1). But unlike Luigi Settembrini, who was able from Santo Stefano to continue to exercise his paternal authority in regard to Gigia and his family in Naples, there was little Gramsci could do for his wife and family in Moscow. 'I feel my inability to do anything real and effective to help you,' he wrote her in 1931; 'I am torn between a feeling of immense tenderness for you who appear to me as a weakness that must immediately be comforted with a physical caress, and a feeling that a great effort of will is necessary on my part to persuade you from afar, with cold and colorless words, that you are nevertheless strong too and that you can and must overcome this crisis' (II: 11). In the end, he realized that it was too late. 'I should have been the one to help you know yourself better, to overcome these contradictions,' he wrote in 1932. 'Ah well! I often think about all the things that I could have and should have done and have not done' (II: 235).

Imprisoned by the Fascists for his political activities, in the end Gramsci was destroyed not so much in his public persona as in his private identity as husband and father. Through the *Quaderni del carcere* his legacy as a thinker survives his imprisonment. The letters he wrote to his family, however, despite their author's desperate efforts to the contrary, do not seem to have had much real effect on the lives of their intended recipients, and this wore heavily on him in the final years of his captivity. Unlike De Gasperi, Gramsci did not believe that he would ever be recompensed – either in this life or afterwards – for his suffering. Nor did he think that his death would help the Communist cause or that his detention was a means for him to take a public position from which he could derive moral satisfaction. He simply thought that the Fascists were killing him. Slowly and painfully. He was right.

The eleven anti-Fascist letter writers who have been considered in this chapter were jailed for periods that ranged from a few weeks for Bassani to nearly two decades for Terracini. This variety of their experiences makes them, when considered as a group, not unlike the Italian patriots of a century earlier. The anti-Fascist prisoners from the 1920s and 1930s, however, lived in an environment much more saturated with information than their Risorgimento counterparts. Because of the greater availability to them – both while in confinement (usually) and before – of texts of all sorts including prison texts, these writers were even more aware than earlier authors of the links between their predicaments and those of celebrated political prisoners of the past. Pellico, especially, continued to be a point of reference, even for those who detested him. *Le mie prigioni*, however, was only one of several descriptions of prison life through whose mediation these later authors attempted to comprehend and then describe their plights. Both the imprisoned Ernesto Rossi, for example, and his mother on the outside read the work of such Risorgimento writers as Orsini, Settembrini, and even the less-known Andryane and Arrivabene. Gramsci was fascinated by whether and under what circumstances Federico Confalonieri had petitioned Emperor Francis I for pardon more than a century earlier – partly because he faced an analogous dilemma. And in his attempts to make sense of his *carcer tetro* (dreary prison), the deeply and eclectically read Carlo Levi consulted a wide group of earlier writers that included such different historical figures as Cellini, Tibullus, and Giovita Scalvini. Even the questioning title of Levi's book is an implicit measuring of his ordeal against those of his predecessors.

Whether or not these anti-Fascist authors knew of specific writings by this or that earlier prisoner, they often reiterate responses to prison articulated earlier by others. The Turinese schoolteacher Augusto Monti's insistence, for example, that his personal ordeal was only one part of his country's suffering mirrors sentiments expressed by the Neapolitan nun Enrichetta Caracciolo nearly a century earlier. On the situational level, the remarkable support Elide Rossi provided her son in a Fascist prison recalls earlier efforts by Anna Filippini Poma and Adelaide Turati in Risorgimento Mantua and turn-of-the-century Turin. Likewise, the alleviation of Giorgio Bassani's dismay in a Ferrara prison thanks to contact with his family recalls comparable reactions by Poma and Tazzoli in nearby Mantua in the 1850s. Terracini's and Ravera's gleeful defiance of the prison censor, moreover, through the ingenious systems for clandestine communications they devised recalls Luigi Pastro's delight in the acrostic sonnets that he wrote 'in Culoz's face.' Finally, the conversion narratives proposed by the secular writers Alicata, Morandi, and Lo Sardo link their prison writing to that of the ubiquitous Pellico. But even though tied to previous texts in the history of prison writing in these ways, the letters by these anti-Fascist prisoners were not attempts to rewrite, much less correct, a collectively produced historical record the way the frequently contentious memoirs of the Spielberg group were. On the contrary, these men and women believed that they were expanding the canon of prison writing for future readers at the same time as they drew support in their own mental and physical struggles from the examples of earlier patriots. This was true even when these forebears did not share their precise political ideologies; it sufficed for the later prisoners that they had struggled in similar circumstances against political oppression. More than ever before in the history of prison writing, these authors felt that they were part of an important continuum of dissent and writing that extended back to the beginnings of the modern Italian nation.

Even though private documents that could be addressed (at least initially) only to members of their authors' families, these letters by Mussolini's prisoners tended as never before to be composed with posterity as well as more immediate recipients in mind. Such documents did not reach this broader public, however, until well after the experiences described in them had become part of Italy's official history and the sentiments articulated in them part of a common national consensus. As has already been indicated, Gramsci's *Lettere dal carcere* did not become available to a mass public until more than two decades after he began to write them in 1926. The letters of Terracini, Ravera, Monti, and Bassani were not released for publication until more than forty years after their authors began their respective detentions, while Lo Sardo's and Levi's works came out nearly half a century after their composition.

One important result of this delay between composition and publication was that when these texts did reach a mass public, they were received in an entirely different political and intellectual climate than that prevailing at the time of their composition. This attached an additional level of significance to them, a further, deferred meaning. Unlike such turn-of-the-century memoirs as those by Pastro, Castromediano, and Rosa with their retrospective views of events of half a century or more earlier, the prison letters by the anti-Fascist activists are documents that belong both to the era in which they were written – the twenty-year duration of Italian Fascism – and to the subsequent and officially anti-Fascist period of the first Italian republic. The paratextual prefaces, notes, explanations, editorial introductions, drawings, photographs, and so on that typically accompany these works accentuate this dual perspective. On the one hand, such texts are clearly testimony of a very immediate sort of a painful struggle against a still prevailing Fascism. But they are also cultural products of a period when opinions that had once been held by a minority and indeed considered subversive had become widely and certainly officially shared. The dual perspective proposed by these publications is particularly evident in Monti's letters, for example, in which passages originally obliterated by the censor (and that their original recipients thus could not read) have, some forty years later, been restored by the ex-prisoner and now editor of his own work. But even without such restoration of originally suppressed passages, all the published letters of these prisoners demand to be read from this double perspective. As bearers of an important deferred meaning of this sort, they are unique in the history of prison writing.[105]

This issue of deferred meaning becomes even more complex in the case of Gramsci's letters. In the abridged, Togliatti-Platone edition of 1947, the Communist leader's *Lettere dal carcere* had been purged of any references by their author to such out-of-favour historical figures as Leon Trotsky or Amadeo Bordiga (1889–1970), a founder of the Italian Communist Party expelled from membership in 1930. It was only with the later, more comprehensive, and philologically rigorous 1965 edition of Gramsci's letters that these references have been restored.[106] In their second edition, therefore, Gramsci's *Lettere dal carcere* can be said to provide a further level of deferred meaning, an additional significance that only after 1965 had become evident to post-Cold War readers. As Gramsci's case reminds us, beyond the censoring, the self-censoring, the construction of both writer and reader on the part of their author – beyond all the other factors conditioning and constraining expression of prison letter writers – when the texts they compose in confinement come to be disseminated to a mass public by what are always more or less disinterested third parties, additional constraints are brought into play. Nowhere is this problem of the reception – arguably the manipulated reception – of prison writings more evident and at such issue in determining the meaning that should be assigned to documents of this sort than in the case of the letters Aldo Moro wrote from prison. So much so that these texts were and still are viewed by many only within quotation marks as the 'letters' that 'Aldo Moro' 'wrote' from 'prison.'

6

The Death of a President / The Effacement of an Author

But when political crimes become confused with ordinary crimes is when these innovators in the theoretical field, which can be surveyed by anyone with a healthy mind, think that they can descend to practical matters and decide, as we have seen, to reach their goals by *any means*, including theft and murder. This, in other words, is because they believe that by killing a few, often entirely innocent victims (something that of course creates a violent reaction in everyone), they can obtain the support that their leaflets and speeches could not produce. Here crime and absurdity are wedded and reduplicated and if a goal is reached, it is the opposite of that which these individuals had set themselves in that they create unpopularity below and the disgust of the wise above.[1]

Shortly after nine o'clock on Thursday morning, 16 March 1978, Member of Parliament Aldo Moro (1916–78), president of Italy's Christian Democrat Party and five-time past president of the country's Council of Ministers – that is, prime minister of Italy – was on his way to church before continuing to a meeting of the Chamber of Deputies.[2] At Palazzo Montecitorio in the centre of Rome that morning a new government was to be presented to the Italian Parliament: an array of Christian Democrat ministers that for the first time since the end of the war had the support of the Italian Communist Party in a 'historic compromise' laboriously brokered by Moro himself.[3] While proceeding along the Via Mario Fani towards the neighbourhood church of Santa Chiara a good distance from the centre of the city, however, Moro's two-car motorcade was forcibly halted by a group of terrorists from the Red Brigades extraparliamentary political organization. Carrying out their attack with dispatch and precision, Brigade members rushed the stalled automobiles, killed all five of

Moro's bodyguards, and sped off with their hostage. Thus began what was not the first nor would be the last but was certainly the most disquieting episode in the ten and more years of political terror in the streets of Italy that came to be known as the 'anni di piombo.'

The 'years of lead' had commenced a decade earlier with the explosion of a neo-Fascist bomb in a bank lobby in Piazza Fontana in downtown Milan. In the resulting carnage sixteen people lost their lives, and more than ninety were wounded. This opening salvo in a war waged against the state by extremist groups from both the political right and left would be echoed by bombings of trains, train stations, and other places of public gathering by right-wing groups; by abductions and shootings of individuals deemed 'enemies of the people' by factions on the left; and by additional widespread violence directed at both persons and property by forces emanating from both ends of the political spectrum.[4]

During the fifty-five days the Red Brigades held him captive, Aldo Moro wrote, as his principal jailer and eventual executioner would testify later, 'constantly.'[5] The texts Moro produced in the makeshift prison on Rome's Via Montalcini where he was held included letters composed at his own initiative directed to his family and prominent political figures, plus a *memoriale* (political memoir) set down at his captors' prodding. In the latter document, a rambling, occasionally incoherent series of personal and political reminiscences, Moro set out his views on the political events of the past thirty years, a period when his party had held power without interruption. In addition to the public texts that appeared in the press during Moro's captivity and his private communications to his family, which can now be read in Aldo Moro, *L'intelligenza e gli avvenimenti, testi 1959–1978*, published by the Fondazione Aldo Moro, other documents have since come to light. During their search in 1978 of a Red Brigades hideout on the Via Monte Nevoso in Milan, police investigating Moro's disappearance found an additional cache of materials concerning the politician and his captors, among them a photocopy of the memoir mentioned above. Twelve years later, when the same apartment on Via Monte Nevoso was undergoing routine remodelling, still more photocopied documents by the prisoner that presumably had been overlooked earlier were discovered. This second group of papers included a slightly different version of the 'memoriale' as it had been published after Moro's death in 1978, plus both rough and fair copies of several letters, some previously unknown to the public. All this material was immediately published in photographic reproduction and transcription by the 'Commissione d'inchiesta sul terrorismo in Italia e sulle cause della mancata individuazione dei responsabili delle stragi' of the Italian Parliament.

Despite the unusual nature of Moro's imprisonment, the letters and memoir the Red Brigades' captive wrote in the 'people's prison' belong to the tradition of prison writing that has been analysed in this study.[6] Moro, however, was a different kind of prisoner from the other writers considered here. First and foremost, he was not held by government powers but by irregular forces determined to overthrow the legally constituted state. A hostage, then, who was facing possible execution rather than a long imprisonment, Moro was eager to protract rather than reduce the length of his confinement. The longer he was confined by his captors, the greater the Christian Democrat politician's chances of being rescued or released, and the longer, meanwhile, he stayed alive. While other writers from similar situations typically describe how slowly time is passing for them – Carlo Levi lamenting, for example, that during his stay in a Fascist jail, time, as he had always known it, had been replaced by an eternity of frustrating artistic immobility – for Moro, time was anything but static, racing forward instead at an alarming rate. As he put it in a letter from the beginning of April, 'time runs swiftly and, unfortunately, there is not enough of it.'[7] It was only towards the end of his imprisonment, when he began to understand that his confinement was going to end in death rather than liberation, that Moro began to turn his thoughts from time's velocity to eternity. In his last writings, the desperate pleading of his earlier communications gives way to an elegiac, valedictory tone not unlike that of the prison letters by the Martyrs of Mantua or the weakened Gramsci's final communications with his family from Turi in the 1930s.[8]

The style Aldo Moro had developed for written and oral communication over the course of his long career was scarcely renowned for either its brevity or its linear logic. In the reflections on the Moro case that he published in 1978, the social commentator and novelist Leonardo Sciascia (1921–89) described this politician's habitual mode of communication as a deliberately incomprehensible 'language of incommunicability.' Elaborating on remarks made earlier by the activist film-maker, novelist, poet, and essayist Pier Paolo Pasolini (1922–75), Sciascia argued that Moro's intent in his public pronouncements was not to communicate but to overwhelm his audience. According to Sciascia, the Christian Democrat politician's habitual public discourse was as impenetrable for most of his listeners as the Latin once used by savants to confound and shame the unlettered. In Sciascia's view, therefore, the dilemma that Moro the prisoner faced in pleading for his release in 1978 was that of having to 'try to *say something* in the language of *not-saying*, to *make himself understood* using the same tools that he had adapted and experimented with in order *not to make himself understood.*'[9] For Sciascia, somewhat cruelly perhaps, Moro's predicament was a fit punishment for his past linguistic sins – a 'contrappasso' like those suffered by the inhabitants of Dante's *Inferno*, who find themselves in painful situations they come to realize are of their own devising. While other historians more sympathetic to the Christian Democrat President have defended Moro's style as a subtle and astute tool for dealing effectively with complex issues not susceptible to simple formulation or solution,[10] most observers would agree that there is a gap between the codified, esoteric, and self-conscious language of Moro's prison writings and their desperate project of practical persuasion. This disparity can be seen, for example, in the tortured preamble to one of Moro's first letters from confinement, a plea for help to Francesco Cossiga that begins, 'Dear Francesco, while I send you a dear greeting, I am induced by difficult circumstances to set out before you, bearing in mind your responsibilities (which I obviously respect) a few precise and realistic considerations' (400). In this prologue to his letter to an old friend, the parenthetical qualifications and ponderous restraint seem inappropriate to the urgency of the life-and-death issues the rest of the letter addresses.

Moro himself was aware of the peculiarities of his public style. When it was suggested that the trying experiences of his confinement had made him someone other than his usual self, he pointed to the style of his prison writings as refutation of this charge. 'I have not been subject to coercion of any sort,' he responded in a letter published on 30 April, 'I have not been drugged, I am writing in my usual style (ugly as that may be) and in my usual handwriting.'[11] What Moro himself dubbed the 'ugliness' of his style was, he insisted, a guarantee of the authenticity of his prison enunciations.

The texts Aldo Moro wrote from what he described as the 'complete and uncontrolled dominion' of Red Brigade captivity were produced in conditions of considerable physical hardship.[12] Confined to a tiny area in which he could sleep, wash, and relieve himself, but not walk around or sit anywhere but on the bed that filled most of the soundproof space constructed for him, Moro knew that his life depended on the persuasiveness of the words he was putting on paper. He also knew that what he wrote had to be approved by his captors before it could be forwarded to its intended destination. But if Moro self-censored what he wrote from prison, the Red Brigades, for their part, do not seem to have found it necessary to interfere significantly with the documents he produced there. In an interview with journalists Mosca and Rossanda some fifteen years after Moro's death, the Brigadist principally responsible for the captive's detention and death stated that 'we made public almost everything that he wrote, the few times when this was not the case was when forwarding his letters was extremely risky ... Why should we, moreover, have hidden any letters? What he was asking for was negotiations involving political prisoners, and that was what we wanted too.'[13] Though the whole matter is still somewhat obscure, Moro's captors do not seem to have exercised their powers to censor nearly as much as the surveillants of some of the other prisoners studied here.[14]

Once approved by his captors, Moro's prison letters were not dispatched to their recipients through the regular postal system. The Red Brigades, evidently, had little faith in the inviolability of their country's mail. Instead of consigning Moro's communications to the Italian postal service, they left them for recovery in such locations as telephone booths or public wastebaskets. In the case of letters to members of the government, these locations would then be identified by telephone calls to selected journalists, who, in turn, would deliver the communications to the addressees indicated – but only after turning over what they had found to their papers.[15] Letters to Moro's family, similarly, were also left in public places, which were then identified by telephone. In these instances, friends of the family served the same mediating function as the journalists did for the recipients of Moro's letters to the government – though with the crucial difference that the letters they recovered did not immediately become a part of the public record and apparently were not automatically shared with the police or other investigating authorities.[16]

The letters by the imprisoned President of the Democrazia Cristiana that appeared in the Italian newspapers during the nearly two months his captivity lasted were thus intended – by the Red Brigades, at least, if not by Moro himself, or at least not at first – for the widest possible public consumption.[17] Though all of Moro's letters were 'ostensible' in that they were read and approved by his jailers before being forwarded to their differing destinations, his letters to his family were 'clandestine' in that, once they had passed Red Brigade surveillance, they were not divulged to anyone but their specific addressees.[18] At the conclusion of one such missive, in fact, Moro admonished his wife that 'nothing of what I am writing, of course [should be communicated] to the press or anyone else' (404). Moro's prison correspondence, then, consisted on the one hand of exceptionally public 'ostensible' letters read by millions of newspaper readers, and on the other, of 'clandestine' notes received only by his family and selected intermediaries that were carefully kept from the public spotlight.

In one of the first letters Moro wrote from Via Montalcini he made explicit mention of the 'filo' or communicative thread for clandestine communication he was hoping to 'tie together' with his secretary, Nicola Rana. In this letter Moro explained to Rana that he wanted to keep the thread between them 'secret for as long as possible' and in this way be able to contact friends in power 'without [causing] dangerous discussions' (399). Along with this cover letter to Rana, Moro included a note of Easter greetings to his wife, reassuring Eleonora Moro that his physical condition was satisfactory, and enclosed a secret communication for Rana to deliver to Interior Minister Francesco Cossiga, a long-time Christian Democrat colleague. However, while the Red Brigades did not object to their prisoner's sending Easter greetings to his family or informing his wife that he was 'well fed and carefully taken care of,' they refused to permit what they considered inappropriate negotiations between their prisoner and the government. Although Moro seems to have been assured that the letter he had written to Cossiga would be treated as 'very confidential,' this communication was not delivered to Moro's secretary but turned over instead by the Red Brigades to the press. In their own 'Communiqué Number 3' sent to journalists with the text of the message to Cossiga, the Red Brigades denounced what they called the 'secret manoeuvres' implicit in Moro's note, a way of conducting business they characterized as 'normal practice for the Christian Democrat Mafia' but counter to their own revolutionary conviction that 'nothing should be hidden from the people.'[19] From this point on, Moro seems to have known that whatever he wrote to individuals such as Cossiga was not 'confidential' at all but likely to end up in the morning papers.

Moro's prison 'Calvary,' as he called it, lasted from 16 March to 9 May 1978. His first letters from confinement – those sent through Rana in the manner described above – reached their recipients towards the end of March, the letter to Cossiga appearing in the papers on 30 March. During April, five more texts by the prisoner were published in the Italian press. Three of these were addressed to then Party Secretary and Moro disciple Benigno Zaccagnini, a fourth to 'la Democrazia Cristiana' collectively. In these communications Moro urged his colleagues to make haste to initiate the proceedings he believed would put an end to his imprisonment.

A fifth text from this period, however, is different from the others. This communication, which first appeared in Rome's *Il messaggero* on 11 April

1978, does not have a specific addressee, though it does bear Moro's name at its conclusion. The document, in fact, seems to have been excerpted from the 'memoriale' Moro was working on in prison rather than conceived from the outset as a letter. In what none the less appeared in the papers as an open letter like the others, Moro complained that his long-held position on hostage negotiations was being distorted in statements to the press by Christian Democrat Senator Paolo Emilio Taviani. Furious at what he considered this self-serving interference in his perilous situation, Moro accused the 'forgetful' Taviani of political opportunism, not only in the Moro situation but throughout his long career. In the present instance, Moro suggested, Taviani's disapproval of negotiations seemed likely to have been dictated by a desire to curry favour with a foreign government (that of the United States or Germany, for example). He ended the letter by accusing his fellow party member of contributing to a climate of 'tension' – a term usually associated with the 'strategia della tensione' embraced by neo-Fascist groups intent on bringing down the Italian state through a studied campaign of terror and confusion.

Even if his remarks about Taviani were not intended for publication in the newspapers (though at this point in his captivity Moro must have known that such was a possibility for all that he wrote), the sharpness of Moro's criticism makes it clear that even in prison the Red Brigades' captive did not consider himself without bargaining chips. In the letters he wrote to Zaccagnini and others, Moro insisted that he was ready to reveal additional, distressing information about his party if negotiations were not begun immediately. The party's imprisoned president was prepared to take such drastic steps because he felt that he had been kidnapped and was now facing death not for who he was personally but because he was a kind of political synecdoche for his captives. In Moro's view, it was the Christian Democrat hierarchy and its activities during three decades of governing that were the real objects of Red Brigade wrath.[20] 'In truth,' he wrote Cossiga about this, 'all of us in the leadership group are on trial and it is our collective operations that are under indictment and for which I am being made to answer.'[21] Several times in his prison correspondence Moro emphasized the collective responsibility his Christian Democrat colleagues bore for his plight, pointing out with considerable vehemence that it was not right that he should 'pay for the entire Democrazia Cristiana' (403).

If the Christian Democrat politicians could do no more than stand by ineffectively while he was made to pay for their misdeeds, Moro made clear, the party and its leadership would be pronouncing his 'death sentence.'[22] In such a case, he wrote Zaccagnini, 'my blood will be on all of your hands, on those of the party and of the country' (411). Urging his friends to understand how the Christian Democrat Party would be just as accountable as his captors if he were executed, Moro twice warned party members in April that 'I will not absolve and I will not justify anyone' (410, 415). In the opinion of Professor of Jurisprudence Aldo Moro, the Christian Democrats' death sentence in his case constituted a deplorable regression to a practice opposed by Italian political thinkers as far back as Cesare Beccaria and meant the reintroduction of a sanction explicitly abolished by the 1948 constitution that Moro, together with such other experts as Umberto Terracini, had helped draft.[23] In an apocalyptic vision of the state of party politics likely to follow on the heels of his colleagues' 'iniquitous and ungrateful' decision, Moro described a 'terrible spiral' in which Christian Democrat politicians would be 'caught up' in a 'vortex' of political destruction subsequent to 'the terrible fact of a decision for death' (415, 410).

Like many other prison writers, Aldo Moro was directing what he wrote from confinement both to people who loved and supported him unconditionally and to others whose backing he was much less sure of. The latter, in this prisoner's case, were not the government censors whose perusal of their intimate thoughts so distressed the other prison writers whose work has been reviewed here, but the intended recipients themselves of his prison writings: Moro's colleagues in the Christian Democrat Party. For their part, these individuals – at least officially – resolutely chose not even to consider the merits of their colleague's arguments in the letters addressed to them. Instead, they insisted that the texts concerned were not really written by their long-time associate at all. Or, if Moro had written them, they continued, then they were not 'morally attributable' to their leader. 'The text of the letter signed Aldo Moro, addressed to the Honourable Zaccagnini,' Moro's party claimed shortly after his letters began to appear in the papers, 'once again reveals the conditions of total coercion in which such documents are written and confirms that this letter too is not *morally attributable to him*.'[24]

With the exception of those to his family, therefore, all of Moro's writings from Red Brigades prison arrived at their destinations already read and interpreted, their content and arguments repudiated in advance. His meanings thus effaced even before his writings reached their intended readers, Moro was erased as an author well before he was physically 'rubbed out' by the Red Brigades.[25] As Adriano Sofri has commented about this stage in the ex-prime minister's captivity, the country's most visible 'public figures deprived Moro of his civil rights, declared that he was someone other than himself, stripped his words of serious implications, and in so doing fooled themselves into thinking that they too were exonerated ... At this point they could no longer have begun to talk with and listen to Moro: he was no longer there.'[26] The absence of a dialectical relationship with his correspondents so ruefully deplored by Gramsci during his imprisonment in the 1930s had become an even more unbridgeable void for the Communist deputy's Christian Democrat counterpart in 1978. Like Gramsci's, Moro's letters amounted to little more than 'stones cast into the darkness.'[27] Moro's prison writing was meant to be the functional equivalent of Cellini's ladder, Pignata's truss, Orsini's saws, or Casanova's *esponton* – an instrument that would enable him to scramble somehow out of prison. The verbal rather than physical tool that he wielded so desperately from the people's prison, however, failed him when he needed it most.

Aldo Moro's prison correspondence is unique in many ways. His letters, for example, constitute a completely one-sided discourse. While in the published versions of many other prison letters the voice of the (almost invariably female) partner in the correspondence is frequently suppressed by a posterity interested only in what a famous man has to say from prison, in the case of Moro's letters there were no responses to be suppressed. During the fifty-five days of his captivity in the Red Brigades' secret location, Moro received only two direct answers to his writings and then in the form of brief notes from his family that appeared as open letters in the newspapers. It is one of the many ironies of the Moro affair that the final, crucial moments in the life of this exceptionally reserved, private individual were played out in a public arena where his increasingly desperate cries for help from what had been his intimate friends echoed vainly in a silent public arena. Despite the immense and often noisy debate his letters excited, in the last days of his life Moro was unable to engage in a real dialogue with the recipients of his writings. He was forced, instead, to reveal his thoughts about the events that had led him to the edge of death in a monologue delivered to an officialdom determined at all costs not to hear what he was saying, almost screaming, to them.

Conclusion:

Sentences and Convictions

How many words expended in these years on pieces of paper that have passed before the censor's vigilant eye. Nowhere else except in prisons are freedom, love, and happiness spoken of with such tenacity.[1]

For the authors whose work has been analysed in the chapters above, writing was more than a diversion from the monotony of prison life. It was an opportunity to shatter the fetters of what Curcio, Valentino, and Petrelli have called the 'definizioni definitorie' used to confine prison inmates not only physically but also linguistically and psychologically.[2] Whether drawn from the muddled Marxist vocabulary of the Red Brigades or proposed in the more academic terms of penology and criminology, the 'defining definitions' applied to all of the prison authors studied here function, in these authors' words, to 'twist one's identity' and thus to 'detach the inmate more and more from the linguistic community from which he came, and thus finally eradicate any memory of it.'[3] But what is at issue here is not only prisoners' memories of the cultural community from which they come, but also, and perhaps more importantly, that community's memory of them. The imperative felt by prison writers to slip the bonds of hostile definitions of who they are, what they have done, and above all how they will be remembered is the founding stimulus for all prison writing. The intense need felt by these authors to contradict a competing account of the meaning of their confinements and their lives is what differentiates the subcategory of prison writing from autobiographical writing in general.[4] Prison letters especially are not only verbal lifelines with existence beyond the constraints of confinement, they are the rejection of an institutional aphasia that threatens to erase the meanings of the individual's life and collocation in history. In the same way, subsequent memoirs are efforts – often triumphalistic ones – to destroy and replace the meaning assigned their authors' imprisonment by the confining authorities at an earlier time.

In confirmation of this notion, it is clear from the opening statement of his *Vita* that Benvenuto Cellini's account of his detention and eventual escape from a papal prison was part of his more general project to dispute his enemies' description of who he was and authenticate his existence as an exceptional individual. One intent of Tasso's letters from Sant'Anna was, to be sure, to atone for the behavioural shortcomings that had led to their author's stay in that institution: but another was to augment his stature as a writer of unusual merit. Casanova's memoirs, by the same token, sought to persuade his audience of their author's personal charm in a process of seduction and domination that was at once a compositional strategy and the main theme of all of his writing. Cellini, Tasso, Pignata, and Casanova all produced their accounts of prison and (except for Tasso) escape in order to mark the distance between their lives and those of ordinary people. Prison, for these writers, helped authenticate their exceptional existences even when, in the case of Giuseppe Pignata, the existence described had no solid historical basis.

Although prison writers after 1815 were just as intent on contextualizing their experiences within the broader setting of their lives as a whole, history rather than just posterity now becomes an essential point of reference. For Pellico, around whose spectacularly successful book the other Spielberg memorialists (as well as a great many subsequent prison authors) circle like secondary planets, what mattered in prison was maintaining faith in God and humanity despite extreme and painful circumstances, in this way attaining a moral victory even in the midst of atrocious suffering. Despite this intention on the part of its author, however, Pellico's book has been read as much for the political as for the pietistic force of its argument.[5] For his part, Pellico's cell-mate and old friend Maroncelli was intent on amending – 'prosthetically' we might say – what he believed was Pellico's incomplete or mutilated record of the significance of their shared captivity and thus of their lives and places in history. Confalonieri also believed that Pellico's account was not 'the whole truth' about their collective captivity, as did Arrivabene. Andryane and Pallavicino, in their mutually discrediting accounts of their Spielberg ordeal propose what are perhaps more explicitly self-serving narratives that also contest what Pellico said, as does Rosa in his different but equally demystifying fashion.

At the same time, each of these memorialists underlines the contributions he has made to a crucial period in Italian and European history. In doing so, these writers are locating the significance of their imprisonment and their lives in a larger context than that imagined by their predecessors. Unlike the Renaissance and eighteenth-century prison writers who came before them, none of these Restoration prisoners were involved in flamboyant escapes. Nor did they waste much of their energy in describing the injustice of their punishments. The principal intention of the Spielberg memorialists was to attest to the mental strength – religious, secular, or some combination of the two – that enabled them to endure frightening ordeals for the sake of a cause passionately espoused, a moral choice they are convinced history will surely vindicate.

The prison writings from later in the century examined here are more varied in both shape and intent than those by the Spielberg inmates, possibly because most of them saw publication only well after Unification. Bini's *Manoscritto di un prigioniero* is a pretext for the development of a young writer's ideas on social injustice and the class struggle as well as an account of a turning-point in its author's life. So, too, the letters Guerrazzi wrote from prison are attempts by a professional man of letters to control such aspects of extra-mural life as the education of his beloved Cecchino, but that reveal to later readers a little-known side of this writer's character. Pastro's triumphalist account of his defiance of his captors through the subversive poetry he was able to write in confinement is a display of his imaginative and unyielding patriotic character. Transgressive writing was also important to the Mantuans Tazzoli and Poma, who, by communicating in often unorthodox ways with their families, strengthened the bonds linking them to both the great traditions of Italian culture and their own precious middle-class origins.

In their prison memoirs and correspondence, Castromediano, Settembrini, and Spaventa were able to denounce the misgovernment of their native South as well as describe extraordinary encounters with a colourful underclass of criminals, brigands, and other marginal individuals. The papal prisoners Galletti and Frignani also documented government malfeasance – in Frignani's case in an institution for the mentally ill as well as in a conventional prison. In all of these otherwise very diverse accounts, confinement was not only a life-threatening but, in the long run, a life-defining experience that these writers are eager to set into a context that is historical as well as personal. In all of their accounts, it is secular history rather than spiritual edification that their writings mean to address.

Conclusion: Sentences and Convictions 189

These texts from the middle of the century, like those by the earlier Spielberg prisoners, are testimony of political sacrifices. But more so than previously, writers from this period are attempting to influence social and political conditions outside prison: in the world of the class struggle for the 'proto-Communist' Bini; in a Lombardy shamefully reduced to an Austrian colony for the Martyrs of Mantua; in a worrisomely backward and anachronistically ruled Kingdom of Two Sicilies for Castromediano, Settembrini, and Spaventa. From the radical Bini to the conservative Castromediano, all these writers were committed – though in different ways and to different degrees – to changes in the societies that surrounded them. Like the prison memoirs of the Spielberg patriots, their books present modest, otherwise unexceptional autobiographical protagonists caught up almost accidentally in exceptional events. For each of these writers – but especially for the Bourbon prisoners serving lengthy terms in generally frightful circumstances – the narrowing of physical autonomy imposed on them by confinement was accompanied by a broadening of social perspectives of a sort that otherwise, one suspects, they would never have experienced.

The challenge that prison presented the activist writers Orsini, Castro, Kuliscioff, Turati, and, in a different way, Caracciolo was, by contrast, how to resist the transformative powers of claustration. In the letters and memoirs by these individuals, all of whom, given the conventions of the times, led irregular sexual existences, the struggle to preserve their distinctive personalities while in confinement is paramount. While these writers are scarcely the first to resent the intrusion of their confinement into the most intimate aspects of their physical and emotional lives, their struggles to safeguard their identities from the normalizing effects of imprisonment are waged more insistently than they were by previous authors. Orsini carries on an intense correspondence with a woman admirer who provides him with both emotional support and the means for a daring escape; Costa and Kuliscioff exchange ardent love letters; Turati is cured of his physical ailments when he is finally able to articulate his political views freely in the clandestine letters he is able to exchange with his mother; Caracciolo struggles to retain her dignity as a woman in the face of the desexualizing forces of the convent. For all of these detainees, claustration fortified rather than altered their social views, vindicated their existences as dissenters, and in this way reinforced their convictions that their sacrifices had not been in vain.

Like their Risorgimento forebears, the anti-Fascists also struggled to preserve their cultural identities in confinement. Whether Catholics or

Communists, painters or novelists, scholars, teachers, or full-time political activists, De Gasperi, Lo Sardo, Terracini, Ravera, Rossi, Monti, Levi, Morandi, Bassani, Alicata, and Gramsci were idealists who viewed imprisonment as a challenge to their physical grit and intellectual coherence. Educated individuals sensitive to the intertextual links between their writings and those of previous political militants, these men and women were acutely aware that the texts they produced while in prison were part of a tradition of liberal protest dating back at least as far as the Risorgimento. The 'lettere dal carcere' each of them penned were evidence of their personal visions of a different arrangement of social relations, a new and superior configuration of society they were convinced would shortly replace outmoded structures. Particularly when published during the reconstruction of Italian society that began immediately after the Second World War, these letters situated their authors' stints in confinement within this effort at renewal, and in this way gave their sacrifices a significance that by the time of these texts' postwar publication was apparent to all.

Aldo Moro's prison letters are different in essential ways from all the other documents examined in this study – and only partly because they were written by a hostage of an anti-State organization. Appearing as they did during the period of radical experimentation in fiction and other kinds of writing that has come to be known as postmodern, Moro's letters were accorded a different reception by their earliest readers than that which greeted all the other prison letters analysed here. Like such novels of this era as Italo Calvino's *If On a Winter's Night a Traveler* (1979) or Antonio Tabucchi's tale of detention, interrogation, and presumed torture and execution, *Pereira Declares* (1994), Moro's communications from Red Brigades prison were read from the beginning with as much attention to the allusions that seemed concealed beneath their overt narrative as they were for their desperate surface message. Approaching them in the spirit of postmodern fiction, virtually all readers of these texts – and especially those who tried to make sense of them while their author was still in captivity – have attempted to understand what Moro was writing by focusing on the material conditions of their production, the good or bad faith of the putative author or authors involved, and the intertextual ties linking them to a tradition of generically similar works – all strategies that are typical of postmodern reading. By considering his letters in this way, Moro's readers were attempting to construct meanings that would both reveal their author's true intent in composing them and provide a significance for his life that could also be applicable to the historical period in which both their author and their readers were distressed participants.

Many of Moro's most touching letters centre on his concern for his young grandchild, Luca. Imprisoned in Austrian-controlled Mantua more than a century before Moro's kidnapping in 1978, the unmarried Luigi Pastro dreamed of the child he hoped to conceive with a woman in an adjoining cell. But the only progeny Pastro produced in Mantua were the acrostic poems 'in barba a Culoz' that he was able to compose there. Writing, for this Treviso physician, was a surrogate for biological creation, his prison texts offspring of his pen rather than his body. The dialectic of substitution and replacement involving both texts and bodies that preoccupied Pastro's imagination while in Mantua is a recurrent theme in the history of prison writing.[6] Unable to embrace the physical bodies of their imprisoned relatives, the addressees of prison letters must direct their concerns and affections onto the bodies of the texts that these loved ones will receive instead. Although they do not serve the same intensely vicarious purpose, prison memoirs, too, dwell perforce on the suffering bodies of their prison authors during a time of unwanted confinement, even if they do so from a safer, retrospective distance.

Such a textualization of the body (and the accompanying corporalization of the text) should not be surprising. Prison itself, for political prisoners, is a detainment intended to prevent additional transgression not so much of the body (as it arguably does for those guilty of rape or assault, for example) but of the spirit. Political prisoners are held in confinement to discourage the promulgation of their nonconformist opinions. But these opinions are harboured within bodies that are innocent as such of wrongdoing and have been detained as if by default. In such circumstances, these protesting bodies often themselves become texts as they are transformed into additional, often unimpeachable witnesses to an ordeal aimed not at them but at what they enclose. The message transcribed on Cellini's head was a written sign, presumably, of God's special concern for the ebullient goldsmith. Carlo Poma's prison writings were validated by the marks left by his body on the soiled linens that he sent home from a Mantua prison. The text of consecration previously inscribed on Tazzoli's body, which was ritually erased in a reversal of his previous elevation to the priesthood, is clear indication that the Church considered his body the appropriate site for its inscription of a text of anathema and degradation. Maroncelli, eager to supply irrefutable proof of the real nature of his prison ordeal, displayed both the stump of his amputated leg and his 'addizioni' in confutation of what he believed was Pellico's otherwise mutilated account of their joint captivity. Andryane attempted to valorize his lost religious prison poem by asserting that it had been composed in blood drawn from the complicitous body of Silvio Pellico. Although they bore very different messages, bodies in all these cases were both witnesses of physical and psychological pain and the emissaries of textual significance.

While the body can authenticate an accompanying or parallel text, it can also confute a competing statement. Giuseppe Galletti considered the marks left on his body by a prison illness a more valid manifestation of his commitment to the rights and duties of humanity than either the decree condemning him to jail or his papal pardon. Unable with words to persuade his fellow officers of the exculpatory circumstances that led to his revelations to the Austrians, Luigi Castellazzo of the Mantua group displayed his scarred buttocks to them instead, calling on his body as a persuasive witness to the torture he believed at least mitigated his capitulation to his interrogators. Just as Church authorities were determined that a consecrating text be erased from Tazzoli's subversive and textually threatening body, Galletti and Castellazzo propose the counter-narratives of their bodies in contravention of their adversaries' opinions of their political integrity. Their bodies, in this way, act in tandem with all the texts that all these authors prepared about their captivities.

But even though the body may be able to authenticate or subvert an accompanying or competing text, it is texts and not bodies that in the long run survive. Prison writing, like any other, is a continuum of written traces of experiences that would otherwise go unattested. This is so even if beyond this writing there is frequently a shadow of still another, as yet unarticulated experience. As has been seen time and again during the history of prison writing in Italy, beneath ostensible prison messages there is often a clandestine text, a more authentic, uncensored communication written in code or invisible ink, or couched in language incomprehensible to the uninitiated. Within the chorus of prison writing over the centuries other texts murmur, texts that cannot be written or if written are now invisible or otherwise lost: texts in some cases of inexpressible passion, in others of ineffable suffering, texts suppressed by the censor or fear of the censor, or by time, editors, or uncomprehending recipients. Despite all attempts by prison authors to master what they write about prison, their textual progeny frequently evade their authors' control. Although he is a historical figure who actually lived, as a prison author Giuseppe Pignata's existence is exclusively textual. Despite his best efforts to dominate all the texts of his confinement – whether the Bible, the

Conclusion: Sentences and Convictions 193

Decameron, or his own memoirs – Casanova became the victim of a linguistically and moralistically editorial deformation of his own writing that lasted nearly two centuries. In his own sometimes very impatient view, at least, Gramsci was unable to make Tatiana understand even his simplest instructions to her, while Aldo Moro was driven to an understandable frenzy at his readers' refusal to read his prison texts simply and without preconceptions. As the texts of their lives slip away from them, all of these authors are prisoners of writing, dissemination, and interpretation just as much as they are of the bricks and mortar of a papal prison, the lead roof of Venice's Piombi, or the soundproof chamber where Moro was held on the Via Montalcini.

As the epigraphs to this book's introductory chapter are meant to suggest, prison authors write first of all for themselves – 'to keep from going crazy' as Naria said, to 'populate the desert' in the words of non-prisoner Bufalino. Unusually self-conscious individuals 'guarded' in more senses than one, these memorialists of their own ordeals have in effect placed themselves at the centre of a personal panopticon where they are both surveillants and surveilled, scrutinizing self-censors and defiant transgressors of prison protocol. For Tito Speri in the middle of the nineteenth century, however, writing from prison – especially by those awaiting execution – was a gesture of utterly transparent significance. 'You can be sure,' Speri wrote, 'that the craze to exaggerate and to falsify the truth is entirely alien to a man who has had the harsh experiences of a prison of this sort. His only wish in such circumstances is to see things dispassionately and to behave in such a way that others, setting all illusions aside, see things as clearly and coolly as when they are seen from between the bars.'[7] But for later prison writers – and their readers – communication from prison has rarely been viewed so straightforwardly. Giancarlo Pajetta has stated bluntly that prison letters by their very nature can never be completely comprehended by readers other than their original recipients. 'All the prison letters were written in code,' he insists about the texts included in his anthology; 'not a single word, not a single affirmation, even the most insistent, not a single bit of news, even the simplest and banal one, meant what an outsider finds in it today.'[8] The letters by anti-Fascist prisoners he has collected, Pajetta emphasizes, never describe such matters as the real nature of their authors' suffering – this partly not to worry their original recipients, partly to deprive the prisoners' captors of an occasion for gloating.[9]

In the analogous case of prison memoirs, Curcio, Valentino, and Petrelli have stressed how difficult it is for ex-prisoners to remember even the simplest details of their previous confinements and insisted that an institutionally induced 'amnesia' has made them incapable of writing anything that is not inadequate or false. Even shortly after their release from confinement, they note, ex-prisoners frequently cannot recall such elementary aspects of their confinement as which items inmates can and cannot receive through the mail. Such a reaction, Curcio, Valentino, and Petrelli conclude, is to be expected when 'as soon as your body emerges from confinement's trance and enters another specific state, your state-dependent memory is also subject to amnesia ... In this way, just as sometimes happens in the case of dreams of great intensity, after a trauma or a shock, you wake up to find that you have forgotten everything. In your past there is a ten-year hole. And you have forgotten the faces, the names, and the addresses of the friends that amidst tears and promises you left beyond the gate on the other side of the awful walls.'[10] Perhaps it is impossible, then, not only for third parties but for prisoners themselves to describe the experience of confinement accurately. Curcio, Valentino, and Petrelli have spoken of a 'unfillable gap that is part of the ... illegible history' of this kind of writing, insisting that any account of confinement must itself remain forcibly incarcerated in the citadel of 'the invisible, the unsaid, the unwritten.' The real circumstances of confinement, these authors maintain, 'can perhaps be lived through, but never observed.'[11]

While escape from prison was possible for such celebrated memorialists of their detention as Cellini, Casanova, Pignata, and Orsini, escape from language and its conventions would seem to be a much more difficult, even impossible project, as Gramsci lamented in the letters of frustration that he wrote towards the end of his confinement. The struggles waged by prison writers against constraints of both a physical and a linguistic nature, however, are part of the appeal their writings offer. Many thinkers, including both Freud and Rousseau, have held that civilization can only exist when social norms inhibiting individual autonomy come to be imposed on an otherwise anarchic human nature. If this is so, then prison can be viewed as a more extreme, non-consensual equivalent of civilization's general normalizing actions, a hyper-civilization founded on mutual hostility rather than a negotiated social contract. Since both in prison and in ordinary life sanctions limiting acceptable conduct tend to be applied selectively and inconsistently, inmates' struggles to protect themselves through their writings are perhaps only extreme cases of more familiar, extra-mural efforts to deal with the threats to identity posed by life in mass society. The intuition of this similarity between prison's radical oppression of individual liberty and the more benign repressions of everyday life does much to explain the suggestive hold that stories of prisoners and prison life exert on readers, movie-goers, and television viewers.[12] Despite the inadequacies of such representations, prison texts command our attention as traces of an experience that we all can respond to at least vicariously, recognizing in these authors' sentences the stories of our own responses to our contingencies, limitations, and constraints, both existential and linguistic.

Notes

Preface

1 'On the other hand,' Gramsci wrote in 1935, 'what has happened was not altogether unforeseeable; you who remember so many things from the past, do you remember when I told you that I was 'going to war? Perhaps it was not very serious on my part, but it was the truth and in reality that is how I felt.' Antonio Gramsci, *Letters from Prison*, II: 351–2; cf. Antonio Gramsci, *Lettere dal carcere*, ed. Sergio Caprioglio and Elsa Fubini, 845.
2 These notebooks have recently begun to be issued in an admirable translation with extensive commentary by Joseph Buttigieg: Antonio Gramsci, *Prison Notebooks*, 1992.
3 For a wide-ranging study of this theme in world literature, see W.B. Carnochan's 'The Literature of Confinement,' in Norval Morris and David J. Rothman, eds., *The Oxford History of the Prison*, 427–55, where there is also a good beginning bibliography.
4 A recent study of the theme of prison in Italian opera, though in the years before the period I have been describing, is Angela Romagnoli's *'Fra catene, fra stili, e fra veleni ...': Ossia della scena di prigione nell'opera italiana (1690–1724)*.
5 See also, for example, the two poems by 1975 Nobel Laureate Eugenio Montale, 'Piccolo testamento' and 'Il sogno del prigioniero,' which close that writer's *La bufera ed altro* of 1956, both of which are set in situations of detainment meant to symbolize the constraints placed on Italian intellectuals during Fascism and afterwards, and to stand as an image for the human condition more generally. The metaphor of prison in Montale's poetry has been studied by Giuseppe Savoca in his 'Montale e la "trappola" della lingua,' *Parole di Ungaretti e di Montale*, 47–60.

Introduction: Writing As Survival

1 Gesualdo Bufalino, 'Le ragioni dello scrivere,' *Cere perse*, 16.
2 Giuliano Naria, in Giuliano Naria and Rosella Simone, *La casa del nulla*, 151.
3 Even so – given the violent aspects of the programs of some of these men and women – they cannot all be considered 'prisoners of conscience' in the sense used by such a group as Amnesty International. For the distinction, see Aryeh Neier, 'Confining Dissent: The Political Prison,' in Morris and Rothman, 391–425.
4 Since they felt no remorse for the purported crimes they had committed, none of these writers would have shared the quite different feelings held by Francesca Mambro, a convicted terrorist from the 1970s. Writing of her existence after prison, Mambro has declared that her new life after detention 'cannot be anything but a walk through a prison. Not necessarily through a state penitentiary, more likely, in fact, through a clean, sweet-smelling, elegant prison ... a spherical one like the world itself or one as infinite as the universe. A prison suitable for a short walk inside or a long one outside – that makes no difference. For our real jailers are our eyes: we have seen certain things – suffering, pain, our own unjust deeds as well as those of others. For this reason, wherever we go (if we do go anywhere), we will never be able to consider ourselves free women.' Laura Braghetti and Francesca Mambro, *Nel cerchio della prigione*, 271.
5 In his preface to Georg Rusche and Otto Kirchheimer's 1939 classic study of crime and punishment, *Punishment and Social Structure*, Thorsten Sellin describes the tautological operation of hegemonic law in which 'the social values which are given the protection of the law, the rules which are enforced by the political power of the state because they are embodied in the criminal code, are those which are deemed desirable by those social groups within the state who have the power to make law' (vii).
6 Giovanni Galletti, *La mia prigionia*, 83.
7 For the different kinds of treatment accorded during the Risorgimento to intellectuals on the one hand and the illiterate masses on the other, see Anna Capelli, *La buona compagnia. Utopia e realtà carceraria nell'Italia del Risorgi-*

mento, 277 and passim. Two anthologies of letters by Italian prisoners of war, authors, that is, who make up still a different and arguably non-political kind of prison population, are Leo Spitzer's *Lettere di prigionieri di guerra italiani 1915–1918*, for the First World War, and Nuto Revelli's *L'ultimo fronte. Lettere di soldati caduti o dispersi nella seconda guerra mondiale*, for the Second.

8 For the architectural history of Italian prisons, see Renzo Dubbini, *Architettura delle prigioni*; other publications on this topic include Giovanni Scarabello, *Carcerati e carceri a Venezia nell'età moderna*, and Aldo Ricci and Giulio Salierno, *Il carcere in Italia*.

9 Sigismondo Castromediano, *Carceri e galere politiche*, II: 35.

10 Other works of value about prison and prisoners include Michael Ignatieff's *A Just Measure of Pain: The Penitentiary in the Industrial Revolution, 1750–1850*, Elissa E. Gelfand's *Imagination in Confinement: Women's Writing from French Prisons*, and John Bender's *Imagining the Penitentiary: Fiction and the Architecture of Mind in Eighteenth-Century England*. For additional contributions to this discussion, see Works Consulted.

11 See, for example, Michelle Perrot's *L'impossible prison*, first published in 1980 in Paris (Editions du Seuil), then in an Italian edition by Rizzoli in Milan in 1981, and the appendix dated 1979 (with rich accompanying notes) of Dario Melossi and Massimo Pavarini's *The Prison and the Factory: Origins of the Penitentiary System*.

12 Although Augusto Monti, in a passage analysed below, writes his daughter that prison does provide him with the chance to think and write without interruption, his assertion is clearly a facetious one meant to console his daughter and defy his captors. For Monti, see below, pp. 154–6.

13 For the censoring of mail to and from inhabitants of insane asylums, see Roy Porter, *A Social History of Madness*, 85, and Renato Curcio, Nicola Valentino, and Stefano Petrelli, *Nel bosco di Bistorco*, n. 181. The classic study on 'total institutions' is Irving Goffman's *Asylums: Essays on the Social Situation of Mental Patients and Other Inmates*. A recent and extremely interesting study of the censoring of letters by non-institutionalized but not for that unconstrained women is Barbara Zaczek's *Censored Sentiments: Letters and Censorship in Epistolary Novels and Conduct Material*.

14 *Carteggio del conte Federico Confalonieri ed altri documenti spettanti alla sua biografia*, I: 497. For a description of a modern prison correspondence in which forbidden communication (in this case of an erotic rather than a political nature) did take place through the shapes themselves of alphabetic signs, see Curcio et al., 295.

15 Silvio Spaventa, *Dal 1848 al 1861. Lettere, scritti, documenti*, 59. Domenico Cirillo, Francesco Pagano, and Vincenzo Russo were Italian patriots active at the time of the Parthenopean Republic in Naples in 1799.
16 Luigi Settembrini, *Ricordanze della mia vita e scritti autobiografici*, 6, 311, 361.
17 Gianni Bisiach, ed., *Pertini racconta gli anni 1915–1945*, 53–4.

1: Predecessors: Prison Writing before 1800

1 Benvenuto Cellini, 'Capitolo sulla prigione,' *Vita di Benvenuto Cellini orefice e scultore fiorentino da lui medesimo scritta, Opere*, 376. 'There's art, and science, within the prisons' plan ... Besides, all prisons have a natural force / To make you eloquent, and fierce and bold, / Debating well of good and ill the source' (*The Autobiography of Benvenuto Cellini*, trans. George Bull, 234). Subsequent quotations from Cellini's *Autobiography* are from this translation, with page numbers indicated in the text.
2 Giuseppe Pignata, also treated in this chapter, was an entirely fictional figure, at least as an author. See the remarks on him that follow, 23–9.
3 For Casanova, see the article by Nicola Mangini in the *Dizionario biografico degli italiani*, XXI: 151–67, and Lydia Flem, *Casanova, the Man Who Really Loved Women*.
4 Swiss historian Jacob Burckhardt lived from 1818 to 1897; his classic *The Civilization of the Renaissance in Italy* was first published in 1860.
5 *Trattato di oreficeria. Opere di Baldassare Castiglione, Giovanni della Casa, Benvenuto Cellini*, ed. Carlo Cordié 1025–6. See also Corinne Lucas, 'L'artiste et l'écriture: *il dire* et *il fare* dans les écrits de Cellini,' 67–97.
6   He who would know God's power and mighty ways
    And how far man may reach to things divine,
    Some time in prison should drag out his days.
    ...
    It may be he's an evil life to mend,
    Give him two years in harsh captivity,
    He'll make a saint, to every man a friend. (232–3)
7 For references by Tasso to eventual collections of his prison letters, see his remarks in 1584 to Angelo Grillo, and in 1585 to Margherita Gonzaga, all in Torquato Tasso, *Lettere*, ed. Cesare Guasti, II: 274, 369. Additional references to Tasso's letters are to this edition and are given in the text.
8 The case, for example, of his appeal for liberation by the people of Naples, first published by Ludovico Antonio Muratori in the eighteenth century and reproduced by Ettore Mazzali in his edition of Tasso's *Lettere*, I: 133.
9 For a contrasting view, see Annibale Caro's description of Cinquecento

letters as communications such that 'many times what they say cannot be understood, they don't know where they are going, they stop, get lost, are intercepted along the way, do not arrive where they are sent nor return to where they are expected, and so very often do not provide us the service that we would have done better had we done it in person,' *Lettere familiari*, I: 223–4.
10 The Neoplatonist Marsilio Ficino (1433–99) wrote, among many other topics, on magic and the nature of the soul.
11 See Carol Ackroyd, ed., *The Technology of Political Control*, 237–42.
12 Giovanni Getto, 'Tra biografia e poesia. L'epistolario,' *Interpretazione del Tasso*, 29.
13 For the equivalency in the eyes of a punishing authority of parricide and lese-majesty, see the Castromediano section of chap. 3 below, p. 83.
14 In a letter to Ottavio Spinola of 1586 he complains that 'I was condemned before being found guilty' (490).
15 Valeria Giordano, ed., *Luoghi del tempo. La percezione del tempo nel carcere e nella società*, 224–5.
16 Guerrini (1845–1916), head librarian at the University of Bologna for many years, wrote several volumes of non-conformist poetry, most of it under the name of Lorenzo Stecchetti. D'Ancona (1835–1914), whose essay on Pignata was originally published in 1886, was a professor at the University of Pisa, where he helped found the 'scuola storica' of academic literary criticism. For other works by him, see Works Consulted.
17 Pignata, *Aventures*, 3. Translation here and in what follows is from the 1725 Cologne edition.
18 *The Adventures of Giuseppe Pignata, Who Escaped from the Prisons of the Inquisition of Rome.*
19 See D'Ancona in his essay in the Sellerio edition of Pignata's *Avventure*, 154 5.
20 Ibid., 165.
21 For a history of judicial torture and its increasing use during this period in European history, see Edward Peters, *Torture*. For its continuing, unauthorized use today, see Antonio Cassese, *Umano-Disumano*.
22 See D'Ancona's essay, 173, where the source, however, for his biographical verifications is a somewhat mysterious unpublished diary from the era lent the scholar by a 'defunct friend' (165). The paper trail for his assertions, therefore, is a rather tenuous one.
23 See Guillén's classic essay, 'Toward a Definition of the Picaresque,' in *Literature as System*, 71–106.
24 Gustave Brunet, *Imprimeurs imaginaires et libraires supposés*, 3, 112.

25 For which see Robert Darnton, *The Literary Underground of the Old Regime*. Though Darnton's study deals with a somewhat later period, he has interesting comments – see especially 44–5 – about the popularity of lurid writing dealing with prison and prisoners.
26 In this regard it is striking to note that the first edition of Cellini's *Vita* as published by Cocchi in Naples in 1728 lists Cologne as its place of publication and none other than Pietro Martello as publisher.
27 Translations here are from the edition by Charles Samaran.
28 Giacomo Casanova, *History of My Life*, 36. All quotations from this work by Casanova are from this edition, and page numbers are given in the text.
29 For the 'transgressive' implications of this choice of a language, see Cynthia Craig's '"Je l'habille souvent à l'Italienne": The Language of Exile in the *Histoire de ma vie*.'
30 John Masters, *Casanova*, 293.
31 Willard R. Trask, 'Introduction,' to Casanova, *History of My Life*, 17.
32 Casanova's *Histoire de ma fuite*, however, as already indicated, had been in circulation since 1788.
33 'Remembering the pleasures I enjoyed, I renew them' is how Trask (29) translates this phrase. For the importance of the concept for Casanova, see Sandro Gentile, '"Jouir par Réminiscence". Su Casanova memorialista,' 103.
34 *Fuite*, 268. Casanova did not like Rousseau: an unflattering portrait of him is included in volume 5 of the *Histoire de ma vie* (221–2; Trask, 223–4), with additional remarks in volume 8, where he accuses the author of the *Confessions* of being fatally bereft of a sense of humour (245; Trask 249).
35 See Franco Fido, 'Casanova "libertino,"' 230.
36 Gentile, 105.
37 The secular Inquisition of the Venetian Republic is not to be confused with the Catholic Inquisition that imprisoned Pignata and that in Venice in this period had less power than it did elsewhere in Italy.
38 Reviewing these later from jail, he admits that 'all these accusations had some basis which gave them an air of probability' even if 'they were all fabrications' (4: 249; cf. also 4: 193).
39 François Roustang, *The Quadrille of Gender: Casanova's Memoirs*, xiii–xiv.
40 For a much less plausible account of a prisoner's encounter with a colony of rats that he claims he succeeded in taming, see Jean Henri Masers de Latude and Simon Nicolas Henri Linguet, *Memoirs of the Bastille*. Another book about imprisonment in Venice from an earlier period is *Il camerotto*, by the seventeenth-century libertine Girolamo Brusoni; Brusoni was held in the 'Giustiniana' prison in that city for about six months.
41 Cellini, *Autobiography*, 216.

42 On this topic, see Maria Luisa Meneghetti, 'Scrivere in carcere nel medioevo.' In this essay, Meneghetti documents a literary tradition of high-born prisoners being confined to towers and other elevations, low-born ones to dungeons.
43 In all the places Casanova was confined in his early life – and there are many instances of confinement and liberation in the first part of his memoirs – he was almost always held somewhere up high. In the Forte Sant'Andrea, for example, he was able to make a sally into the city by climbing out his cell window directly onto the mast of a waiting boat. In the episode when he definitively lost his virginity to either Marton or Nanette Savorgnan (it was dark at the time and the two sisters were in many ways remarkably alike), he did his cavorting in an upstairs bedroom. Then there is the episode of the 'lazzaretto' at Ancona, where he made somewhat incongruous love vertically downward from an upper room, thanks to the agility of a cooperative Greek slave girl detained in quarters below (1: 212–17).
44 In the second story of the Fourth Day of that work – a tale also set in Venice – Boccaccio describes how Frate Alberto similarly manifests himself, not 'in forma d'agnolo' (in the shape of an angel) but 'in forma d'uomo' (in the shape of a man), to a gullible and vain Monna Lisabetta, who is eager to welcome the lusty apparition into her bedroom.
45 For the importance of mastering writing for Casanova throughout his life, see Flem, 11.
46 In his article on Cellini for the *Dizionario biografico degli italiani* Nino Borsellino says bluntly of the episode in the *Vita* of the escape from Castel Sant'Angelo that 'Casanova imitated it in his *History of My Flight from the Piombi*' (448).
47 Flem agrees, noting on the first page of her book how Casanova's escape from the Piombi was 'the emblem of his life' (3).
48 For a similar identification between 'vivo' or 'I live' and 'scrivo' or 'I write' (though in an entirely different emotional context) see Gabriele D'Annunzio, *Il secondo amante di Lucrezia Buti*, in volume 2 of his *Prose di ricerca di lotta ..., Tutte le opere*, 390 ff.

2: The Spielberg: Concealment and Refutation

1 Stendhal [Marie Henri Beyle], *La Chartreuse de Parme, Romans et Nouvelles*, ed. Henri Martineau, II: 397.
2 For these problems in Italian historiography see Clara M. Lovett, *The Democratic Movement in Italy, 1830–1976*, 1–7. Anarchist and Socialist prisoners of the later nineteenth century are treated in chapter 4.

3 Victor Brombert, *The Romantic Prison*, 4.
4 For information, including photographs, about this citadel-prison and the later museum, a complex destroyed by bombing in the 1940s, see Renato Bertacchini, *Pellico, Maroncelli, Confalonieri, Pallavicino allo Spielberg*.
5 Alessandro D'Ancona, *Federico Confalonieri*, 51.
6 For all of them, see John Morris Roberts, *The Mythology of the Secret Societies*.
7 There is a copy of the law specifying capital punishment for such association in Alessandro Luzio, *Il processo Pellico-Maroncelli secondo gli atti ufficiali segreti*, 553–6.
8 Antonio Cassese documents the use of similar practices today in *Umano-Disumano*.
9 Luzio, 243.
10 Egidio Bellorini, 'Silvio Pellico,' *Enciclopedia italiana*, XXVI: 633–5.
11 Barbara Allason, *Vita di Silvio Pellico*, 464, is one of the many who has repeated this phrase.
12 Attilio Marinari, 'Silvio Pellico tra rivolta e rassegnazione,' 361.
13 Blaise Pascal, *Pensées and The Provincial Letters*, 66.
14 Chap. 18. To facilitate consultation of *Le mie prigioni*, I refer to it by chapter rather than page numbers, and give these references in the text. For an American echo of the many 'faux Dauphins' who proliferated in Europe during this period, see 'the Duke and the Dauphin' of Mark Twain's *The Adventures of Huckleberry Finn* (1884).
15 In a letter to Henri de Bombelles, Prince Metternich remarked bitterly about the work that 'one would be tempted to believe that Monsieur Pellico has come out of prison less reformed than he was when he went in' (Allason, 310–11). For more on the book's early reception, see the introduction by Egidio Bellorini to Silvio Pellico's *Le mie prigioni ed altri scritti scelti*, xxxvii–xl.
16 Mario Milani, 'Una lettura de *Le mie prigioni*, oggi,' 35.
17 First published in 1804, Alfieri's work was explicitly inspired – as its author states on the book's first page – by 'amore di me medesimo' or 'love for myself.'
18 The actual documents alluded to, however, have been recovered from Austrian police archives and are often reproduced in annotated editions of Pellico's book.
19 The episode in *Le mie prigioni*, it should be clear, is quite different from Casanova's earlier opening of the *Orlando furioso* at random in a semi-serious (though very successful) attempt to find out when he would be released from prison. For Pellico and Zanze, see especially María Rosa Menocal, 'Bondage: Pellico's Francescas.'
20 Pellico's description of what he is writing might suggest that the text in

question is a first draft of the *I doveri degli uomini* that he published after release from the Spielberg. There is nothing in that work, however, that would seem to require such intricate concealment.

21 Another example of a text dealing with intimate matters that is first written and then erased (though not without leaving palimpsests beneath) is that proposed by Sigmund Freud as a figure for the operations of the mind in general, especially as it chooses to remember or forget. See his 1924 essay 'The Mystic Writing Pad' in *The Standard Edition of the Complete Psychological Works of Sigmund Freud*, XIX: 227–32.

22 Upon release from prison, Foresti emigrated to the United States, where he was the second (after Lorenzo Da Ponte) professor of Italian literature at Columbia University. After Foresti became a U.S. citizen in 1853, President Pierce appointed him United States consul to Genoa, but because of the appointee's radical political views the nomination was not ratified by the Savoy government. Foresti was later reappointed to the same post by President Buchanan and this time did receive the Savoy kingdom's *exequatur*. There is information about him in Atto Vannucci's *I martiri della libertà italiana dal 1794 al 1848*, II: 451–95, and in an anonymous article in the *Atlantic Monthly* of 1859 (25: 526–40). His memoirs were translated and published by Howard R. Marraro in the *Columbia University Quarterly* XXIV (1932): 441–75. In the same publication the following year Marraro followed up this translation with a comprehensive article about this figure titled 'Eleuterio Felice Foresti.' See also Giuseppe Monsagrati, 'Felice Foresti,' *Dizionario bibliografico degli italiani*, XLVIII: 797–804.

23 In the essay 'Il palinsesto dell'autobiografia: Pellico e D'Azeglio' in his 1982 collection, *Dall'anima al sottosuolo*, Giorgio Barberi-Squarotti argues that the invisible text Pellico writes on the Piombi table is an account of 'youthful experiences and political commitments' that cannot be included in the account of religious edification he is composing. 'In order for *Le mie prigioni* to be written,' this critic says, 'it is necessary for the rest of Silvio's biography to be set down, it is true, but also erased since this is a matter that concerns only Silvio (and God, precisely the entity to whom secret confession is made). The work contains no moral except in regard to Pellico; it does not and cannot recommend anything exemplary or positive to his reader' 179, 184.

24 A recent biography is Anna Maria Mambelli's *Piero Maroncelli. Una vita per la libertà e la giustizia*.

25 See his letter to the *Courrier Français* of 1833 in Silvio Pellico, *Le mie prigioni*, ed. Silvia Spellanzon, 401.

26 For all of this, see the article 'Il testo autentico dei "Capitoli aggiunti"' by Henri Bédarida.

27 When *Le mie prigioni* was published in 1832, some of the members of Pellico's group – in particular, Federico Confalonieri – were still in the Spielberg; Pellico's reticence about certain topics may have been due to concern about possible reprisals affecting his still-detained comrades. Such scruples did not seem to have inhibited Maroncelli, however.

28 Allason, *Vita di Silvio Pellico*, 313–14, n. 464. Later research in the Viennese archives has made it clear that Pavlovich did indeed take advantage of his pastoral position to try to extract political information from his charges. Luzio states, for example, that it is 'without any doubt' that this cleric 'had been told to forward to the Emperor every political secret that was disclosed to him' (530).

29 See Pellico, chap. 44, Maroncelli in *Le mie prigioni*, ed. Spellanzon, 38.

30 Bédarida, 734. The recently rediscovered Italian original of Pellico's additions to his work reveals that in his French version of *Le mie prigioni* Latour did not publish Pellico's additional chapters in their entirety but cut them instead – a further rewriting by Pellico's French publisher of Pellico's rewriting of Maroncelli's rewriting him.

31 Letter in the Maroncelli archives at Forlì, quoted by Mambelli, 135. In regard to imprisonment in general, Curcio, Valentino, and Petrelli have noted how 'the body in confinement is an amputated body' (*Nel bosco di Bistorco*, 62), while in *Le prigioni degli altri*, Adriano Sofri has also described prison life as 'mutilata' (64).

32 A well-known poet and man of letters in later life, Foscolo (1778–1827) had been a friend of Pellico's in his early years.

33 Silvio Pellico, *Epistolario*, ed. Guglielmo Stefani, 194–5, 400–2.

34 Pellico, *Lettere milanesi (1815–'21)*, ed. Mario Scotti, 501. For the whole matter see Scotti's 'Introduzione,' 'Nota al testo,' and the photocopies of the mutilated documents in question that he includes.

35 For him see Luigi Ambrosoli, 'Federico Confalonieri,' *Dizionario biografico degli italiani*, XXVII: 772–7, and the essays edited by Giorgio Rumi, *Federico Confalonieri aristocratico progressista*.

36 Details in D'Ancona, *Federico Confalonieri*, 140 and passim.

37 *Carteggio*, 2: 695, emphasis by Confalonieri.

38 Ibid., 139.

39 Federico Confalonieri, *Memorie e lettere*, 15. Further references to this edition are given in the text and notes by page numbers only.

40 For more on the guard who provided Confalonieri with paper for the writing of his memoirs, see below, p. 57.

41 There are photographs of these fingernail pens and toilet-paper stationery in Bertacchini, *Pellico*.

42 These texts, plus additional letters to and about Confalonieri, are available in

Gallavresi's *Carteggio*. Among the texts reproduced there are two clandestine messages smuggled from prison by Matilde Dembowski, the same Milanese beauty who fascinated both Foscolo and Stendhal and was immortalized by the latter in his *De l'amour*. For more about her see Michel Crouzet, *Stendhal*.

43 In chapter 75 of *Le mie prigioni*, Pellico denied there was clandestine communication in or out of the Spielberg. But this was not true. Confalonieri did write secretly from prison, doing so, Gallavresi explains, 'by means of palimpsests beneath the letters of the commercial houses Bretschneider of Vienna and Bagus Carron of Trieste,' (646). See also Alexandre-Philippe Andryane, *Mémoires d'un prisonnier d'état au Spielberg*, III: 263.

44 Even after the Spielberg prisoners were deprived of the books brought with them from Italy – a measure taken to punish them 'in the same area where they have sinned' (230) – Confalonieri was able to obtain clandestine copies of Pascal's *Pensées* and St Augustine's *Confessions*. Read in prison, he reports, these works had a particularly powerful effect on him, possibly because 'the light of eternal truth, no matter how splendid it might be, abhors the world's tumult to seek out days of silence and solitude and in this way be able to descend into your heart' (228).

45 In his comment on this matter, D'Ancona distinguishes between 'Silvio Pellico, a person of feminine nature, born for the vague images of poetry' who 'emerged from prison an ascetic' and 'Confalonieri, a person of virile nature, born for the active life' who 'emerged from prison a believer' (175). Confalonieri's struggles with his conscience while in prison were also of great interest to another political leader who spent many years in prison, the anti-Fascist Antonio Gramsci. For his reaction in 1932 to the likelihood Confalonieri may have asked the emperor for a pardon at this point in his confinement, see Gramsci's *Lettere dal carcere*, 627 (*Letters from Prison*, II: 177).

46 For him, see Umberto Coldagelli, 'Giovanni Arrivabene,' *Dizionario biografico degli italiani*, 325–7. Coldagelli, while praising Arrivabene's efforts on behalf of Unification and his accomplishments in economics, criticizes his 'aristocratic and paternalistic attitude towards the working classes' and points out how 'his stance towards the social question further reveals the limits of his paternalistic philanthropy.'

47 Giovanni Arrivabene, *An Epoch of My Life*, 30. Subsequent references are given in the text.

48 Andryane, IV: 361–2, Andryane's emphasis. Further references to his work are indicated in the text and notes by volume and page numbers only.

49 Though not, at first, in England. See Michele Lupo Gentile, '*Le memorie di un prigioniero* di Alessando Andryane.'

50 I: 131. For the persistence of this mode of communication among prisoners, see the section in chap. 3 about Pastro's love affair through wall tapping in

Mantua and *Wall Tappings*, an anthology of women's writing from prison edited by Judith A. Scheffler.
51 By contrast with what Andryane suggests about his own conduct in captivity, Sandonà calls him 'one of the sorriest figures to appear on the scene of the political uprisings of this period,' suggesting that 'he blurted out everything he knew' because he believed that by so doing he would be granted immunity or a reduction of his sentence. Augusto Sandonà, *Contributo alla storia dei processi del Ventuno e dello Spielberg*, 168.
52 Confalonieri, *Carteggio*, 1092.
53 For Pellico's reservations, see his *Epistolario*, ed. Stefani, 162–3, 172–3.
54 The term 'romanzo' or 'novel' is Pallavicino's, for whom see below, pp. 59–63.
55 *Epistolario*, 163. Here Pellico is using a variant of Pallavicino's last name.
56 Ibid., 172. Alessandro D'Ancona, in his book on Confalonieri, has compared this bickering to the mutual pecking of two chickens being carried to the slaughter in a famous passage in Manzoni's *I promessi sposi* (D'Ancona, 108).
57 Giorgio Pallavicino, *Memorie di Giorgio Pallavicino*, I: 14. Further references to this edition are given in the text.
58 Tommaseo, who was born in Dalmatia in 1802 and died in 1874, was a well-known lexicographer, novelist, and man of letters.
59 Giorgio Pallavicino, *Spilbergo e Gradisca*, 20. Further references to this work are given in the text.
60 This is the opinion of Ugoberto Alfassio Grimaldi in the preface to his edition of Gabriele Rosa and Silvio Pellico, *Due patrioti allo Spielberg*.
61 Mario Menghini, 'Gabriele Rosa,' *Enciclopedia italiana*, XXX: 107.
62 Denis Mack Smith, *Mazzini*, 6.
63 Grimaldi, in Rosa and Pellico, 14–15. Further references to Rosa's memoir are to Grimaldi's edition and are given in the text.
64 Gabriele Rosa, *Federico Confalonieri*.
65 His *Autobiografia* was first made public posthumously in 1912 as part of the centennial celebration of its author's birth, which also saw the erection in Iseo of a monument to this patriot and author. See Grimaldi, in Rosa and Pellico, 10.
66 In 1832, as already mentioned, Confalonieri was still in jail, where he was known, Rosa reports, to 'marvel' when he heard of *Le mie prigioni*'s publication (84).

3: Bodies Politic

1 Luigi Settembrini, *Lettere dall'ergastolo*, 361.
2 For this counterpart of Milan's *Conciliatore* and Genoa's *Indicatore genovese*, see Franco Della Peruta, *Mazzini e i rivoluzionari italiani*, 14–18.

3 Carlo Bini, *Scritti*, 348.
4 Carlo Bini, *Il manoscritto di un prigioniero e altro*, ed. Mario Ambel and Marziano Guglielminetti; *Manoscritto di un prigioniero*, in Gaetano Trombatore, ed., *Memorialisti dell'Ottocento*, I: 260.
5 Bini, *Il manoscritto di un prigioniero* (1978), 124. Further references to this edition are given in the text and notes by page numbers only.
6 For his activities of this sort, see Alma Borgini, 'Carlo Bini traduttore.'
7 Page 96. Whether one agrees with the gruff suggestion made years later by Bini's fellow Tuscan, the novelist Federigo Tozzi (1883–1920), that 'Bini found Pellico antipatico – otherwise we would not have his book' (*Realtà di ieri e di oggi*), there is little doubt that Bini considered the *Manoscritto di un prigioniero* – written in 1833, one year after publication of *Le mie prigioni* – his response to Pellico.
8 For Livorno in Bini's day, see Della Peruta, passim, esp. 134–7; Sebastiano Timpanaro, 'Alcuni chiarimenti su Carlo Bini,' *Antileopardiani e neomoderati nella sinistra italiana*; Nicola Badaloni, 'Guerrazziani e sansimoniani,' 26–40; and David G. Lo Romer, *Merchants and Reform in Livorno 1814–1868*.
9 The son of a woodworker in a family of venerable traditions but little wealth, Guerrazzi became a successful lawyer as well as a nationally acclaimed writer and political figure. In *The Democratic Movement in Italy, 1830–1976*, Clara M. Lovett takes him as an example of the many Risorgimento patriots who, thanks to special skills or unusual gumption, rose dramatically on the social ladder during the period (82).
10 Giuseppe Petronio, ed., *Dizionario enciclopedico della letteratura italiana*, III: 220.
11 Guerrazzi's most famous work, *L'assedio di Firenze* (The Siege of Florence), was banned in Italy in its author's lifetime, but during the ban enjoyed such notoriety that, according to a biographer: 'whoever had the good fortune to acquire a copy of it, even at a steep price, held on to it like a sacred object,' while 'others who were less lucky or less rich, borrowed it from a friend or a relative and copied it out in the silence of the night' (Giovanni Pirodda, 'Giuseppe Mazzini e il romanticismo democratico,' 334). Today, however, like most of Guerrazzi's other works, his most famous historical novel is, if not unreadable, certainly not widely read. For other contemporary testimony, see Luigi Pastro, *Ricordi di prigione dell'unico superstite dei condannati di Mantova dal 1851 al 1853*, 15.
12 Benedetto Croce, for example, in an essay originally published in 1914, described Guerrazzi's correspondence from prison as his 'best prose,' holding that in his letters from confinement the often bombastic novelist and playwright 'abandoned his attempts to fire minds and told and talked about himself and personal matters,' and in this way 'came out looking admirable.'

Benedetto Croce, *La letteratura italiana per saggi storicamente disposti*, III: 285. The poet and man of letters Giosue Carducci (1835–1907), who edited a selection of Guerrazzi's letters (1880–2), also had high praise for these texts, possibly because their author's unbuttoned and sometimes stormy style is very much like Carducci's own in his more argumentative, informal writing.

13 Francesco Domenico Guerrazzi, *Lettere*, ed. Giosue Carducci, I: 102. Further references are to this edition and are given in the text. For the prison writing of Sacco and Vanzetti, see Charles Klopp, '"Waiting for the Hanger": The Letters of Sacco and Vanzetti.'

14 Both Carducci and Federico Martini, who also issued a volume of Guerrazzi's letters in Turin in 1891, were none the less so impressed by the wisdom of Guerrazzi's advice to Cecchino that they suggested that abridged editions of his letters be required reading in the Italian public schools. See the note by Luca Toschi to his edition of *L'epistolario di F.D. Guerrazzi, con il catalogo ...*, 13.

15 As such, they may be compared to such collections as the two edited by Piero Malvezzi and Giovanni Pirelli, *Lettere di condannati a morte della Resistenza italiana (8 settembre 1943–25 aprile 1945)* and *Lettere di condannati a morte della Resistenza europea*.

16 For details of this law, see Alessandro Luzio, *I martiri di Belfiore e il loro processo*, 160–1.

17 Pastro, *Ricordi*, 110. All further references to this edition are indicated in the text by page numbers only.

18 Pastro's lines might be translated as 'Stay with the canon / postpone your graduation / there are never [enough] brave men / to make thrones tremble.' The complete text of the sonnet is as follows:

    A V I Ta, amico, e al mio vigor mi riede
    S E L A Diva, che coli ne le profonde
    M I   S Tiche fonti a te scrutar concede
    U P E Trilli mortai salute asconde;

    O R R Ibil morbo, il sai, che il cor mi fiede
    V O T E, e tarde il sangue rende le onde,
    E D O Na al corpo non vital mercede
    R I   P Aratrice, ma languor vi offende!

    I   M O Lai!! Ma al profano è sorda lega!
    T' A S Colterà, se il chiedi, il sol tuo merto
    R I   P Arar puote alla mia sorte rea!

   O S O N nulla sperar? Chè non ardisci?
   N O N Offre in van chi cinto ha il crin d'un serto!
   I N I Nganno non son ... vien ... mi guarisci!   (*Ricordi*, 112)

To produce the acrostic message, the fourth letter of line 1 should be read first, then the fourth letter of lines, 2, 3, and so on down to line 14, a procedure that generates the message: 'T'attien al canon.' For the other three lines, the letters in the third position of all fourteen lines should be read, then those in the second and the first. Since Pastro admits that as a sonnet, his poem 'is almost inexplicable,' it is perhaps not necessary to attempt to translate it.

19 The documents of various kinds that the Mantua patriots produced in prison have been transmitted principally through two secondary sources: Luigi Martini's *Il confortatorio di Mantova* (Mantua, 1867; second edition, 1870–1 with several revised versions since) and Alessandro Luzio's *I martiri di Belfiore e il loro processo* (Milan, 1905, 1908, and 1916; revised and augmented edition 1924). For both Martini and Luzio – to whom he devotes an entire chapter – see Mario Vaini, *Mantova nel Risorgimento. Itinerario bibliografico*; for Luzio, Walter Maturi, *Interpretazioni del Risorgimento*, 432–46, and Antonio Gramsci, *Il Risorgimento, Opere* 4, 119–23; for Martini, Anselmo Guido Pecorari, 'Il confortatorio di Mons. Luigi Martini e l'Indice,' and the essays edited by Luigi Bosio and Giancarlo Manzoli in *Mons. Luigi Martini e il suo tempo (1803–1877)*.

20 Tazzoli's and Grazioli's degradations were apparently performed with the approval of church authorities in Rome but carried out over the protests of the local hierarchy. For a detailed account of the ceremony see Martini, I: 190–208.

21 After its initial surreptitious circulation, this pamphlet was republished by Luzio in 1886, and again in 1959 by the Comitato di Mantova of the Istituto per la Storia del Risorgimento Italiano.

22 See Luzio, *I martiri di Belfiore*, 213, for a facsimile of this document.

23 Texts in Luzio, *I martiri di Belfiore*, 331–63, and in Edoardo Piva, 'Lettere e versi inediti di un martire di Belfiore,' *Miscellanea di studi critici pubblicati in onore di Guido Mazzoni*, II: 405–25.

24 Martini, I: 138. 'As you know well, my Silvio, I am no poet / But when there burns irresistibly in my breast / A gently reciprocated affection, / Who would forbid even a donkey to sing? / So allow me to set down these few verses / Even though they must soon be dispersed by the breeze.'

25 Invisible ink made from lemon juice was still being used by Red Brigades prisoners in the 1970s. See Alberto Franceschini, *Mara Renato e io*, 127.

26 All quotations from Luzio, *I martiri di Belfiore*, 337–8; further references to this source are given in the text.
27 'The rich treasure of knowledge that adorned his mind led to his being sought out and rendered him distinctive in the most cultured settings' is how his relative Angelo Poma described him; see the collective volume edited by his mother, Anna Filippini Poma, *Cenni biografici e scritti vari di Anna Filippini Poma e del dottore Carlo Poma martire dell'Indipendenza italiana*, 75.
28 For the projected but finally abandoned plan by these conspirators to assassinate Rossi, a project that can be seen to foreshadow the political shootings and murders of the 1970s, see Martini, I: 287; Luzio, *I martiri di Belfiore*, 66ff. and 129ff. For comment on this Risorgimento activity on the part of the Mantuans by a member of the extraparliamentary left of the 1970s, see Adriano Sofri, *Memoria*, 227.
29 Anna Poma, 110; further references to this work are indicated in the text and notes by page numbers only.
30 Luzio, *I martiri di Belfiore*, 382, 388.
31 Ibid., 428ff.
32 For a similar ploy by Tito Speri, see ibid., 466. A modern example involving a prisoner of the Fascists who sent messages home in the slots for his collar stays is documented by Ferdinando Cordova in 'Alcune lettere inedite di un condannato a morte della resistenza romana.'
33 When Poma found it necessary to smear brick dust or other substances on his linen so that he could consign it to the laundry as quickly as possible, he was at pains to warn the attentive readers of these texts of what he had done, 'so that they would not be frightened or disgusted ' (414) by what they were handling.
34 Anna Poma's edition of the correspondence and other texts she exchanged with her incarcerated son is a rare instance in the history of prison writing in Italy because it presents not just one but both voices in the prison dialogue. For the suppression of the other, female voice in another famous prison correspondence, that of Antonio Gramsci with Tatiana Schucht, see Teresa De Lauretis, 'The Left Hand of History.'
35 'There is so much sweetness in your name / That I find nothing else that resembles it, / And in the great suffering that, alas!, has come over my soul, / I seek your benediction as if that of God. / Through you I find rest and the tempest / That has stormed my soul is stilled; / Serenity returns to my brow / And I bravely await the bitter contest. / When I speak with you in this horrible prison, / Despite my poor prospects / I still feel your vivid presence near me. / Just as in the first days of my life, / When you moved silently

near my cradle, / I could feel you there and smiled in my sleep' (Anna Poma, 89.) The poem is included by Ettore Janni in his *Poesia della patria ed eredità del risorgimento: I poeti minori dell'Ottocento*, II: 89.

36 See her epithalamium for her daughter (Carlo's sister) Teresa in which the martyred son and brother appears in a mystic apotheosis from which he first blesses his sister and new brother-in-law, and then proclaims the importance of religion, 'source of all virtue,' in the struggle for national liberation – a sentiment that the historical Carlo Poma would not necessarily have shared with his mother.

37 Luigi Settembrini, *Lettere dall'ergastolo*, 404. Further references to this work in the text and notes are marked *Lettere*.

38 Mario Themelly, in *Lettere*, xiii.

39 For the numbers, see Raffaello Ricci, 'Carceri e galere politiche nel regno di Napoli,' 559, and Luigi Settembrini, *Ricordanze della mia vita*, 342. By contrast, Adriano Sofri estimates that in a much more populous Italy since the 'years of lead' of the 1970s 'about six thousand "political" detainees have spent time in Italian prisons.' *Le prigioni degli altri*, 140.

40 Castromediano, *Carceri e galere politiche*, I: 135. Further references to this work are indicated in the text and notes by volume and page numbers only.

41 Francesco Gabrieli, 'Il duca bianco.'

42 Luigi Agnello, 'Sigismondo Castromediano,' *Dizionario biografico degli italiani*, XXII: 245.

43 For his life, in addition to the works by Gabrieli, Ricci, and Agnello cited above, see the 'Cenno biografico' by Brizio de Sanctis appended to Castromediano, II: 209–49; Giuseppe De Matteis, 'Sigismondo Castromediano'; Carolina Pironti, 'Carlo Poerio e Sigismondo Castromediano'; and Aldo Vallone, 'Il Risorgimento salentino-napoletano nelle parti inedite delle "Memorie" di S. Castromediano.' In 1995 the Comune of Cavallino and the Provincial Administratio of Lecce published Castromediano's *Lettere dal carcere*, edited by Giuseppe Barletta and Michele Paone; in 1996 the same two entities published his *Scritti di storia di arte*, edited by Michele Paone. I am grateful to Antonio Cassiano, Director of the Museo Provinciale 'Sigismondo Castromediano' of Lecce, for providing me with copies of these two important publications.

44 The phrase translated is from a letter by Castromediano quoted by De Matteis, 1229. On the last page of his memoir, Castromediano speaks of a 'bitterness worse than any he experienced while in prison: the bitterness of honest souls torn by the ingratitude of ordinary people, the bitterness of one who is proud of his past and yet cannot defend himself from the deadly lies levelled against him' (II: 208).

45 For conditions in the prisons of the Kingdom of Two Sicilies in Castromediano's time see Capelli, 95–106.
46 In one of his letters to Duke Alfonso, which has already been quoted, Tasso had made a similar connection between the two kinds of transgression. See above, p. 21.
47 Elena Croce comments on this practice in regard to Silvio Spaventa in her *Silvio Spaventa*, 73.
48 I: 265. For an autobiographical account of the life of another southern brigand of the period see P. Masi's *Mémoires de Gasparone rédigées par P. Masi, son compagnon dans la montagne et dans la prison*.
49 For the beggar, see I: 292. There is evidence that, while the regime treated prisoners who had received life sentences relatively benignly, those like Castromediano who had been given a term sentence were subjected to treatment expressly designed to kill them in detention (Ricci, 561).
50 I: 302–3. For similar sentiments expressed by the nuns who served as guardians at the women's prison at Trani in the 1930s, see Camilla Ravera, *Diario di trent'anni: 1913–1943*, 538.
51 Ricci, 562.
52 Published only a few years after Settembrini's work, De Sanctis's study was strongly influenced by Hegelian philosophy and is much less anti-clerical than Settembrini's *Lezioni*. It is probably the most influential – and maybe the best – history of Italian literature ever written.
53 The first edition of the *Ricordanze* was published in Naples in 1879, three years after Settembrini's death, with a preface by De Sanctis. For the publishing history of this work, see Mario Themelly's 'Nota al testo' in Settembrini, *Ricordanze*, lv–lxxi. Additional references to this edition are indicated in the text.
54 Ibid., lvi.
55 'Difesa di Luigi Settembrini scritta per gli uomini di buon senso dedicata alla Gran Corte criminale di Napoli,' *Ricordanze*, 427. There is a description of this imprisonment in the first part of the *Ricordanze*.
56 For details of the accusations, see *Ricordanze*, 423.
57 *Ricordanze*, 6 *infra*, 311, and 361 where there are passages about the experience from Settembrini's diary of 1854–5.
58 A book-length meditation on the term by a present-day 'ergastolano' is Nicola Valentino's *Ergastolo*.
59 For more about this institution, see *Lettere*, 5–6; *Ricordanze*, 315. There is an illustration of the building in Silvio Spaventa's *Lettere a Felicetta*, 48ff.
60 For Settembrini's putting on weight, see *Lettere*, 134, 571, 573. Spaventa also grew fat, as Settembrini notes, 418. For the use of meat and wine, 318, for

lobsters 378. The 'politici' also ate with cutlery brought from home (*Lettere a Felicetta*, 121), were served a kind of coffee in bed by 'comuni' they had hired as servants (*Lettere*, 12, and cf. *Lettere a Felicetta*, 154, where Spaventa also speaks of having a 'servo'). During one hot summer they were even provided three times with snow from Ischia (*Lettere a Felicetta*, 26). While in forced residence on the island of Ustica in 1926, Gramsci also put on weight. See his remarks in a letter to Sraffa, *Lettere*, 26, *Letters*, 53.

61 Entry of 23 January 1855 from his 'Diario 1854–5' in *Ricordanze*, 394.
62 Settembrini, *Lettere*, 48. Aldo Moro's captors, Anna Laura Braghetti has revealed, fitted out the apartment in the Via Montalcini where the president of the Christian Democrat Party was held with, among other things, a cage with two imprisoned canaries, which later – unlike Moro – escaped. See her *Il prigioniero*, 31, 73–4.
63 Elena Croce, 77.
64 *Lettere*, 35–6. If this ritualized interaction between prisoners and the authorities detaining them suggests such later meditations on prison life as those by Franz Kafka in his story, 'In the Penal Colony,' the theatrical production by Santo Stefano inmates during this same carnival featuring prisoners 'dressed as generals, colonels, captains, princes, lords, princesses, young girls in love, etc.' (*Lettere*, 36) seems a startling prefiguration of certain of the works of Jean Genêt. Carlo Emilio Gadda reports that in the prisoner-of-war camp where he was interned during the First World War, the prisoners also put on theatrical productions. See his *Giornale di guerra e di prigionia*, 193–4; Camilla Ravera too is reported to have written a 'commediola' that was presumably then performed while she was in prison at Trani; see below, p. 224 n. 35. For information about theatrical productions by prisoners in the 1980s, including one of Genêt's *Haute Surveillance* (*Deathwatch*), see Maria Ponce de León, *Meccanismi di sopravvivenza: Letteratura carceraria contemporanea in Italia. Poesia, narrativa e teatro 1970–1997*, 122–32.
65 *Lettere*, 52–3; for Castromediano, see above, p. 86.
66 Castromediano I: 15; see Themelly's comments in his introduction to Settembrini's *Ricordanze*, xiii.
67 A modern edition is Luigi Settembrini, *I neoplatonici*, ed. Raffaele Cantarella.
68 Like other writers of this period, Settembrini is aware of the precedent Pellico represents for his own prison writing. Though convinced that 'Italy will not rise up by force of paternosters,' he concedes that Pellico, 'by describing the cruel torments endured by one man, makes you think about all the generous individuals who in those dark ten years in prisons throughout Italy endured what were even crueller torments that they could not describe to the world in appropriate words of the sort used by Pellico, a

person who it is evident spoke not only for himself but for them all.' Luigi Settembrini, *Lezioni di letteratura italiana dettate nell'università di Napoli*, III: 326, 324. While in prison, Settembrini also read Cellini and Tasso (*Lettere*, 47, 143).

69 After the death of his parents in the Casamicciola earthquake of 1883, the young Croce lived for a period with his uncle Silvio in Rome; for the latter's 'intertextual' first name, see Elena Croce, 10.
70 Castromediano, *Carceri e galere politche*, II: 127
71 Silvio to Bertrando Spaventa in Spaventa, *Dal 1848 al 1861*, 120.
72 In 1849, when Bertrando was a tutor in the household of fellow exiles Prince and Princess Pignatelli, he gave all of his salary to Silvio. When the Pignatellis discovered what he was doing, they doubled Bertrando's salary and even after Bertrando had left their service they continued to send money to his imprisoned brother. See Elena Croce, 64.
73 Spaventa *Dal 1848*, 96.
74 Spaventa, *Lettere a Felicetta*, 81. Further references to these letters are given in the text.
75 Spaventa, *Dal 1848*, 166–7.
76 For his astonished recognition of just how good his health was at this stage of his life, see Settembrini, *Lettere*, 407, 418.
77 For a similar title devised for similar reasons in more recent years, see Sofri, *Le prigioni degli altri*.
78 Galletti, 46. Further references to this edition are given in the text.
79 For prison conditions in the pontifical states in general during this period, see Capelli, 83–9.
80 Galletti, 273. See also Lovett, 135. For comments by Galletti on the carabinieri, see Galletti, 39.
81 For a different kind of bodily marking as testimony – that is, contemporary prisoners' employment of tattoos as signs of their inner freedom – see the illustration to Valentino, *Ergastolo*, 101–6.
82 Angelo Frignani, *Angelo Frignani e il suo libro 'La mia pazzia nelle carcere'. Memorie autobiografiche di un patriotto romagnolo per la prima volta pubblicate in Italia*, ed. Luigi Rava, xc. Further references to this edition appear in the text.
83 It was translated into French, German, and English as, respectively, *Ma folie dans les prisons, memoires d'Angelo Frignani* (Paris: Truchy, 1840); *Mein Wahnsing in Kerker* (Leipzig, 1842); and *Nil desperandum; or, the narrative of an escape from Italian dungeons, translated from the memoirs of Angelo Frignani* (London: T.C. Newby, 1859).
84 Tommasini, 39–40, 78. Franz Anton Mesmer had died in Austria in 1805; Mary Shelley's *Frankenstein, or the Modern Prometheus* was first published in 1818.

85 As indicated in note 43 above, Castromediano's letters from prison to his parish priest have now been collected and published with the Gramscian title, Sigismondo Castromediano, *Lettere dal carcere*. Of the writers in the previous group, by contrast, only Confalonieri left both letters and a memoir.
86 For more information on the fascinating figure of Luigi Castellazzo see Alfonso Scirocco, 'Luigi Castellazzo,' *Dizionario biografico degli italiani*, XXI: 661–4; Simonetta Bono, 'Luigi Castellazzo ed i processi di Mantova del 1852–53 alla luce di alcuni documenti inediti'; and Charles Klopp, 'The Corpus and Bodies of Prison Discourse in Risorgimento Mantua.' Two articles that comment on connections between Castellazzo's confessions and those of repentant Italian terrorists of the 1970s are Maria Berlinguer, 'Luigi Castellazzo, il "pentito"'; and Walter Boni, 'Luigi Castellazzo, il "convertito" della congiura di Belfiore.' Castellazzo is also known for the novel *La Lombardia nel 1848*, which he published under the pseudonym of Anselmo Rivalta (Florence: Tipografia Garibaldi, 1862).

4: Authority, Desire, and Dissent: Serving the Revolution

1 Anna Kuliscioff, from an article in *Il secolo* of 1880, quoted in Franco Damiani and Fabio Rodriguez, eds., *Anna Kuliscioff. Immagini, scritti, testimonianze*, 46.
2 Enrichetta Caracciolo, *Misteri del chiostro napoletano*, 189.
3 Albert M. Ghisalberti calls this association 'bad insurrectional literature rather than an alarming preparation for true uprisings.' See his edition of Felice Orsini, *Lettere*, xii.
4 See Felice Orsini, *Alla gioventù italiana*, *Lettere*, xiv.
5 Felice Orsini, *The Austrian Dungeons in Italy: A Narrative of Fifteen Months' Imprisonment and Final Escape from the Fortress of S. Giorgio*, 162.
6 See Elizabeth Adams Daniels, *Jessie White Mario: Risorgimento Revolutionary*.
7 Michael St John Packe, *Orsini: The Story of a Conspirator*, 221; for Orsini's jubilation at the contract for his English writings, see his letter to Emma Herwegh in Alessandro Luzio, *Felice Orsini. Saggio bibliografico*, 68.
8 For details see Packe and Daniels.
9 Felice Orsini, *Memorie politiche*, ed. Marchetti and Pergameni, 6.
10 For a brief sketch of this fascinating woman, see 'The Italian Connection: Emma Herwegh and Her Circle' in Gordon A. Craig's *The Triumph of Liberalism: Zurich in the Golden Age*.
11 A note to the 1962 Milan edition by Marchetti and Pergameni lists eleven editions of the *Memorie* between 1858 and 1865 alone: *Memorie politiche*, 7.
12 Packe, 226. 'How to Be a Revolutionary' can now be read in the Ghisalberti edition of Orsini's *Lettere*, 268ff.

13 Both Packe and Ghisalberti speculate about this.
14 Luzio, *Felice Orsini*, 213.
15 Martini, *Il confortatorio di Mantova*, 216.
16 Visited in the spring by another prison official, who complimented him on his 'studious habits' and asked when his project would be completed, Orsini replied that his book would be ready 'shortly' (Martini, 160; cf. *Memorie*, 240). A short three days later, indeed, he was on his way to Switzerland.
17 *Austrian Dungeons*, 58. Orsini himself, writing to Emma about his life, had also noted how 'willpower and disdain for life plus wanting to escape no matter those who would wish us dead ... is leading me towards something that seems more a novel than reality' (*Lettere*, 189). For more about Orsini's lost manuscript, see *Austrian Dungeons*, 163; *Memorie*, 242.
18 Those by Guerrazzi, for example.
19 *Memorie*, 194.
20 *Austrian Dungeons*, 171.
21 Giuliano Procacci, *Storia degli italiani*, 391.
22 The Partito Socialista Italiano (Italian Socialist Party), for example, was founded in 1892.
23 Anna Kuliscioff, *Lettere d'amore a Andrea Costa, 1880–1909*, ed. Pietro Albonetti, 94. Further references to this edition are indicated in the text and notes by page numbers only.
24 For a similar declaration by a later activist and political prisoner, see Mario Alicata's 1943 remarks in his *Lettere e taccuini di Regina Coeli*, 67–8.
25 For the date of her birth see Albonetti in Kuliscioff's *Lettere d'amore*, 17, n. 2, and Rosalia Colombo Ascari, 'Feminism and Socialism in Anna Kuliscioff's Writings,' in Robin Pickering-Iazzi, ed., *Mothers of Invention: Women, Italian Fascism, and Culture*.
26 For Kropotkin as a prison writer, see his *In Russian and French Prisons*.
27 Karl Marx, *La corrispondenza di Marx e Engels con italiani. 1848–1895*, ed. Giuseppe Del Bo, 515–17, quoted by Albonetti on p. 128 of his collection of the Kuliscioff letters. For more information on her early life, see Jan Marinus Meijer, *Knowledge and Revolution: The Russian Colony in Zurich (1870–1873)*.
28 Page 141, cf. similar remarks on 145 and 209–10 where she says that 'instead of a bedroom, I would prefer a cell with bars.'
29 The events of May 1898 have been famously described by the Socialist novelist and polemicist Paolo Valera in *Le terribili giornate del maggio '98*, ed. Enrico Ghidetti. On this occasion, Costa too – in Milan independently from Kuliscioff and Turati – was imprisoned by the Milanese authorities.
30 Of these sentences, however, they served eight and fourteen months respectively.
31 Page 158. Fifty years later, under the stricter censoring of the Fascist regime,

it would not have been possible for a prisoner to describe detention as 'unexpected and illegal.'
32 Although jail regulations usually forbid writing in languages the censor assigned to reading them does not know, for some reason the person in charge of monitoring Costa's and Kuliscioff's mail decided not to interfere with these expressions of feeling. For more on secret languages for expressing erotic emotions in censored letters and the lively interest taken in them by one linguistically curious and extremely well prepared Austrian censor during the First World War, see Leo Spitzer's introduction to his *Lettere di prigionieri di guerra italiani 1915–1918*.
33 For Cafiero and his political break with Costa during this same period see Pier Carlo Masini, *Storia degli anarchici italiani. Da Bakunin a Malatesta (1862–1892)*, chap. 10; and Nunzio Pernicone, *Italian Anarchism, 1864–1892*.
34 For trenchant comment on Kuliscioff's relations with both Costa and Turati, see Alessandro Roveri, *Giovinezza e amori di Anna Kuliscioff*.
35 Filippo Turati, *Carteggio. Vol. I: 1898–99*, collected by Alessandro Schiavi, ed. Franco Pedone, 611. Further references to this collection are indicated in the text.
36 Pages 85–6; Prampolini (1859–1930), was one of the founders of the Italian Socialist Party.
37 An earlier woman prisoner of interest was Eleonora Fonseca Pimentel of Naples (1752–99); see also the section on Camilla Ravera in the chapter to follow and the books by Elissa E. Gelfand and by Judith A. Scheffler listed in Works Consulted.
38 It was only later that the industrial workers of nearby Milan united with their agricultural comrades in what would become the classic labour coalition. For Costa see Andrea Costa, 'Annotazioni autobiografiche per servire alle Memorie della vita,' *Movimento operaio* 4, no. 2 (1952): 314–56; Andreina De Clementi, 'Andrea Costa,' *Dizionario biografico degli italiani*, XXX: 128–44; Gino Cerrito, *Andrea Costa nel socialismo italiano*; Manuel Gonzales, *Andrea Costa and the Rise of Socialism in the Romagna*; and Lilla Lipparini, *Andrea Costa rivoluzionario*.
39 Costa wrote a novel, too, in his case a utopian one. There is information about it in De Clementi.
40 Despite its title (which was first attached to Costa's manuscript on publication in *Movimento operaio* 4, no. 2 (1952)), this work consists of scattered notes on topics that include his prison readings of Carlyle, Nietzsche, and American history, his musings on the future of the Socialist movement, his complaints about the effects of confinement on the imagination, and reminiscences of his early life.
41 Kuliscioff, 181. 'Oh how sadly through the iron bars/ The winter day

penetrates into the cell! / Oh how mournfully the sparrows sing / How sepulchral the silence seems. / And what phantoms from the insistent fog / Arise here and pass before me! / What strange phantoms! And how the soul / Oppressed seeks to find comfort in you! / As you with a smile now draw nearer; / I see the earth flower at your steps. / The fog clears when struck by the rays of your eyes / The sky turns blue and the sun begins to shine!'

42 Paolo Pillitteri, *Anna Kuliscioff. Una biografia politica*, 67. Charcot (1825–93) was also Sigmund Freud's teacher during the early part of Freud's career.
43 Turati, *Carteggio*, I: 115.
44 Renato Giusti, ed., 'Lettere dal carcere ad Enrico Ferri di Anna Kuliscioff, Andrea Costa e Filippo Turati (maggio-agosto 1898),' 323.
45 'For Kuliscioff,' writes Maria Casalini about the encounter with Turati that was to develop into a lasting relationship, 'hurt and disappointed by Costa's unstable passion, it must have been especially pleasing to be the object of the reassuring attentions of Turati, with whom, above all, she shared the unresolvable and fundamental contradiction between the impossibility of giving up a traditional, upper bourgeois life style and the equally powerful desire for the realization of Socialism's egalitarian ideals.' *La signora del socialismo italiano. Vita di Anna Kuliscioff*, 81.
46 'The truth of the matter,' writes Paolo Pillitteri about the latter's relation with Kuliscioff, 'is that Andrea Costa carried with him the ancient and irremovable curse of all Italian men: that peculiar mixture of jealousy and prejudice. For this reason his relationship with Anna could not help but be interwoven with misunderstandings, disapproval, and tension' (40).
47 Once he was released from prison and restored to Parliament, one of Turati's first actions was to propose a series of prison reforms. While imprisoned he had intended to write an article that would be 'a breakthrough on prison psychology that will make the country shudder. Nobody has the slightest idea!' (see his clandestine letter to his mother in *Carteggio*, I: 121).
48 For these two pamphlets, see the note in ibid., 114.
49 Ibid., 216–17.
50 Luigi Settembrini, *Lettere dall'ergastolo*, 292–3, n. 2.
51 The characterization of her claustration as an 'ergastolo' is Caracciolo's own: Caracciolo, 234.
52 Caracciolo's memoir has been reissued twice in recent years: in 1964 by Giordano in Naples with the title *Le memorie di una monaca napoletana*, and in 1986 by Giunti of Florence as *Misteri del chiostro napoletano*, with a 'Nota critica' by the historian and novelist Maria Rosa Cutrufelli.
53 She also served briefly as inspector of schools, a position to which she was named by Garibaldi. For this and other information about her see Ales-

sandra Briganti, 'Enrichetta Caracciolo,' *Dizionario biografico degli italiani*, XIX: 348–9.
54 For this aspect of his character, see especially the documentation in Packe.

5: Answering Gramsci: The Anti-Fascists

1 For the seventeen years from 1926, when the special tribunals were first instituted, until 1943 and the Liberation, Spriano counts more than 5,000 anti-Fascists in jail, 10,000 in *confino* (forced residence), 21,000 made to appear in court, and 160,000 'warned' or kept under special surveillance by the police. See Paolo Spriano, *Storia del Partito comunista italiano*, II: 358.
2 'So long as the influx continues into the prisons and forced residence, so long as the special courts are functioning,' the captious Rossi wrote his mother from a Fascist prison cell, 'you can continue to have hope in our people. As little as thirty years ago, I believe, a political system like the present one would have been able to stay in power without special courts or special laws. Everything else notwithstanding, from the point of view of forming character, a certain progress has been made.' Ernesto Rossi, *Elogio della galera. Lettere 1930–1943*, 135.
3 Barbara Allason, 'Epistolari,' 314–16. The Turinese Germanist, translator, and novelist Allason lived from 1877 to 1968. Allason's *Memorie di un'antifascista 1919–1940*, published in Rome, Florence, and Milan in 1945, was one of the few prison writings by anti-Fascists to be published in Italy before Gramsci's 1947 *Lettere*.
4 Croce's review has been reprinted in volume two of his *Scritti vari e discorsi politici*.
5 Calvino's introduction, translated by William Weaver, has been reprinted as the preface to the English edition of Calvino's *Il sentiero – The Path to the Nest of Spiders*, trans. Archibald Colquhoun.
6 The literature of the Nazi death camps is a special subgroup of the literature of detention. Since prisoners destined for extermination were forbidden any correspondence with the outside world, writing about the *lagers* is perforce almost entirely in the form of survivor memoirs. For this literature see, among many others, Renato Giusti, 'Appunti sulla letteratura dei lager.'
7 For an excellent anthology of letters by anti-Fascist prisoners and internees, see Giancarlo Pajetta's *Lettere di antifascisti dal carcere e dal confino*. Some well-known Italian political or cultural figures imprisoned by the Fascists who have preferred not to publish their prison letters include the left-wing activists Riccardo Bauer (but see his memoir, *Quello che ho fatto. Trent'anni di lotte e di ricordi*), Giorgio Amendola, Pietro Nenni, and many others. Still

other documents of this sort did not survive the confusion of the war, occupation, and civil war, among them Leone Ginzburg's diaries from confinement in 1935–6, for which see the introduction to Leone Ginzburg, *Scritti*, xxxvi; and Arturo Colombo, 'L'esempio di Leone Ginzburg (con l'ultima lettera a Natalia).'

8 Alcide De Gasperi, *Lettere dalla prigione, 1927–1928*, 82; further references are to this edition and are given in the text. For De Gasperi, see Piero Craveri, 'Alcide De Gasperi,' *Dizionario biografico degli italiani*, XXXVI: 79–114; Elisa Carrillo, *Alcide De Gasperi: The Long Apprenticeship*; and Maria Romani Catti De Gasperi, *De Gasperi, uomo solo*.
9 Carrillo, 12–13.
10 Ibid., 67–74.
11 Ibid., 71–2.
12 De Gasperi, *Lettere*, 169; Carrillo, 94; Catti De Gasperi, 122.
13 Although he did suffer from digestive irregularities, De Gasperi was not in nearly as poor health as such other prisoners of the period as the Communists Lo Sardo and Gramsci, both of whom were in effect killed by the harsh conditions of their confinement.
14 He repeatedly compares his sufferings with those of saints Augustine (21), Peter, and Paul (67, 58), with Job (38), and even with 'the great Innocent Convict,' Christ himself (32).
15 Francesco Lo Sardo, *Epistolario dal carcere (1926–1931)*, 240.
16 For a review of his life as a Communist activist, see the 'Memoriale' Lo Sardo presented in his own defence to the special tribunal in Pajetta I: 191.
17 Both the first edition of 1984 and second augmented edition of 1988 of Lo Sardo's letters were published in Verona by Edizioni del Paniere. References here are to the 1984 edition and are made in the text.
18 For reactions to Lo Sardo's death by fellow Turi inmate Gramsci, see the account by Athos Lisa in *Memorie. In carcere con Gramsci*, 95; and the comments by Tania Schucht to Piero Sraffa in the latter's *Lettere a Tania per Gramsci*, 229.
19 Umberto Terracini, *Sulla svolta. Carteggio clandestino dal carcere 1930–31–32*, 59. Further references to this work appear in the text.
20 Umberto Terracini, *Al bando dal Partito. Carteggio clandestino dall'isola e dall'esilio*, ed. Alessandro Coletti, 170. For the circumstances of Terracini's expulsion from the party by the Ventotene collective, see this work passim, and Ravera, *Diario di trent'anni*, 613, where Terracini's friend and political comrade insists that the ostracism of the two Communists in 1932 was based on 'imprecise information and was part of the inevitably abstract thinking of that isolation from real life, plus a return to schematics and dogmatisms

that the party, despite certain backsliding, was already surpassing and rejecting.'
21 See also Umberto Terracini, 'Ricordi e riflessioni di un rivoluzionario professionale,' 249–66; and the commemorative volume *Umberto Terracini nella storia contemporanea*.
22 In addition to Terracini's *Sulla svolta*, see Spriano, *Storia*, II: 210–307.
23 Some letters in the volume were sent to the party through another prisoner's correspondence with his sister: *Sulla svolta*, 71.
24 There are details about this in Terracini's introduction to *Sulla svolta*, 9. Although most of the communications devised in this way seem to have reached their destination, in a few cases (see 58) part of the clandestine message was erased by the censor's obliterations of portions of the ostensible letter.
25 Ibid., 18, n. 5. This method of clandestine communication was later discovered by prison authorities; see Tania Schucht to Piero Sraffa, *Lettere a Tania*, 81.
26 Terracini explained that his prolixity in this 'papiello' was due to his having '24 hours a day and 364 days a year free for its elaboration.' (*Sulla svolta*, 38).
27 Letter 1 in *Sulla svolta*, 15–18; this event, which Spriano has characterized as 'an episode about which there has been endless discussion from 1938 until today' (*Storia* II: 262), has been famously described by Ignazio Silone in his *Via d'uscita* of 1965 and in the collective work by Silone, Richard Wright, Arthur Koestler, and André Gide, *The God That Failed*, of 1949.
28 Terracini, 'Ricordi e riflessioni,' 261. After the lengthy preventative detention preceding his trial, Terracini had written something similar about his mental state to his wife. 'Sometimes,' he told Alma Lex then, 'when I would suddenly find myself immersed in some empty and nebulous fantasy, or else when after half a page of a "serious" letter my brain turned torpid and my eyes began to close, I asked myself whether, as the final effect of these mishaps, I was not going to become a bit dehumanized. The trial has reassured me in this regard: it's not going too badly at all; my mental machine is functioning perfectly' (Pajetta, II: 376–7).
29 Spriano, *Storia*, II: 158.
30 Camilla Ravera, *Lettere al Partito e alla famiglia*, 231.
31 The women's prison at Trani should not be confused with the institution for men at nearby Turi, where Gramsci and Lo Sardo were confined.
32 Others in this tradition more contemporary with Ravera include the anti-Fascist women prisoners discussed in Laura Mariani's *Quelle dell'idea. Storie di detenute politiche 1927–1948*. For a connection between Ravera and Anna Kuliscioff see Damiani, 145; Pillitteri, 186. In the special prison-and-prisoners

issue of *Il ponte*, March 1949, there are two contributions by women prisoners, Bice Rizzi from the First World War period, and Adele Bei from the Resistance (325–36, 372–7). For the different treatments accorded male and female prisoners in an earlier period in France, see O'Brien, 52–74. Writing by criminal women prisoners, with specific reference to France, has been studied by Gelfand; chap. 2 of *Imagination in Confinement* is devoted to women's prisons.

33 Ravera, *Diario*, 534.
34 Ibid., 518. In regard to Pellico, however, Anna Gobetti points out that while the earlier author described reawakening on his first morning in jail as a 'horrendous thing,' Ravera insisted in her first letter home to her family that 'I can assure you that I am not too bad off even here.' See the documentation on this period of Ravera's life in Ada Gobetti, *Vita in carcere e al confino, con lettere e documenti*, 65–6. Although this book is frequently catalogued under Gobetti's name, the material in it is mostly by Ravera.
35 While in prison Ravera even managed to write a *commediola* (little comedy) that the nuns later put on in the prison theatre to celebrate the name day of the Mother Superior (Gobetti, 68). The text for this performance, an event that brings to mind the analogous carnival festivities on Santo Stefano nearly one hundred years earlier described by Settembrini – see p. 90 – has not survived.
36 Gobetti, 62. The OVRA was the Fascist secret police.
37 *Lettere al Partito e alla famiglia*, xx and note; see also Rita Palumbo, *Camilla Ravera racconta la sua vita*, 97. For the story of the botched shooting of Vecchi in Paris, see Ravera, *Diario*, 526 and Palumbo, *Camilla Ravera racconta*, 96, as well as Spriano, II: 291–3, where the implications of the incident for the party are also detailed. Further references to Ravera's letters in *Lettere al Partito e alla famiglia* are indicated in the text and notes by page numbers only.
38 Gobetti, 28.
39 Page 66. For examples of correspondence from prison in which names of supposed relatives were really references to political comrades, see the documents by prison and police authorities about Sandro Pertini's mail, collected by Vico Faggi in *Sandro Pertini. Sei condanne, due evasioni*, 207–54. In one of these texts the Fascist prefect of Savona notes to a superior that the prisoner Pertini does not have a nephew named Nino living in Nice, while another hand (that of his superior) has noted on the document that the 'nephew' is in fact the anti-Fascist Anacreonte Costa (232–4).
40 Ravera, *Diario*, 528.
41 Ibid., 551.
42 Page 112; see also the similar passages on 132, 157, etc., of *Lettere*.

43 'If only he is not too sick: that would be good enough for me!' Among other allusions to Gramsci is the letter dated 8 January 1935, in which Ravera expresses her satisfaction that 'Antonio' has agreed, at the party's urging, to consider the possibility of seeking parole.
44 Pages 98, 99. For Sraffa's relationship with Gramsci during his imprisonment, see below.
45 Page 124. Compare the letter a few pages later where she declares that 'I am happy that you have finally sent your little students home' (135).
46 For Ravera's position on 'the three' while she was still in Paris, see Spriano, *Storia*, II: 250.
47 Ravera, *Diario*, 566.
48 Ernesto Rossi, *Miserie e splendori del confino di polizia. Lettere da Ventotene 1939–1943*, 152. See also his *Elogio della galera*; Elide Rossi, *Lettere ad Ernesto*; the volume of 'Scritti e testimonianza' gathered by Giuseppe Armani in *Ernesto Rossi, un democratico ribelle. Cospirazione antifascista, carcere, confino*; Angelo Corsetti, 'Ernesto Rossi'; Giuseppe Fiori, *Una storia italiana. Vita di Ernesto Rossi*.
49 Charles F. Delzell, 'Antifascism,' in Philip V. Cannistraro, ed., *Historical Dictionary of Fascist Italy*, 25; see also Fiori, *Una storia italiana*, 89–192.
50 Quoted in Corsetti, 54. For Rossi's own preference for a utopian rather than a scientific Socialism, see *Elogio*, 201.
51 Condemned by the special tribunal for his anti-Fascist activities, Rossi was deprived of both his rank in the military reserve and his pension as a wounded veteran; *Elogio*, 15, 83–4.
52 Rossi, *Miserie e splendori*, 60.
53 For the extremely important role he played in disposing of Allied war materials left in Italy after the war and his subsequent considerable public service, see Fiori, *Una storia italiana*, 221ff.
54 Ibid., 242–97.
55 Unfortunately, there are no complete letters in the *Lettere ad Ernesto*, their editor having preferred to prune the more than 5,000 pages of Elide Rossi's communications to her son in favour of selected 'excerpts that ... can best reveal the personality of Signora Elide' (xvii).
56 In this regard, see the remarks on Anna Filippini Poma's correspondence with her son, Carlo, discussed above in chap. 3, 79–80 and notes 34 and 36 to chap. 3. For more on Elide Rossi, see Fiori, *Una storia italiana*, 3–18 and passim.
57 Elide Rossi, *Lettere ad Ernesto*, xix, see also 93. Further references to this collection are made in the text.
58 See Ernesto Rossi's comments in his *Critica del capitalismo* (in Corsetti, 54) on

his feelings at being permitted after eight years to write down his reactions to what he had been reading.
59 Pages 211–12. The phrase printed in italics (*'Who are forced to live like animals'*) had been obliterated by the censor but later became visible once more.
60 Fiori, who has written about both Rossi and Gramsci, also believes that Rossi's prison letters should be compared to the Communist deputy's *Quaderni* rather than to his prison letters: *Una storia italiana*, 118.
61 Augusto Monti, *Lettere a Luisotta*, 16. Further references to this collection are given in the text.
62 See the note by Luisa Monti Sturani, ibid., 25–6.
63 Note by Luisa Monti Sturani, ibid., 12.
64 William Arrowsmith goes on to say about 'I mari del Sud' (South Seas) that 'without Monti's example, it is doubtful the poem would have been written, certainly not as it is written.' Cesare Pavese, *Hard Labor*, 207. Pavese and Monti exchanged several letters when the older man was in jail; for them see Attilo Dughera, 'Monti e Pavese: Storia di un'amicizia attraverso le lettere.'
65 Monti's court-assigned lawyer – who as such was not due a fee – extorted money from the family instead. *Lettere a Luisotta*, 3, 25–6.
66 Some notion of the atmosphere that prevailed during the period when Monti and Terracini were confined at this institution can now be gleaned thanks to the publication of some of the official prison records. See Natoli, Foa, and Ginzburg, eds., *Il registro. Carcere politico di Civitavecchia 1941–1943*. The material printed in this volume is from a slightly later time period than that when Monti was imprisoned.
67 For the classical and medieval idea of prison as a refuge from the greater prison that is the world, see Witt, *Existential Prisons*, 1–15.
68 Rodolfo Morandi, *Lettere al fratello, 1937–1943*, 112–13.
69 While Levi and Morandi had already enjoyed some success in the 1930s, they moved to real prominence in the country's cultural power structure only after 1945. For an analysis of the special problems facing intellectuals in postwar Italy who grew up under Fascism, see Albertoni, Antonini, and Palmieri, eds., *La generazione degli anni difficili*.
70 Alicata was one of the collaborators on the screenplay of Luchino Visconti's crypto-anti-Fascist film, *Ossessione*. For prison as a conversion experience for him, see what Giorgio Amendola says in his preface to Alicata, *Lettere e taccuini di Regina Coeli*, vii.
71 Carlo Levi, *E' questo il 'carcer tetro'? Lettere dal carcere 1934–35*, 30, 95, 96, 83; all further references to this edition are indicated in the text.
72 Renato Curcio has noted how during his imprisonment in the 1980s and 1990s, watches and clocks were forbidden to prisoners, a procedure that

exaggerated this sensation of living outside time. Renato Curcio, *La soglia*, 94.
73 Pia Vivarelli, 'Carlo Levi. Disegni e riflessioni dal carcere,' in Carlo Levi, *Disegni dal carcere 1934. Materiali per una storia*, 30.
74 In the 'Pagine di un diario ritrovato' (Pages of a Rediscovered Diary), which is printed second in his book, Bassani speaks at one point of 'when I got out of prison last year.' Since this essay is dated 1940, this would place his imprisonment itself sometime in 1938 or 1939. Giorgio Bassani, *Di là dal cuore*.
75 Ibid., 12.
76 The depriving of an individual of this identity by a tyrannical state is the theme of such later works by Bassani as *Gli occhiali d'oro* (*The Gold-Rimmed Spectacles*), of 1958.
77 See Gramsci's letter to Tania Schucht of 25 January 1932, *Letters from Prison*, II: 131 and Sraffa, *Lettere a Tania per Gramsci*, 73, where Sraffa suggests to his sister-in-law that Gramsci might be persuaded to review Morandi's work.
78 Morandi, *Lettere al fratello*, 35. Further references to this work are given in the text.
79 Alicata, *Lettere e taccuini di Regina Coeli*, 187 (his emphasis). Further references to this work are given in the text.
80 For the phrase by Kulisçioff, see Turati, *Carteggio*, 244.
81 Gramsci, *Letters from Prison*, ed. Rosengarten, I: 347. Further references to Gramsci's letters in this edition are given in the text.
82 For letters dealing with Gramsci's life and work for the party before his arrest in 1926, see his *Lettere 1908–1926*, ed. Santucci.
83 There is an immense bibliography on this topic. Good recent summaries of the situation include Paolo Spriano, *Antonio Gramsci and the Party: The Prison Years*; Rosengarten's introduction and notes to Gramsci, *Letters from Prison*, and Valentino Gerratana's introductory essay, 'Gramsci e Sraffa' in Sraffa, *Lettere a Tania*, xiii–lv. A provocative, carefully documented, and highly original account of Gramsci's imprisonment viewed in the context of his entire life and Communist beliefs is provided by Aurelio Lepre in *Il prigioniero. Vita di Antonio Gramsci*. I regret not having been able to make greater use of Lepre's very recent work in my comments on Gramsci here.
84 See Sraffa to Togliatti in 1932 on the importance of finding material for their comrade to write on in prison, even though 'one must, of course, find a topic whose political content can be passed off under the guise of literature' (Sraffa, 225).
85 The most complete collection of Gramsci's prison letters in any language is that edited by Frank Rosengarten and translated by Raymond Rosenthal.

Columbia University Press has also begun to bring out the *Prison Notebooks* in English in an admirably annotated edition by Joseph A. Buttigieg.
86 Paolo Spriano, 'Nota introduttiva,' to Antonio Gramsci, *Lettere dal carcere*, xvii.
87 They are, in this sense, similar to the texts left posterity by the Martyrs of Mantua, as well as to the letters from prison by Lo Sardo.
88 All of Gramsci's prison communications were, it seems, of the 'ostensible' sort, though there is a report of a clandestine message dealing with the 'svolta' of 1930 that was smuggled into prison for him. For this supposed communication in invisible ink, see Ezio Riboldi, *Vicende socialiste*, 182–3.
89 So Maria-Antonietta Macciocchi reports on the basis of an interview she had with Piero Sraffa in Cambridge. See her *Pour Gramsci*, 290.
90 Gerratana, in his edition of Sraffa's *Lettere a Tania*, xxx, has described the Sraffa of this period as a 'communist without a party.' For him in general, see Jean-Pierre Potier, *Piero Sraffa – Unorthodox Economist (1898–1983)*.
91 For Sraffa's correspondence about Gramsci with Tatiana Schucht, see his *Lettere a Tania*.
92 In her introduction to Tatiana Schucht's *Lettere ai familiari*, Mimma Paulesu Quercioli says that at least some of Tatiana's mail for Giulia was sent by diplomatic pouch or through friends travelling to Russia rather than by regular mail. Whether this prevented such communications from being read by the Soviet authorities is perhaps still open to question.
93 For this project see Frank Rosengarten, 'Gramsci's "Little Discovery": Gramsci's Interpretation of Canto 10 of Dante's *Inferno*.'
94 Gerratana comments astutely that 'the tie with Sraffa should be seen ... not only as a *means* for connecting Gramsci in a material sense with the Party, but also as a *source* for the nurturing and stimulation of his intellectual life.' Sraffa, xxvi.
95 Rosengarten estimates that Gramsci's wife wrote her husband a total of perhaps forty letters during his more than ten years of confinement.
96 Aldo Natoli, for example, puts all of Giulia's letters from November 1934 until her husband's death in April 1937 into the latter category and is able to identify other times during their correspondence when letters from her are either missing or lost. See his *Antigone e il prigioniero. Tania Schucht lotta per la vita di Gramsci*, 170.
97 Commentators have proposed explanations of Giulia Schucht Gramsci's health problems that range from the purely physical to the condition itself of being a woman in a patriarchal society. For the latter position, see Adele Cambria, *Amore come rivoluzione. Tre sorelle per un rivoluzionario, le lettere*

inedite della moglie e delle cognate di Antonio Gramsci, la risposta alle Lettere dal carcere. Con il testo teatrale Nonostante Gramsci.

98 Quoted in Natoli, *Antigone e il prigioniero*, 224.
99 For Gramsci's dilemma, see also Giuseppe Donghi, 'Dialoghi e monologhi nelle *Lettere dal carcere* di Antonio Gramsci. Aspetti di un'analisi semiotica.' Curcio, Valentino, and Petrelli, similarly, have described the 'anguish' of a prisoner forced to 'see his own reflection exclusively in his own words,' going on to say that 'in this case, in fact, over time the mirror sends nothing back but dead images, because without living relationships there can be no living words.' *Nel bosco di Bistorco*, 111.
100 After being retrieved from prison with his other belongings and then hidden, with Sraffa's connivance, in the vaults of the Banca Commerciale Italiana, Gramsci's prison notebooks were dispatched by Tatiana, via American Express, to safety in the Soviet Union. See Tatiana's letter in Sraffa, 195.
101 Natoli, *Antigone e il prigioniero*, 184.
102 Sraffa, who insisted on calling Tatiana Schucht 'voi' rather than 'tu' throughout their long correspondence, never seems to have been very fond of his link in Italy with the imprisoned Gramsci and often lost patience with Schucht's dilatoriness and apparent inability to follow instructions. For an angry passage in which he accuses her of having caused a 'disaster,' see Sraffa, 108.
103 Terracini, *Sulla svolta*, 86.
104 'Because desire lies between the needs to which the body responds and the demands that speech articulates,' a student of epistolary writing has commented about this problem more generally, 'it is always a gap in language that cannot be filled, and consequently, every discourse of desire is a critique of language: it cannot encapsulate, enclose, sum up desire – much less satisfy it.' Linda S. Kauffman, *Discourses of Desire: Gender, Genre, and Epistolary Fictions*, 301.
105 Although it might be objected that letters by earlier prisoners – those of Kulisçioff, Turati, or Costa, for example – were also published many years after their composition and thus also belong to two different historical periods, they were not brought to the public in an era in which the cause for which these activists struggled had so definitively triumphed. By the explicit terms of the 1948 Italian Constitution, after all, the Italian republic is an officially anti-Fascist state.
106 For this matter, see Rosengarten's introduction to Antonio Gramsci, *Letters from Prison*, and Stephen Gundle, 'The Legacy of the Prison Notebooks: Gramsci, the PCI and Italian Culture in the Cold War Period.' Gundle

notes, in regard to the letters, that 'the sections omitted ... contained politically awkward observations as well as doubts and fears that in some respects detracted from the image of sure conviction and unflinching heroism that the party sought to convey' (138).

6: The Death of a President / The Effacement of an Author

1 Cesare Lombroso, *Gli anarchici*, 34–5. Emphasis in original.
2 Moro habitually stopped for a moment of prayer and reflection before proceeding to his political appointments of the day. For these and other details about the last weeks of his life, see Robert Katz, *Days of Wrath*.
3 For a succinct but thorough account of Moro's early life and politics as they led up to the 'historic compromise,' as well as an exhaustive description of the court proceedings associated with Moro's murder, see Richard Drake, *The Aldo Moro Murder Case*.
4 For a beginning bibliography on this much discussed topic, see, in addition to the works already cited by Katz and Drake, the entries in Works Consulted by Beverly Allen, Alberto Arbasino, Armenia Balducci, Nanni Balestrini, Francesco M. Biscione, Giorgio Bocca, Luigi Bonante, Anna Laura Braghetti, Salvatore Bussu, Aniello Coppola, Gian Paolo Cresci, Renato Curcio, Donatella Della Porta, Uri Eisenzweig, Lucrezia Escudero, Enrico Fenzi, Franco Ferrarotti, Sergio Flamigni, Alberto Franceschini, Carlo Ginzburg, Luigi Guicciardi, Henner Hess, the Italian Parliament, Alison Jamieson, Robert J. Kelly, Sergio Lenci, Brunello Mantelli, Silvana Mazzocchi, Indro Montanelli, Sue Ellen Moran, Mario Moretti, Aldo Moro, David Moss, Giuliano Naria, Antonio Negri, Diego Novelli, Gino Pallotta, Giovanni Palombarini, Michele Pistillo, Adriano Prosperi, Alain Saudan, Leonardo Sciascia, Alessandro Silj, Adriano Sofri, Mario Sossi, Dominique Venner, Vittorio Vettori, Robin Erica Wagner-Pacifici, Leonard Weinberg, and Giuseppe Zupo.
5 Mario Moretti, *Brigate rosse. Una storia italiana*, intervista di Carla Mosca e Rossana Rossanda, 134. For Moro's incessant writing see also Anna Laura Braghetti, *Il prigioniero*, 98.
6 Braghetti explicitly compares the letters Moro wrote from his prison to those included in the Malvezzi and Pirelli anthology of *Lettere di condannati a morte della Resistenza italiana*, commenting that when she read her father's copy of the Resistance letters as a schoolgirl she did so 'weeping tears of rage and sometimes wondering how I would have behaved in similar circumstances.' *Il prigioniero*, 101.
7 Aldo Moro, *L'intelligenza e gli avvenimenti. Testi 1959–1978*, ed. Bozzo, Medici,

and Mongillo, 402. Further translations of Moro's letters made from the texts in this edition are indicated in the text and in the notes by page numbers only.

8 For one of the many comparisons between Moro and Gramsci made by commentators on the Moro case, see the volume of documents sympathetically edited by Gian Paolo Cresci, *Moro. I giorni del tormento,* where the section devoted to the letters from the Via Montalcini is subtitled *Lettere dal 'carcere'* – a characterization (and use of quotation marks) meant to indicate both the similarities and the differences between Moro's letters and those of his Communist predecessor. A similar tactic was evidently followed by the editors of Sigismondo Castromediano's *Lettere dal carcere* of 1995.

9 Leonardo Sciascia, *L'affaire Moro,* 16, Sciascia's emphasis. Moretti, too, was admittedly baffled by the language of his prisoner's public statements: 'When he wrote the "memoriale,"' he says about this, 'he had in mind those who hold the keys to his language and know what he is talking about. He did not think, I believe, that I could really understand. And in fact I didn't understand. It was clear that he was denouncing misdeeds of every kind, disclosing names and circumstances that should have made the Palace tremble. But for us at that moment it wasn't the scandals that mattered. We were not there to ruin anyone's career; we were aiming higher than that' (Moretti, 156). Braghetti's description of Moro's language is similar; see *Il prigioniero,* 37–9.

10 See, for example, Gino Pallotta, *Aldo Moro. L'uomo la vita le idee,* 201.

11 Page 416. A later autopsy of Moro's body confirmed that he had not been drugged and was in generally good health.

12 Page 400. The second adjective in the phrase quoted would seem to mean that in Moro's view the Red Brigades were frustratingly and frighteningly unresponsive to compromise, co-optation, or other strategies for political control of the sort that he and his colleagues were accustomed to employing in the adversarial situations they knew best.

13 Moretti, 149. In *Il prigioniero,* a later but equally firsthand account of Moro's imprisonment, Braghetti does speak of letters that Moretti decided not to send, pointing out that Moro's captors concentrated on the more narrowly political missives, while those to the family 'were taken to their destinations if they contained indications that were helpful in our projects of the time, or because of humanitarian considerations' (100).

14 A comparison of what was apparently the first draft of one of Moro's letters with the final version as published by the newspapers is nevertheless instructive. In a letter to Benigno Zaccagnini that appeared in the papers on 5 April, Moro had written 'it is not difficult to imagine the consequences I

will have to pay,' while in what was evidently the draft, the phrase was 'pay with a sentence of death.' In the published document, similarly, Moro spoke of a 'political trial in which there are foreseeable developments and consequences' instead of 'in which I have already been found guilty' and mentioned how 'I remember how [Communist Party Secretary Enrico] Berlinguer used to say that the Red Brigades' major reaction was going to take place just as the agreement is reached ... As has happened, at my expense,' a phrase that was omitted entirely in the final version. In the draft, Moro had also described himself as a 'hostage' instead of a 'political prisoner' and had noted how he was writing 'with complete lucidity, or at least as much as someone can have after fifteen days in exceptional circumstances.' In the final version this became 'with complete lucidity and without having suffered any sort of physical coercion.' For the two texts, see Moro, 402–6, and the report of the *Commissione parlamentare d'inchiesta sul terrorismo in Italia*, 83–4.

15 To demonstrate their efficiency and presumed ubiquity, as well as to guarantee that what they sent would be sure to appear in a newspaper somewhere, the Red Brigades took pains to disseminate what Moro had written not just to journalists in Rome but to their counterparts in Turin, Genoa, and Milan as well, timing their telephone calls so that the papers in the four cities were informed simultaneously where they could find the texts in question (Moretti, 138–9).

16 Intermediaries for Moro's mail to his family included the politician's personal secretary, Nicola Rana; his parish priest, Don Antonello Mennini; and a student from the law classes he taught at the University of Rome, Maria Luisa Familiari. Despite the precaution of communicating through these trusted third parties, Moro believed that some of his prison writings had been intercepted and, as he put it, 'sequestered' – apparently, to his mind, by the authorities. In the documents discovered in 1990, Moro expressed his fears that previous dispatches, including two last wills and testaments sent for safekeeping to his family, had been seized in this way. It is not clear what happened to these documents: they could, of course, have been impounded by the Red Brigades themselves.

17 Sciascia notes how the dissemination of Moro's message to the press 'inflated the Red Brigades' action to an almost mythical degree and guaranteed that their theoretical and practical communications would enjoy extremely wide diffusion' (77).

18 Some twelve of these letters have still not been released to the public by the Moro family, though they have been examined by the authorities; in the volume published by the Italian Parliament they are indicated by blank pages and the rubric 'scritto non pubblicato' or 'unpublished writing.'

19 Giorgio Bocca, *Il caso Moro*, 43.
20 The Red Brigades had in fact first considered kidnapping Prime Minister Giulio Andreotti rather than Moro, the latter becoming their actual victim almost by chance. See Moretti, 115–16.
21 Page 400. Or, as Moretti paraphrased his prisoner's views in this regard, 'I have come to such a tremendous pass not because they [that is, the Red Brigades] find me antipatico but because I am President of the Democrazia Cristiana. I am not here to answer for myself, but for all of you' (146–7).
22 The phrase appears in the draft form only of the letter to Zaccagnini. See n. 14 above.
23 Page 410. Terracini's prison experience under the Fascists has been treated in the previous chapter. Beccaria (1738–94) was the author of the influential work on imprisonment and capital punishment *Dei delitti e delle pene (On Crimes and Punishments)* of 1764.
24 Sciascia, 58. For similar reactions by other political colleagues of Moro, see Adriano Sofri, *L'ombra di Moro*, 174–5. Taviani, for example, declined even to discuss the accusations about him in the April letter to the papers, declaring that he did not intend 'to get into an argument with the Red Brigades' (Sciascia, 73).
25 For a chilling, firsthand account of his fatal shooting, see Moretti, 167–9.
26 Sofri, *L'ombra di Moro*, 43. Something similar happened to Moro's image in his treatment in the Italian press, where the only newspapers that took an independent position in regard to the Moro case seem to have been the radical organs *Lotta continua* and *Il manifesto*. A thorough and carefully documented account of press response to the entire situation is available in Alessandro Silj, *Brigate Rosse-Stato. Lo scontro spettacolo nella regia della stampa quotidiana*. For decidedly more unsympathetic reactions to Moro's abduction and death, by contrast, on the part of factory workers in Italy's industrialized north, see the interviews gathered by Brunello Mantelli and Marco Revelli in their *Operai senza politica*.
27 For another analogy between Moro and Gramsci, two prisoners 'abandoned by their friends while in the hands of the enemy,' see the article by Sciascia in *La stampa* of 17 March 1989.

Conclusion: Sentences and Convictions

1 Laura Braghetti, in Braghetti and Mambro, 264.
2 Curcio, Valentino, and Petrelli, 110.
3 Ibid., 111. It is because inmates are aware of this linguistic threat to their

identities that they feel the need to create the special jargons that exist in prisons everywhere. For a study of such a language in an American maximum security prison see Inez Cardozo-Freeman, *The Joint: Language and Culture in a Maximum Security Prison*. For prison argot in nineteenth-century French prisons, see O'Brien, 77–89.

4 'Prison has the power,' notes Marianella Sclavi, 'to totally identify an inmate with his crime' (*Ridere dentro. Un seminario sull'umorismo in carcere con Renato Curcio, Maurizio Iannelli, Stefano Petrelli, e Nicola Valentino*, 61). Franca Ongaro Basaglia has also noted how women detained in Italian mental hospitals become subject to a similar 'nullification of their persons' and are thus 'rendered objects without life, without a history save the anonymous one of the abnormality of their behaviour.' See her preface to Giuliana Morandini's *... e allora mi hanno rinchiusa*, v.

5 Adriano Sofri, like Pellico both a successful journalist and a prisoner of a mistrusted state, has commented about his predecessor's strategy in regard to secular and divine authority. 'Pellico,' he remarks, 'is no stronger than the others – quite the contrary. But he behaves ... according to a traditional model of passive aggressiveness that he has hoarded up out of his own weakness. His self-sacrifice is complete and even rather unctuous. But his surrender to constituted authority has venom in its tail: if, in fact, the turnkey's omnipotence must cede to that of the prosecutor, and the latter's is eclipsed by that of His Majesty the Emperor – all of them must bow down before God's supreme power. God is called maliciously to account in every line of *Le mie prigioni* to diminish and finally crush the power of jailers and despots, while at the same time preserving the prisoner from the sin of lese-majesty' (*Le prigioni degli altri*, 58–9).

6 The prisoner Nicola Valentino commented in an interview in 1996 with Maria Ponce de León how writing in prison 'substitutes for the absence of a body' and is 'therefore a help, a medicine, a cure, but also the sign of a sickness, a difficulty' (Ponce de León, *Meccanismi di sopravvivenza*, 218).

7 Luzio, *I martiri di Belfiore*, 494–5.

8 Pajetta, *Lettere di antifascisti dal carcere e dal confino*, I: xvi.

9 Giorgio Amendola (1907–80), a former prisoner of the Fascists from Pajetta's generation and a PCI leader in the postwar years, agrees with this, pointing out that the letters he and his comrades wrote from Fascist prisons 'were never sincere' (*Un'isola*, 102).

10 Curcio et al., 200. In support, in this regard, of what these inmates have written, prison administrator Mariapia Frangeamore agrees that prison memoirs by their very nature describe an experience that is '"revisited,"

made into a novel, in any case changed in the process of a later retelling.' See her essay, 'In carcere,' in Giordano, 221.
11 Curcio et al., 373.
12 For the even more radical idea that non-criminals at some level admire lawbreakers because they 'perform psychological functions for noncriminals – gratifying their antisocial impulses, reassuring them of their comparative innocence, and assuaging their guilt through vicarious punishment,' see Duncan, 117, and the entire section entitled 'A Strange Liking: Our Admiration for Criminals.'

Works Consulted

Ackroyd, Carol, ed. *The Technology of Political Control.* London: Pluto Press, 1980.
Agnello, Luigi. 'Sigismondo Castromediano.' *Dizionario biografico degli italiani.* Rome: Istituto dell'Enciclopedia Italiana. Vol. 22, 1979: 245.
Albertoni, Ettore A., Ezio Antonini, and Renato Palmieri, eds. *La generazione degli anni difficili.* Bari: Laterza, 1962.
Alfieri, Vittorio. *Vita rime e satire di Vittorio Alfieri.* Ed. Luigi Fassò. Turin: UTET, 1965.
Alicata, Mario. *Lettere e taccuini di Regina Coeli.* Turin: Einaudi, 1977.
Allason, Barbara. 'Epistolari.' *Nuova Antologia* 440 (1947): 314–16.
– *Memorie di un'antifascista 1919–1940.* Rome, Florence, and Milan: Edizioni U [1945].
– *Vita di Silvio Pellico.* Milan: Mondadori, 1933.
Allen, Beverly. 'The Telos, Trope and Topos of Italian Terrorism.' *SubStance* 53 (1987): 37–43.
Altman, Janet. *Epistolarity: Approaches to a Form.* Columbus: Ohio State University Press, 1981.
Ambrosoli, Luigi. 'Federico Confalonieri.' *Dizionario biografico degli italiani.* Rome: Istituto dell'Enciclopedia Italiana. Vol. 27, 1982: 772–7.
Amendola, Giorgio. *Un'isola.* Milan: Rizzoli, 1981.
– *Lettere a Milano: 1939–1945.* Rome: Editori Riuniti, 1980.
Amoroso, Giuseppe. *Lettere di patrioti italiani del Risorgimento.* Bologna: Cappelli, 1971.
Andryane, Alexandre-Philippe. *Mémoires d'un prisonnier d'état au Spielberg par A. Andryane, compagnon de l'illustre Comte Confalonieri.* 4 vols. Paris: Ladvocat, 1837–8.
Anonymous. 'E. Felice Foresti.' *Atlantic Monthly* 25 (1859): 526–40.
Ansaldo, Giovanni. *L'antifascista riluttante. Memorie del carcere e del confino, 1926–1927.* Bologna: Il Mulino, 1992.

Apostoli, Francesco. *Lettere Sirmiensi per servire alla storia della deportazione dei cittadini cisalpini in Dalmazia ed Ungheria*. Milan: 1801.
Arbasino, Alberto. *In questo stato*. Milan: Garzanti, 1978.
Armani, Giuseppe. *Ernesto Rossi, un democratico ribelle. Cospirazione antifascista, carcere, confino*. Parma: Guanda, 1975.
Arrigoni, Carlo. *Luigi Pastro il medico inquisito nei processi di Venezia e Mantova (1851–53)*. Milan: Libreria Lombarda, 1914.
Arrivabene, Giovanni. *An Epoch of My Life. Memoirs of Count John Arrivabene*. London, 1862.
Ascari, Rosalia Colombo. 'Feminism and Socialism in Anna Kuliscioff's Writings.' In Robin Pickering-Iazzi, ed., *Mothers of Invention: Women, Italian Fascism, and Culture*. Minneapolis: University of Minnesota Press, 1995.
Aventi, Giuseppe. *Diario di Ventotene*. Milan: All'Insegna del Pesce d'Oro, 1975.
Bachelard, Gaston. *La Poétique de l'espace*. Paris: PUF, 1958.
Badaloni, Nicola. 'Guerrazziani e sansimoniani.' *Democratici e socialisti livornesi nell'Ottocento*. Rome: Editori Riuniti, 1966.
Balducci, Armenia, Giuseppe Ferrara, and Robert Katz. *Il caso Moro*. Naples: Pironti, 1987.
Balestrini, Nanni. *Gli invisibili*. Milan: Bompiani, 1987.
Barberi-Squarotti, Giorgio. 'Il palinsesto dell'autobiografia: Pellico e D'Azeglio.' *Dall'anima al sottosuolo. Problemi della letteratura dell'Ottocento da Leopardi a Lucini*. Ravenna: Longo, 1982.
Barbiera, Carlo Raffaelo. *Simpatie. Studi letterari*. Milan: Battezzati, 1877.
Bassani, Giorgio. *Di là dal cuore*. Milan: Mondadori, 1984.
– *Gli occhiali d'oro*. Milan: Mondadori, 1958.
Battistini, Andrea. 'L'autobiografia e il superego dei generi letterari.' *Annali d'italianistica* 4 (1986): 7–29.
Bauer, Riccardo. *Quello che ho fatto. Trent'anni di lotte e di ricordi*. Milan and Bari: Cariplo-Laterza, 1987.
Bazzotti, Ugo, ed. *Le carceri dei martiri di Belfiore nel Castello di San Giorgio*. Mantua: Comune di Mantova, 1985.
Beccaria, Cesare. *Dei delitti e delle pene*. Ed. Gianni Francioni. Edizione Nazionale delle Opere di Cesare Beccaria. Milan: Mediobanca, 1984.
Bédarida, Henri. 'Nel centenario delle "Mie prigioni." Il testo autentico dei "Capitoli aggiunti."' *Convivium* 4 (1932): 717–39.
Bellomo, Bino. *Lettere censurate*. Milan: Longanesi, 1975.
Bellorini, Egidio. 'Silvio Pellico.' *Enciclopedia italiana*. Rome, 1935. Vol. 26, 1981: 633–5.
– 'Silvio Pellico e Federico Confalonieri.' *Giornale storico della letteratura italiana* 41 (1903): 344–53.

Bender, John. *Imagining the Penitentiary: Fiction and the Architecture of Mind in Eighteenth-Century England*. Chicago: University of Chicago Press, 1987.
Berlinguer, Maria. 'Luigi Castellazzo, il "pentito,"' *Gazzetta di Mantova*, 8 December 1983.
Bertacchini, Renato. *Pellico, Maroncelli, Confalonieri, Pallavicino allo Spielberg*. Florence: La Nuova Italia, 1966.
– 'Le "Ricordanze" di Settembrini. Proposte per una lettura.' *Italianistica* 7 (1978): 264–81.
Berti, Enrico. 'F.D. Guerrazzi da Palazzo Vecchio alle Murate.' *Rassegna storica del Risorgimento* 57 (1970): 592–604.
Biloni, Vincenzo. *Tito Speri da Brescia*. Florence: Bemporad, 1933.
Bini, Carlo. *Manoscritto di un prigioniero*. In Gaetano Trombatore, ed., *Memorialisti dell'Ottocento*. Naples and Milan: Ricciardi, 1953. I: 179–224.
– *Il manoscritto di un prigioniero e altro*. Ed. Mario Ambel and Marziano Guglielminetti. Bologna: Cappelli, 1978.
– *Scritti*. Florence: Le Monnier, 1900.
– *Scritti editi e postumi di Carlo Bini*. Florence: Le Monnier, 1869.
Biscione, Francesco M., ed. *Il memoriale di Aldo Moro rinvenuto in via Monte Nevoso a Milano*. Rome: Coletti, 1993.
Bisiach, Gianni, ed. *Pertini racconta gli anni 1915–1945*. Milan: Mondadori, 1983.
Blanchot, Maurice. *Le livre à venir*. Paris: Gallimard, 1959.
Bocca, Giorgio. *Il caso Moro*. Milan: Bompiani, 1978.
– *Noi terroristi*. Milan: Garzanti, 1985.
– *Il terrorismo italiano 1970–1978*. Milan: Rizzoli, 1978.
Boggs, Carl. *Gramsci's Marxism*. London: Pluto Press, 1976.
Bonante, Luigi, ed. *Dimensioni del terrorismo politico*. Milan: Franco Angeli, 1979.
Boni, Walter. 'Luigi Castellazzo, il "convertito" della congiura di Belfiore.' *Gazzetta di Mantova*, 20 December 1983.
Bono, Simonetta. 'Luigi Castellazzo ed i processi di Mantova del 1852–53 alla luce di alcuni documenti inediti.' *Rassegna storica del Risorgimento* 43 (1956): 87–123.
Borgini, Alma. 'Carlo Bini traduttore.' *Rassegna della letteratura italiana* 68 (1964): 382–98.
Borsellino, Nino. 'Benvenuto Cellini.' *Dizionario biografico degli italiani*. Rome: Istituto dell'Enciclopedia Italiana. Vol. 23, 1979, 440–55.
Bosio, Luigi and Giancarlo Manzoli, eds. *Mons. Luigi Martini e il suo tempo (1803–1877). Convegno di studi nel centenario della morte*. Mantua: Accademia Virgiliana and Diocesi di Mantova, 1978.
Bourget, Paul. *Sensations d'Italie*. Paris: Plon, 1891.

Braghetti, Anna Laura, with Paola Tavella. *Il prigioniero*. Milan: Mondadori, 1998.
Braghetti, Laura, and Francesca Mambro. *Nel cerchio della prigione*. Milan: Sperling and Kupfer, 1995.
Brand, Charles Peter. *Torquato Tasso: A Study of the Poet and of His Contribution to English Literature*. Cambridge: Cambridge University Press, 1965.
Briganti, Alessandra. 'Enrichetta Caracciolo.' *Dizionario biografico degli italiani*. Rome: Istituto dell'Enciclopedia Italiana. Vol. 19, 1976: 348–9.
Brombert, Victor. *The Romantic Prison*. Princeton: Princeton University Press, 1978.
Brunet, Gustave. *Imprimeurs imaginaires et libraires supposés: Étude bibliographique*. Paris: Tross, 1866.
Brusoni, Girolamo. *Il camerotto*. Venice: F. Valuavense, 1645.
Bruss, Elizabeth. *Autobiographical Acts: The Changing Situation of a Literary Genre*. Baltimore, MD: Johns Hopkins University Press, 1976.
Bufalino, Gesualdo. *Cere perse*. Palermo: Sellerio, 1985.
Bulferetti, Luigi. *Cesare Lombroso*. Turin: UTET, 1975.
Busoni, Jaurès. *Confinati a Lipari*. Milan: Vangelisti, 1980.
– *Nel tempo del fascismo*. Rome: Editori Riuniti, 1975.
Bussu, Salvatore. *Un prete e i terroristi*. Milan: Mursia, 1988.
Buttigieg, Joseph A. 'Il paradosso Gramsci.' *Belfagor* 52 (1997): 509–15.
Caddeo, R. *L'attentato di Felice Orsini*. Milan, 1933.
Calamandrei, Piero, ed. *Carceri. Esperienze e documenti. Il Ponte* 5 (1949).
Calvino, Italo. *The Path to the Nest of Spiders*. Trans. Archibald Colquhoun. New York: Ecco, 1976.
– *Romanzi e racconti*. 2 vols. Milan: Mondadori, 1991–2.
– *Il sentiero dei nidi di ragno*. Turin: Einaudi, 1947.
Cambria, Adele. *Amore come rivoluzione. Tre sorelle per un rivoluzionario, le lettere inedite della moglie e delle cognate di Antonio Gramsci, la risposta alle Lettere dal carcere: con il testo teatrale Nonostante Gramsci*. Milan: Sugar, 1976.
Cammett, John M. *Antonio Gramsci and the Origins of Italian Communism*. Stanford, CA: Stanford University Press, 1967.
– *Bibliografia gramsciana, 1922–1988*. Rome: Editori Riuniti, 1991.
– 'Communist Women and the Fascist Experience.' In Jane Slaughter and Robert Kern, eds., *European Women on the Left*. Westport, CT: Greenwood Press, 1981. 163–77.
Candido, Salvatore. 'Da Belfiore alle Fosse Ardeatine.' *Capitolium*, October 1973.
Canosa, Romano. *Storia del manicomio in Italia dall'unità a oggi*. Milan: Feltrinelli, 1979.
Capelli, Anna. *La buona compagnia. Utopia e realtà carceraria nell'Italia del Risorgimento*. Milan: Franco Angeli, 1988.

Caracciolo, Enrichetta. *Misteri del chiostro napoletano*. Florence: Giunti, 1986.
Cardozo-Freeman, Inez. *The Joint: Language and Culture in a Maximum Security Prison*. Springfield, IL: Charles Thomas, 1984.
Carnochan, W.B. *Confinement and Flight*. Berkeley and Los Angeles: University of California Press, 1977.
Caro, Annibale. *Lettere familiari*. Ed. Aulo Greco. 3 vols. Florence: Le Monnier, 1957–61.
Carrillo, Elisa. *Alcide De Gasperi: The Long Apprenticeship*. Notre Dame, IN: University of Notre Dame Press, 1965.
Casalini, Maria. *La signora del socialismo italiano. Vita di Anna Kuliscioff*. Rome: Editori Riuniti, 1987.
Casanova, Giacomo. *Histoire de ma fuite des prisons de la République de Venise, qu'on appelle les Plombs, écrite à Dux en Bohéme 1787*. Ed. Charles Samaran. Paris: Bossard, 1922.
– *History of My Life: First Translated into English in Accordance with the Original French Manuscript by Willard R. Trask*. Intro. by Willard R. Trask. Baltimore, MD: Johns Hopkins University Press, 1997.
– *Mémoires de J. Casanova de Seingalt: Écrits par lui-même*. Paris: La Sirène, 1926.
– *Histoire de ma vie*. 12 vols. Paris: Plon, 1960.
Cassese, Antonio. *Umano-Disumano. Commissariati e prigioni nell'Europa d'oggi*. Bari: Laterza, 1994.
Castel, Robert. *The Regulation of Madness: Origins of Incarceration in France*. Berkeley and Los Angeles: University of California Press, 1989.
Castellazzo, Luigi (under the pseudonym of Anselmo Rivalta). *La Lombardia nel 1848*. Florence: Tipografia Garibaldi, 1862.
Castromediano, Sigismondo. *Carceri e galere politiche*. 2 vols. Lecce: Salentina, 1895.
– *Lettere dal carcere*. Ed. Giuseppe Barletta and Michele Paone. Galatina: Salentina, 1995
– *Scritti di storia di arte*. Ed. Michele Paone. Galatina: Salentina, 1996.
Catalano, Gabriele. 'Settembrini: "Martire dei Borboni," e oltre.' *Il ponte* 34 (1978): 197–215.
Catti De Gasperi, Maria Romani. *De Gasperi, uomo solo*. Milan: Mondadori, 1964.
Cellini, Benvenuto. *The Autobiography of Benvenuto Cellini*. Trans. with intro. by George Bull. London: Penguin Books, 1988.
– *Opere*. Milan: Rizzoli, 1968.
– *Trattato di oreficeria. Opere di Baldassare Castiglione, Giovanni della Casa, Benvenuto Cellini*. Ed. Carlo Cordié. Milan and Naples: Ricciardi, 1960.

Cerrito, Gino. *Andrea Costa nel socialismo italiano*. Rome: La Goliardica, 1982.
Ceva, Bianca. *1930: Retroscena di un dramma*. Milan: Ceschina, 1955.
Childs, J. Rives. *Casanova: A New Perspective*. New York: Paragon House, 1988.
Cohen, Stanley, and Laurie Taylor. *Psychological Survival: The Experience of Long-Term Imprisonment*. New York: Pantheon, 1972.
Coldagelli, Umberto. 'Giovanni Arrivabene.' *Dizionario biografico degli italiani*. Rome: Istituto dell'Enciclopedia Italiana. Vol. 4, 1962: 325–7.
Coletti, Alessandro. *Il governo di Ventotene. Stalinismo e lotta politica tra i dirigenti del PCI al confino*. Milan: La Pietra, 1978.
Colombo, Arturo. 'L'esempio di Leone Ginzburg (con l'ultima lettera a Natalia).' *Nuova Antologia* 572 (1994): 178–91.
Colombo, Giorgio. *La scienza infelice. Il museo di antropologia criminale di Cesare Lombroso*. Turin: Boringhieri, 1975.
Confalonieri, Federico. *Carteggio del conte Federico Confalonieri ed altri documenti spettanti alla sua biografia*. Ed. Giuseppe Gallavresi. 3 vols. Milan: Ripalta, 1910–13.
– *Memorie e lettere*. Ed. Gabrio Casati. Milan: Hoepli, 1889.
Consoli, Domenico. *Critici romantici*. Rome: Nuova Spada, 1979.
Coppola, Aniello. *Moro*. Milan: Feltrinelli, 1976.
Cordova, Ferdinando. 'Alcune lettere inedite di un condannato a morte della resistenza romana.' *Historica* 27 (1974): 3–9.
La correspondance (Edition, fonctions, signification): Actes du colloque franco-italien, Aix-en-Provence, 5–6 October 1983. Aix: 1984–5.
Corsetti, Angelo. 'Ernesto Rossi.' *Belfagor* 18 (1963): 29–71.
Cortesi, Luigi. *Turati giovane. Scapigliatura, positivismo, marxismo*. Milan: Edizioni Avanti!, 1962.
Costa, Andrea. 'Annotazioni autobiografiche per servire alle Memorie della vita.' *Movimento operaio* 6 (1952): 314–56.
Craig, Cynthia C. '"Je l'habille souvent à l'italienne": The Language of Exile in the *Histoire de ma vie*.' *Romance Languages Annual* 4 (1992): 209–15.
Craig, Gordon A. *The Triumph of Liberalism: Zurich in the Golden Age, 1830–1869*. New York: Macmillan, 1988.
Craveri, Piero. 'Alcide De Gasperi.' *Dizionario biografico degli italiani*. Rome: Istituto dell'Enciclopedia Italiana. Vol. 36, 1988: 79–114.
Cresci, Gian Paolo, ed. *Moro. I giorni del tormento*. Rome: Cinque Lune, 1985.
Croce, Benedetto. *La letteratura della nuova Italia. La letteratura italiana per saggi storicamente disposti*. Vol. 3. Bari: Laterza, 1961.
– *Scritti vari e discorsi politici*. Vol. 2. Bari: Laterza, 1963.
Croce, Elena. *Silvio Spaventa*. Milan: Adelphi, 1969.
Crouzet, Michel. *Stendhal*. Paris: Flammarion, 1990.

Cugusi, P. *Evoluzione e forme dell'epistolografia latina nella tarda repubblica e nei primi due secoli dell'impero con cenni sull'epistolografia preciceroniana.* Rome, 1983.
Curcio, Renato. *A viso aperto.* Ed. Mario Scialoja. Milan: Mondadori, 1993.
- *L'alfabeta d'Esté.* Bologna: Sensibili alle Foglie, 1988.
- *La mappa perduta.* Rome: Sensibili alle Foglie (Progetto Memoria), 1994.
- *La soglia.* Rome: Sensibili alle Foglie, 1994.
- *WHKY,* Rome, 1985.
Curcio, Renato, Nicola Valentino, and Stefano Petrelli. *Nel bosco di Bistorco.* Rome: Sensibili alle Foglie, 1990.
D'Ancona, Alessandro. *Federico Confalonieri.* Milan: Treves, 1898.
- *Viaggiatori e avventurieri.* Florence: Sansoni, 1874.
D'Annunzio, Gabriele. *Tutte le opere di Gabriele D'Annunzio.* Milan: Mondadori, 1968.
D'Eaubonne, Françoise. *Les écrivains en cage.* Paris: André Balland, 1970.
Damiani, Franco, and Fabio Rodriguez, eds. *Anna Kuliscioff. Immagini, scritti, testimonianze.* Milan: Feltrinelli, 1978.
Daniels, Elizabeth Adams. *Jessie White Mario: Risorgimento Revolutionary.* Athens: Ohio University Press, 1972.
Darnton, Robert. *The Literary Underground of the Old Regime.* Cambridge, MA: Harvard University Press, 1982.
Davies, Ioan. *Writers in Prison.* Oxford: Basil Blackwell, 1990.
Davis, John A. *Conflict and Control: Law and Order in Nineteenth-Century Italy.* London: Macmillan, 1988.
De Clementi, Andreina. 'Andrea Costa.' *Dizionario biografico degli italiani.* Rome: Istituto dell'Enciclopedia Italiana. Vol. 30, 1984: 128–44.
De Gasperi, Alcide. *Lettere dalla prigione, 1927–1928.* Milan: Mondadori, 1955.
De Lauretis, Teresa. 'The Left Hand of History.' *Heresies* 1 (1977–8): 23–6.
De Man, Paul. 'Autobiography As De-Facement.' *The Rhetoric of Romanticism.* New York: Columbia University Press, 1984.
De Matteis, Giuseppe, 'Sigismondo Castromediano.' *Rassegna storica del Risorgimento* 25 (1938): 1221–39.
Della Peruta, Franco. *Mazzini e i rivoluzionari italiani.* Milan: Feltrinelli, 1974.
Della Porta, Donatella. *Il terrorismo di sinistra.* Bologna: Il Mulino, 1990.
Delzell, Charles F. 'Antifascism.' In Philip V. Cannistraro, ed., *Historical Dictionary of Fascist Italy.* Westport, CT: Greenwood Press, 1982.
Derla, Luigi. 'Pietro Borsieri moralista.' *Letteratura e politica tra la Restaurazione e l'Unità.* Milan: Vita e Pensiero, 1977. 165–87.
Derrida, Jacques. *The Post Card: From Socrates to Freud and Beyond.* Chicago: University of Chicago Press, 1987.
- *Writing and Difference.* Chicago: University of Chicago Press, 1987.

Di Scala, Spencer. *Dilemmas of Italian Socialism: The Politics of Filippo Turati.* Amherst: University of Massachusetts Press, 1980.
Dombroski, Robert S. *Antonio Gramsci.* Boston: G.K. Hall, 1989.
Donghi, Giuseppe. 'Dialoghi e monologhi nelle *Lettere dal carcere* di Antonio Gramsci. Aspetti di un'analisi semiotica.' *Studi italiani di linguistica teorica e applicata* 11 (1982): 119–40.
Drake, Richard. *The Aldo Moro Murder Case.* Cambridge: Harvard University Press, 1995.
– *The Revolutionary Mystique and Terrorism in Contemporary Italy.* Bloomington: Indiana University Press, 1989.
Dubbini, Renzo. *Architettura delle prigioni. I luoghi e il tempo della punizione (1700–1880).* Milan: Franco Angeli, 1986.
Dughera, Attilo. 'Monti e Pavese. Storia di un'amicizia attraverso le lettere.' In Giovanni Tesio, ed., *Augusto Monti nel centenario della nascita.* Turin: Centro Studi Piemontesi, 1982. 55–65.
Duncan, Martha Grace. *Romantic Outlaws, Beloved Prisons: The Unconscious Meaning of Crime and Punishment.* New York: New York University Press, 1996.
Echaurren, Pablo, and Valerio Fioravanti. *Rebibbia Rhapsody.* Rome: Stampa Alternativa, 1996.
Écrire publier lire les correspondances: Actes du Colloque International: 'Les Correspondances.' Nantes, 1983.
Eisenzweig, Uri. 'Terrorism in Life and in Real Literature.' *Diacritics* 18 (1988): 32–42.
Eisinstein, Maria. *L'internata numero 6. Donne fra i reticolati del campo di concentramento.* Rome: D. De Luigi, 1944.
Escudero, Lucrezia. 'Il caso Moro. Manipolazione e riconoscimento.' *Problemi dell'informazione* 3 (1978).
Fabbrini, Ivano. *I gerani di Trani.* Rome: Sensibili alle Foglie, 1996.
Fabio, Emilio. 'Mostra del Risorgimento mantovano (1848–1866).' *Rassegna storica del Risorgimento* 42 (1955): 498–513.
Faccioli, Giulio. *La scuola della sventura, ossia inspirazioni e reminiscenze d'un carcere.* Verona: Merlo, 1862.
Faggi, Vico. *Sandro Pertini. Sei condanne, due evasioni.* Milan: Mondadori, 1978.
Falaschi, Giovanni. 'Interventi redazionali negli anni trenta.' *Belfagor* 40 (1985): 497–528.
Fatini, Giuseppe. 'Bini e Guerrazzi al Forte Stella.' *Nuova Antologia* 476 (1959): 47–64.
Fenzi, Enrico. *Armi e bagagli. Un diario dalle Brigate Rosse.* Genoa: Costa and Nolan, 1987.

Ferrarotti, Franco. *L'ipnosi della violenza*. Milan: Rizzoli, 1980.
Ferriani, Lino. *Delinquenti che scrivono*. Como: Omarini, 1899.
Fido, Franco. 'At the Origins of Autobiography in the 18th and 19th Centuries: The *Topoi* of the Self.' *Annali d'italianistica* 4 (1986): 168–80.
– 'Casanova.' *Il paradiso dei buoni compagni*. Padua: Antenore, 1988.
– 'Casanova "libertino."' *Forum Italicum* 16 (1982): 230–40; reprinted in *Il paradiso dei buoni compagni* (Padua: Antenore, 1988), 137–46.
Fiori, Giuseppe. *Una storia italiana. Vita di Ernesto Rossi*. Turin: Einaudi, 1997.
– *Vita di Antonio Gramsci*. Bari: Laterza, 1966.
Firpo, Luigi. 'Correzioni d'autore coatte.' *Studi e problemi di critica testuale*. Bologna: Commissione per i Testi di Lingua, 1961. 143–87.
Flamigni, Sergio. *La tela del ragno. Il delitto Moro*. Milan: Kaos, 1993.
Flem, Lydia. *Casanova, the Man Who Really Loved Women*. New York: Farrar, Straus, and Giroux, 1997.
Foa, Vittorio. *Il cavallo e la torre. Riflessioni su una vita*. Turin: Einaudi, 1991.
Fontana, Enzo. *Mia linfa mio fuoco*. Rimini: Guaraldi, 1996.
Forest, Eva. *From a Spanish Prison*. New York: Random House and Moon Books, 1976.
Foresti, Felice. *The Fate of the Carbonari: Memoirs of Felice Foresti*. Ed. Howard R. Marraro. *Columbia University Quarterly* 24 (1932): 441–75.
Le forme del diario. *Quaderni di retorica e poetica* 2 (1985).
Forni, Dante. *Storia di uno di noi*. Venice: Marsilio, 1980.
Forti-Lewis, Angelica Paola. *Italia autobiografica*. Rome: Bulzoni, 1986.
Foucault, Michel. *Discipline and Punish: The Birth of the Prison*. New York: Random House, 1979.
– *Language, Counter-Memory, Practice*. Ed. Donald F. Bouchard. Ithaca: Cornell University Press, 1977.
– *Madness and Civilization*. New York: Random House, 1973.
– 'La scrittura di sè.' *Aut-Aut*, 1983, 5–18.
Franceschini, Alberto. *Mara Renato e io. Storia dei fondatori delle BR*. Milan: Mondadori, 1988.
Franklin, H. Bruce. *The Victim as Criminal and Artist: Literature from the American Prison*. New York, 1978.
Freud, Sigmund. *The Standard Edition of the Complete Psychological Works of Sigmund Freud*. Vol. 19. London: Hogarth Press, 1961.
Frignani, Angelo. *Angelo Frignani e il suo libro 'La mia pazzia nelle carceri'. Memorie autobiografiche di un patriotto romagnolo per la prima volta pubblicate in Italia*. Ed. Luigi Rava. Bologna: Zanichelli, 1899.
Fubini Leuzzi, Mario. 'Carlo Bini.' *Dizionario biografico degli Italiani*. Rome: Istituto dell'Enciclopedia Italiana. Vol. 10, 1968: 506–10.

Gabrieli, Francesco. 'Il duca bianco.' *Il Ponte* 8 (1952): 1794–9.
Gadda, Carlo Emilio. *Giornale di guerra e di prigionia*. Florence: Sansoni, 1955.
Galletti, Giovanni. *La mia prigionia*. Bologna: Vitali, 1870.
Gelfand, Elissa E. *Imagination in Confinement: Women's Writing from French Prisons*. Ithaca, NY: Cornell University Press, 1983.
Gentile, Michele Lupo. 'Le memorie di un prigioniero di Alessando Andryane.' *Il Risorgimento* 9 (1957): 216–20.
Gentile, Sandro. '"Jouir par Réminiscence". Su Casanova memorialista.' *Rassegna della letteratura italiana* 84 (1980): 101–11.
Getto, Giovanni. *Interpretazione del Tasso*. Naples: Edizioni scientifiche italiane, 1949.
Gével, Claude. *Deux carbonari: Napoleon III e Felice Orsini*. Paris: Émile-Paul Frères, 1934.
Ghini, Celso. *Gli antifascisti al confino: 1926–1943*. Rome: Editori Riuniti, 1971.
Giacomelli, Angelo. *Reminiscenze della mia vita politica negli anni 1848–1853*. Florence: Barbèra, 1893.
Giacometti, Parolo. *Come vennero salvate all'amore degli italiani – imperando ancora l'Austria – le spoglie sacre dei martiri di Belfiore*. Mantua: Voce di Mantova, 1930.
Giannone, Pietro. *Vita scritta da lui medesimo*. Ed. Sergio Bertelli. Milan: Feltrinelli, 1960.
Ginzburg, Carlo. *Il giudice e lo storico. Considerazioni in margine al processo Sofri*. Turin: Einaudi, 1991.
Ginzburg, Leone. *Scritti*. Turin: Einaudi, 1964.
Giordano, Valeria, ed. *Luoghi del tempo. La percezione del tempo nel carcere e nella società*. Rome: Consiglio Regionale del Lazio, 1989.
Giuntella, Vittorio E. 'Mito e realtà del Risorgimento nei lager tedeschi.' *Rassegna storica del Risorgimento* 69 (1982): 387–98.
Giusti, Renato. 'Appunti sulla letteratura dei lager.' *Atti e memorie del Museo del Risorgimento di Mantova* 13 (1976): 53–89.
– 'Inventario dei documenti esistenti presso il Museo del Risorgimento di Mantova.' *Rassegna storica del Risorgimento* 42 (1955): 654–9.
– 'Il Museo del Risorgimento di Mantova.' *Rassegna storica del Risorgimento* 62 (1975): 490–7.
– 'La nascita e l'affermarsi dell'idea nazionale a Mantova nel secolo XIX.' *Rassegna storica del Risorgimento* 71 (1984): 3–12.
– 'Lettere dal carcere ad Enrico Ferri di Anna Kuliscioff, Andrea Costa e Filippo Turati (maggio–agosto 1898).' *Bollettino storico mantovano* 4 (1956): 310–29.
– *Memorialisti italiani dell'Ottocento*. Mantua: L'Arco, 1957.
Gladstone, William. *A Second Letter to the Earl of Aberdeen, on the State Prosecutions of the Neapolitan Government*. London: J. Murray, 1851.

Gobetti, Ada. *Vita in carcere e al confino, con lettere e documenti*. Parma: Guanda, Centro Studi Piero Gobetti, 1969.
Goffman, Irving. *Asylums: Essays on the Social Situation of Mental Patients and Other Inmates*. New York: Anchor, 1961.
Gonzales, Manuel. *Andrea Costa and the Rise of Socialism in the Romagna*. Washington, DC: University Press of America, 1980.
Gramsci, Antonio. *Forse rimarrai lontana. Lettere a Iulca*. Ed. Mimma Paulesu Quercioli. Rome: Albatros/Editori Riuniti, 1987.
– *Lettere dal carcere*. Ed. Sergio Caprioglio and Elsa Fubini. Turin: Einaudi, 1965.
– *Lettere dal carcere*. Ed. Antonio Santucci. 2 vols. Editrice *L'Unità*, 1988.
– *Lettere dal Carcere: A Selection Translated and Introduced by Hamish Henderson*. Edinburgh: Zwan, 1988.
– *Lettere dal carcere. Una scelta a cura di Paolo Spriano*. Turin: Einaudi, 1971.
– *Lettere 1908–1926*. Ed. Antonio A. Santucci. Turin: Einaudi, 1992.
– *Letters from Prison*. Ed. Frank Rosengarten. Trans. Raymond Rosenthal. 2 vols. New York: Columbia University Press, 1994.
– *Nuove lettere di Antonio Gramsci, con altre lettere di Piero Sraffa*. Ed. Antonio Santucci. Rome: Editori Riuniti, 1986.
– *Pre-Prison Writings*. Ed. Richard Bellamy. Cambridge: Cambridge University Press, 1994.
– *Prison Notebooks*. Ed. with an intro. Joseph A. Buttigieg. Trans. Joseph A. Buttigieg and Antonio Callari. New York: Columbia University Press, 1992.
– *Il Risorgimento. Opere* 4. Turin: Einaudi, 1954.
– *Vita attraverso le lettere*. Ed. Giuseppe Fiori. Turin: Einaudi, 1994.
Grechi, Gian Franco. 'Teresa Casati Confalonieri nell'universo femminile del Manzoni.' *Otto/Novecento* 16 (1992): 37–43.
Greenberg, David F. *Crime and Capitalism: Readings in Marxist Criminology*. Palo Alto, CA: Mayfield, 1981.
Grisoni, Dominique, and Robert Maggiori. *Lire Gramsci*. Paris: Citoyens, 1973.
Gubar, Susan. 'The "Blank Page" and the Issues of Female Creativity.' *Critical Inquiry* 8 (1981): 23–63.
Guerrazzi, Francesco Domenico. *L'epistolario di F.D. Guerrazzi, con il catalogo delle lettere edite e inedite*. Ed. Luca Toschi. Florence: Olschki, 1978.
– *Lettere*. 2 vols. Ed. Giosue Carducci. Livorno: F. Vigo, 1880–82.
– *Lettere*. Ed. Ferdinando Martini. Turin: Roux, 1891.
– *Lettere e discorsi*. Florence: Franceschini, 1863.
– *Lettere inedite di F.D. Guerrazzi a Giuseppe Scarlata*. Ed. Nicola Giordano. Palermo: Denaro, 1966.
– *Note autobiografiche*. Florence: Le Monnier, 1899.

Guglielminetti, Marziano. *Memoria e scrittura. L'autobiografia da Dante a Cellini*. Turin: Einaudi, 1977.
– *La 'vita' di Benvenuto Cellini*. Turin: Giappichelli, 1974.
Guicciardi, Luigi. *Il tempo del furore. Il fallimento della lotta armata raccontato dai protagonist*. Milan: Rusconi, 1988.
Guillemot, Étienne. 'Andryane (Alexandre-Philippe).' *Dictionnaire de Biographie Française*. Paris: Letouzey, 1936.
Guillén, Claudio. *Literature as System*. Princeton: Princeton University Press, 1971.
Gundle, Stephen. 'The Legacy of the Prison Notebooks: Gramsci, the PCI and Italian Culture in the Cold War Period.' In Christopher Duggan and Christopher Wagstaff, eds., *Italy in the Cold War: Politics, Culture and Society 1948–58*. Oxford: Berg, 1995. 131–47.
Harlow, Barbara. *Barred: Women, Writing, and Political Detention*. Wesleyan, 1993.
– *Resistance Literature*. New York: Methuen, 1987.
Hepworth, Mike, and Bryan S. Turner. *Confession: Studies in Deviance and Religion*. London: Routledge and Kegan Paul, 1982.
Hess, Henner. *La rivolta ambigua. Storia sociale del terrorismo italiano*. Florence: Sansoni, 1991.
Holub, Renate. *Antonio Gramsci: Beyond Marxism and Postmodernism*. London: Routledge, 1992.
Hostetter, Richard. *The Italian Socialist Movement: Origins (1860–1882)*. Princeton: Van Nostrand, 1958.
Hughes, H. Stuart. *Prisoners of Hope: The Silver Age of the Italian Jews 1924–1974*. Cambridge, MA: Harvard University Press, 1983.
I processi spielberghiani. Rome: Tipografia del Senato, 1937.
Ignatieff, Michael. *A Just Measure of Pain: The Penitentiary in the Industrial Revolution, 1750–1850*. New York: Pantheon, 1978.
Ingrao, Pietro. *Le cose impossibili*. Rome: Editori Riuniti, 1990.
Invernizzi, Irene. *Il carcere come scuola di rivoluzione*. Turin: Einaudi, 1973.
Italy. Parlamento. Commissione parlamentare d'inchiesta sul terrorismo in Italia. *Relazione sulla documentazione rinvenuta il 9 ottobre 1990, in via Monte Neroso, a Milano*. Rome: Tipografia del Senato, 1991.
Jamieson, Alison. *The Heart Attacked: Terrorism and Conflict in the Italian State*. London: Marion Boyars, 1989.
Janni, Ettore. *Poesia della patria ed eredità del Risorgimento. I poeti minori dell'Ottocento*. Vol 2. Milan: Rizzoli, 1955.
Joll, James. *Antonio Gramsci*. New York: Penguin Books, 1977.
Juin, Hubert, Françoise d'Eaubonne, and Marc Kravetz, eds. 'La littérature et les prisons.' *Magazine littéraire* 71 (December 1972).
Katz, Robert. *Days of Wrath: The Ordeal of Aldo Moro*. Garden City, NY: Doubleday, 1980.

Kauffman, Linda S. *Discourses of Desire: Gender, Genre, and Epistolary Fictions.* Ithaca, NY: Cornell University Press, 1986.
Kelly, Robert J. 'Terrorism and Intrigue: The Red Brigades – Aldo Moro's Murder – and the Gladio Affair.' *Italian Journal* 5 (1991): 14–21.
Klopp, Charles. 'The Corpus and Bodies of Prison Discourse in Risorgimento Mantua.' *Esperienze letterarie* 17 (1992): 25–51.
– 'Giuseppe Pignata, Seventeenth-Century Virtual Author.' *Essays in Honor of Albert Mancini. Italiana* 8 (1997): 185–93.
– 'Inklings and Effacements in Silvio Pellico's *Le mie prigioni.*' *Italica* 68 (1991): 195–203.
– '*La mia pazzia* di Angelo Frignani. Follia e intertestualità nella memorialistica del primo Ottocento.' *Il Veltro* 40 (1996): 157–61.
– '"Waiting for the Hanger": The Letters of Sacco and Vanzetti.' In Pietro Frassica, ed., *Studi di filologia e letteratura italiana in onore di Maria Picchio Simonelli.* Alessandria: Edizioni dell'Orso, 1992, 159–66.
Kropotkin, Peter. *In Russian and French Prisons.* London, 1887.
Kulisciof, Anna. *Lettere d'amore a Andrea Costa, 1880–1909.* Ed. Pietro Albonetti. Milan: Feltrinelli, 1976.
La Vigna, Claire. *Anna Kuliscioff: From Russian Populism to Italian Socialism.* New York: Garland, 1991.
Laffin, John. *Codes and Ciphers. Secret Writing through the Ages.* London: Abelard-Schuman, 1964.
Latude, Jean Henri Masers de, and Simon Nicolas Henri Linguet. *Memoirs of the Bastille.* Trans. and intro. by J. and S.F. Mills Whitham. London: George Routledge, 1927.
Lejeune, Philip. *On Autobiography.* Minneapolis: University of Minnesota Press, 1989.
Lenci, Sergio. *Colpo alla nuca.* Rome: Editori Riuniti, 1988.
Lepre, Aurelio. *Il prigioniero. Vita di Antonio Gramsci.* Bari: Laterza, 1998.
La lettera familiare. Quaderni di retorica e poetica 1 (1985).
Lettere dei caduti della R.S.I. A cura dell'Associazione Nazionale delle Famiglie dei Caduti e Dispersi della Repubblica Sociale Italiana. N.p., 1975.
Lettres d'écrivains. Revue des Sciences Humaines 195 (1984).
Levaillant, Maurice. *Chateaubriand, Mme Récamier et les mémoires d'outre-tombe (1830–1850).* Paris, 1939.
Levi, Carlo. *Disegni dal carcere 1934. Materiali per una storia.* Rome: De Luca, 1983.
– *E' questo il 'carcer tetro'? Lettere dal carcere 1934–35.* Genoa: Il Melangolo, 1991.
Lewes, W. David. *From Newgate to Dannemora: Rise of the Penitentiary in New York 1746–1848.* Ithaca, NY: Cornell University Press, 1965.
Li Causi, Girolamo. *Il lungo cammino. Autobiografia 1906–1944.* Rome: Editori Riuniti, 1974.

Liburdi, Enrico. 'Belfiore nella lirica patriottica del tempo e nella contemporanea. Tito Speri e Pier Fortunato Calvi.' *Rassegna storica del Risorgimento* 42 (1955): 320–7.
Lipparini, Lilla. *Andrea Costa rivoluzionario*. Milan: Longanesi, 1977.
Lisa, Athos. *Memorie. In carcere con Gramsci*. Milan: Feltrinelli, 1973.
Lo Romer, David G. *Merchants and Reform in Livorno 1814–1868*. Berkeley and Los Angeles: University of California Press, 1987.
Lo Sardo, Francesco. *Epistolario dal carcere (1926–1931)*. Verona: Edizione del Paniere, 1984.
Lograsso, Angelina H. 'Piero Maroncelli in America (da documenti inediti).' *Rassegna storica del Risorgimento* 15 (1928): 894–948.
Lollini, Massimo. 'Literature and Testimony in Gramsci's *Letters from Prison*: The Question of Subjectivity.' *Canadian Review of Comparative Literature* 23 (1966): 519–29.
– 'Il velo della letteratura e le sofferenze del soggetto nel carcere di Gramsci.' *Il piccolo Hans* 81 (1994): 91–112.
Lombroso, Cesare. *Gli anarchici*. Turin: Bocca, 1895.
– *Palimsesti del carcere*. Turin: Bocca, 1888.
Lovett, Clara M. *The Democratic Movement in Italy, 1830–1976*. Cambridge, MA: Harvard University Press, 1982.
Lubiani, Giorgio. 'Ritratti critici di contemporanei. Augusto Monti.' *Belfagor* 12 (1957): 288–302.
Lucas, Corinne. 'L'artiste et l'écriture: *il dire* et *il fare* dans les écrits de Cellini.' In Charles Fiorato, ed. *Culture et professions en Italie*. Paris: Publications de la Sorbonne, 1989. 67–97.
Luzio, Alessandro. *Felice Orsini. Saggio bibliografico*. Milan: Cogliati, 1914.
– *I martiri di Belfiore e il loro processo*. Milan: Cogliati, 1908.
– *Il processo Pellico-Maroncelli secondo gli atti ufficiali segreti*. Milan: Cogliati, 1903.
Macciocchi, Maria-Antonietta. *Pour Gramsci*. Paris: Editions du Seuil, 1974.
Mack Smith, Denis. *Mazzini*. New Haven: Yale University Press, 1994.
– *Victor Emmanuel, Cavour, and the Risorgimento*. London: Oxford, 1971.
Magnaghi, Alberto. *Un'idea di libertà. San Vittore '79 – Rebibbia '82*. Rome: Manifestolibri, 1985.
Maier, Bruno, and Paolo Semama. *Antonio Gramsci. Introduzione e guida allo studio dell'opera gramsciana*. Florence: Le Monnier, 1978.
Malvezzi, Piero, and Giovanni Pirelli, eds. *Lettere di condannati a morte della Resistenza europea*. Turin: Einaudi, 1954.
– *Lettere di condannati a morte della Resistenza italiana (18 settembre 1943 – 25 aprile 1945)*. Turin: Einaudi, 1966.

Mambelli, Anna Maria. *Piero Maroncelli. Una vita per la libertà e la giustizia.* Ravenna: Longo, 1991.
Mancini, Augusto. 'Carlo Bini e il Risorgimento.' *Nuova Antologia* 453 (1951): 247–53.
Mancini, Fausto. *Le carte di Andrea Costa conservate nella biblioteca comunale di Imola.* Rome: Quaderni della Rassegna degli Archivi di Stato, 1964.
Mangini, Nicola. 'Giacomo Casanova.' *Dizionario biografico degli italiani.* Rome: Istituto dell'Enciclopedia Italiana. Vol. 21, 1978: 151–67.
Mantelli, Brunello, and Marco Revelli, eds. *Operai senza politica.* Rome: Savelli, 1979.
Mariani, Gaetano. 'Carlo Bini ovvero un "pastiche" mancato.' *Ottocento romantico e verista.* Naples: Giannini, 1972.
– 'Un esemplare testo romantico. Le "Ricordanze" del Settembrini.' *Ottocento romantico e verista.* Naples: Giannini, 1972.
Mariani, Laura. *Quelle dell'idea. Storie di detenute politiche 1927–1948.* Bari: De Donato, 1982.
Marinari, Attilio. 'Silvio Pellico tra rivolta e rassegnazione.' In Carlo Muscetta, ed., *La letteratura italiana, storia e testi,* vol. 7, Part 1, *Il primo ottocento. L'età napoleonica e il risorgimento.* Bari: Laterza, 1977. 359–65.
Markus, Stefano. 'I processi di Mantova e i moti ungheresi.' *Rassegna storica del Risorgimento* 42 (1955): 363–70.
Marraro, Howard R. 'Eleuterio Felice Foresti.' *Columbia University Quarterly* 25 (1933): 34–64.
Martelli, Mino. *Andrea Costa e Anna Kuliscioff. Rivelazioni sulla coppia da nuovi documenti.* Rome: Edizioni Paoline, 1980.
Marti, Mario. 'L'epistolario come "genere" e un problema editoriale.' *Nuovi contributi dal certo al vero. Studi di filologia e di storia.* Ravenna: Longo, 1980.
Martini, Luigi. *Il confortatorio di Mantova negli anni 1851-52-55.* Mantua: Comune di Mantova, 1962.
Marx, Karl, and Friedrich Engels. *La corrispondenza di Marx e Engels con italiani. 1848–1895.* Ed. Giuseppe Del Bo. Milan: Feltrinelli, 1964.
Masi, P. *Mémoires de Gasparone rédigées par P. Masi, son compagnon dans la montagne et dans la prison.* Paris, 1867.
Masini, Pier Carlo. *Storia degli anarchici italiani. Da Bakunin a Malatesta (1862–1892).* Milan: Rizzoli, 1974.
Massano, Riccardo. 'Silvio Pellico "milanese."' *Da Dante al Novecento. Studi critici offerti a Giovanni Getto.* Milan: Mursia, 1970.
Masters, John. *Casanova.* New York: Bernard Geis, 1969.
Maturi, Walter. *Interpretazioni del Risorgimento.* Turin: Einaudi, 1962.
Mauro, Walter. *Invito alla lettura di Antonio Gramsci.* Milan: Mursia, 1981.

Mazzetti, Anton. *I processi del '21 nel carteggio di Antonio Mazzetti*. Rome: Tipografia del Senato, 1939.
Mazzocchi, Silvana. *Nell'anno della tigre. Storia di Adriana Faranda*. Milan: Baldini and Castoldi, 1994.
Meijer, Jan Marinus. *Knowledge and Revolution: The Russian Colony in Zurich (1870–1873)*. Assen (Netherlands): Van Gorcum, 1955.
Melossi, Dario, and Massimo Pavarini. *The Prison and the Factory: Origins of the Penitentiary System*. London: Macmillan, 1981.
Meneghetti, Maria Luisa. 'Scrivere in carcere nel medioevo.' In Pietro Frassica, ed., *Studi di filologia e letteratura italiana in onore di Maria Picchio Simonelli*. Alessandria: Edizioni dell'Orso, 1992. 185–99.
Menghini, Mario. 'Enrico Tazzoli.' *Enciclopedia italiana*, 33. Rome, 1937, 502.
– 'Gabriele Rosa.' *Enciclopedia Italiana*, 30. Rome, 1936, 107.
Menocal, María Rosa. 'Bondage: Pellico's Francescas,' *Writing in Dante's Cult of Truth from Borges to Boccaccio*. Durham, NC: Duke University Press, 1991. 51–88.
Mercenaro, Pietro, and Vittorio Foa. *Riprendere tempo. Un dialogo con postilla*. Turin: Einaudi, 1982.
Milani, Mario. 'Una lettura de *Le mie prigioni*, oggi.' In Aldo A. Mola, ed., *Saluzzo e Silvio Pellico nel 150° de Le mie prigioni. Atti del Convegno di Studio, Saluzzo, 30 ottobre, 1983*. Turin: Centro Studi Piemontesi, 1984. 31–41.
Minuz, Fernanda. 'Gli intellettuali socialisti e la scienza. I dibattiti nella "Critica sociale" (1891–1898).' *Studi sulla cultura filosofica italiana fra Ottocento e Novecento*. Bologna: CLUEB, 1982.
Mirri, Mario. 'Alexandre-Philippe Andryane.' *Dizionario biografico degli italiani*. Rome: Istituto dell'Enciclopedia Italiana. Vol. 3, 1961: 164–9.
Mitford, Jessica. *Kind and Usual Punishment: The Prison Business*. New York: Vintage, 1974.
Modona, Guido Neppi. 'Carcere e società civile.' *Storia d'italia*, vol. 5, *I documenti*. Turin: Einaudi, 1973, 1903–98.
Mola, Aldo A., ed. *Saluzzo e Silvio Pellico nel 150° de Le mie prigioni. Atti del Convegno di Studio, Saluzzo, 30 ottobre, 1983*. Turin: Centro Studi Piemontesi, 1984.
Monsagrati, Giuseppe. 'Felice Foresti,' *Dizionario biografico degli italiani*. Rome: Istituto dell'Enciclopedia Italiana. Vol. 48, 1997: 797–804.
Montanelli, Indro, and Mario Cervi. *L'Italia degli anni di piombo (1965–1978)*. Milan: Rizzoli, 1992.
Monti, Augusto. *Lettere a Luisotta*. Turin: Einaudi, 1977.
Montini, Renzo U. 'Sei lettere inedite dei carbonari polesani (16 marzo 1824).' *Rassegna storica del Risorgimento* 42 (1955): 379–92.

- 'Tre suppliche inedite di Federico Confalonieri.' *Rassegna storica del risorgimento* 29 (1942): 83–90.
- 'Vita americana di Pietro Borsieri.' *Rassegna storica del Risorgimento* 41 (1954): 467–76.

Morabito, Leo, ed. *Museo del Risorgimento*. Genoa: Comune di Genova, 1987.

Moran, Sue Ellen, ed. *Court Depositions of Three Red Brigadists*. Santa Monica: Rand Corporation, 1986.

Morandi, Rodolfo. *Lettere al fratello, 1937–1943*. Turin: Einaudi, 1959.

- *Storia della grande industria in Italia*. Bari: Laterza, 1931.

Morandini, Giuliana ... *e allora mi hanno rinchiusa*. Milan: Bompiani, 1977.

Morello, Paolo. *Lettere di un prigioniero italiano alla sua donna*. Florence: Società tipografica, 1848.

Moretti, Mario. *Brigate rosse. Una storia italiana*. Intervista di Carla Mosca e Rossana Rossanda. Prefazione di Rossana Rossanda. Milan: Anabasi, 1994.

Moro, Aldo. *L'intelligenza e gli avvenimenti. Testi 1959–1978*. Ed. G.B. Bozzo, M. Medici, and D. Mongillo. Milan: Garzanti, 1979.

Morris, Norval, and David J. Rothman, eds. *The Oxford History of the Prison: The Practice of Punishment in Western Society*. New York: Oxford, 1995.

Moss, David. *The Politics of Left-Wing Violence in Italy, 1969–85*. London: Macmillan, 1989.

Muscetta, Carlo. 'Gramsci in carcere.' *Realismo neorealismo controrealismo*. Milan: Garzanti, 1976.

Museo Civico del Risorgimento e della Resistenza R. Giusti. *L'età del Risorgimento*. Mantua: Comune di Mantova, n.d.

Naria, Giuliano, and Rosella Simone. *La casa del nulla*. Naples: Pironti, 1988.

Natoli, Aldo. *Antigone e il prigioniero. Tania Schucht lotta per la vita di Gramsci*. Rome: Editori Riuniti, 1990.

- 'Gramsci in carcere, il partito, il comintern.' *Belfagor* 43 (1988): 167–88.

Natoli, Aldo, Vittorio Foa, and Carlo Ginzburg, eds. *Il registro. Carcere politico di Civitavecchia 1941–1943*. Rome: Editori Riuniti, 1994.

Negri, Antonio. *Pipe-line. Lettere da Rebibbia*. Turin: Einaudi, 1983.

Nerenberg, Ellen Victoria. *Habeas Corpus: The Gendered Subject in Prison. The Prose of Containment in Mid-Twentieth Century Italian Literature*. Ph.D. dissertation, University of Chicago, 1993.

Nisco, Niccola. *Ferdinando II e il suo reame*. Naples: Morano, 1888.

Novelli, Diego, and Nicola Tranfaglia. *Vite sospese. Le generazioni del terrorismo*. Milan: Garzanti, 1988.

O'Brien, Patricia. *The Promise of Punishment: Prisons in Nineteenth-Century France*. Princeton: Princeton University Press, 1982.

Occhipinti, Maria. *Una donna di Ragusa*. Milan: Feltrinelli, 1976.
Olivier, L'Abbé. *L'infortuné Napolitain ou les aventures du Seigneur Rozelli*. Augsberg, 1768.
Orsini, Felice. *The Austrian Dungeons in Italy: A Narrative of Fifteen Months' Imprisonment and Final Escape from the Fortress of S. Giorgio*. London: G. Routledge, 1856.
– *Felice Orsini ed Emma Herwegh. Nuovi documenti*. Ed. Alessandro Luzio. Florence: Le Monnier, 1937.
– *Geografia militare della penisola italiana*. n.p., 1852.
– *Lettere*. Ed. Albert M. Ghisalberti. Rome: Vittoriano, 1936.
– *Memoirs and Adventures of Felice Orsini*. Trans. George Carbonel. Edinburgh: Constable, 1857.
– *Memorie politiche*. Ed. Leopoldo Marchetti and Elena Larsimont Pergameni. Milan: Rizzoli, 1962.
Packe, Michael St John. *Orsini: The Story of a Conspirator*. Boston: Little, Brown, 1957.
Padovani, Tullio. *L'utopia punitiva. Il problema delle alternative alla detenzione nella sua dimensione storica*. Milan: Giuffrè, 1981.
Pajetta, Giancarlo, ed. *Lettere di antifascisti dal carcere e dal confino*. 2 vols. Rome: Editori Riuniti, 1962–3.
Palla, Marco. 'Il Gramsci abbandonato.' *Belfagor* 41 (1986): 581–6.
Palladini, Arrigo. *Via Tasso. Carcere nazista*. Rome: Istituto Poligrafico e Zecca dello Stato, 1986.
Pallavicino, Giorgio. *Memorie di Giorgio Pallavicino*. 3 vols. Turin: Roux Frassati, 1895.
– *Spilbergo e Gradisca. Scene del carcere duro in Austria*. Turin: Stamperia dell'Unione, 1856.
Pallotta, Gino. *Aldo Moro. L'uomo la vita le idee*. Milan: Massimo, 1979
Palombarini, Giovanni. *7 aprile. Il processo e la storia*. Venice: Arsenale Cooperativa, 1982.
Palumbo, Rita. *Camilla Ravera racconta la sua vita*. Milan: Rusconi, 1985.
Panizzari, Giorgio. *Libero per interposto ergastolo*. Milan: Kaos, 1990.
Parca, Gabriele, ed. *Voci dal carcere femminile*. Milan: Rizzoli, 1982.
Pascal, Blaise. *Pensées and The Provincial Letters*. New York: Random House, 1941.
Pascal, Roy. *Design and Truth in Autobiography*. Cambridge, MA: Harvard University Press, 1960.
Pasolini, Pier Paolo. *Empirismo eretico*. Milan: Garzanti, 1981.
Pastro, Luigi. *Ricordi di prigione dell'unico superstite dei condannati di Mantova dal 1851 al 1853*. Milan: Cogliati, 1915.

Paternostro, Rocco. *La poetica dell'assenza*. Rome: Bulzoni, 1990.
Pavese, Cesare. *Hard Labor*. Trans. William Arrowsmith. Baltimore, MD: Johns Hopkins University Press, 1979.
Pecorari, Anselmo Guido. 'Il confortatorio di Mons. Luigi Martini e *l'Indice*.' *Civiltà mantovana* 9 (1977): 282–8.
Pellico, Silvio. *Epistolario*. Ed. Guglielmo Stefani. Florence: Le Monnier, 1856.
– *Lettere milanesi (1815–'21)*. Ed. Mario Scotti. Turin: Supplemento 28 al *Giornale storico della letteratura italiana*. 1963.
– *Le mie prigioni*. Milan: Mursia, 1971.
– *Le mie prigioni*. Ed. Silvia Spellanzon. Milan: Rizzoli, 1984.
– *Le mie prigioni*. Ed. Gaetano Trombatore. *Memorialisti dell'Ottocento*, vol. 1. Milan and Naples: Ricciardi, 1953. 17–175.
– *Le mie prigioni. Con le addizioni di Piero Maroncelli*. Milan: Rizzoli, 1984.
– *Le mie prigioni ed altri scritti scelti*. Ed. and intro. Egidio Bellorini. Milan: Vallardi, 1907.
– *My Prisons*. Ed. I.G. Capaldi. London: Oxford University Press, 1963.
Pernicone, Nunzio. *Italian Anarchism, 1864–1892*. Princeton: Princeton University Press, 1993.
Perrot, Michelle. *L'impossibile prigione*. Milan: Rizzoli, 1981.
Pessina, Anna. 'Luigi Settembrini e la difficile adolescenza del figlio Raffaele in una corrispondenza inedita con Antonio Panizzi.' *Rassegna storica del Risorgimento* 71 (1984): 36–42.
Peters, Edward. *Torture*. London: Basil Blackwell, 1985.
Petronio, Giuseppe, ed. *Dizionario enciclopedico della letteratura italiana*. 6 vols. Bari: Laterza, 1966–70.
Pieroni Bortolotti, Franca. *Socialismo e questione femminile in Italia 1892–1922*. Milan: Gabriele Mazzotta, 1974.
Pignata, Giuseppe. *The Adventures of Giuseppe Pignata, Who Escaped from the Prisons of the Inquisition of Rome*. Trans. Arthur Symonds. New York: Sears, 1931.
– *Les Aventures de Joseph Pignata echappé des prisons de l'Inquisition de Rome*. Cologne: Pierre Marteau, 1725.
– *Le avventure di Giuseppe Pignata fuggito dalle carceri dell'Inquisizione di Roma*. Palermo: Sellerio, 1980.
Pillitteri, Paolo. *Anna Kuliscioff. Una biografia politica*. Venice: Marsilio, 1986.
Pirodda, Giovanni. 'Giuseppe Manzzini e il romanticismo democratico.' In Carlo Muscetta, ed., *La letteratura italiana storia e testi*. Vol. 7, 2: *Il primo Ottocento. L'età napoleonica e il Risorgimento*. Bari: Laterza, 1975.
Pironti, Carolina. 'Carlo Poerio e Sigismondo Castromediano.' *Nuova Antologia* 241 (1912): 319–40.

Pistillo, Michele. *Gramsci come Moro?* Rome: Lacaita, 1989.
Pitrè, Giuseppe. *Del Sant'Uffizio a Palermo e di un carcere di esso.* Vol. 26 of *Opere complete di Giuseppe Pitrè*. Rome: Società Editrice del Libro Italiano, 1940.
Pittorru, Fabio. *Torquato Tasso. L'uomo, il poeta, il cortigiano.* Milan: Bompiani, 1982.
Piva, Edoardo. 'Lettere e versi inediti di un martire di Belfiore.' *Miscellanea di studi critici pubblicati in onore di Guido Mazzoni*. Florence: Tipografia Galileiana, 1907.
Podda, Luigi. *Dall'ergastolo*. Milan: La Pietra, 1976.
Poma, Anna Filippini. *Cenni biografici e scritti vari di Anna Filippini Poma e del dottore Carlo Poma martire dell'Indipendenza italiana*. Mantua: Segna, 1867.
Ponce de León, Maria. *Meccanismi di sopravvivenza. Letteratura carceraria contemporanea in Italia. Poesia, narrativa e teatro 1970–1997*. Ph.D. dissertation, Northwestern University, 1998.
Porter, Charles A., ed. *Men/Women of Letters*. *Yale French Studies* 71 (1986).
Porter, Roy. *A Social History of Madness*. London: Weidenfeld and Nicolson, 1987.
Potier, Jean-Pierre. *Piero Sraffa – Unorthodox Economist (1898–1983)*. London: Routledge, 1991.
Praticò, Giovanni. 'Le fonti per la storia del Risorgimento nell'Archivio di Stato di Mantova con particolare riguardo ai Martiri di Belfiore.' *Rassegna storica del Risorgimento* 42 (1955): 393–409.
Price Zimmerman, T.C. 'Confession and Autobiography in the Early Renaissance.' In Anthony Molho and John Tedeschi, eds., *Renaissance Studies in Honor of Hans Baron*. Dekalb: Northern Illinois University Press, 1971. 121–40.
Priestley, Phillip. *Victorian Prison Lives: English Prison Biography 1830–1914*. New York: Methuen, 1985.
Procacci, Giuliano. *Storia degli italiani*. Bari: Laterza, 1975.
Prosperi, Adriano. 'A Pisa con Adriano Sofri.' *Paragone* 486 (1990): 86–94.
Quondam, Amedeo, ed. *Le 'carte messaggiere'. Retorica e modelli di comunicazione epistolare. Per un indice dei libri di lettere del Cinquecento*. Rome: Bulzoni, 1981.
Ragonese, Gaetano. 'Francesco Domenico Guerrazzi.' *Letteratura italiana. I minori*, vol. 3. Milan: Marzorati, 1961. 2555–82.
Ravera, Camilla. *Breve storia del movimento femminile in Italia*. Rome: Editori Riuniti, 1978.
– *Diario di trent'anni. 1913–1943*. Rome: Editori Riuniti, 1973.
– *La donna italiana dal primo al secondo Risorgimento*. Rome: Edizioni di Cultura Sociale, 1951.
– *Lettere al Partito e alla famiglia*. Rome: Editori Riuniti, 1979.

Ravindranathan, T.R. *Bakunin and the Italians*. Kingston and Montreal: McGill-Queen's University Press, 1988.
Re, Luigi. *La satira patriottica nelle scritte murali del Risorgimento*. Brescia: Vannini, 1933.
Resta, Gianvito. *Studi sulle lettere del Tasso*. Florence: Le Monnier, 1957.
Revelli, Nuto. *L'ultimo fronte. Lettere di soldati caduti o dispersi nella seconda guerra mondiale*. Turin: Einaudi, 1971.
Rezzaghi, Albany. 'La congiura di Belfiore nelle memorie inedite del cospiratore Attilio Mori.' *Rassegna storica del Risorgimento* 42 (1955): 410–17.
Riboldi, Ezio. *Vicende socialiste*. Milan: Azione Comune, 1964.
Ricci, Aldo, and Giulio Salierno. *Il carcere in Italia. Inchiesta sui carcerati, i carcerieri e l'ideologia carceraria*. Turin: Einaudi, 1971.
Ricci, Raffaello. 'Carceri e galere politiche nel regno di Napoli.' *Nuova Antologia* 61 (1896): 558–71.
Rinieri, Ilario. *La verità storica del processo Pellico-Maroncelli*. Rome: Befani, 1904.
Rivalta, Anselmo. See Castellazzo, Luigi.
Roberts, John Morris. *The Mythology of the Secret Societies*. New York: Scribner's, 1979.
Romagnoli, Angela. *'Fra catene, fra stili, e fra veleni ...'. Ossia della scena di prigione nell'opera italiana (1690–1724)*. Lucca: Libreria Musicale Italiana, 1995.
Romagnoli, Sergio. 'Francesco Domenico Guerrazzi e il romanzo storico.' *Manzoni e i suoi colleghi*. Florence: Sansoni, 1984.
Romano, Aldo. *Storia del movimento socialista in Italia*. 3 vols. Bari: Laterza, 1966–7.
Romano, Ruggiero. 'Rodolfo Morandi.' *Belfagor* 15 (1960): 437–54.
Romano, Salvatore Francesco. *Antonio Gramsci*. Turin: UTET, 1965.
Rosa, Gabriele. *Federico Confalonieri*. Brescia: Apollonio, 1890.
Rosa, Gabriele, and Silvio Pellico. *Due patrioti allo Spielberg*. Ed. Ugoberto Alfassio Grimaldi. Milan: Palazzi, 1971.
Rosengarten, Frank. 'Gramsci's Arrest.' *Italian Culture* 7 (1986–9): 71–80.
– 'Gramsci's "Little Discovery": Gramsci's Interpretation of Canto 10 of Dante's *Inferno*.' *Boundary* 1 (Spring 1986): 71–90.
– 'Three Essays on Antonio Gramsci's *Letters from Prison*.' *Italian Quarterly* 25–6 (1984): 7–40.
Rossi, Elide. *Lettere ad Ernesto*. Florence: La Nuova Italia, 1958.
Rossi, Ernesto. *Elogio della galera. Lettere 1930/1943*. Bari: Laterza, 1968.
– *Miserie e splendori del confino di polizia. Lettere da Ventotene 1939–1943*. Milan: Feltrinelli, 1981.
– *La pupilla del Duce*. Parma: Guanda, 1956.

Rothman, David J. *The Discovery of the Asylum: Social Order and Disorder in the New Republic.* Glenview, IL: Scott, Foresman, 1971.
Roustang, François. *The Quadrille of Gender: Casanova's Memoirs.* Stanford, CA: Stanford University Press, 1988.
Roveri, Alessandro. *Giovinezza e amori di Anna Kuliscioff.* Florence: Atheneum, 1993.
Rumi, Giorgio, ed. *Federico Confalonieri aristocratico progressista.* Milan and Bari: Cariplo-Laterza, 1987.
Rusche, Georg, and Otto Kirchheimer. *Punishment and Social Structure.* New York: Columbia University Press, 1939.
Sandonà, Augusto. *Contributo alla storia dei processi del Ventuno e dello Spielberg. Dagli atti officiali segreti degli archivi di Stato di Vienna e dal carteggio dell'imperatore Francesco I co' suoi ministri e col presidente del Senato Lombardo-Veneto del Tribunale supremo di Giustizia (1821–1838).* Milan: Bocca, 1911.
Santucci, Antonio A. *Gramsci.* Rome: Newton and Compton, 1996.
Saudan, Alain. *Analyse sémiotique de 'l'affaire Aldo Moro.'* Groupe de Recherches sémio-linguistiques, Centre National de la recherche scientifique, Paris, 1983 [*Actes Sémiotiques-Documents,* V, 41, 1983].
Savio, Carlo Fedele. 'Silvio Pellico liberale e credente.' *Archivio storico del movimento liberale italiano.* Saluzzo: Tipografia Vescovile S. Vincenzo, 1900.
Savoca, Giuseppe. 'Montale e la "trappola" della lingua.' *Parole di Ungaretti e Montale.* Rome: Bonacci, 1993. 47–60.
Scarabello, Giovanni. *Carcerati e carceri a Venezia nell'età moderna.* Rome: Istituto dell'Enciclopedia Italiana, 1979.
Scheffler, Judith A., ed. *Wall Tappings: An Anthology of Writings by Women Prisoners.* Boston: Northeastern University Press, 1986.
Schiavi, Alessandro. *Anna Kuliscioff.* Rome: Opere Nuove, 1955.
– *Filippo Turati attraverso le lettere ai corrispondenti (1880–1925).* Bari: Laterza, 1947.
Schucht, Tatiana. *Lettere ai familiari.* Rome: Editori Riuniti, 1991.
Sciascia, Leonardo. *L'affaire Moro.* Palermo: Sellerio, 1978.
Scirocco, Alfonso. 'Luigi Castellazzo.' *Dizionario biografico degli italiani.* Rome: Istituto dell'Enciclopedia Italiana. Vol. 21, 1978: 661–4.
Sclavi, Marianella. *Ridere dentro. Un seminario sull'umorismo in carcere con Renato Curcio, Maurizio Iannelli, Stefano Petrelli, e Nicola Valentino.* Milan: Anabasi, 1993.
Scotti, M. 'Lettere inedite di Pietro Borsieri a Luigi e Silvio Pellico.' *Giornale storico della letteratura italiana* 434 (1964): 243–64.
Seeing through 'Paradise.' Artists and the Terezín Concentration Camp. Boston: Massachusetts College of Art, 1991.

Settembrini, Luigi. *Lettere dall'ergastolo.* Ed. Mario Themelly. Milan: Feltrinelli, 1962.
- *Lettere edite e inedite 1860–1876.* Ed. Anna Pessina. Naples: Società Editrice Napoletana, 1983.
- *Lezioni di letteratura italiana dettate nell'università di Napoli.* 3 vols. Naples: Morano, 1909.
- *I neoplatonici.* Ed. Raffaele Cantarella. Milan: Rizzoli, 1977.
- *Opere scelte di Luigi Settembrini.* Ed. Luigi Negri. Turin: UTET, 1955.
- *Ricordanze della mia vita e scritti autobiografici.* Ed. Mario Themelly. Milan: Feltrinelli, 1961.

Siliprandi, Francesco. *Scritti e memorie.* Ed. Renato Giusti. Mantua: Amministrazione Provinciale di Mantova, 1959.

Silj, Alessandro. *Brigate Rosse-Stato. Lo scontro spettacolo nella regia della stampa quotidiana.* Florence: Vallecchi, 1978.

Sofri, Adriano. *Memoria.* Palermo: Sellerio, 1990.
- *L'ombra di Moro.* Palermo: Sellerio, 1991.
- *Le prigioni degli altri.* Palermo: Sellerio, 1993.

Solerti, Angelo. *Vita di T. Tasso.* Turin, 1895.

Sossi, Mario. *Nella prigione delle BR.* Milan: Editoriale Nuova, 1979.

Sparacino, Calogero. *Diario di prigionia.* Milan: La Pietra, n.d.

Spaventa, Silvio. *Dal 1848 al 1861. Lettere, scritti, documenti.* Ed. Benedetto Croce. Bari: Laterza, 1923.
- *Lettere a Felicetta.* Ed. Mario Themelly. Naples: Edizioni Scientifiche Italiane, 1977.

Spierenburg, Pieter. *The Prison Experience: Disciplinary Institutions and Their Inmates in Early Modern Europe.* New Brunswick: Rutgers University Press, 1991.

Spinazzola, Vittorio. 'Il motivo della tentazione nell'opera del Pellico.' In Emilio Cecchi e Natalino Sapegno, eds., *Storia della letteratura italiana.* Vol. 7, *L'ottocento.* Milan: Garzanti, 1969. 984–99.

Spinelli, Altiero. *Come ho tentato di diventare saggio.* Bologna: Il Mulino, 1984.
- *Il lungo monologo.* Rome: Edizioni dell'Ateneo, 1968.
- *Il manifesto di Ventotene.* Naples: Guida, 1982.

Spitzer, Leo. *Lettere di prigionieri di guerra italiani 1915–1918.* Turin: Boringhieri, 1976.

Spriano, Paolo. *Antonio Gramsci and the Party: The Prison Years.* London: Lawrence and Wishart, 1979.
- *Socialismo e classe operaia a Torino dal 1892 al 1913.* Turin: Einaudi, 1958.
- *Storia del Partito comunista italiano.* 5 vols. Turin: Einaudi, 1967–75.

Springer, Beverly Tanner. 'Anna Kuliscioff: Russian Revolutionist, Italian

Feminist.' In Jane Slaughter and Robert Kern, eds. *European Women on the Left*. Westport, CT: Greenwood Press, 1981. 13–27.

Sraffa, Pietro. *Lettere a Tania per Gramsci*. Ed. Valentino Gerratana. Rome: Editori Riuniti, 1991.

Stefanoni, Franco. *Manicomio italiano. Inchiesta su follia e psichiatra*. Rome: Editori Riuniti, 1998.

Stendhal [Beyle, Marie Henri]. *La Chartreuse de Parme. Romans et Nouvelles*. Ed. Henri Martineau. Paris: Gallimard, 1952.

Stille, Alexander. *Benevolence and Betrayal: Five Italian Jewish Families under Fascism*. New York: Summit, 1991.

Stone, Jennifer. 'Italian Freud: Gramsci, Giulia Schucht, and Wild Analysis.' *October* 28 (1984): 105–24.

Suzzara Verdi, Paride. *Patria e cuore*. Milan: Boniotti, 1861.

Tabucchi, Antonio. *Pereira Declares*. New York: New Directions, 1995.

Tasso, Torquato. *Lettere*. Ed. Ettore Mazzali. Turin: Einaudi, 1978.

– *Lettere di Torquato Tasso*. Ed. Cesare Guasti. 5 vols. Florence: Le Monnier, 1853–5.

Tazzoli, Enrico. 'Lettere e versi inediti di un martire di Belfiore (Enrico Tazzoli).' *Miscellanea di studi critici pubblicati in onore di Guido Mazzoni*. Florence: Seeber, 1907. 2: 405–25.

– *Memorie di Don Enrico Tazzoli sulle cause della congiura del 1850*. Mantua: Istituto per la Storia del Risorgimento Italiano, 1959.

– *Memorie inedite di Don Enrico Tazzoli al gen. Culoz sulle cause della congiura del 1850*. Mantua: Segna, 1886.

Tellini, Gino. *L'arte della prosa*. Florence: La Nuova Italia, 1995.

Terracini, Umberto. *Al bando dal Partito. Carteggio clandestino dall'isola e dall'esilio*. Ed. Alessandro Coletti. Milan: La Pietra, 1976.

– 'Ricordi e riflessioni di un rivoluzionario professionale.' *Belfagor* 31 (1976): 249–66.

– *Sulla svolta. Carteggio clandestino dal carcere*. Ed. Alessandro Coletti. Milan: La Pietra, 1975.

Tesio, Giovanni, ed. *Augusto Monti nel centenario della nascita*. Turin: Centro Studi Piemontesi, 1982.

Themelly, Mario, ed. *Luigi Settembrini nel centenario della morte*. Naples: Società Nazionale di Scienze, Lettere e Arti, 1977.

Thomas, Paul. *Karl Marx and the Anarchists*. London: Routledge and Kegan Paul, 1980.

Timpanaro, Sebastiano. 'Alcuni chiarimenti su Carlo Bini.' *Antileopardiani e neomoderati nella sinistra italiana*. Pisa: ETS, 1982.

Toschi, Luca. 'Il rifiuto di Carlo Bini livornese.' *Belfagor* 34 (1979): 249–62.

Tozzi, Federigo. *Realtà di ieri e di oggi*. Milan: Alpes, 1928.

Tramarollo, Giuseppe. 'Carlo Bini nella letteratura di prigione.' *Nuova Antologia* 543 (1980): 217–25.
Trombatore, Gaetano, ed. *Memoralisti dell'Ottocento*. Vol. 1. Milan and Naples: Ricciardi, 1953.
Turati, Filippo. *Carteggio. Vol. I: 1898–99; Vol II: 1900–1909*. Collected by Alessandro Schiavi. Ed. Franco Pedone. Turin: Einaudi, 1977.
– *I cimiteri dei vivi (per la riforma carceraria)*. Rome: Tipografia della Camera dei Deputati, 1904.
Turchi, Emma. *La felicità è la lotta*. Venice: Marsilio, 1976.
Ugolini, Luigi. *Regina coeli (dieci mesi di carcere fascista 1940–41)*. Milan: Ceschina, 1970.
Umberto Terracini nella storia contemporanea. Alessandria: Edizioni dell'Orso, 1987.
Vaini, Mario. *Mantova nel Risorgimento. Itinerario bibliografico*. Mantua: Biblioteca Comunale di Mantova, 1976.
Valacarenghi, Marina. *I manicomi criminali*. Milan: Gabriele Mazzotta, 1975.
Valentino, Nicola. *Ergastolo*. Rome: Sensibili alle Foglie, 1994.
Valera, Paolo. *Le terribili giornate del maggio '98*. Ed. Enrico Ghidetti. Bari: De Donato, 1973.
Vallone, Aldo. 'Il Risorgimento salentino-napoletano nelle parti inedite delle "Memorie" di S. Castromediano.' *Rassegna storica del Risorgimento* 45 (1958): 550–72.
– 'Settembrini letterato attraverso testi inediti.' *Accademie e biblioteche d'Italia* 45 (1977): 23–40.
Vannucci, Atto. *I martiri della libertà italiana dal 1794 al 1848*. 2 vols. Milan: Prato, 1887.
Varaut, Jean-Marc. *Poètes en prison de Charles d'Orleans à Jean Genet*. Paris: Perrin, 1989.
Venner, Dominique. *Treize Meurtres exemplaires*. Paris: Plon, 1988.
Venturi, Franco. *Utopia and Reform*, Cambridge: Cambridge University Press, 1971.
Vettori, Vittorio. *Diario apocrifo di Aldo Moro prigioniero*. Palermo: Mazzoni, 1982.
Vidali, Vittorio. *Giornale di bordo*. Milan: Vangelista, 1977.
Vittoria, Albertina. 'Mario Alicata.' *Dizionario biografico degli italiani*. Rome: Istituto dell'Enciclopedia Italiana. Vol. 34, 1988: 61–5.
Wagner-Pacifici, Robin Erica. *The Moro Morality Play: Terrorism as Social Drama*. Chicago: University of Chicago Press, 1986.
Weinberg, Leonard, and William Lee Eubank. *The Rise and Fall of Italian Terrorism*. Boulder, CO: Westview Press, 1987.
Weintraub, Karl Joachim. *The Value of the Individual: Self and Circumstances in Autobiography*. Chicago: University of Chicago Press, 1978.

Wilkinson, James. *The Intellectual Resistance in Europe*. Cambridge, MA: Harvard University Press, 1981.
Witt, Mary Ann Frese. *Existential Prisons: Captivity in Mid-Twentieth-Century French Literature*. Durham, NC: Duke University Press, 1985.
Wood, Mary Elene. *The Writing on the Wall: Women's Autobiography and the Asylum*. Urbana and Chicago: University of Illinois Press, 1994.
Zaczek, Barbara. *Censored Sentiments: Letters and Censorship in Epistolary Novels and Conduct Material*. Newark: University of Delaware Press, 1997.
Zagaria, Riccardo. 'Intorno al Guerrazzi scrittore.' *Giornale storico della letteratura italiana* 94 (1929): 241–70.
Zangrande, Ruggero. *Il lungo viaggio attraverso il fascismo. Contributo alla storia di una generazione*. 2 vols. Milan: Garzanti, 1962.
Zilliacus, Laurin. *Mail for the World: From the Courier to the Universal Postal Union*. New York: John Day, 1953.
Zupo, Giuseppe, and Vincenzo Marini Recchia. *Operazione Moro. I fili ancora coperti di una trama politica criminale*. Milan: Franco Angeli, 1984.

Index

Acerbo, Giacomo, 134
Ackroyd, Carol, 201 n11
Agnelli, Giovanni, 155
Agnello, Luigi, 213, nn42, 43
Albertoni, Ettore A., 226 n69
Albonetti, Piero, 111, 112, 218 n27
Alexander I (of Russia), 48
Alfieri, Vittorio, 31, 40, 41, 43, 204 n17
Alfonsi, Filippo, 25–6, 27, 109
Alicata, Mario, vii, 157, 159, 161–3, 164, 174, 190, 218 n24
Allason, Barbara, 132, 204 nn11, 15, 206 n28, 221 n3
Allen, Beverly, 230 n4
Ambel, Mario, 209 n4
Ambrosoli, Luigi, 206 n35
Amendola, Giorgio, 221 n7, 226 n70, 234 n9
Amnesty International, 198 n3
Amoretti, Giuseppe, 147
Anderlini, Paolo, 100–1
Andreotti, Giulio, 233 n20
Andryane, Alexandre-Philippe, 55–9, 60, 61, 62, 63, 64, 74, 85, 103, 104, 153, 174, 187, 192, 207 n43
Antonini, Ezio, 226 n69
Arbasino, Alberto, 230 n4

Aretino, Pietro, 18
Ariosto, Ludovico, 34
Armani, Giuseppe, 225 n48
Arrivabene, Giovanni, 54–5, 58, 68, 153, 174, 187
Arrivabene, Marianna, 75
Arrivabene, Teresa Giacomelli, 76
Arrowsmith, William, 226 n64
Ascari, Rosalia Colombo, 218 n25
Augustine, Saint, 53, 158, 207 n44, 222 n14
Aventine Succession, 134
Avogaro, Giuseppe, 73

Badaloni, Nicola, 209 n8
Bakunin, Mihail Aleksandrovich, 107, 111, 113, 130
Balbi, Marin, 34, 35, 45
Balducci, Armenia, 230 n4
Balestrini, Nanni, 230 n4
Banca Commerciale Italiana, 229 n100
Barberi-Squarotti, Giorgio, 205 n23
Barletta, Giuseppe, 213 n43
Bartolozzi, Teresa, 46
Basaglia, Franca Ongaro, 234 n4
Bassani, Giorgio, 157, 159–60, 161, 163, 173, 174, 175, 190

264 Index

Bastille (Parisian prison), 38
Bauer, Riccardo, 221 n7
Bava Beccaris, Fiorenzo, 113
Beccaria, Cesare, 184, 233 n23
Bédarida, Henri, 205 n26, 206 n30
Bei, Adele, 224 n32
Bellorini, Egidio, 204 nn10, 15
Bender, John, 199 n10
Bergson, Henri, 158
Berlinguer, Enrico, 232 n14
Berlinguer, Maria, 217 n86
Bertacchini, Renato, 204 n4
Beyle, Marie Henri. *See* Stendhal.
Bianchi, Nicomede, 47–8
Bini, Carlo, 3, 67–70, 72, 78, 83, 101, 126, 188, 189
Biscione, Francesco M., 230 n4
Bisiach, Gianni, 100 n17
Bocca, Giorgio, 230 n4, 233 n19
Boccaccio, Giovanni, 34–5, 45
Boethius, xii
Boito, Arrigo, xiii
Bombelles, Henri de, 204 n15
Bonante, Luigi, 230 n4
Bonaparte, Napoleon, 71
Boni, Walter, 217 n86
Bonizzoni, Giuseppina Perlasca, 74
Bono, Simonetta, 217 n86
Bordiga, Amadeo, 176
Borgini, Alma, 209 n6
Borsellino, Nino, 37, 203 n46
Bosio, Ferdinando, 77
Bosio, Luigi, 211 n19
Bozzo, G.B., 230 n7
Bragadin, Matteo Giovanni, 32
Braganti, Alessandra, 220 n53
Braghetti, Anna Laura, 186, 198 n4, 215 n62, 230 nn4, 6, 231 nn9, 13, 233 n1
Briche, Odoardo, 47

Brigate Rosse. *See* Red Brigades.
Brombert, Victor, 6, 38
Brunet, Gustave, 28
Brusoni, Girolamo, 202 n40
Buchanan, James, 205 n22
Bufalino, Gesualdo, 193, 198 n1
Bull, George, 200 n1
Buonarotti, Filippo, 55
Burckhardt, Jacob, 13, 200 n4
Bussu, Salvatore, 230 n4
Buttigieg, Joseph, 197 n2, 228 n85

Caesar, Julius, 158
Cafardo, Giuseppe, 24, 29
Cafiero, Carlo, 115
Calvino, Italo, 133, 190
Cambria, Adele, 228 n97
Camorra (criminal organization), 81, 84–5, 86, 87, 102
Campanella, Tommaso, 158
Cannistraro, Philip V., 225 n49
Cantarella, Raffaele, 215 n67
Capelli, Anna, 198 n7, 214 n45, 216 n79
Capponi, Gino, 49
Caprioglio, Sergio, 197 n1
Caracciolo, Enrichetta, 5, 106, 125–30, 144, 174, 189
Caracciolo, Francesco, 125
Carbonari, 4, 39, 46, 48, 54, 63
Carbonel, George, 108
Carcere Nuovo (Roman prison), 96
Cardozo-Freeman, Inez, 234 n3
Carducci, Giosue, 117–18, 119, 210 nn12, 14
Carlyle, Thomas, 219 n40
Carmine (Neapolitan prison), 81, 86
Carnochan, W.B., 197 n3
Caro, Annibale, 200 n9
Carrillo, Elisa, 222 nn8, 9, 10, 11, 12

Casalini, Maria, 220 n45
Casanova, Giacomo, xii, xiv, 12, 29–37, 38, 40, 41, 45, 108, 109, 110, 116, 185, 187, 193, 194, 204 n19
Casati, Camillo, 52
Casati, Gabrio, 49
Cassese, Antonio, 201 n21, 204 n8
Cassiano, Antonio, 213 n43
Cassola, Carlo, 41
Castel San Giorgio (Mantua castle and prison), 5, 78, 96, 106–11
Castel Sant'Angelo (Roman castle and prison), 3, 13, 14, 15, 27, 33, 104, 109
Castellazzo, Luigi (Anselmo Rivalta), 104, 192, 217 n86
Castlereagh, Lord 48
Castromediano, Sigismondo, 5, 80, 81–7, 88, 90, 92, 101, 102, 107, 175, 188, 189, 201 n13, 213 nn43, 44, 217 n85, 231 n8
Cataneo, Maurizio, 19
Catti De Gasperi, Maria Romani, 222 nn8, 12
Cellini, Benvenuto, xii, xiv, 3, 10, 12, 13–18, 22, 25, 26, 27, 29, 31, 32, 35, 36, 37, 83, 104, 108, 109, 110, 116, 128, 129, 152, 158, 174, 185, 187, 191, 194, 216 n68
censors and censorship: in prison and other institutions generally 8–9, 199 n13; of Tasso's letters, 19; of *Le mie prigioni* by the Church, 47; by Pellico of published versions of his own letters, 47–8; Andryane's reaction to, 56; of letters by later Risorgimento patriots, 103; by subsequent editors or family members, 103; by Austria of nineteenth-century prison narratives, 107–8; by Fascists as compared to nineteenth-century Italian governments, 218–19 n31; of Russian words in the Costa-Kuliscioff correspondence, 219 n32; by Leo Spitzer as Austrian censor, 219 n32; addressed in his letters by Turati, 121–2, 124; inhibiting force for Morandi, 161; of Gramsci's letters, 166–7; defied by Ravera and Terracini, 174; foiled by time for Monti's letters, 176; case of Aldo Moro, 180–1
Cerrito, Gino, 219 n38
Cervantes Saavedra, Miguel de, 158
Champollion, Jean-François, 57
Charcot, Jean-Martin, 121
Charles Albert (= Carlo Alberto, of Savoy), 48
Charles V (of Austria), 13
Christian Democrat Party (DC or Democrazia cristiana), 6, 133, 134, 177–85
Cicero, Marcus Tullius, 19, 158
Cirillo, Domenico, 9
Civitavecchia (Italian prison at), 155, 226 n66
clandestine communication, 10, 80; in invisible ink, 9, 52, 76, 109, 141, 211 n25; on cigarette papers rolled up in a ball of wax, 9; written in blood, 9, 43, 77; pricked out with a pin, 49; as palimpsests in ostensible commercial letters, 307 n43; not employed by Gramsci, 9, 228 n88; by Confalonieri, 49–52, 57, 207 n43; existence in the Spielberg denied by Pellico, 207 n43; by whistling, 57; by tapping on the wall, 57, 64, 74, 207–8 n50; by

bribing or persuading prison personnel, 57, 124; through coded poetry, 73; written by Tazzoli on bandages, 77; through Carlo Poma's laundry, 78–9, 212 n33; through other prisoners' laundry, 212 n32; arranged for her son by Adelaide Turati, 124; by Terracini, 141–2; unwittingly erased by censor, 223 n24; in 'magical letters' by Ravera, 145–50; for Aldo Moro, 181–2
Clemens, Samuel L., 204 n14
Clement VII (Pope), 13
Cocchi, Antonio, 13, 202 n26
codes and ciphers: used by Pellico, 44; in poetry by Pastro, 73, 210–11 n18; in Tazzoli's ledger, 74; in the form of Russian words in the Costa-Kuliscioff correspondence, 114–15; in Ravera's 'magical' letters, 145–50; for Pajetta in all prison letters, 193
Coldagelli, Umberto, 207 n46
Coletti, Alessandro, 222 n20
Colombo, Arturo, 222 n7
Colquhoun, Archibald, 221 n5
Commissione parlamentare d'inchiesta sul terrorismo in Italia, 178, 232 nn14, 18
Communist Party. *See* Italian Communist Party.
Comte, Auguste, 122, 124
Confalonieri, Federico, 4, 8, 48–54, 55, 56, 57, 59, 61, 63, 65, 68, 83, 163, 174, 187, 206 n27, 208 n66
Confalonieri, Teresa Casati, 8, 49, 51, 52, 53, 55, 57, 116
Coppola, Aniello, 230 n4
Cordié, Carlo, 200 n5

Cordova, Ferdinando, 212 n32
Corriere della sera, 112
Corsetti, Angelo, 225 nn48, 50, 58
Cossiga, Francesco, 180, 182, 183
Costa, Anacreonte, 224 n39
Costa, Andrea, 4, 41, 103, 111–21, 125, 126, 129–30, 135, 159, 170, 189, 218 n29, 220 nn45, 46, 229 n105
Costa, Andreina, 117, 120, 219 nn38, 39
Courrier Français, 205 n25
Craig, Cynthia, 202 n29
Craig, Gordon A., 217 n10
Craveri, Piero, 222 n8
Cresci, Gian Paolo, 230 n4, 231 n8
Croce, Benedetto, 9, 92, 132, 161, 169, 209 n12, 216 n69
Croce, Elena, 89, 214 n47, 216 nn69, 72
Crouzet, Michel, 207 n42
Culoz, Karl von, 74, 77, 174, 191
Curcio, Renato, 186, 193–4, 199 nn13, 14, 206 n31, 226 n72, 229 n99, 230 n4, 234 n4
Cutrufelli, Maria Rosa, 128, 220 n52

D'Ancona, Alessandro, 23, 24, 26, 27, 49, 201 nn16, 22, 204 n5, 206 n36, 207 n45, 208 n56
D'Annunzio, Gabriele, 203 n48
D'Azeglio, Massimo, 92, 158, 205 n23
D'Este, Alfonso II, 18, 21, 22, 36
D'Este, Ippolito, 17
D'Este, Lucrezia, 22
Da Ponte, Lorenzo, 205 n22
Da Vinci, Leonardo, 14
Damiani, Franco, 217 n1, 223 n32
Daniels, Elizabeth Adams, 217 nn6, 8
Dante Alighieri, 16, 34, 78, 137, 158, 169, 180

Darnton, Robert, 202 n25
De Amicis, Edmondo, 41
De Gasperi, Alcide, 133–7, 138, 140, 164, 173, 190
De Latour, Antoine, 45, 46, 206 n30
De Lauretis, Teresa, 212 n34
De Matteis, Giuseppe, 213 nn43, 44
De Sanctis, Brizio, 213 n43
De Sanctis, Francesco, 87, 214 nn52, 53
De' Gabrielli, Pietro, 24, 27, 37
Defoe, Daniel, 158
Del Bo, Giuseppe, 218 n27
Della Peruta, Franco, 208 n2, 209 n8
Della Porta, Donatella, 230 n4
Delzell, Charles F., 225 n49
Dembowski, Matilde, 116, 207 n42
Descartes, René, 92
Diderot, Denis, 158
Donghi, Giuseppe, 229 n99
Drake, Richard, 230 n3
Dubbini, Renzo, 199 n8
Dughera, Attilo, 226 n64
Duncan, Martha Grace, 6, 7, 235 n12

Einaudi, Giulio, 154
Eisenzweig, Uri, 230 n4
Eliot, George, 158
Engels, Friedrich, 113
escape from captivity: by Cellini, 15–16; by Pignata, 25–7; by Casanova, 29, 33–4; twice planned but aborted by Confalonieri, 57; rejected by Castromediano, 86; planned for Settembrini, 90; by Orsini, 106–11; of caged canaries from Moro's prison, 215 n62
Escudero, Lucrezia, 230 n4

Faggi, Vico, 224 n39

Familiari, Maria Luisa, 232 n16
Farnese, Pier Luigi, 13, 14, 16, 17
Fenzi, Enrico, 230 n4
Ferdinand II (of Kingdom of Two Sicilies), 5, 80, 82, 84, 86, 87
Ferrara (Italian prison at), 174
Ferrarotti, Franco, 230 n4
Ferri, Enrico, 220 n44
Fichte, Johan Gottlieb, 158
Ficino, Marsilio, 20, 201 n10
Fido, Franco, 202 n35
Fiori, Giuseppe, 53, 56, 225 nn48, 49, 226 n60
Flamigni, Sergio, 230 n4
Flem, Lydia, 200 n4, 203 nn45, 48
Foa, Vittorio, 154, 226 n66
Foresti, Felice, 45, 205 n22
Forte Della Stella (Elba prison), 68, 69, 78
Foscolo, Ugo, 47, 48, 206 n32
Foucault, Michel, 6, 8
Franceschini, Alberto, 211 n25, 230 n4
Franchi, Ausonio, 108
Francis I (of Austria), 48, 174
Francis I (of France), 13
Frangeamore, Mariapia, 22, 23, 234–5 n10
Franklin, Benjamin, 71
Freud, Sigmund, 194, 205 n21, 220 n42
Frignani, Angelo, 46, 95, 97–101, 102, 104, 123, 128, 188
Fubini, Elsa, 197 n1

Gabrieli, Francesco, 213 nn41, 43
Gadda, Carlo Emilio, 215 n64
Gallavresi, Giuseppe, 52, 207 nn42, 43
Galletti, Giovanni, 4, 5, 46, 95–7, 101, 102, 104, 188, 192

Garibaldi, Giuseppe, 90, 125, 220 n53
Gelfand, Elissa E., 199 n10, 219 n37, 224 n32
Genêt, Jean, 215 n64
Gentile, Giovanni, 161
Gentile, Michele Lupo, 207 n49
Gentile, Sandro, 202 nn33, 36
Gerratana, Valentino, 227 n83, 228 nn90, 94
Getto, Giovanni, 20
Ghidetti, Enrico, 218 n29
Ghisalberti, Albert M., 217 nn3, 12, 218 n13
Giannone, Pietro, 80
Gide, André, 223 n27
Gigante, Antonio, 146
Ginzburg, Carlo, 226 n66, 230 n4
Ginzburg, Leone, 154, 222 n7
Giolitti, Giovanni, 120
Giordano, Umberto, xiii
Giordano, Valeria, 201 n15, 235 n10
Giovane Italia. *See* Young Italy.
Giusti, Renato, 220 n44, 221 n6
Giustiniana (Venetian prison), 202 n40
Giustizia e Libertà (political movement), 4, 150, 154, 158, 160
Gobetti, Ada, 145, 149, 224 nn34, 35, 38
Goethe, Johan Wolfgang, 158
Goffman, Irving, 199 n13
Goldoni, Carlo, 31
Gonzaga, Margherita, 18, 200 n7
Gonzales, Manuel, 219 n38
Gorki, Maxim, 158
Gradisca (Austrian prison), 60
Gramsci, Antonio, vii, xi–xii, xiv, 4, 5, 7, 9, 23, 103, 118, 122, 132–3, 135, 137, 138, 140, 142, 143, 144, 147, 148, 150, 154, 157, 163–73, 179, 185, 190, 193, 194, 197 n1, 207 n45, 211 n19, 212 n34, 215 n60, 217 n85, 225 n43, 226 n60
Gramsci, Peppina, 168
Grazioli, Bartolomeo, 74, 211 n20
Grillo, Angelo, 200 n7
Grimaldi, Ugoberto Alfassio, 63, 208 nn60, 63, 65
Guasti, Cesare, 200 n7
Guerrazzi, Franceschino Michele (Cecchino), 71, 93, 188
Guerrazzi, Francesco Domenico, 68, 70–2, 82, 93, 96, 102, 103, 104, 188, 218 n18
Guerrini, Olindo, 23, 201 n16
Guglielminetti, Marziano, 209 n4
Guicciardi, Luigi, 230 n4
Guillén, Claudio, 201 n23
Gundle, Stephen, 229 n106

Hegel, Georg Wilhelm Friedrich, 92, 214 n52
Herwegh, Emma, 108, 109, 110, 116, 217 nn7, 10, 218 n17
Hess, Henner, 230 n4
Homer, 91
Horace (Quintus Horatius Flaccus), 110, 158
Huxley, Aldous, 158

Ignatieff, Michael, 199 n10
Il messaggero, 182
ink: invisible, 9, 52, 76, 109, 141, 211 n25; made from blood, 9, 43, 57–8, 76–7, 104; from urine and brick dust, 16, 104; from herbs or medicine, 50, 158; from wine, 96; from starch, 141
Isgrò, Michele, 143, 164
Italian Communist Party (PCI,

PCd'I), 4, 6, 138, 140, 144, 146–50, 157, 164, 165, 167, 176, 177
Italian Socialist Party (PSI), 111–25, 147, 160, 164, 165, 218 n22, 219 n36

Jamieson, Alison, 230 n4
Janni, Ettore, 213 n35
Jesus Christ, 222 n14
Job, 222 n14

Kafka, Franz, 215 n64
Kant, Immanuel, 92, 158
Katz, Robert, 230 n2
Kauffman, Linda S., 229 n104
Kelly, Robert J., 230 n4
Keynes, John Maynard, 167
Kipling, Rudyard, 158
Kirchheimer, Otto, 198 n5
Koestler, Arthur, 223 n27
Kropotkin, Peter, 113
Kuliscioff, Andreina. *See* Costa, Andreina.
Kulisciolf, Anna, 4, 41, 106, 111–24, 125, 126, 129–30, 135, 162, 170, 189, 218 n30, 220 nn45, 46, 223 n32, 229 n105

Labriola, Antonio, 113
Laforgue, Jacques, 30
Latude, Jean Henri Masers de, 202 n40
Lecce (prisons at), 81, 84, 86
Leibniz, Gottfried Wilhelm von, 158
Lenci, Sergio, 230 n4
Leonetti, Alfonso, 142, 148
Leopardi, Giacomo, xiii, 69
Lepre, Aurelio, 227 n83
Levi, Carlo, 157–9, 160, 161, 162, 163, 174, 175, 179, 190, 226 n69
Lex, Alma, 141, 142, 223 n28

Linguet, Simon Nicolas Henry, 202 n40
Lipparini, Lilla, 219 n38
Lisa, Athos, 222 n18
Lo Romer, David, 209 n8
Lo Sardo, Ciccino, 139
Lo Sardo, Francesco, 134, 137–40, 142, 143, 153, 164, 174, 175, 190, 228 n87
Lo Sardo, Giovannino, 139
Lo Sardo, Teresina, 139
Lombroso, Cesare, 230 n1
Longinus, 158
Louis XIV (of France), 28
Louis XVII (of France), 41
Lovelace, Richard, vii
Lovett, Clara M., 203 n2, 209 n9, 216 n80
Lucas, Corinne, 200 n5
Lucian, 91
Luzio, Alessandro, 204 n7, 206 n28, 210 n16, 211 nn19, 21–3, 212 nn26, 28, 31, 217 n7, 218 n14, 234 n7

Macaulay, Thomas Babington, 158
Macciocchi, Maria-Antonietta, 228 n89
Mack Smith, Denis, 208 n62
madness: Tasso's worries about, 19–22; of Maroncelli at the end of his life, 24; feigned by Frignani, 98–102; considered by Turati, 121, 123; feared by Caracciolo, 128
Mainolda (Mantua prison), 78, 103
Malvezzi, Piero, 210 n15
Mambelli, Anna Maria, 205 n24, 206 n31
Mambro, Francesca, 198 n4
Mangini, Nicola, 200 n4
Mann, Thomas, 28
Mantelli, Brunello, 230 n4, 233 n26

Mantua, Martyrs of. *See* Martyrs of Mantua.
Manzoli, Giancarlo, 211 n19
Manzoni, Alessandro, xiii, 208 n56
Marchetti, Leopoldo, 217 nn9, 11
Marchionni, Carlotta, 46
Mariani, Laura, 223 n32
Marinari, Attilio, 204 n12
Maroncelli, Piero, 43, 45–8, 49, 51, 52, 53, 54, 63, 65, 103, 163, 187, 191
Marraro, Howard R., 205 n22
Marteau, Pierre (Pietro Martello), 23, 24, 28, 29, 202 n26
Martini, Federico, 210 n14
Martini, Luigi, 110, 211 n19, 212 n28, 218 nn15, 16
Martyrs of Mantua, 3, 5, 72–80, 83, 102, 106, 110, 114, 162, 179, 189, 192, 228 n87
Marx, Karl, 107, 111, 130, 218 n27
Mascagni, Pietro, 115, 116
Masi, P., 214 n48
Masini, Pier Carlo, 219 n33
Masters, John, 202 n30
Matteotti, Giacomo, 134, 138
Maturi, Walter, 211 n19
Mazzali, Ettore, 200 nn7, 8
Mazzini, Giuseppe, 63, 70, 74, 107, 108, 111
Mazzocchi, Silvana, 230 n4
Medici, Cosimo de', 13
Medici, M., 230 n7
Meijer, Jan Marinus, 218 n27
Melossi, Dario, 199 n11
Meneghetti, Maria Luisa, 203 n42
Menghini, Mario, 208 n61
Mennini, Antonello, 232 n16
Menocal, María Rosa, 204 n19
Mesmer, Franz Anton, 216 n84

Metastasio, Pietro, 34
Metternich, Klemens von, 47, 48, 50, 204 n15
Mila, Massimo, 154, 157
Milani, Mario, 204 n16
Minghetti, Mario, 92
Mongillo, M., 230 n7
Monsagrati, Giuseppe, 205 n22
Montale, Eugenio, 197 n5
Montanelli, Giuseppe, 70
Montanelli, Indro, 230 n4
Montefusco (Neapolitan prison), 81, 85, 87
Montesarchio (Neapolitan prison), 81, 86
Monti, Augusto, 3, 103, 126, 150, 154–6, 157, 159, 161, 162, 168, 174, 175, 176, 190, 199 n12, 226 n64
Monti Sturani, Luisa, 154, 156, 226 nn62, 63
Moran, Sue Ellen, 230 n4
Morandi, Rodolfo, 103, 156–7, 159, 160–1, 162, 163, 174, 190, 226 n69, 227 n77
Morandini, Giuliana, 234 n4
Moretti, Mario, 230 n4, n5, 231 nn9, 13, 232 n15, 233 nn21, 25
Moro, Aldo, xiii, xiv, 3, 5, 176, 177–85, 190–1, 193, 215 n62, 230 n4
Moro, Eleonora, 182
Morris, Norval, 197 n3
Mosca, Carla, 181, 230 n5
Moss, David, 230 n4
Murate (Tuscan prison), 103
Muratori, Ludovico Antonio, 200 n7
Mussolini, Benito, xiii, 132, 134, 155, 164, 166, 170, 175

Napoleon III, emperor of France, 107
Naria, Giuliano, 193, 198 n2, 230 n4

Natoli, Aldo, 170, 226 n66, 228 n96, 229 n98
Negri, Antonio, 230 n4
Neier, Aryeh, 198 n3
Nelson, Horatio, 125
Nenni, Pietro, 221 n7
Nietzsche, Friedrich Wilhelm, 219 n40
Nievo, Ippolito, 158
Novelli, Diego, 230 n4

O'Brien, Patricia, 6, 224 n32, 234 n3
Oliva, Antonio, 24
Olivier, L'Abbé, 23, 24
Ordine nuovo, 140, 144, 164
Orlandini, Silvio, 48
Orsini, Felice, 106–11, 112, 116, 117, 129–30, 132, 152, 153, 174, 185, 189, 194
Orsini, Girolama, 16
Orsini, Orso, 117
OVRA (Fascist Secret Police), 145, 166

Packe, Michael St John, 217 nn7, 8, 12, 218 n13, 221 n54
Pagano, Francesco, 9
Pajetta, Giancarlo, 154, 193, 221 n7, 222 n16, 223 n28
Pallanza (Lombard prison), 121
Pallavicino, Giorgio, 59–63, 68, 98, 187, 208 n54
Pallotta, Gino, 230 n4, 231 n10
Palmieri, Renato, 226 n69
Palombarini, Giovanni, 230 n4
Palumbo, Rita, 221 n37
Panizzi, Antonio, 90, 125
Pannunzio, Mario, 151
Paone, Michele, 213 n43
paper and paper-substitutes for writing in prison: writing table surface for Pellico, 44; toilet paper for Confalonieri, 50; and for Andryane, 57; pages of a novel for Andryane, 58; cell walls for Andryane, 58; bandages for Tazzoli, 77; laundry for Poma, 78–9, 104; printed books for Terracini, 141; and for Ravera, 147; letters from home for Levi, 158–9
Papio, Angelo, 20
pardon(s) sought or not sought by prisoners: Tasso, 21–2; Confalonieri, 53, 207 n45; Castromediano, 86; Kuliscioff, 116; Monti, 155; Gramsci in the case of Confalonieri, 174
Parini, Giuseppe, 40
Parri, Ferruccio, 151
Parthenopean Republic, 125, 200 n15
Partito d'Azione (Action Party), 151, 158
Partito Radicale (Radical Party), 151
Pascal, Blaise, 41, 42, 53, 207 n44
Pasolini, Pier Paolo, 179
Pastro, Luigi, 5, 72–4, 75, 77, 79, 82, 83, 102, 107, 159, 165, 174, 175, 188, 191, 207–8 n50, 209 n11
Paul III (Pope), 13, 15, 17
Paul, Saint, 222 n14
Pavarini, Massimo, 199 n11
Pavese, Cesare, 154, 155, 156, 157
Pavlovich, Stefan, 47, 51–2, 53, 56, 85, 206 n28
Pecorari, Anselmo Guido, 211 n19
Pedone, Franco, 219 n35
Pellico, Silvio, xi–xii, xiv, 5, 10, 30, 38, 39, 40–5, 46, 47, 48, 51, 52, 53, 55, 56, 58, 59, 61, 63, 64, 65, 68, 72, 82–3, 92, 95, 97, 104, 107, 108, 128, 131, 132, 133, 135, 137, 141, 152, 158, 163, 174, 187, 191, 192, 206 n27, 207

nn43, 45, 209 n7, 215–16, n68, 224 n34, 234 n5
pens: made from wood splinter, 16; from sticks and fingernails, 50; from straw or wood, 57; from fish bone, 96
People's Prison, 3, 178–9, 193, 215 n62. *See also* Via Montalcini.
Pergameni, Elena Larsimont, 217 nn9, 11
Pernicone, Nunzio, 219 n33
Perrot, Michelle, 199 n11
Pertini, Sandro, 9, 224 n39
Perugia (prison at), 113, 115, 144, 145
Peter, Saint, 222 n14
Peters, Edward, 201 n21
Petrarch, Francesco, 158
Petrelli, Stefano, 186, 193–4, 199 nn13, 14, 206 n31, 229 n99, 234 n4
Petronio, Giuseppe, 209 n10
Pickering-Iazzi, Robin, 218 n25
Pierce, Franklin, 205 n22
Pignata, Giuseppe, 23–9, 36, 65, 83, 108, 109, 110, 185, 187, 192, 194, 200 n2
Pignatelli, Prince and Princess, 216 n72
Pilliteri, Paolo, 220 nn42, 46, 223 n32
Pimentel, Eleonora Fonseca, 219 n37
Piombi (Venetian prison), 10, 29, 32–3, 38, 41, 54
Pirandello, Luigi, 99, 100, 102, 170
Pirelli, Giovanni, 210 n15
Pirodda, Giovanni, 209 n11
Pironti, Carolina, 213 n43
Pistillo, Michele, 230 n4
Pius IX (Pope), 96
Piva, Edoardo, 211 n23
Platone, Felice, 132, 146, 176
Poerio, Carlo, 82, 213 n43

Polo, Marco, xii
Poma, Angelo, 212 n27
Poma, Anna Filippini, 78–9, 174, 212 nn27, 34, 225 n56
Poma, Carlo, 72, 74, 77–80, 93, 102, 103, 104, 118, 159, 174, 188, 191, 213 n36
Poma, Teresa, 213 n36
Ponce de León, Maria, 215 n64, 234 n6
Ponza, island of, 144
Popular Party, 134
Porter, Roy, 199 n13
Potier, Jean-Pierre, 228 n90
Prampaloni, Camillo, 116, 219 n36
prison: cause of madness, 19–22; convents and, 5–6, 125–9, 133, 145, 151; as hermitage, 133; death and, 7–8; unpleasant aspects of, vii, viii, 7, 19–22: for Tasso, 71; for Guerrazzi, 83–5; for Castromediano, 115; for Kuliscioff, 115; strengthens spirit, 17–18, 144; as gilded cage, 68; different for the poor and for the rich, 69; opportunity for reflection, 78; cause of spiritual contamination, 90–2; as 'Nirvana,' 155; conducive to secular conversion, 161, 162–3; as trope for tyranny beyond prison walls, 87, 126, 155; difficulty of writing in, 7, 20, 50, 91, 118, 159, 169–73, 186–95, 229 n99; reading in: for Casanova, 34–5; for Pellico and Zanze, 43–4; for Confalonieri, 51, 207 n44; forbidden Pastro, 73; of smuggled texts for Poma, 78; forbidden Castromediano, 85; on Santo Stefano for Settembrini and Spaventa, 89

prisoners of conscience, 198 n3
prisons. *See* Bastille; Carcere Nuovo; Carmine; Castel San Giorgio; Castel Sant'Angelo; Civitavecchia; Ferrara; Forte Della Stella; Giustiniana; Gradisca; Lecce; Mainolda; Montefusco; Montesarchio; Murate; Pallanza; People's Prison; Perugia; Piombi; Procida; Rebibbia; Regina Coeli; Saint Peter's; San Michele; San Vittore; Sant'Andrea; Sant'Anna; Santa Margherita; Santo Stefano; Spielberg; Theresienstadt; Torre di Nona; Trani; Turi; Vicaria
Procacci, Giuliano, 218 n21
Procida (Neapolitan prison island), 81, 84–5, 86
Prosperi, Adriano, 230 n4
Puccini, Giacomo, xiii

Quercioli, Mimma Paulesu, 228 n92

Rana, Nicola, 182, 232 n16
Rava, Luigi, 97, 101, 216 n82
Ravera, Camilla, 5, 52, 103, 143–50, 153, 154, 165, 174, 175, 190, 214 n50, 215 n64, 219 n37, 222 n20, 223 n32
Ravera, Carlo, 148
Ravera, Cesare, 146
Ravera, Elena, 148
Ravezzoli, Paolo, 142, 148
reading in prison. *See* prison, reading in.
Rebibbia (Roman prison), 22
Red Brigades, xiii, 3, 177–85, 186, 211 n25, 231 n12, 232 nn15–17, 233 nn20, 21, 24
Regina Coeli (Roman prison), vii, 5, 134, 135, 156, 162, 164, 218 n24

Revelli, Marco, 233 n26
Revelli, Nuto, 199 n7
Riboldi, Ezio, 228 n88
Ricci, Aldo, 199 n8
Ricci, Raffaello, 213 nn39, 43, 214 n51
Rivalta, Anselmo. *See* Castellazzo, Luigi.
Rizzi, Bice, 224 n32
Roberts, John Morris, 204 n6
Rodriguez, Fabio, 217 n1
Romagnoli, Angela, 197 n4
Romains, Jules, 158
Rosa, Gabriele, 63–5, 111, 133, 151, 175, 187
Rosengarten, Frank, 227 nn83, 85, 228 nn93, 95, 229 n106
Rosenstein, Anna. *See* Kuliscioff, Anna.
Rosenthal, Raymond, 227 n85
Rossanda, Rossana, 181, 230 n5
Rosselli, Carlo, 150
Rossi, Elide, 151–3, 168, 174, 225 nn48, 55
Rossi, Ernesto, 103, 126, 132, 150–4, 168, 171, 174, 190, 221 n2
Rossi, Filippo, 78, 212 n28
Rothman, David J., 197 n3
Rousseau, Jean-Jacques, 13, 31, 194, 202 n34
Roustang, François, 32–3, 35
Roveri, Alessandro, 219 n34
Rozielli, Seigneur, 23, 24
Rumi, Giorgio, 206 n35
Rusche, Georg, 198 n5
Russo, Vincenzo, 9

Sacco, Nicola, 210 n13
Saint Peter's (Roman prison) 27
Salierno, Giulio, 199 n8
Salvotti, Antonio, 40, 42, 46, 60

Samaran, Charles, 27
San Giorgio (Mantua prison). See Castel San Giorgio.
San Michele (Venetian prison), 54
San Vittore (Turinese prison), 5
Sand, George, 158
Sandonà, Augusto, 208 n51
Sant'Andrea (Venetian fort and prison), 203 n43
Sant'Angelo (Roman prison). See Castel Sant'Angelo.
Sant'Anna (Ferrarese prison), xii, 18, 19, 22, 104, 187
Santa Margherita (Milanese prison), 5, 8, 41, 43, 52, 64, 83, 131
Santo Stefano (Neapolitan prison island), 4, 9, 80, 88–95, 102, 103, 125, 173, 224 n35
Santucci, Antonio, 227 n82
Sardou, Victorien, 116
Saudan, Alain, 230 n4
Savoca, Giuseppe, 197 n5
Scalvini, Giovita, 158, 174
Scarabello, Giovanni, 199 n8
Scheffler, Judith A., 208 n50, 219 n37
Schiavi, Alessandro, 219 n35
Schiller (Spielberg prison guard), 41, 57, 145
Schucht, Apollon Alexandrovich 169
Schucht, Giulia, 167, 168, 169, 171, 173, 228 nn92, 96, 97
Schucht, Tatiana, 7, 167, 168, 169, 170, 171, 173, 193, 212 n34, 222 n18, 223 n25, 227 n77, 228 nn91, 92, 229 n102
Sciascia, Leonardo, 179–80, 230 n4, 232 n17, 233 nn24, 27
Scirocco, Luigi, 217 n86
Sclavi, Marianella, 234 n4
Scotti, Mario, 48, 206 n34
Scribe, Eugène, 116

secret, invisible, or unreadable texts: 10, 66; on Cellini's forehead, 10, 17; on Pellico's writing table, 10, 43–5, 205 n23; musical, by Pignata, 25; by Arrivabene, 55; in Andryane's self-censored correspondence, 56; described or alluded to by Andryane, 58; hidden in Turati's letters, 122; in Gramsci's letters, 172
Sellin, Thorsten, 198 n4
Settembrini, Gigia, 89, 91, 92, 93
Settembrini, Giulia, 89, 92
Settembrini, Luigi, xiv, 4, 9, 10, 80, 81, 87–92, 102, 103, 104, 124, 125, 152, 153, 173, 174, 188, 189, 208 n1, 213 n39, 224 n35
Settembrini, Raffaele (father of Luigi), 88
Settembrini, Raffaele (son of Luigi), 92
Sforza, Riario, 126
Shaw, George Bernard, 116
Shelley, Mary, 216 n84
Silj, Alessandro, 230 n4, 233 n26
Silone, Ignazio, 223 n27
Simone, Rosella, 198 n2
Sofri, Adriano, vii, 184–5, 206 n31, 212 n28, 213 n39, 216 n77, 230 n4, 233 n24, 234 n5
Soradaci, Francesco, 34
Sossi, Mario, 230 n4
Spaventa, Bertrando, 92, 93, 94, 216 n72
Spaventa, Silvio, 4, 9, 80, 89, 92–5, 102, 103, 104, 112, 125, 151, 170, 188, 189, 214 nn47, 59, 60, 216 n69
Spellanzon, Silvia, 205 n25
Speri, Tito, 78, 193, 212 n32
Spielberg (Austrian prison), xii, 4,

38–66, 67, 68, 74, 85, 89, 104, 128, 141, 162, 163, 205 n20, 207 n43
Spinola, Ottavio, 201 n14
Spinoza, Baruch, 92, 158
Spitzer, Leo, 199 n7, 219 n32
Spriano, Paolo, 221 n1, 223 nn22, 27, 29, 224 n37, 225 n46, 227 n83, 228 n86
Sraffa, Piero, 148, 167, 168–9, 215 n60, 222 n18, 223 n15, 227 nn77, 83, 228 nn89, 91, 229 n102
Stalin, Joseph, 141, 142, 165
Stefani, Guglielmo, 206 n33, 208 n53
Stendhal (Marie Henri Beyle), 38, 118, 207 n42
Sterne, Laurence, 68
Stowe, Harriet Beecher, 40
Sturani, Luisa Monti, 226 nn62, 63
suicide: attempted by Cellini, 16; possible for Pellico, 45; attempted by Felice Foresti, 45; of Pellico's friend, Odoardo Briche, 47; attempted by Caracciolo, 128
Symonds, Arthur, 23

Tabucchi, Antonio, 190
Tangentopoli, 6
Tasca, Angelo, 140
Tasso, Bernardo, 18
Tasso, Torquato, xii, 12, 18–23, 25, 26, 32, 33, 35, 36, 37, 83, 104, 116, 121, 128, 158, 187, 216 n68
Taviani, Paolo Emilio, 183, 233 n24
Tazzoli, Enrico, 72, 74–7, 79, 93, 102, 103, 104, 118, 141, 159, 174, 188, 191, 192, 211 n20
Tazzoli, Silvio, 75
Terracini, Umberto, 4, 5, 52, 140–3, 144, 147, 148, 153, 154, 155, 164, 165, 171, 173, 174, 175, 184, 190

Themelly, Mario, 213 n38, 214 n53, 215 n66
Theresienstadt (Austrian prison), 83
Tibullus, Albius, 174
Timpanaro, Sebastiano, 209 n8
Tofin (Mantua fisherman), 110
Togliatti, Palmiro, 132, 140, 167, 176, 227 n83
Tolstoy, Leo Nikolayevich, 158
Tommaseo, Niccolò, 61, 62, 63, 208 n58
Tommasini, Giacomo, 98–9
Torre di Nona (Roman prison), 16
torture, of prisoners, 26, 104, 162, 201 n21, 217 n86
Toschi, Luca, 210 n14
Tozzi, Federigo, 209 n7
Trani (Italian prison at), 144, 145, 214 n50, 215 n64
Trask, Willard R., 202 n31
Tresso, Pietro, 142, 148
Trombatore, Gaetano, 209 n4
Trotsky, Leon, 176
Turati, Adelaide, 121–4, 168, 174
Turati, Filippo, 4, 41, 103, 111–13, 115–17, 120–5, 128, 129–30, 135, 138, 168, 171, 189, 218 n30, 220 n45, 229 n105
Turi (Italian prison at), xii, 163, 164, 165, 179

Ugolini, Giorgio, 14–15, 16
Ulisse, Felicetta, 93–5, 104, 112, 170
Ustica, island of, 171

Vaini, Mario, 211 n19
Valentino, Nicola, 186, 193–4, 199 nn13, 14, 206 n31, 214 n58, 216 n81, 229 n99, 234 nn4, 6
Valera, Paolo, 218 n29
Vallone, Aldo, 213 n43

Vannucci, Atto, 205 n22
Vanzetti, Bartolomeo, 71
Vecchi, Eros, 146, 224 n37
Venner, Dominique, 230 n4
Ventotene, island of, 140, 144, 151
Verdi, Giuseppe, xiii
Vettori, Vittorio, 230 n4
Via Montalcini, 178, 182, 193, 215 n62, 231 n8. *See also* People's Prison.
Via Monte Nevoso, 178
Viareggio Prize, 132
Vicaria (Neapolitan prison), 93
Virgil, 34
Visconti, Luchino, 226 n70
Vivarelli, Pia, 227 n73
Von Schütz, Wilhelm, 30

Wagner-Pacifici, Robin Erica, 230 n4
Weaver, William, 221 n5
Weinberg, Leonard, 230 n4
White, Jessie Meriton (Jessie White Mario), 107, 108, 116
Wilde, Oscar, 116
Witt, Mary Ann Frese, 6, 226 n67
Wright, Richard, 223 n27
writing materials. *See* ink; paper and paper substitutes; pens

Years of Lead (1970s), xiii, xv, 6, 178, 198 n4, 213 n39, 217 n86
Young Italy (Giovane Italia) political movement, 63, 74, 88

Zaccagnini, Benigno, 182, 184, 231 n14
Zaczek, Barbara, 199 n13
Zasulich, Vera, 113
Zupo, Giuseppe, 230 n4

OHIO UNIVERSITY LIBRARY
Please return this book as soon as you have
finished with it. In order to avoid a fine it must
be returned by the last date stamped below.